POLICING:

A VIEW FROM THE STREET

Edited by

PETER K. MANNING
Michigan State University

JOHN VAN MAANEN
Massachusetts Institute of Technology

GOODYEAR PUBLISHING COMPANY, INC.
Santa Monica, California

Acknowledgments

We would like to thank certain institutions and departments which were supportive to this project in a variety of ways, both direct and indirect. The Law Enforcement Assistance Administration, and in particular, the Institute of Law Enforcement and Criminal Justice funded much of the research reported here and granted Professor Manning a visiting fellowship in 1974–75. During the period in which this book took shape, Professor Manning has been a member of the Departments of Sociology and Psychiatry at Michigan State University and a Visiting Research Scholar at University of London, Goldsmiths' College. Professor Van Maanen has been a member of the Organization Studies Group in the Sloan School of Management at the Massachusetts Institute of Technology and a Visiting Assistant Professor in the School of Organization and Management at Yale University. Certain individuals deserve mention here too. Nancy Emery, Ella Schrader, Felicia Pettygrew, and Carol Sanders executed many of the necessary tasks associated with the production of this book, and we are grateful for their assistance. Perhaps belatedly, we are also deeply appreciative of the day-to-day solace, tolerance, and encouragement of our families, in whose debt we comfortably find ourselves.

Y-6836-4

Current Printing (last digit):
10 9 8 7 6 5 4 3 2 1

Printed in the United States of America

Library of Congress Cataloging in Publication Data

Main entry under title:

Policing.

    1. Police—Addresses, essays, lectures.
I. Manning, Peter K. II. Van Maanen, John.
HV7921.P58   363.2   77-19343
ISBN 0-87620-683-6

About the Authors

Egon Bittner is a Professor of Sociology at Brandeis University. His extensive theoretical and empirical writings include the book, *The Functions of the Police in Modern Society* (1971).

Donald Black is an Associate Professor of Sociology at Yale University. He has written numerous articles and is the author of *The Behavior of Law* (1976).

Richard N. Harris received his PhD in Sociology from Tufts University. He is the author of *The Police Academy: An Inside View* (1973).

Peter K. Manning is a Professor of Sociology at Michigan State University. He is the author of numerous articles and several books including *Police Work* (1977).

Lawrence J. Redlinger is an Associate Professor in the School of Behavioral Science at the University of Texas, Dallas. He has written several articles drawing upon his extensive fieldwork concerned with illicit drug markets and the police.

Jonathan Rubenstein received his PhD from Harvard University in History and is currently associated with the Center for Policy Research in New York City. He is the author of *City Police* (1973).

Harvey Sacks, until his recent and untimely death, was a Professor of Social Science at the University of California, Irvine. He was a key figure in the development of a phenomenological sociology and had written extensively in sociolinguistics, conversational analysis, and ethnomethodology.

Larry L. Tifft is an Associate Professor of Sociology at Central Michigan University. He is the author of several articles on policing including "The Cop Personality Revisited" (1974).

John Van Maanen is an Associate Professor of Organizational Studies at the Massachusetts Institute of Technology. He has written numerous articles and edited several books including *Organizational Careers: Some New Perspectives* (1977).

John A. Webster is an Associate Professor of Criminology at the University of Illinois. He is the author of *The Realities of Police Work* (1973).

James Q. Wilson is a Professor of Government at Harvard University. He is the author of numerous articles and books including *Thinking About Crime* (1975).

Contents

Contents

Preface

After spending eight nights observing the work of patrolmen, Jerome Skolnick, in an otherwise pioneering and exemplary study of the behavioral side of the law, wrote in 1966: ". . . patrol work is minimally connected with legal processing. To be sure, some street behavior is relevant to the patrolman's role as a legal actor. On the street, the policeman has the greatest potential for discretionary judgement not to invoke the criminal law, a decision of major legal consequence for those involved. Nevertheless, I thought that the typical activities of a patrolman were not those of a *law* officer, but rather those of a *peace* officer" (p. 33). This rather vague distinction was apparently viewed by Skolnick to be meaningful enough so that he could conclude a few lines further that "law enforcement is not to be found in its most significant and interesting forms on the street."

On the basis of this statement, one wonders not only where these most "interesting and significant forms" are to be found but, perhaps more critically, what Professor Skolnick means by his usage of the phrase "law enforcement" in this context? Regarding the latter complications, several interpretations are possible. For instance, Skolnick may be suggesting, quite accurately, that law enforcement per se occupies only a small fraction of a patrolman's everyday activities, which are dominated by those of a more mundane and servicelike nature. He may also be noting that what many patrolmen do in the name of the law is, in itself, not very legal—either procedurally or substantively. Finally, Skolnick may be arguing, again quite accurately, that the police rarely have much to do with the formal legal work that accompanies the cases they funnel into the criminal justice machinery. That is, the legal decisions surrounding the eventual disposition of cases sent forward by the police are most often made by people other than the police; in particular, by prosecutors, whose actions on now legally defined matters are made with their own specific interests in mind. Certainly, all of these possible meanings are sound and consistent with the available evidence. Yet, when this sort of reasoning is used to direct our attention away from patrolmen, it obfuscates some rather stark and compelling facts about the pivotal and critical role patrolmen do play in the law enforcement.

First, the patrol division of any metropolitan police agency consumes more resources, both financial and human, than all other divisions combined. Second, far more arrests, for whatever purposes, are enacted by patrolmen going about their everyday routine than are made elsewhere in police organizations. Third, all policemen, from chief to proverbial station-house broom, receive their initiation to the police life as patrolmen, and it is from working a beat that their later understandings of the law enforcement mission must necessarily derive. Fourth, whether keeping the peace by chatting idly with the neighborhood locals in one's district or enforcing the law by sending a .38-caliber snub-nosed bullet through the back of a fleeing felon, police work is primarily a reactive, not a proactive, business. And the locus of such reaction lies at the bottom of police organizations, where there may be little division of labor among the men but, nonetheless, a plethora of fundamental police tasks to perform. To argue that patrolmen are not central figures in the patterns of law enforcement is futile no matter how much one wishes to make of the patrolman's peculiar position in the scheme of things legal.

At any rate, a major premise lying behind this book of readings is simply that we consider the essence of police work to be located at the ground level. In fact, we have called this book *Policing* not simply to distinguish it from other police books on the market (though there is that objective too), but to emphasize the active character of law enforcement. And, as the police themselves are fond of saying, most of the action is to be found down among the "troops" who are working the street at the patrol level. Certainly, other somewhat specialized aspects of police work are significant as well, but often these more glamorous and dramatic pursuits hide the plain fact that the activities of any police agency are dominated by the hard-slogging work of the patrolman who must go about his duties among the social debris and clutter of city streets. These are the activities of our interest.

We have selected readings for this book that reflect, primarily, a concern for a theoretical understanding of the police. We are not interested here in merely detailing the world as the policeman (or social scientist) might see it; rather, we wish to be able to suggest, first, why the world is viewed in such a fashion, and, second, what the consequences are that flow from such a view. Thus, we are asking the reader to take a step backward with us and consider how it is that any social world can be said to exist. This theoretical perspective bends toward the edicts of phenomenological sociology and is infused with something of the neo-Marxian view that reality does not produce itself nor does it stalk about with a label. The social worlds within which people live are ongoing creations, and considerable work is required to maintain them. The implication of this view stands conventional wisdom on its head, for truth in the social world follows a believing-is-seeing prescription and not one that regards seeing-as-believing.

In line with the above bias and passion, the reader should also be forewarned that we have chosen to emphasize empirical work based upon the field-work tradition in sociology. No doubt because we both work primarily out of this mode, firsthand ethnographic or participant-observation reports seem to convey to us the richness of any investigated social sphere in a more lively and telling fashion than reports grounded upon survey or archival materials. This perhaps represents a drawback to the material presented here, since field data often suffers from a lack of comparative concepts and are usually far more suitable for the building, not the testing, of theoretical supposition. Nevertheless, a number of urban police settings are examined in the various selections of this book, and the data reported from them we feel are remarkably consistent across key issues. Furthermore, since firsthand, *in situ* data are emphasized in the readings, we have provided an epilogue to the book which describes in some detail how one field worker went about his task. The generality of this account cannot be established of course, though we believe that many of the major concerns raised in doing ethnographic work in police organizations are covered. With some cautious optimism and a bow to the traditions established at the University of Chicago in the 1920s and 1930s, we should also note that there seems to be something of a rebirth of this methodological genre in the social sciences today—although there will no doubt continue to be continuing legal, moral, and procedural difficulties in pursuing participant-observation research within law enforcement agencies.

Summarily, we have chosen to select readings that are close to our own substantive and methodological interests and have, as a matter of course, included much of our own work in this anthology. Not insignificantly, we have emphasized the active nature of police work in both the title and in the organization of the book. The sections that follow are thought to flow in something of a natural order. We begin in Part I with a consideration of the historical processes and changing cultural arrangements that have provided the police with their rather loose mission and mandate within this society. We move, in Part II, to examine the present-day context in which policing is accomplished. Part III deals with the various tactics, including administrative, operational, and individual, used when performing various police tasks; and Part IV investigates these general tactics within the framework of the everyday practice of policing, taking, as a primary focus, the street-level encounters between the police and the public. Part V closes the book and, to some degree, brings us full circle, for it is concerned with how the dicta of police work are learned and transmitted from generation to generation of policemen. Here we come face to face with the fact that many of the portraits of the police sketched in this book seem to arrest the passage of time. By offering only single frames from a continuous reel, some portraits may become instantly obsolete. Since police departments have, within the last decade, become something of the organizational parvenu among public service agencies because of the tremendous flow of dollars pumped into them by federal programs, dramatic changes in the patterns of law enforcement may be immanent. However, we think this possibility is very unlikely, for policing has displayed a massive resistance to change across the years. Whether this traditional "conservativism" is viewed as positive or negative depends on one's values. But, values aside for the moment, we feel there are some altogether sound theoretical reasons which account for such a stable state of affairs. And we believe these reasons are laid out rather persuasively in the materials to follow.

Peter K. Manning
John Van Maanen

PART ONE
BACKGROUND TO POLICING

The present form and function of any police organization is linked to the history of its development, the present cultural definition of its purpose and extent of its legitimate control and authority, and the ways in which the organization symbolizes how it carries out its charter. These matters, although conceptually distinct, are in fact, closely intertwined. For purposes of introduction, we will discuss these broad concerns in the following fashion. First, we briefly examine the emergence and development of the police mandate as it originated historically in Great Britain. Second, we look at the American transformation of the English version of the police mandate. Finally, we note some of the more salient structural and symbolic features that characterize policing in the United States. Many of these same themes are, of course, echoed across the parts and articles that make up this book; nonetheless, it is useful to present them here together as a way of framing the evolutinary canvas upon which the actions of the police in present day society can be portrayed.

In the so-called classic discussions on the emergence of the "modern" police in the early decades of the nineteenth century, there is a distinct and somewhat ethnocentric bias which regards the invention of the police, as represented by the Parliamentary Police Act of 1829 authored by Sir Robert Peel, to be a rather reasonable and altogether rational response to certain chaotic social conditions that were then prevalent in London (Reith, 1956; Lee, 1901; Critchley, 1967). From this perspective, organizing a formal police agency represented simply the culmination of certain relentless trends occurring in British society, if not all of "civilization." Other not so classic but equally crude arguments suggest that the police in England were the product of some ill-defined conspiracy of some similarly ill-defined ruling classes to repress the peculiarly well defined working classes (Parks, 1970). An unusually articulate and sophisticated version of this theory on the origins of the police has been advanced by Silver (1967), wherein he argues that the modern police stem from the elites' fear and dread of the "rabble" or "dangerous classes" in the populace. Somewhere between, no doubt, lies the answer; for, as Manning (1977) has shown, neither the sinister and dark conspiracy theories or the romantic versions of British humanity and good sense can fully explain, on their own, the complicated and diverse political movements which led to the establishment of the English police.

However, some themes have been articulated and more or less agreed upon by all scholars examining the origins of the police in Britain. First, the basic legitimacy of the English government at the time the police emerged seems to be unquestioned. Second, there appears to have been a consensus among the various political forces of the day that a police organization, if there were to be one, must have only limited powers and be controlled by the crown through civil servants responsible to the home secretary. It would, in a sense, be a limited national force housed in London—although subsequent acts of Parliament in 1839 and 1855 were to broaden the scope of policing to the larger provinces and eventually to the entire nation. Third, the police were to be concerned primarily with civil, order-maintaining functions. In other words, they would be representatives of the crown but would be no more than citizens in uniform, with very limited arrest powers. Fourth, the police would be unarmed and strictly accountable to political bodies. Finally, regional and ethnic variations were apparently respected in the United Kingdom. Indeed, it took some time before the London model could be adapted to Scotland, Ireland, and Wales, where the legal systems were shaped (and continue to be shaped) by quite distinct regional and political influences. In these themes, then, policing, as we know it, had its origins.

The *American* police did not simply inherit the English model intact, even though it appeared in modified form in the United States some ten years after it had been institutionalized by Parliament in London. Furthermore, the elements of policing that were adopted in America were more or less grafted on other organizational forms borrowed in somewhat diffused form from the English: the constable, the sheriff, and the watch systems of local policing (Chapman and St. Johnston, 1962). Indeed, the police model that took root in the United States was altered by several features of the society and of the police response to them. In particular, violence; pluralism; the American attachment to, and belief in, the law; and a fascination with police technology have all played a part in creating a unique American brand of policing.

Emerging at a time when the population of the country was moving west and consequently had a deep involvement in, and emphasis upon, individualism and self-protection, policing in America has always reflected frontier notions of law, order, and justice. Even today policing in the United States is action-oriented, disdainful of the general "stay-at-home" public, and heavily involved with weaponry and its use. Furthermore, ethnic pluralism, a given in America since the late nineteenth and early twentieth centuries, has been the continual basis for most political and economic struggles. Thus, the police as instruments of order maintenance have been placed squarely in the middle of such struggles and have become something of a lightning rod for controversy. This was as true yesterday as it is today. And the police, despite their best efforts, have never been able to extract themselves from this locus of conflict. Unlike the British, the police were adopted piecemeal by communities in America as the need for and power behind their services took shape and surfaced. Policing in the United States has been and is now localistic in both form and sensitivity. It is far more responsive to community elites than to national trends.

As Peter K. Manning, in an article written in the late 1960s, points out in the first selection presented in Part I, symbolically, the police in the United States have chosen to cope with the basic organizational problem of survival in particular ways. In fact, they have cast their claims for community prestige and respect (translated into political and budgetary support) in the form of several common themes that are rather plainly American. By and large, they have publicly defined their role as violent; technologically sophisticated; crime-related; professionally oriented; and have, in many ways, determined that they must be viewed by the community in only these ways. It is interesting to note, as Manning does, that Peel, the founder of the English police, hoped that the police might reduce crime but would nonetheless avoid the use of repressive legal sanctioning and a military-like presence in society. Additionally, Peel hoped that the police might manage public order nonviolently and perhaps control the possible discord that might arise between the police and the policed by serving the public interest in a subtle, nondramatic, and almost invisible fashion (Reith, 1956; Radelet, 1973:5). From this standpoint, it can be argued that the American police represent something of a mirror image of Peel's optimistic vision insofar as they rarely seek to prevent crime, characteristically utilize violence, and certainly symbolize a most dramatic and military-like presence in the community by virtue of their equipment, speech, and action. Indeed, as Manning illustrates graphically in his essay, the American police seize upon occasions for police control; seek proactive, crime-oriented activities as a verification of their effectiveness; and in general mobilize, at every opportunity, their powers to intervene directly and authoritatively in the private lives of the citizenry.

Relatedly, perhaps the most significant feature of American policing is its violent character. Egon Bittner argues in the second essay displayed in this section that force is applied typically, not atypically, by the police in the United States when they are faced with a problematic situation. Violence, then, must be seen as both the symbolic action and the symbolic source of legitimation for the American police. Thus, from Bittner's analysis concerning the centrality of force in shaping the police role and from Manning's observations of the basis on which the police symbolize their claims for public trust and support, we can derive a set of defining characteristics to fit the American police. From this perspective, the police can be seen as: (1) a representation of the coercive potential and its enactment in society—the application of force in everyday affairs—that is (2) backed by law and the conventional institutions of the community, and (3) that reflects the interest of those who control and define the situations that require the use of authority. Of all the suasive forces acting on the police, these three are clearly the most enduring conditions and pressures under which policing is shaped.

In practice, the actions of the American police are very much a response to the organizational form that surrounds them. This organizational form has become highly elaborated internally in most departments, while externally the form has remained much the same in appearance for the past 150 years. The police present themselves as bureaucratically organized in rhetorical terms. That is, although the police claim to operate within the bureaucratic model, critical aspects of policing represent what Manning (1977) calls "situationally justified actions." These are actions that become rationalized after the fact because, from the police actors' perspective, certain situations literally demand intervention. Such actions are to be contrasted with the police claim that they act as they do because certain rules prescribe certain responses. As Bittner shows, how to intervene might be defined, but when, where, and with whom the police should intervene cannot be defined clearly. In fact, for all practical purposes, interventions are considered by the police to be matters of individual discretion, though one would not guess this is so by listening to the public rhetoric of the police. Summarily, the organizational form surrounding the police can be thought of as a "symbolic bureaucracy." To paraphrase Jacobs (1969:414), symbolic bureaucracies are organizations which maintain an image of complete adherence to bureaucratic rules while internally they conform to such rules little or not at all.

The public image of the police, when combined with the diverse tasks performed in the organization, the discretion of the officers at the operating levels, and the vulnerability of the police to local political pressures, creates an interesting, if explosive, paradox. Indeed, the paramilitary facade of the organization is contradicted by the internally decentralized, officer-centered mode of operation. This is put well by Clark and Sykes (1974:473) when they remark that much of the bureaucratizing potential of police organizations such as the uniforms, chain of command, formalized training programs, and the like is "neutralized by the debureaucratizing effects of relatively isolated and atomized police operations in detached individual or two-man patrol or investigative teams, under weak or nonexistent supervision, operating within an organizational ethos of the individualization of each case and each officer's solution to it."

Let us raise now a rather significant question. If the police are not controlled by the law (as both Manning and Bittner suggest) but rather *use* the law as a resource to rationalize and gain public support for their interventions into the body politic, why do we even talk about, and conceive of, the police as a "law enforcement agency"? To answer this question, several interrelated hypotheses can be advanced. First, in a society as complex, pluralistic, and conflicted as ours, the law is one of the few sources of legitimacy—something Americans tend to believe stands above regional, class, racial, or individual interest. In essence, we operate with a mythological conception of the state as a reflection of the society. Both of them are thought to be governed by law and laws, not by individuals. The police, insofar as they are able to gain an association in the public mind with the moral order embodied in the law, gain respectability and legitimacy; thus, they are able to exercise much authority in their task. Second, it is possible to argue that the law also provides the police with an additional source of legitimacy in that the courts, not the police, must contend with the effects of police actions. Even when police actions may have been conceived of, and accomplished on, a very ill defined and shaky legal basis, the law can serve as a secondary source of justification. As Bittner suggests, since the police lack a clear set of legal rules to guide their interventions, the courts provide only post facto control. And, simply because the police receive retrospective validation by the courts, this does not mean that the police have acted in line with any a priori court-defined parameters. They may try of course to act in a thoroughly legal manner, and some professional departments do attempt to act in line with court cases and prosecutor's standards, but it is always a conflictual and troublesome matter to do so. In most jurisdictions, there is constant conflict between the prosecutor's office, the courts, and the police. They each have different roles, information and authority. To wit, whereas the police must gather "facts" for conviction, the prosecutor's office is responsible for achieving a conviction, and the courts are presumably expected to "serve justice." Thus, in essence, the final decision on police actions tends to be held by the courts after the fact. Third, no doubt the police are as convinced as the rest of us that social problems can be solved by the application of planned investments. In short, the police believe that more officers, more money, more equipment, and more law can and will bring success. Since in a capitalistic society organizations are judged by what they produce, the police have attempted to define their "product" as "crime control" and, in their rhetoric, symbolize this notion by delivering to the public a product efficiently produced. In this sense, their efforts are very American. It remains to be seen, however, whether legalistic crime control in the manner in which the police speak of it is truely sensitive to their efforts. Fourth, the collective morale of the police depends, to a large degree, upon the assertion that they perform feats of daring much of the time. "Real police work" means crook-catching to the police and public alike, and it is this aspect of their work that is publicly proclaimed as the dominant mission of the organization rather than the more mundane and boring paperwork, service work, and dirty work which actually occupies some 80 to 90 percent of the police time. Finally, it can be argued that the police accept this version because it also serves to coerce the public to compliance. The public in the United States, unlike that in England, does not share a common conception of manners, of civility, of deference to one another. Rather, there are enormously diverse standards of propriety and demeanor that differ by region, class, ethnicity, age, sex, race, and urban or rural residence. The police face uncertain responses from those with whom they deal and hence tend to try to redefine any intervention situation as a legal problem wherein they can increase their resources to command compliance by using force if necessary.

The real dilemma of American policing as depicted here is that as the police become more and more professional and, in fact, more and more constrained by the law they so frequently invoke in their pronouncements and actions, the public they serve is asking for more and more police activities that affirm and maintain the social order of an area in the form of more foot patrols, community-based policing, and the like. It would appear, therefore, that more legalistic interventions under these conditions will exacerbate rather than reduce the very problems people presently face with the police. Conversely, the demand for crime control, as the public defines it, is important, persistent, and salient. Should the police fail in this instrumental function, they will be confronted with a significant proportion of the public that questions their every activity. Ironically, if the police define their role as limited to crime control and if they fail in this role, they are likely to lose more support than if they had claimed that their interests, functions, and obligations were considerably broader.

We shall continue to confront this dilemma throughout this book, for the police are evaluated—and evaluate themselves—against functions they rarely perform (arrest and crime control), deny the reality of functions they frequently perform, and do not take credit for many of their functions which are in fact very significant to their public—incidental help, finding lost children, supplying information, assisting at accidents, and so forth. In practical terms, then, the ways in which the English mandate has been transformed in America results in a narrowing of the function of the police, a restriction of their symbolic claims, and a more uneasy and politically volatile mandate. It cannot be said, of course, that the police have intentionally sought this outcome on their own, but certainly many of their best efforts have resulted in the present paradoxical situation.

The Police:
Mandate, Strategies,
and Appearances

*Peter K. Manning**

I. INTRODUCTION

All societies have their share of persistent, chronic problems—problems of life, of death, problems of property and security, problems of man's relationship to what he consecrates. And because societies have their quota of troubles, they have developed ways in which to distribute responsibility for dealing with them. The division of labor that results is not only an allocation of functions and rewards, it is a moral division as well. In exchange for money, goods, or services, these groups—such as lawyers or barbers or clergymen or pharmacists—have a *license* to carry out certain activities that others may not. This license is a legally defined right, and no other group or groups may encroach upon it.[1]

The right to perform an occupation may entail the permission to pick up garbage or to cut open human bodies and transfer organs from one to another. What it always involves, however, is a series of tasks and associated attitudes and values that set apart a specialized occupational group from all the others. Further, the licensed right to perform an occupation may include a claim to the right to define the proper conduct of others toward matters concerned with the work. The claim, if granted, is the occupation's *mandate*. The mandate may vary from a right to live dangerously to the right to define the conditions of work and functions of related personnel.

The professional mandate is not easily won, of course, for clients are often unwilling to accept the professional definition of their problem. Professions claim a body of theory and practice to justify their right to discover, define, and deal with problems. The medical profession, for example, is usually considered the model of a vocation with a secure license and mandate. Yet even in medicine the client may refuse to accept the diagnosis; he may change physicians or fail to follow doctor's orders or insist upon defining his troubles as the product of a malady best cured by hot lemonade or prayer. The contraction and expansion of an occupation's mandate reflects the concerns society has with the services it provides, with its organization, and with its effectiveness. In times of crisis, it is the professions that are questioned first.[2]

---

[1]See Everett C. Hughes, *Men and Their Work* (New York: The Free Press, 1958), chap. 6; idem, "The Study of Occupations," in *Sociology Today,* ed. R. K. Merton, Leonard Broom, and L. S. Cottrell (New York: Basic Books, 1959), pp. 442–458 (footnotes renumbered—eds.).

[2]Hughes, *op. cit.*

*I would like to thank Howard S. Becker, Jerome H. Skolnick, and Jack D. Douglas for helpful comments and criticism on this essay.

REPRINTED FROM: J. D. Douglas (ed.) *Crime and Justice in American Society.* Indianapolis: Bobbs-Merrill, *1971* (149–172; 180–193).

Some occupations are not as fortunate as others in their ability to delimit a societal "trouble" and deal with it systematically. The more power and authority a profession has, the better able it is to gain and maintain control over the symbolic meanings with which it is associated in the public's mind. As we have become less concerned with devils and witches as causes of mental illness, clergymen have lost ground to psychiatrists who have laid claim to a secular cure for madness; in this sense, mental illness is a product of the definitions supplied by psychiatry. A profession, therefore, must not only compete with its clientele's definitions, it must also defend itself against the definitions of competing groups. Is a backache better treated by a Christian Scientist, an osteopath, a chiropractor, a masseuse, or an M.D.? Professional groups whose tools are less well-developed, whose theory is jerry-built or unproved, and who are unable to produce results in our consumer-oriented society will be beset with public doubt, concern, and agitation. In other words, these are the groups that have been unable to define their mandate for solving social "troubles" in such a way that it can be accomplished with ease and to the satisfaction of those they intend to serve.

The police have trouble. Among the many occupations now in crisis, they best symbolize the shifts and strains in our changing socio-political order. They have been assigned the task of crime prevention, crime detection, and the apprehension of criminals. Based on their legal monopoly of violence, they have staked out a mandate that claims to include the efficient, apolitical, and professional enforcement of the law. It is the contention of this essay that the police have staked out a vast and unmanageable social domain. And what has happened as a result of their inability to accomplish their self-proclaimed mandate is that the police have resorted to the manipulation of *appearances*.

We shall attempt to outline the nature of the police mandate, or their definition of social trouble, their methods of coping with this trouble, and the consequences of their efforts. After developing a sociological analysis of the paradoxes of police work and discussing the heroic attempts—*strategies*—by police to untangle these paradoxes, we shall also consider the recommendations of the President's crime commission[3] and assess their value as a means of altering and improving the practical art of managing public order.

To turn for the moment to "practical matters," the same matters to which we shall return before concluding, the troubles of the police, the problems and paradoxes of their mandate in modern society, have become more and more intense. Police today may be more efficient in handling their problems than were the first bobbies who began to patrol London in 1829. Or they may not be. There may or may not be more crime. Individual rights may or may not be greatly threatened by crime or crime-fighters, and the enforcement of law in view of recent Supreme Court decisions may or may not be a critical issue in crime control. The police may or may not have enough resources to do their job,

---

[3]The President's Commission on Law Enforcement and Administration of Justice (hereafter cited as President's Commission). *The Challenge of Crime in a Free Society* (Washington, D.C.: U.S. Government Printing Office, 1967); and idem. *Task Force Report: The Police* (Washington, D.C.: United States Government Printing Office, 1967).

and they may or may not be allocating them properly. Peace-keeping rather than law enforcement may or may not be the prime need in black communities, and the police may or may not need greater discretionary powers in making an arrest. But however these troubles are regarded, they exist. They are rooted deeply in the mandate of the police.

Some Sociological Assumptions

This essay makes several assumptions about occupations, about people as they execute occupational roles, about organizations as loci or structures for occupational activities, and about the nature of society. Not all activity taking place "on the job" can be construed as "work"; goldbricking is not unknown in American society and some professionals have even been known to use their places of work to conduct business somewhat outside the mandate of their organization. An individual's "organizational" behavior varies with what the organization is said to require or permit, with his particular place in the organizational hierarchy, and with the degree of congruence between the individual's personal definition of his role and the organization's definition of his role. In a given situation, then, organizational rules and regulations may be important sources of meanings ("He's working hard"), or other criteria may provide more relevant meanings of behavior ("He can't be expected to work. His wife just had a baby"). The ways in which people explain or account for their own organizational activities and those of others are problematic. How do people refer to their organizational roles and activities? How do they construct their moral obligations to the organization? What do they think they owe the organization? How does this sense of obligation and commitment pattern or constrain them in another role—the role of golfer or father or politician?

People as they perform their roles are actors. They are alert to the small cues that indicate meaning and intention—the wink, the scowl, the raised eyebrow. Those who attend to these behavioral clues are the audience. All actors try to maximize the positive impression they make on others, and both experience and socialization provide them with a repertoire of devices to manage their appearance.

People as actors in roles must also make assumptions about their audience. The politician, for example, must make certain assumptions about his constituency, the lawyer certain assumptions about clients. Assumptions are an important part of urban life. Some actors with white faces, for instance, may make certain assumptions about others with black faces, that they will be ill-mannered or badly educated and that any request for directions is a prelude to a holdup. Assumptions are not simply individual in nature; they are shared, patterned, and passed on from one social group to the next.

One of the most important aspects of assumptions, however, is that they are the basis for strategies.[4] Strategies arise from the need of organizations and individuals to cope with persistent social problems about which assump-

---

[4]The important, sociological notions of "strategy" and "tactics" come from military theory and game theory. See, for example, Erving Goffman, *The Presentation of Self in Everyday Life* (Garden City, N.Y.: Doubleday, 1959).

Reflected Appraisal

tions have been made. Strategies are often a means of survival in a competitive environment; they can be inferred from the allocation of resources or from the behavior and pronouncements of an organization. In short, strategies assist any organization within the society in managing its appearance and in controlling the behavior of its audience.

All organizations and individuals, we assume, are bent on maximizing their impressions in order to gain control over an audience.[5] The audience for the police is diverse; it should be considered many audiences. For the police must convince the politicians that they have used their allocated resources efficiently; they must persuade the criminals that they are effective crimefighters; they must assure the broader public that they are controlling crime. Rather than a single rhetoric—the "use of words to form attitudes or induce actions in other human agents"[6]—directed toward convincing one audience, the police must develop many rhetorics. Linguistic strategies to control audiences are only one of many ploys used by the police organization to manage its impression. Not all the results of the use of rhetorics are intended; the consequence of the rhetorical "war on crime" in Detroit in the fall of 1969, to cite one example, was a continued advance in the city's downtown crime rate. Moreover, rhetoric can take on different meanings even within the organizational hierarchy. To patrolmen, the term "professionalism" means control over hours and salary and protection from arbitrary punishment from "upstairs"; to the chief and the higher administrators, it relates to the public-administration notions of efficiency, technological expertise, and standards of excellence in recruitment and training.

Tactics are the means by which a strategy is implemented. If the strategy is to mount a war on crime, then one tactic might be to flood the downtown area with scooter-mounted patrolmen. Tactics, in other words, are the ways in which one group of people deals with others in face-to-face encounters. How does the policeman handle a family quarrel in which the wife has the butcher knife and the husband already knows how sharp it is? Strategies pertain to general forms of action or rhetoric while tactics refer to the specific action or the specific words used to best meet a specific, problematic situation.[7] The tactic of flattery may be far more effective—and safer—in wresting the butcher knife than a leap over the kitchen table.

All occupations possess strategies and tactics, by means of which they attempt to control their most significant audiences. However, our analysis must do more than describe the existence of such means of creating impressions. So far as the police are concerned, impression management, or the construction of appearances, cannot substitute for significant control of crime. To maintain the dramaturgic metaphor, we suggest that there are significant flaws and

---

[5]*Ibid.*

[6]Kenneth Burke, *A Grammar of Motives and a Rhetoric of Motives* (New York: Meridian Books, 1962), p. 565.

[7]D. W. Ball makes this distinction between rhetoric and what he terms "situated vocabularies" in "The Problematics of Respectability," in Jack D. Douglas, ed., *Deviance and Respectability* (New York: Basic Books, 1970).

contradictions in the performance of the police that cast a serious doubt on the credibility of their occupational mandate.

The mandate of the police is fraught with difficulties, many of them, we shall argue, self-created. They have defined their task in such a way that they cannot, because of the nature of American social organization, hope to honor it to the satisfaction of the public. We will argue that the appearances that the police create—that they control crime and that they attain a high level of efficiency—are transparent on close examination, that they may, in fact, be created as a sop to satisfy the public's impossible expectations for police performance. By utilizing the rhetoric of crime control, the police claim the responsibility for the social processes that beget the illegal acts. They cannot control these social processes that are embedded in American values, norms, and cultural traditions. Creating the appearance of controlling them is only a temporizing policy; it is not the basis for a sound, honorable mandate.

The police mandate and the problems it creates in American society are our central concern. We will rely on the concepts of actor, organization, and audience, of mandate, and of strategy and appearances. We will show that the police mandate, as presently defined, is full of contradictions. We will further demonstrate that the strategies and tactics of the American police are failing in a serious way to meet the need of controlling crime.

The Occupational Culture of the Police

Before beginning an analysis of the police mandate, a brief comment is necessary about the occupational culture of our law enforcers. The American police act in accord with their assumptions about the nature of social life, and their most important assumptions originate with their need to maintain control over both their mandate and their self-esteem. The policeman's self is an amalgam of evaluations made by the many audiences before whom he, as social actor must perform: his peers, his family, his immediate superiors and the higher administrators, his friends on and off duty. His most meaningful standards of performance are the ideals of his *occupational culture*. The policeman judges himself against the ideal policeman as described in police occupational lore and imagery. What a "good policeman" does is an omnipresent standard. The occupational culture, however, contains more than the definition of a good policeman. It contains the typical values, norms, attitudes, and material paraphernalia of an occupational group.

An occupational culture also prompts the *assumptions* about everyday life that become the basis for organizational strategies and tactics. Recent studies of the occupational culture of the police allow the formulation of the following postulates or assumptions, all of which are the basis for police strategies to be discussed later:

1. People cannot be trusted; they are dangerous.

2. Experience is better than abstract rules.

3. You must make people respect you.

4. Everyone hates a cop.

5. The legal system is untrustworthy; policemen make the best decisions about guilt or innocence.

6. People who are not controlled will break laws.

7. Policemen must appear respectable and be efficient.

8. Policemen can most accurately identify crime and criminals.

9. The major jobs of the policeman are to prevent crime and to enforce laws. laws.

10. Stronger punishment will deter criminals from repeating their errors.[8]

Some qualifications about these postulates are in order. They apply primarily to the American noncollege-educated patrolman. They are less applicable to administrators of urban police departments and to members of minority groups within these departments. Nor do they apply accurately to nonurban, state, and federal policemen.

We shall now describe the paradoxes of the police mandate, the strategies of the police in dealing with their troubles, and some of the findings and recommendations of the President's crime commission as they bear on the current attempt by the police to make a running adjustment to their problems.

II. THE "IMPOSSIBLE" MANDATE

The police in modern society are in agreement with their audiences—which include their professional interpreters, the American family, criminals, and politicians—in at least one respect: they have an "impossible" task. Certainly, all professionals have impossible tasks insofar as they try to surmount the problems of collective life that resist easy solutions. The most "successful" occupations, however, have managed to construct a mandate in terms of their own vision of the world. The policeman's mandate, on the other hand, is defined largely by his publics—not, at least at the formal level, in his own terms.

Several rather serious consequences result from the public's image of the police. The public is aware of the dramatic nature of a small portion of police work, but it ascribes the element of excitement to all police activities. To much of the public, the police are seen as alertly ready to respond to citizen demands,

---

[8]These postulates have been drawn from the work of Michael Banton, *The Policeman in the Community* (New York: Basic Books, 1965); the articles in *The Police: Six Sociological Essays,* ed. David Bordua (New York: John Wiley & Sons, 1967), esp. those by Albert J. Reiss and David Bordua, and John H. McNamara; Arthur Niederhoffer, *Behind the Shield* (Garden City, N.Y.: Doubleday, 1967); Jerome Skolnick, *Justice Without Trial* (New York: John Wiley & Sons, 1966); and William A. Westley, "Violence and the Police," *American Journal of Sociology,* 59 (July 1953), 34–41; idem, "Secrecy and the Police," *Social Forces,* 34 (March 1956), 254–257; idem, "The Police: Law, Custom and Morality," in Peter I. Rose, ed. *The Study of Society* (New York: Random House, 1967). See also James Q. Wilson, *Varieties of Police Behavior: The Management of Law and Order in Eight Communities* (Cambridge, Mass.: Harvard University Press, 1968); idem, "The Police and Their Problems: A Theory," *Public Policy,* 12 (1963), 189–216; idem, "Generational and Ethnic Differences Among Police Officers," *American Journal of Sociology,* 69 (March 1964), 522–528.

as crime-fighters, as an efficient, bureaucratic, highly organized force that keeps society from falling into chaos. The policeman himself considers the essence of his role to be the dangerous and heroic enterprise of crook-catching and the watchful prevention of crimes.[9] The system of positive and negative sanctions from the public and within the department encourages this heroic conception. The public wants crime prevented and controlled; that is, it wants criminals caught. Headlines herald the accomplishments of G-Men and F.B.I. agents who often do catch dangerous men, and the reputation of these federal authorities not infrequently rubs off on local policemen who are much less adept at catching criminals.

In an effort to gain the public's confidence in their ability, and to insure thereby the solidity of their mandate, the police have encouraged the public to continue thinking of them and their work in idealized terms, terms, that is, which grossly exaggerate the actual work done by police. They do engage in chases, in gunfights, in careful sleuthing. But these are rare events. Most police work resembles any other kind of work: it is boring, tiresome, sometimes dirty, sometimes technically demanding, but it is rarely dangerous. Yet the occasional chase, the occasional shoot-out, the occasional triumph of some extraordinary detective work have been seized upon by the police and played up to the public. The public's reponse has been to demand even more dramatic crook-catching and crime prevention, and this demand for arrests has been converted into an index for measuring how well the police accomplish their mandate. The public's definitions have been converted by the police organization into distorted criteria for promotion, success, and security. Most police departments promote men from patrol to detective work, a generally more desirable duty, for "good pinches"—arrests that are most likely to result in convictions.[10] The protection of the public welfare, however, including personal and property safety, the prevention of crime, and the preservation of individual civil rights, is hardly achieved by a high pinch rate. On the contrary, it might well be argued that protection of the public welfare could best be indexed by a low arrest rate. Because their mandate automatically entails mutually contradictory ends—protecting both public order and individual rights—the police resort to managing their public image and the indexes of their accomplishment. And the ways in which the police manage their appearance are consistent with the assumptions of their occupational culture, with the public's view of the police as a social-control agency, and with the ambiguous nature of our criminal law.

---

[9] Although the imagery of the police and their own self-definition coincide on the dangers of being a policeman, at least one study has found that many other occupations are more dangerous. Policemen kill six times as many people as policemen are killed in the line of duty. In 1955, Robin found that the rate of police fatalities on duty, including accidents, was 33 per 100,000, less than the rate for mining (94), agriculture (55). construction (76), and transportation (44). Between 1950 and 1960, an average of 240 persons were killed each year by policemen—approximately six times the number of policemen killed by criminals. Gerald D. Robin, "Justifiable Homicide by Police Officers," *Journal of Criminal Law, Criminology and Police Science*, 54 (1963), 225–231.

[10] Niederhoffer, *Behind the Shield*, p. 221.

The Problematic Nature of Law and Order

The criminal law is one among many instrumentalities of social control. It is an explicit set of rules created by political authority; it contains provisions for punishment by officials designated with the responsibility to interpret and enforce the rules which should be uniformly applied to all persons within a politically defined territory.[11] This section discusses the relationships between the laws and the mores of a society, the effect of the growth of civilized society on law enforcement, and the problematic nature of crime in an advanced society. The differential nature of enforcement will be considered as an aspect of peace-keeping, and will lead to the discussion of the police in the larger political system.

A society's laws, it is often said, reflect its customs; it can also be said that the growth of the criminal law is proportionate to the decline in the consistency and binding nature of these mores. In simpler societies, where the codes and rules of behavior were well known and homogeneous, sanctions were enforced with much greater uniformity and predictability. Social control was isomorphic with one's obligations to family, clan, and age group, and the political system of the tribe. In a modern, differentiated society, a minimal number of values and norms are shared. And because the fundamental, taken-for-granted consensus on what is proper and respectable has been blurred or shattered, or, indeed, never existed, criminal law becomes a basis of social control. As Quinney writes, "Where correct conduct cannot be agreed upon, the criminal law serves to control the behavior of all persons within a political jurisdiction."[12]

Social control through the criminal law predominates in a society only when other means of control have failed. When it does predominate, it no longer reflects the mores of the society. It more accurately reflects the interests of shifting power groups within the society. As a result, the police, as the designated enforcers of a system of criminal laws, are undercut by circumstances that accentuate the growing differences between the moral order and the legal order.

One of these complicating circumstances is simply the matter of social changes, which further stretch the bond between the moral and the legal. The law frequently lags behind the changes in what society deems acceptable and unacceptable practice. At other times, it induces changes, such as those pertaining to civil rights, thereby anticipating acceptable practice. The definition of crime, then, is a product of the relationship between social structure and the law. Crime, to put it another way, is not a homogeneous entity.

The perspective of the patrolman as he goes about his daily rounds is a legalistic one. The law and the administrative actions of his department provide him with a frame of reference for exercising the mandate of the police. The of crime, then, is a product of the relationship between social structure and the

---

[11]See Richard Quinney, "Is Criminal Behavior Deviant Behavior?" *British Journal of Criminology*, 5 (April 1965), 133 . The material in this section draws heavily from Quinney. See also R. C. Fuller, "Morals and the Criminal Law," *Journal of Criminal Law, Criminology and Police Science*, 32 (March–April 1942), 624–630.

[12]Quinney, *op. cit.*, p. 133.

citizen, on the other hand, does not live his life in accordance with a legalistic framework; he defines his acts in accordance with a moral or ethical code provided him by his family, his religion, his social class. For the most part, he sees law enforcement as an intervention in his private affairs.

No matter what the basis for actions of private citizens may be, however, the patrolman's job is one of practical decision-making within a legalistic pattern. His decisions are expected to include an understanding of the law as a system of formal rules, the enforcement practices emphasized by his department, and a knowledge of the specific facts of an allegedly illegal situation. The law includes little formal recognition of the variation in the private arrangement of lives. Even so, the policeman is expected to take these into account also. No policeman can ever be provided with a handbook that could tell him, at a moment's notice, just what standards to apply in enforcing the law and in maintaining order. Wilson summarizes the difficulty inherent in law enforcement as follows:

> Most criminal laws define *acts* (murder, rape, speeding, possessing narcotics), which are held to be illegal; people may disagree as to whether the act should be illegal, as they do with respect to narcotics, for example, but there is little disagreement as to what the behaviour in question consists of. Laws regarding disorderly conduct and the like assert, usually by implication, that there is a condition ("public order") that can be diminished by various actions. The difficulty, of course, is that public order is nowhere defined and can never be defined unambiguously because what constitutes order is a matter of opinion and convention, not a state of nature. (An unmurdered person, an unraped woman, and an unpossessed narcotic can be defined so as to be recognizable to any reasonable person.) An additional difficulty, a corollary of the first, is the impossibility of specifying, except in the extreme case, what degree of disorder is intolerable and who is to be held culpable for that degree. A suburban street is quiet and pleasant; a big city street is noisy and (to some) offensive; what degree of noise and offense, and produced by whom, constitutes disorderly conduct"?[13]

The complexity of law enforcement stems from both the problem of police "discretion" and the inherent tensions between the maintenance of order and individual rights. The law contains rules on how to maintain order; it contains substantive definitions of crime, penalties for violations, and the conditions under which the commission of a crime is said to have been intended.[14] Further, the law contains procedures for the administration of justice and for the protection of the individual. The complexities of law enforcement notwithstanding, however, the modern policeman is frequently faced with the instant problem of defining an action as either legal or illegal, of deciding, in other words, whether to intervene and, if so, what tactic to use. He moves in a dense web of social action and social meanings, burdened by a problematic, complex array of ever-changing laws. Sometimes the policeman must quickly decide very abstract matters. Though a practitioner of the legal arts, his tools

---

[13]Wilson, *op. cit.*, pp. 21–22.

[14]Skolnick, *op cit.*, pp. 7–8, 9.

at hand are largely obscure, ill-developed, and crude. Wtih little formal training, the rookie must learn his role by absorbing the theories, traditions, and
personal whims of experienced patrolmen.

Police Work as Peace Keeping [15]

The thesis of two recent major works on the police, Wilson's *The Varieties of
Police Behavior* and Skolnick's *Justice Without Trial*, can be paraphrased as
follows: the policeman must exercise discretion in matters involving life and
death, honor and dishonor, and he must do so in an environment that he perceives as threatening, dangerous, hostile, and volatile. He sees his efficiency
constrained by the law and by the police organization. Yet, he must effectively
manage "disorder" in a variety of unspecified ways, through methods usually
learned and practiced on the job. As a result of these conditions, the policeman,
in enforcing his conception of order, often violates the rights of citizens.

Many observers of police work regard the primary function of a policeman
as that of a *peace-keeper*, not a *law enforcer*. According to this view, police
spend most of their time attending to order-maintaining functions, such as
finding lost children, substituting as ambulance drivers, or interceding in
quarrels of one sort or another. To these observers, the police spend as little as
10 to 15 per cent of their time on law enforcement—responding to burglary
calls or trying to find stolen cars. The large-scale riots and disorders of recent
years accounted for few police man-hours. Wilson illustrates the peace-keeping
(order maintenance) and law-enforcement distinction this way:

> The difference between order maintenance and law enforcement is not
> simply the difference between "little stuff" and "real crime" or between
> misdemeanors and felonies. The distinction is fundamental to the police
> role, for the two functions involve quite dissimilar police actions and
> judgments. Order maintenance arises out of a dispute among citizens
> who accuse each other of being at fault; law enforcement arises out of the
> victimization of an innocent party by a person whose guilt must be
> proved. Handling a disorderly situation requires the officer to make a
> judgment about what constitutes an appropriate standard of behavior;
> law enforcement requires him only to compare a person's behavior with a
> clear legal standard. Murder or theft is defined, unambiguously, by
> statutes; public peace is not. Order maintenance rarely leads to an arrest;
> law enforcement (if the suspect can be found) typically does. Citizens
> quarreling usually want the officer to "do something," but they rarely
> want him to make an arrest (after all, the disputants are usually known
> or related to each other). Furthermore, whatever law is broken in a quar-
> rel is usually a misdemeanor, and in most states, an officer cannot make

---

[15]This perspective on police work is emphasized by Wilson *op. cit.;* Banton, *op. cit.;*
and Skolnick, *op. cit.* In addition, see the more legalistically oriented work of Wayne R.
LaFave, *Arrest,* ed. F. J. Remington (Boston: Little, Brown, 1965); Joseph Goldstein.
"Police Discretion Not to Invoke the Legal Process: Low-Visibility Decisions in the Administration of Justice." *Yale Law Journal,* 69 (1960), 543–594; and Herman Goldstein,
"Police Discretion: The Ideal Versus the Real," *Public Administration Review,* 23 (September 1963), 140–148.

a misdemeanor arrest unless one party or the other will swear out a formal complaint (which is even rarer)[16]

The complexity of the law and the difficulty in obtaining a complainant combine to tend to make the policeman underenforce the law—to overlook, ignore, dismiss, or otherwise erase the existence of many enforceable breaches of the law.

Some researchers and legalists have begun to piece together a pattern of the conditions under which policemen have a tendency not to enforce the law. From a study of police in three Midwestern states, LaFave has concluded that two considerations characterize a decision not to arrest. The first is that the crime is unlikely to reach public attention—for example, that it is of a private nature or of low visibility—and the second is that underenforcement is unlikely to be detected or challenged.[17] Generally, the conditions under which policemen are less likely to enforce the law are those in which they perceive little public consensus on the law, or in which the law is ambiguous. LaFave found that policemen are not apt to enforce rigorously laws that are viewed by the public as dated, or that are used on the rare occasions when the public order is being threatened.

There is a certain Benthamic calculus involved in all arrests, a calculus that is based on pragmatic considerations such as those enumerated by LaFave. Sex, age, class, and race might also enter into the calculus of whether the law should be enforced. In a case study of the policeman assigned to skid row, Bittner illustrates the great degree of discretion exercised by the policeman. Yet the law, often reified by the policeman, is rarely a clear guide to action—despite the number of routine actions that might be termed "typical situations that policemen perceive as *demand conditions* for action without arrest."[18]

In the exercise of discretion, in the decision to enforce the law or to underenforce, the protection of individual rights is often at stake. But individual rights are frequently in opposition to the preservation of order, as a totalitarian state exemplifies in the extreme. The police try to manage these two contradictory demands by emphasizing their peace-keeping functions. This emphasis succeeds only when a consensus exists on the nature of the order (peace) to be preserved. The greater the difference in viewpoint between the police and the public on the degree and kind of order to be preserved, the greater will be antagonism between the two; the inevitable result of this hostility will be "law breaking."

The resolution of the contradictions and complexities inherent in the police mandate, including the problems of police discretion, of individual rights, of law enforcement and peace-keeping, is not helped, however, by the involvement of police in politics. Politics only further complicates the police

[16]James Q. Wilson, "What Makes a Better Policeman?" *Atlantic*, 223 (March 1969), 131.

[17]LaFave, *op. cit.*

[18]Egon Bittner, "The Police on Skid-Row: A Study of Peace-Keeping." *American Sociological Review*, 32 (October 1967), 699–715.

mandate. The law itself is a political phenomenon, and at the practical level of enforcing it, the local political system is yet another source of confusion.

The Police in the Political System

In theory, the American police are apolitical. Their own political values and political aims are supposed to be secondary to the institutional objective of law enforcement. In practice, however, police organizations function in a political context; they operate in a public political arena and their mandate is defined politically. They may develop strategies to create and maintain the appearance of being apolitical in order to protect their organizational autonomy, but they are nonetheless a component of American political machinery. There are three reasons why the police are inextricably involved in the political system, the first and most obvious being that the vast majority of the police in this nation are locally controlled.

> [Among the 40,000 law-enforcement agencies in the United States], there are only 50 . . . on the federal level . . . 200 on the state level. The remaining 29,750 agencies are dispersed throughout the many counties, cities, towns, and villages that form our local governments . . . . Only 3,050 agencies are located in counties and 3,700 in cities. The great majority of the police forces—33,000—are distributed throughout boroughs, towns, and villages.[19]

In 1966 there were 420,000 full- and part-time law-enforcement officers and civilians employed by police agencies in the United States. Most of them—371,000—were full-time employees; about 11 per cent—46,000—were civilians. Of the full-timers, 23,000 served at the federal level of government, 40,000 at the state level, and the remaining 308,000, or 83 per cent of the total, were divided between county and local political jurisdictions. Of the 308,000, somewhat more than 197,000 were employees of counties, cities under 250,000, townships, boroughs, and villages; the balance of 110,500 served in the 55 American cities with populations of more than 250,000. The number of police personnel in any one type of political division varied widely, of course. For example, on the county level of government, the roster of the 3,050 sheriff's offices in the United States ranged from a one-man force in Putnam County, Georgia, to a 5,515-man force in Los Angeles County.

What all these figures indicate is the massive dispersal of police authority—and political authority—throughout the nation. What these figures also indicate is the existence of overlapping laws governing law enforcement. Further, they show that the responsibility for maintaining public order in America is decentralized, and that law-enforcement officers are largely under the immediate control of local political authorities.

The second reason why the police are an integral part of the political system is this: law is a political entity, and the administration of criminal law unavoidably encompasses political values and political ends. The police are directly related to a political system that develops and defines the law, itself a

---

[19]President's Commission, *Task Force Report: The Police*, pp. 7, 8–9

product of interpretations of what is right and proper from the perspective of different politically powerful segments within the community.

The third reason why the police are tied to the political system emanates from the second: the police must administer the law. Many factors pattern this enforcement, but they all reflect the political organization of society. The distribution of power and authority, for example, rather than the striving for justice, or equal treatment under the law, can have a direct bearing on enforcement.

Because law enforcement is for the most part locally controlled, sensitivity to local political trends remains an important element in police practice. Since the police are legally prohibited from being publicly political, they often appeal to different community groups, and participate sub rosa in others, in order to influence the determination of public policy. Community policy, whether made by the town council or the mayor or the city manager, affects pay scales, operating budgets, personnel, administrative decisions, and, to some extent, organizational structure. The police administrator must, therefore, be responsive to these controls, and he must deal with them in an understanding way. He must be sensitive to the demands of the local politicians—even while maintaining the loyalty of the lower ranks through a defense of their interests.

There are several direct effects of the political nature of the police mandate. One is that many policemen become alienated; they lose interest in their role as enforcers and in the law as a believable criterion. The pressures of politics also erode loyalty to the police organization and not infrequently lead to collusion with criminals and organized crime.

The policeman's exposure to danger, his social background, low pay, low morale, his vulnerability in a repressive bureaucracy all conspire to make him susceptible to the lures of the underhanded and the appeals of the political. Studies summarized by Skolnick[20] reveal a political profile of the policeman as a conservative, perhaps reactionary, person of lower-class or lower-middle-class origin, often a supporter of radical right causes, often prejudiced and repressive, often extremely ambivalent about the rights of others. The postulates or assumptions of the police culture, the suspiciousness, fear, low self-esteem, and distrust of others are almost diametrically opposed to the usual conception of the desirable democratic man.

Thus, the enforcement of some laws is personally distasteful. Civil-rights legislation, for example, can be anathema. Or truculence can be the reaction to an order relaxing controls in ghettos during the summer months. It is the ambivalence of policemen toward certain laws and toward certain local policies that fragments loyalty within a department and causes alienation.

There is another consequence of the political nature of the police mandate: the police are tempted. They are tempted not to enforce the law by organized crime, by the operators of illegal businesses such as prostitution, and by fine "law-abiding," illegally parked citizens. All too frequently, the police submit to temptations, becoming in the process exemplars of the corruption typical of

---

[20]Jerome Skolnick, ed., *The Politics of Protest* (New York: Simon & Schuster, 1969), pp. 252–253.

modern society, where the demand for "criminal services" goes on at the station house.[21]

Police and politics within the community are tightly interlocked. The sensitivity of the police to their political audiences, their operation within the political system of criminal justice, and their own personal political attitudes undermine their efforts to fulfill their contradictory mandate and to appear politically neutral.

The Efficient, Symptom-Oriented Organization

The Wickersham report, the Hoover administration's report on crime and law enforcement in the United States, was published in 1931. This precursor of the Johnson administration's *The Challenge of Crime in a Free Society* became a rallying point for advocates of police reform. One of its central themes was the lack of "professionalism" among the police of the time—their lack of special training, their corruption, their brutality, and their use of illegal procedures in law enforcement. And one of its results was that the police, partly in order to demonstrate their concern with scientific data gathering on crime and partly to indicate their capacity to "control" crime itself, began to stress crime statistics as a major component of professional police work.

Crime statistics, therefore—and let this point be emphasized—became a police construction. The actual amount of crime committed in a society is unknown—and probably unknowable, given the private nature of most crime. The *crime rate*, consequently, is simply a construction of police activities. That is, the crime rate pertains only to "crimes known to the police," crimes that have been reported to or observed by the police and for which adequate grounds exist for assuming that a violation of the law has, in fact, taken place. (The difference between the *actual* and *known crimes* is often called the "dark figure of crime.") Of course, the construction of a crime rate placed the police in a logically weak position in which they still find themselves. If the crime rate is rising, they argue that more police support is needed to fight the war against crime; if the crime rate is stable or declining, they argue that they have successfully combated the crime menace—a heads-I-win-tails-you-lose proposition.

In spite of their inability to control the commission of illegal acts (roughly, the actual rate), since they do not know about all crime, the police have claimed responsibility for crime control, using the crime rate as an index of their success. This use of the crime rate to measure success is somewhat analogous to their use of a patrolman's arrest rate as an indication of his personal success in law enforcement. Questions about the actual amount of crime and the degree of control exercised are thus bypassed in favor of an index that offers great potential for organizational or bureaucratic control. Instead of grappling with the difficult issue of defining the ends of police work and an

---

[21]There are several popular treatments of police corruption, none of them very good. Ralph L. Smith *The Tarnished Badge* (New York: Thomas Y. Crowell, 1965); Ed Cray, *The Big Blue Line* (New York: Coward-McCann, 1967).

operational means for accomplishing them, the police have opted for "efficient" law-enforcement defined in terms of fluctuations of the crime rate. They have transformed concern with undefined ends into concern with available means. Their inability to cope with the causes of crime—which might offer them a basis for defining their ends—shifts their "organizational focus" into symptomatic concerns, that is, into a preoccupation with the rate of crime, not its reasons.

This preoccupation with the symptoms of a problem rather than with the problem itself is typical of all bureaucracies. For one characteristic of a bureaucracy is goal-displacement. Bureaucratic organizations tend to lose track of their goals and engage in ritual behavior, substituting means for ends. As a whole, bureaucracies become so engrossed in pursuing, defending, reacting to, and, even, in creating immediate problems that their objective is forgotten. This tendency to displace goals is accelerated by the one value dear to all bureaucracies—efficiency. Efficiency is the be-all and end-all of bureaucratic organizations. Thus, they can expend great effort without any genuine accomplishment.

The police are burdened with the "efficiency problem." They claim to be an efficient bureaucratic organization, but they are unable to define for themselves and others precisely what it is they are being efficient about. In this respect, they do not differ from other paper-shuffling organizations. The police's problem is that the nature of their work is uncertain and negatively defined. It is uncertain in the absence of a consensus not only between the police and the public but also among themselves as to what the goals of a police department should be. It is defined in the negative because the organization punishes its members—patrolmen—for violating departmental procedures but offers no specifications on what they should do or how they should do it.

What do the police do about the problematic nature of law, about the problems arising from their involvement with politics, about their preoccupation with the symptoms of crime rather than the causes? Do they selectively adopt some strategies at the expense of others? Do they vacillate? Are the roles of the organization's members blurred? Before answering these questions, let us examine how the police, through various strategies, manage their appearance before the public. The questions will then be easier to answer.

III. MAJOR STRATEGIES OF THE POLICE

The responsibilities of the police lead them to pursue contradictory and unattainable ends. They share with all organizations and occupations, however, the ability to avoid solving their problems. Instead, they concentrate on managing them through strategies. Rather than resolving their dilemmas, the police have manipulated them with a professional eye on just how well the public accepts their dexterity. Thus, law enforcement becomes a self-justifying system. It becomes more responsive to its own needs, goals, and procedures than to serving society. In this section, we will show the ways in which the police have followed the course of most other bureaucratic institutions in society, responding to their problems by merely giving the appearance of facing them while simultaneously promoting the trained incapacity to do otherwise.

The two primary aims of most bureaucracies, the police included, are the maintenance of their organizational autonomy and the security of their members. To accomplish these aims, they adopt a pattern of institutional action that can best be described as "professionalism." This word, with its many connotations and definitions, cloaks all the many kinds of actions carried out by the police.

The guise of professionalism embodied in a bureaucratic organization is the most important strategy employed by the police to defend their mandate and thereby to build self-esteem, organizational autonomy, and occupational solidarity or cohesiveness. The professionalization drives of the police are no more suspect than the campaigns of other striving, upwardly mobile occupational groups. However, since the police have a monopoly on legal violence, since they are the active enforcers of the public will, serving theoretically in the best interests of the public, the consequences of their yearnings for prestige and power are imbued with far greater social ramifications than the relatively harmless attempts of florists, funeral directors, and accountants to attain public stature. Disinterested law enforcement through bureaucratic means is an essential in our society and in any democracy, and the American police are certainly closer to attaining this ideal than they were in 1931 at the time of the Wickersham report. Professionalism qua professionalism is unquestionably desirable in the police. But if in striving for the heights of prestige they fail to serve the altruistic values of professionalism, if their professionalism means that a faulty portrait of the social reality of crime is being painted, if their professionalism conceals more than it reveals about the true nature of their operations, then a close analysis of police professionalism is in order.

Police professionalism cannot be easily separated in practice from the bureaucratic ideal epitomized in modern police practice. The bureaucratic ideal is established as a means of obtaining a commitment from personnel to organizational and occupational norms. This bureaucratic commitment is designed to supersede commitments to competing norms, such as obligations to friends or kin or members of the same racial or ethnic group. Unlike medicine and law, professions that developed outside the context of bureaucracies, policing has always been carried out, if done on a full-time basis, as a bureaucratic function.

Modern police bureaucracy and modern police professionalism are highly articulated, although they contain some inherent stresses that are not our present concern. The strategies employed by the police to manage their public appearance develop from their adaptation of the bureaucratic ideal. These strategies incorporate the utilization of *technology* and *official statistics* in law enforcement, of *styles of patrol* that attempt to accommodate the community's desire for public order with the police department's preoccupation with bureaucratic procedures, of *secrecy* as a means of controlling the public's response to their operations, of *collaboration* with criminal elements to foster the appearance of a smoothly run, law-abiding community, and of a *symbiotic relationship* with the criminal justice system that minimizes public knowledge of the flaws within this largely privately operated system.

IV. THE EFFECTIVENESS OF POLICE STRATEGIES

The police have developed and utilized the strategies outlined above for the purpose of creating, as we have said, the appearance of managing their troublesome mandate. To a large extent, they are facilitated in the use of these strategies, in being able to project a favorable impression, by a public that has always been apathetic about police activity. Moreover, what activity the public does observe is filtered through the media with its own special devices for creating a version of reality. The public's meaning of police action is rarely gathered from first-hand experience, but from the constructed imagery of the media—which, in turn, rely upon official police sources for their presentation of the news. The police for their part, understandably, manipulate public appearances as much as they possibly can in order to gain and maintain public support.

The specific strategies used by the police to create a publicly suitable image were described in Section III: the guise of professionalism; the implementation of the bureaucratic ideal of organization; the use of technology, official statistics, and various styles of patrol; secrecy; collaboration with corrupt elements; and the establishment of a symbiotic relationship with the courts. This section will present evidence by which to evaluate these strategies. The term "effectiveness" is used only in the context of how well these devices accomplish the ends which the public and the police themselves publicly espouse; the recommendations and evaluations of the President's crime commission will be central in making judgments of police effectiveness. This appraisal of how well the police manipulate their appearance will also be a guideline for evaluating the recommendations of the commission's task force report on the police.

Professionalism and the Bureaucratic Ideal

The assumptions of professionalism and of a bureaucratic organization include a devotion to rational principles and ends that may then be translated into specific work routines having predictable outcomes. The police are organized in a military command fashion, with rigid rules and a hierarchy governing operations. However, the patrolman, the lowest man in the hierarchy—and usually the least well-trained and educated—is in the key position of exercising the greatest amount of discretion on criminal or possibly criminal activities. Especially in his peace-keeping role and in dealing with minor infractions (misdemeanors), the patrolman has wide discretionary power concerning if, when, why, and how to intervene in private affairs.

Police work must both rely on discretion and control it. Excessive inattention and excessive attention to infractions of the law are equally damaging to a community. However, the complexity of the law, its dynamic and changing properties, the extensiveness of police department regulations, policies, and procedures, and the equivocal, relativistic nature of crime in regard to certain situations, settings, persons, and groups make it impossible to create a job description that would eliminate the almost boundless uncertainty in police patrol.

Neither professionals nor bureaucrats, however, have yet found an effective means of controlling discretion. If an organization cannot control those of its members with the greatest opportunity to exercise discretion, it flounders in its attempts to accomplish its stated purposes. Two general principles suggest why the police have not been able to control discretion. The first has to do with the general problem of control and the second with the specific nature of police work.

Men are unwilling to submit completely to the will of their organizational superiors. Men will always attempt to define and control their own work. Control means the right to set the pace, to define mistakes, to develop standards of "good" production and efficiency. But as surely as superiors seek to control the quality and the extent of work performed by their subordinates in a hierarchy, just as surely will they meet with attempts to reshape and subvert these controls.

In the specific instance of police bureaucracies, the patrolman conceives of himself as a man able to make on-the-spot decisions of guilt or innocence. He does not think of himself as a bureaucratic functionary nor as a professional. Further, since the police organization itself has become far more interested in efficiency than in purpose, since it is unable to specify its overall objectives, the patrolman finds it difficult, if not impossible, to demonstrate that necessary devotion to rational ends required of professionalism and bureaucratic organizations. Until police departments are able to control the amount and kind of discretion exercised by their members, and until the police are able, with the help of lawyers and other citizens, to develop positive means of motivation and reward in line with clear, overall policy directives, the failure of what we have called the professionalism-bureaucracy strategy is an absolute certainty.

Technology, Statistics, and the Crime Rate

This section will evaluate the strategy of technology in the control and prevention of crime, the use of statistics, and the significance of the so-called crime rate. Given the sociological nature of crime, let it be said immediately that present technology deals with unimportant crime and that the F.B.I. index of crimes, by which we base judgments of police effectiveness, is biased and an unrealistic reflection of the actual crime rate.

One of the striking aspects of the President's crime commission report is the thoroughly sociological nature of the document. The discussion of the causes of crime in the first two chapters points to the growth of urbanism, anonymity, the breakdown in social control, and the increasing numbers of frustrated and dissatisfied youth who have always constituted the majority of known lawbreakers. There are no labels such as "evil people," "emotionally disturbed," "mentally ill," or "criminally insane." The first set of recommendations under prevention in the summary pages of the report are "sociological": strengthen the family, improve slum schools, provide employment, reduce segregation, construct housing. All these matters are patently and by definition out of the control of the police.

There is every evidence that the police themselves subscribe to a thoroughly social, if not sociological, definition of the causes of crime—that is, that crime is the manifestation of long-established social patterns and structures which ensnare and implicate the police and the criminals as well as the general public. And they are doubtless correct.

Surveys done by the President's crime commission revealed that there are always contingencies in the information police receive about a crime even before they are able to investigate it. These contingencies involve such matters as the nature of the relationship between the victim and the offender and whether or not the victim believes the police are competent to investigate and solve the crime. Computer technology depends on informational "input." On that point, the police seem both unable to define what sort of information would be useful and unable to obtain, and probably never can obtain in a democratic society, information that would make them better able to enforce the law.

The facts in the problem of "crime prevention" overwhelmingly doom the present professionally based notion that the application of science and technology will begin to ease the distress the police feel as they face the escalating demands of their audiences. Also, it would be easier to assess the value of the technology strategy if we were able to define exactly to what end the technology would be applied and in what ways it could be expected to work.

Styles of Patrol

Police strategy is subject to many contingencies. It is a basic principle of public administration that policy made at the higher echelons of an organization will be effective only if each successively lower level of the organization complies with that policy and is capable of carrying it out. It is also a truism that participants at the lowest level in the hierarchy are the most "difficult" to mobilize and integrate into the organization. A style of patrol is basically the manner in which an administrative police policy is executed. The policy may prescribe that the patrolman overlook certain types of illegal acts; it may order that he minimally enforce particular laws or be sensitive to and strictly enforce others. If the administrative order setting a patrol style does not win the cooperation of the patrolman it is certain to fail. Thus, the success of any high-echelon policy that involves the performance of the patrolman is contingent upon his compliance with that policy. If the administrator's orders are not binding on the patrolman, no distinctive style of patrol will result; all that will be demonstrated will be the responses of the patrolman to other aspects of his social environment, especially, how his fellow patrolmen perform.

The success of this strategy is dependent upon the capacity of the administrator to create loyalty to his internal policies. With the rise of police unions, the discontent of the black patrolman, low pay, and relatively less security for the policeman, organizational control is a major problem in all the large police departments of the country—with Los Angeles possibly the single exception.

The effectiveness of the watchman, legalistic, and service styles of patrol will also depend on the degree of political consensus among the community groups patrolled, the clarity of the boundaries of community neighborhoods, competition between the police and self-help or vigilante groups, and the relative importance of nonoccupational norms in enforcement practices—that is, the importance of racial or ethnic similarities between the patrolman and the people in his neighborhood. If a clear social consensus on the meaning of the law and what is expected of the police can be established within a community, a well-directed policy of control over police patrol is the most logical and rational approach to police work. In some communities, largely suburban and middleclass, the police can carry out what their public demands and a degree of harmony exists. This consensus is absent in our inner cities.

Secrecy and Collaboration

The use of secrecy by the police is, as we have pointed out, a strategy employed not only to assist them in maintaining the appearance of political neutrality but to protect themselves against public complaints. Secrecy also helps to forestall public efforts to achieve better police service and to secure political accountability for police policy. Police collaboration with criminal elements—corruption, in other words—has much the same effect since it decreases the pressure to enforce "unenforceable" laws against certain segments of the police's clientele.

These two strategies were among the major concerns of the President's crime commission task force on police. The task force's report devoted major attention to the fact that political forces influence police actions and policies. The report affirmed the political nature of police work; what concerned the writers of the report was the nature and type of political influence on police actions. Their recommendations, furthermore, were based on their recognition of the fact that the police have been fairly successful in managing the appearance of being apolitical.

There are several reasons why the police strategies of secrecy and collaboration will continue in force: (1) as long as the client—the public—is seen as the enemy, the police will treasure their secrecy and use it to engineer public consent to their policies and practices; (2) as long as a new political consensus is not formed on the nature and type of police control necessary in society as a whole, the organized, self-serving survival aims of police organizations will emerge victorious. Any well-organized consensual, secretive organization can resist the efforts of an unorganized public, managed by rhetoric and appearances, to reform it; (3) as long as there remains a lack of consensus on the enforcement of many of our "moralistic" laws, police corruption and selective law enforcement will continue. Collaboration to reduce adversary relationships with the criminal segment of society will always be an effective strategy—providing a sudden upsurge in public morality doesn't temporarily subject the police to a full-scale "housecleaning." Replacements would, of course, be subject to the same pressures and would, in all likelihood, eventually take the same line of least resistance.

One solution to corruption is said to be better educated, more professional policemen. By recruiting better educated men, the more professionalized police departments also seek to diminish the expression of political attitudes on the job and the tendency of policemen to form political power groups based on their occupation. These are also assumptions made by the crime commission's task force on police. There is, however, no evidence that college-educated or better-paid policemen are "better policemen"; nor is there any evidence that "better men" alone will solve the essentially structural problems of the occupation.

We can tentatively conclude from this review that corruption will remain with us as long as laws remain which stipulate punishments for actions on which a low public consensus exists. It will remain when there is likely to be a low visibility of police performance, and it will remain while there is a high public demand for illegal services—gambling, prostitution, abortion—and the concomitant need of the police for information on these services from the practitioners themselves.

Symbiosis and Justice

Although the police have the principal discretion in the field with reference to the detection, surveillance, and appraisal of alleged offenders, the final disposition of a criminal case must be made in the courts. The police are thus dependent on the courts in a very special way for their successes. The ideal model of the criminal-justice system makes the police essentially the fact gatherers and apprehenders, while the courts are to be the decision-makers.

The police attempt to appear efficient has led them as we have noted before, to seek the good pinch, the arrest that will stand up in court. With victimless crimes, such as those involving gambling or drugs or prostitution, the police control the situation since they alone decide whether an offense has been committed and whether they have a legal case against the offender. To control the success rate in these cases, the police create a gaggle of informants, many of whom are compelled to give the police evidence in order to stay free of a potential charge against themselves for a violation similar to the one they are providing information about. In the case of more serious crimes, the problems are more complex; in these cases the police must rely on other informants, and their discretion on arrests and charges are more often exercised by administrators and prosecuting attorneys.

In the prosecution stage, the bureaucratic demands of the court system are paramount. Abraham Blumberg describes these demands and the tension between efficiency and "due process":

> The dilemma is frequently resolved through bureaucratically ordained shortcuts, deviations and outright rule violations by the members of the courts, from judges to stenographers, in order to meet production norms. Because they fear criticism on ethical as well as legal grounds, all the significant participants in the court's social structure are bound into an organized system of complicity. Patterned, covert, informal breaches, and evasions of "due process" are accepted as routine—they are institutionalized—but are nevertheless denied to exist.[22]

The net effect of this strain within the court system is to produce a higher rate of convictions by means of encouraging a plea of guilty to a lesser charge. As far as the police are concerned, then, the strategy of symbiosis is sound.

There are several undesirable effects of this symbiosis. First, it encourages corruption by permitting the police to make decisions about the freedom of

---

[22]Abraham Blumberg, *Criminal Justice* (Chicago: Quadrangle Press, 1967), p. 69.

their informants; it gives them an illegal hold and power over them, and thus it undercuts the rule of law. Second, many offenders with long criminal records are either granted their freedom as informants or allowed to plead guilty to lesser charges in return for the dismissal of a more serious charge. Skolnick calls this the "reversal of the hierarchy of penalties," because the more serious crimes of habitual criminals are prosecuted less zealously than the minor violations of first offenders. Third, it helps blur the distinction between the apprehension and prosecution aspects of our criminal-justice system.

V. CONCLUSIONS AND PROPOSED REFORMS

The allocation of rewards in a society represents both its division of labor and its configuration of problems. Ironically, the allocation of rewards is also the allocation of societal trouble. Societal trouble in a differentiated society is occupational trouble. The ebb and flow of rewards emanating from the division of labor becomes structured into persistent patterns that are sustained by continuous transactions among organizations and occupational groups. Occupational structures reflect societal structures, but they reflect them in ways that have been negotiated over time. The negotiation is based upon the universal human proclivity to differentiate roles, organizations, and occupations. The more dependent an organization is upon its environment for rewards, the more likely it is to rely on the management and presentation of strategies to establish the appearance of autonomy.

Organizations without a high degree of autonomy in the environments in which they operate are greatly constrained by the internal pressure of competing aims and roles of members. The agreement on problems, goals, values, and self-concepts that emerges from occupational socialization and functioning is a strong basis for influencing organizational direction. The occupational standards in this case subvert the rule of law as a system of norms outside the informal norms of the occupation. The policeman's view of his role and his occupational culture are very influential in determining the nature of policing. The basic source of police trouble is the inability of the police to define a mandate that will minimize the inconsistent nature of their self-expectations and the expectations of those they serve.

The problems derived from a contradictory mandate remain unaffected by the efforts of the institution to solve them; they do, however, take the shape into which they have been cast by institutional functionaries. Cooley long ago discussed the process of institutional ossification, the process by which institutions stray from serving the needs of their members and their publics, thereby losing the loyalty of those within and the support of those without. The consequences of institutional ossification as related to the police are twofold. First, the police begin to search for a so-called higher order of legitimacy; they make appeals to morality, to patriotism, to "Americanism," and to "law and order" to shore up eroded institutional charters and to accelerate their attempts to control and manipulate their members and clients. Second, the police, as they develop a far greater potential for controlling those they serve through their presentational strategies, come to serve themselves better than ever before.

The problem of the police is, essentially, the problem of the democratic society, and until the central values and social structures of our society are modified (and I think we are seeing such a modification), there can be no real change in the operation of social control. The needed changes are, by and large, not those dealt with in the crime commission report. And this is telling. For an eminently sociological document, it did not focus on the heart of the problem: our anachronistic, moralistic laws, with which the police are burdened, and our dated political system, which is unable to bring political units into a state of civil accountability. The focus of the report and recommendations was predictably on symptoms of crime, not on causes of crime. The "managerial focus" of the report, or its public-administration bias, outlined needed reforms, but not ways in which to implement them, and the problem of efficiency was never really faced.

Not surprisingly for a political document having a variety of public functions, the report has little to say about the nature of the present criminal laws. It dwells, like the police themselves, on means, not ends. As Isidore Silver points out in a critique of the report, more than one-half the crimes committed do not harm anyone: more than one-third are for drunkenness, and a small but important portion are for other "crimes without victims." Most crimes are committed by juveniles who inexplicably "grow out" of their criminality. In 1965, 50 per cent of the known burglaries and larcenies were committed by youths under 18.[23] The report does note what was a central point of our discussion of the political nature of crime, that police corruption is, in almost every instance, a consequence of trying to enforce admittedly unenforceable laws. The demand for services provided by homosexuals, by gamblers, prostitutes, and abortionists is high, and the supply is legally made unavailable to anyone who wants to remain in the so-called "law-abiding" category. The laws, in effect, create the crime and the criminals.

Changes in laws to reduce their absolutistic element and to free people who deviate with little harm to others from the onus of criminalization cannot be accomplished without a parallel change in the nature of police accountability. As we have seen, the strategies of secrecy and rhetoric used by the police play on the fears of society and provide a basis for police control. The managerial reforms contained in the task force report—more public debate on and greater internal and external control over police actions—are needed. Even more urgently required are specific ways in which the cities can control the police and make them strictly accountable for their actions—methods, that is, which go a good deal further than merely disposing of the chief or convening a judicial review board. To give city governments this kind of control over the police, however, entails the reorganization of police departments themselves so that their goals are clear and defined and so that the occupational rewards within the police organization are aligned with public goals.

---

[23]Isidore Silver, Introduction to *The Challenge of Crime in a Free Society* (New York: Avon Books, 1968), p. 25. The President's Commission, *Task Force Report: The Courts,* discusses substantive criminal law, however, and does make some suggestions for legal change.

Three interrelated organizational changes must be made to insure that police attend to the job of maintaining public order. One is to reorganize police departments along functional lines aimed at peace-keeping rather than law enforcement; the second is to allocate rewards for keeping the peace rather than for enforcing the law; the third is to decentralize police functions to reflect community control without the diffusion of responsibility and accountability to a central headquarters.

Present police departments are organized in a military fashion; orders move down the line from the chief to departmental sections assigned law-enforcement functions. These sections usually include such divisions as traffic, patrol, records, detective, juvenile, intelligence, crime-lab, and communications. The principal basis for the assignment of functions, however, is law enforcement;[24] what is needed is a new set of organizational premises so that the basis for the assignment of functions is not law enforcement but the maintenance of order. As Wilson explains:

> If order were the central mission of the department, there might be a "family disturbance squad," a "drunk and derelict squad," a "riot control squad," and a "juvenile squad"; law enforcement matters would be left to a "felony squad." Instead, there is a detective division organized, in the larger departments, into units specializing in homicide, burglary, auto theft, narcotics, vice, robbery, and the like. The undifferentiated patrol division gets everything else. Only juveniles tend to be treated by specialized units under both schemes, partly because the law requires or encourages such specialization. The law enforcement orientation of most departments means that new specialized units are created for every offense about which the public expresses concern or for which some special technology is required.[25]

What is called for, then, is a new organizational pattern that will provide a domestic unit (as is now being tried in New York City), a juvenile unit, and a drunk unit with a detoxification center, all with a peace-keeping orientation and peace-keeping functions. Only a felony squad and perhaps a riot squad should be used to enforce the law.

One of the obvious ways in which to improve the morale of the patrolman is to let him do a greater amount of investigative work and to take on the responsibility for "solving" some of the crimes originating with his patrol. Rewards could then be allocated in accord with the more limited ends of peace-keeping—for instance, in rewarding a patrolman for a decline in the number of drunks who reappear in court. Since no comprehensive policy can be imagined to guide order maintenance, limited ends for various departments must be developed and subjected to public review. The key is to allow the policeman to develop judgment about the motives and future intentions of people with whom he comes in contact, and to reward him for peace-keeping, not "good pinches" alone.

This reappraisal of the allocation of rewards means, of course, that there

---

[24]President's Commission, *Task Force Report: The Police,* charts on pp. 46–47.
[25]Wilson, *op. cit.,* p. 69.

must be greater coordination of police and other agencies within the criminal-justice system in order to increase the benefits to the client (the offender or the criminal) and break down the isolation of the police.[26] To allow the policeman to assume greater peace-keeping responsibilities would allow him to play a functional role parallel to that of the better general practitioner of medicine: the referral specialist, the coordinator of family health, the source of records and information, and the family friend and counselor. Such an organizational change in the policemen's function would, naturally enough, make community control of the police a greater possibility. It would begin to bridge the chasm between the police and many hostile segments within the public, a process that could be facilitated by the creation of a community-relations division within police departments.

The third needed modification of the present structure of police work is the development of decentralized operations. One of the major social trends of the last ten years has been the increase in the lack of attachment people have for their major institutions. Police today suffer from a crisis of legitimacy, and this crisis is heightened by their failure to promote a sense of commitment to their operations by the citizens they serve. One way in which to introduce commitment and a sense of control over the police by members of a community is to make the police more accessible. St. Louis, for example, has experimented with "storefront" police stations, staffed by a few men who are available as advisers, counselors, protectors, and friends of the people in the immediate neighborhood. If the police should begin to differentiate the role of the patrolman to include the functions of a peace-keeping community agent, the control of these agents should reside in the community. Thus public participation in the decision-making processes of the police would begin at the precinct or neighborhood level; it would not be simply in the form of a punitive civilian review board or a token citizen board at headquarters.

We began with the notion of trouble, police trouble, the troublesome mandate of the policeman. There will be little succor for him as long as our social structure remains fraught with contradictory value premises, with fragmented political power and the consequent inadequate control of the police, with the transformation of public trusts into institutional rights. There will be little succor for him as long as our political agencies resist moving to de-moralize our criminal laws. As it is, we can expect that the management of crime through police strategies and appearances will continue to be a disruptive element in American society.

---

[26]See John P. Clark, "The Isolation of the Police: A Comparison of the British and American Situations," in John Scanzoni ed., *Readings in Social Problems* (Boston: Allyn & Bacon, 1967), pp. 384–410. See also David Bordua, "Comments on Police-Community Relations," mimeographed (Urbana: University of Illinois, n.d.).

The Functions of The Police in Modern Society

Egon Bittner

I. THE CAPACITY TO USE FORCE AS THE CORE OF THE POLICE ROLE

The quest for peace by peaceful means is one of the culture traits of modern civilization. This aspiration is historically unique. For example, the Roman Empire was also committed to the objectives of reducing or eliminating warfare during one period of its existence, but the method chosen to achieve the *Pax Romana* was, in the language of the poet, *debellare superbos*, i.e., to subdue the haughty by force. Contrary to this, our commitment to abolish the traffic of violence requires us to pursue the ideal by pacific means. In support of this contention we pointed to the development of an elaborate system of international diplomacy whose main objective it is to avoid war, and to those changes in internal government that resulted in the virtual elimination of all forms of violence, especially in the administration of justice. That is, the overall tendency is not merely to withdraw the basis of legitimacy for all forms of provocative violence, but even from the exercise of provoked force required to meet illegitimate attacks. Naturally this is not possible to a full extent. At least, it has not been possible thus far. Since it is impossible to deprive responsive force entirely of legitimacy, its vestiges require special forms of authorization. Our society recognizes as legitimate three very different forms of responsive force.

First, we are authorized to use force for the purpose of self-defense. Though the laws governing self-defense are far from clear, it appears that an attacked person can counterattack only after he has exhausted all other means of avoiding harm, including retreat, and that the counterattack may not exceed what is necessary to disable the assailant from carrying out his intent. These restrictions are actually enforceable because harm done in the course of self-defense does furnish grounds for criminal and tort proceedings. It becomes necessary, therefore to show compliance with these restrictions to rebut the charges of excessive and unjustified force even in self-defense.[1]

The second form of authorization entrusts the power to proceed coercively to some specifically deputized persons against some specifically named persons. Among the agents who have such highly specific powers are mental hospital attendants and prison guards. Characteristically, such persons use force in carrying out court orders; but they may use force only against named persons who are remanded to their custody and only to the extent required to implement a judicial order of confinement. Of course, like everybody else, they may also act within the provisions governing self-defense. By insisting on the

---

[1]"Justification for the use of Force in the Criminal Law," *Stanford Law Review*, 13 (1961), 566–609 *Footnotes renumbered—eds.*

REPRINTED FROM: Egon Bittner, *The Functions of The Police in Modern Society*, Washington, D.C.: U.S. Government Printing Office, *1971* (36–47; 52–62).

high degree of limited specificity of the powers of custodial staffs, we do not mean to deny that these restrictions are often violated with impunity. The likelihood of such transgressions is enhanced by the secluded character of prisons and mental institutions, but their existence does not impair the validity of our definition.

The third way to legitimize the use of responsive force is to institute a police force. Contrary to the cases of self-defense and the limited authorization of custodial functionaries, the police authorization is essentially unrestricted. Because the expression "essentially" is often used to hedge a point, we will make fully explicit what we mean by it. There exist three formal limitations of the freedom of policemen to use force, which we must admit even though they have virtually no practical consequences. First, the police use of deadly force is limited in most jurisdictions. Though the powers of a policeman in this respect exceed those of citizens, they are limited nevertheless. For example, in some jurisdictions policemen are empowered to shoot to kill fleeing felony suspects, but not fleeing misdemeanor suspects. It is scarcely necessary to argue that, given the uncertainties involved in defining a delict under conditions of hot pursuit, this could hardly be expected to be an effective limitation.[2] Second, policemen may use force only in the performance of their duties and not to advance their own personal interests or the private interests of other persons. Though this is rather obvious, we mention it for the sake of completeness. Third, and this point too is brought up to meet possible objections, policemen may not use force maliciously or frivolously. These three restrictions, and nothing else, were meant by the use of the qualifier "essentially." Aside from these restrictions there exist no guidelines, no specifiable range of objectives, no limitations of any kind that instruct the policeman what he may or must do. Nor do there exist any criteria that would allow the judgment whether some forceful intervention was necessary, desirable, or proper. And finally, it is exceedingly rare that police actions involving the use of force are actually reviewed and judged by anyone at all.

In sum, the frequently heard talk about the lawful use of force by the police is practically meaningless and, because no one knows what is meant by it, so is the talk about the use of minimum force. Whatever vestigial significance attaches to the term "lawful" use of force is confined to the obvious and unnecessary rule that police officers may not commit crimes of violence.

---

[2]"At common law, the rule appears to have been that an officer was entitled to make a reasonable mistake as to whether the victim had committed a felony, but a private person was not so entitled. Thus strict liability was created for the private arrester, and he could not justifiably kill, if the victim had not actually committed a felony. Several modern cases have imposed this standard of strict liability even upon the officer by conditioning justification of deadly force on the victim's actually having committed a felony, and a number of states have enacted statutes which appear to adopt this strict liability. However, many jurisdictions, such as California, have homicide statutes which permit the police officer to use deadly force for the arrest of a person 'charged' with felony. It has been suggested that this requirement only indicates the necessity for reasonable belief by the officer that the victim has committed a felony." *Ibid.,* pp. 599–600.

Otherwise, however, the expectation that they may and will use force is left entirely undefined. In fact, the only instructions any policeman ever receives in this respect consist of sermonizing that he should be humane and circumspect, and that he must not desist from what he has undertaken merely because its accomplishment may call for coercive means. We might add, at this point, that the entire debate about the troublesome problem of police brutality will not move beyond its present impasse, and the desire to eliminate it will remain an impotent conceit, until this point is fully grasped and unequivocally admitted. In fact, our expectation that policemen will use force, coupled by our refusals to state clearly what we mean by it (aside from sanctimonious homilies), smacks of more than a bit of perversity.

Of course, neither the police nor the public is entirely in the dark about the justifiable use of force by the officers. We had occasion to allude to the assumption that policemen may use force in making arrests. But the benefit deriving from this apparent core of relative clarity is outweighed by its potentially misleading implications. For the authorization of the police to use force is in no important sense related to their duty to apprehend criminals. Were this the case then it could be adequately considered as merely a special case of the same authorization that is entrusted to custodial personnel. It might perhaps be considered a bit more complicated, but essentially of the same nature. But the police authority to use force is radically different from that of a prison guard. Whereas the powers of the latter are incidental to his obligation to implement a legal command, the police role is far better understood by saying that their ability to arrest offenders is incidental to their authority to use force.

Many puzzling aspects of police work fall into place when one ceases to look at it as principally concerned with law enforcement and crime control, and only incidentally and often incongruously concerned with an infinite variety of other matters. It makes much more sense to say that the police are nothing else than a mechanism for the distribution of situationally justified force in society. The latter conception is preferable to the former on three grounds. First, it accords better with the actual expectations and demands made of the police (even though it probably conflicts with what most people would say, or expect to hear, in answer to the question about the proper police function); second, it gives a better accounting of the actual allocation of police manpower and other resources; and, third, it lends unity to all kinds of police activity. These three justifications will be discussed in some detail in the following.

The American city dweller's repertoire of methods for handling problems includes one known as "calling the cops." The practice to which the idiom refers is enormously widespread. Though it is more frequent in some segments of society than in others, there are very few people who do not or would not resort to it under suitable circumstances. A few illustrations will furnish the background for an explanation of what "calling the cops" means.[3]

---

[3]The illustrations are taken from field notes I have collected over the course of fourteen months of intensive field observations of police activity in two large cities. One is located in a Rocky Mountain State, the other on the West Coast. All other case vignettes used in the subsequent text of this report also come from this source.

Two patrolmen were directed to report to an address located in a fashionable district of a large city. On the scene they were greeted by the lady of the house who complained that the maid had been stealing and receiving male visitors in her quarters. She wanted the maid's belongings searched and the man removed. The patrolmen refused the first request, promising to forward the complaint to the bureau of detectives, but agreed to see what they could do about the man. After gaining entrance to the maid's room they compelled a male visitor to leave, drove him several blocks away from the house, and released him with the warning never to return.

In a tenement, patrolmen were met by a public health nurse who took them through an abysmally deteriorated apartment inhabited by four young children in the care of an elderly woman. The babysitter resisted the nurse's earlier attempts to remove the children. The patrolmen packed the children in the squad car and took them to Juvenile Hall, over the continuing protests of the elderly woman.

While cruising through the streets a team of detectives recognized a man named in a teletype received from the sheriff of an adjoining county. The suspect maintained that he was in the hospital at the time the offense alleged in the communication took place, and asked the officers to verify his story over their car radio. When he continued to plead innocence he was handcuffed and taken to headquarters. Here the detectives learned that the teletype had been cancelled. Prior to his release the man was told that he could have saved himself grief had he gone along voluntarily.

In a downtown residential hotel, patrolmen found two ambulance attendants trying to persuade a man, who according to all accounts was desperately ill, to go to the hospital. After some talk, they helped the attendants in carrying the protesting patient to the ambulance and sent them off.

In a middle-class neighborhood, patrolmen found a partly disassembled car, tools, a loudly blaring radio, and five beer-drinking youths at the curb in front of a single-family home. The home-owner complained that this had been going on for several days and the men had refused to take their activities elsewhere. The patrolmen ordered the youths to pack up and leave. When one sassed them they threw him into the squad car, drove him to the precinct station, from where he was released after receiving a severe tongue lashing from the desk sergeant.

In the apartment of a quarreling couple, patrolmen were told by the wife, whose nose was bleeding, that the husband stole her purse containing money she earned. The patrolmen told the man they would "take him in," whereupon he returned the purse and they left.

What all these vignettes are meant to illustrate is that whatever the substance of the task at hand, whether it involves protection against an undesired imposition, caring for those who cannot care for themselves, attempting to solve a crime, helping to save a life, abating a nuisance, or settling an explosive dispute, police intervention means above all making use of the capacity and authority to overpower resistance to an attempted solution in the native habitat of the problem. There can be no doubt that this feature of police work is uppermost in the minds of people who solicit police aid or direct the attention of the police to problems, that persons against whom the police proceed have this feature in mind and conduct themselves accordingly, and that every conceivable police intervention projects the message that force may be, and may have to be, used to achieve a desired objective. It does not matter whether the persons who seek police help are private citizens or other government officials, nor does it matter whether the problem at hand involves some aspect of law enforcement or is totally unconnected with it.

It must be emphasized, however that the conception of the centrality of the capacity to use force in the police role does not entail the conclusion that the ordinary occupational routines consist of the actual exercise of this capacity. It is very likely, though we lack information on this point, that the actual use of physical coercion and restraint is rare for all policemen and that many policemen are virtually never in the position of having to resort to it. What matters is that police procedure is defined by the feature that it may not be opposed in its course, and that force can be used if it is opposed. This is what the existence of the police makes available to society. Accordingly, the question, "What are policemen supposed to do?" is almost completely identical with the question, "What kinds of situations require remedies that are non-negotiably coercible?"[4]

Our second justification for preferring the definition of the police role we proposed to the traditional law enforcement focus of the role requires us to review the actual police practices to see to what extent they can be subsumed under the conception we offered. To begin we can take note that law enforcement and crime control are obviously regarded as calling for remedies that are non-negotiably coercible. According to available estimates, approximately one-third of available manpower resources of the police are at any time committed to dealing with crimes and criminals. Though this may seem to be a

---

[4]By "non-negotiably coercible" we mean that when a deputized police officer decides that force is necessary, then, within the boundaries of this situation, he is not accountable to anyone, nor is he required to brook the arguments or opposition of anyone who might object to it. We set this forth not as a legal but as a practical rule. The legal question whether citizens may oppose policemen is complicated. Apparently resisting police coercion in situations of emergency is not legitimate; see Hans Kelsen, *General Theory of Law and State*, (New York: Russel & Russel, 1961), pp. 278–279, and H. A. L. Hart, *The Concept of Law* (Oxford: Clarendon Press, 1961), pp. 20–21. Common law doctrine allows that citizens may oppose "unlawful arrest," 6 *Corpus Juris Secundum*, Arrest #13, p. 613; against this, the Uniform Arrest Act, drafted by a committee of the Interstate Commission on Crime in 1939, provides in Section 5, "If a person has reasonable grounds to believe that he is being arrested by a peace officer, it is his duty to refrain from using force or any weapons in resisting arrest regardless of whether or not there is a legal basis for the arrest," S. B. Warner, "Uniform Arrest Act," *Vanderbilt Law Review*, 28 (1942), 315–347. At present, at least twelve states are governed by case law recognizing the validity of the Common Law doctrine, at least five have adopted the rule contained in the Uniform Arrest Act and at least six have case law or statutes that give effect to the Uniform Arrest Act rule. That the trend is away from the Common Law doctrine and in the direction of the Uniform Arrest Act rule is argued in Max Hochanadel and H. W. Stege, "The Right to Resist an Unlawful Arrest: An Outdated Concept?" *Tulsa Law Journal*, 3 (1966), 40–46. I am grateful for the help I received from 35 of the 50 State Attorney General Offices from whom I sought information concerning this matter.

relatively small share of the total resources of an agency ostensibly devoted to crime control, it is exceedingly unlikely that any other specific routine police activity, such as traffic regulation, crowd control, supervision of licensed establishments, settling of citizens' disputes, emergency health aids, ceremonial functions, or any other, absorb anywhere near as large a share of the remaining two-thirds. But this is precisely what one would expect on the basis of our definition. Given the likelihood that offenders will seek to oppose apprehension and evade punishment, it is only natural that the initial dealings with them be assigned to an agency that is capable of overcoming these obstacles. That is, the proposed definition of the role of the police as a mechanism for the distribution of non-negotiably coercive remedies entails the priority of crime control by direct inference. Beyond that, however, the definition also encompasses other types of activities, albeit at lower level or priority.

Because the idea that the police are basically a crimefighting agency has never been challenged in the past, no one has troubled to sort out the remaining priorities. Instead, the police have always been forced to justify activities that did not involve law enforcement in the direct sense by either linking them constructively to law enforcement or by defining them as nuisance demands for service. The dominance of this view, especially in the minds of policemen, has two pernicious consequences. First, it leads to a tendency to view all sorts of problems as if they involved culpable offenses and to an excessive reliance on quasilegal methods for handling them. The widespread use of arrests without intent to prosecute exemplifies this state of affairs. These cases do not involve errors in judgment about the applicability of a penal norm but deliberate pretense resorted to because more appropriate methods of handling problems have not been developed. Second, the view that crime control is the only serious, important, and necessary part of police work has deleterious effects on the morale of those police officers in the uniformed patrol who spend most of their time with other matters. No one, especially he who takes a positive interest in his work, likes being obliged to do things day-in and day-out that are disparaged by his colleagues. Moreover, the low evaluation of these duties leads to neglecting the development of skill and knowledge that are required to discharge them properly and efficiently.

It remains to be shown that the capacity to use coercive force lends thematic unity to all police activity in the same sense in which, let us say, the capacity to cure illness lends unity to everything that is ordinarily done in the field of medical practice. While everybody agrees that the police actually engage in an enormous variety of activities, only a part of which involves law enforcement, many argue that this state of affairs does not require explanation but change. Smith, for example, argued that the imposition of duties and demands that are not related to crime control dilutes the effectiveness of the police and that the growing trend in this direction should be curtailed and even reversed.[5] On the face of it this argument is not without merit, especially if one considers

---

[5]Smith, B. *Police Systems in the United States*, (New York: Harper & Row, 2nd, rev. ed.), 1960.

that very many of those activities that are unrelated to law enforcement involve dealing with problems that lie in the field of psychiatry, social welfare, human relations, education, and so on. Each of these fields has its own trained specialists who are respectively more competent than the police. It would seem preferable, therefore, to take all those matters that belong properly to other specialists out of the hands of the police and turn them over to those to whom they belong. Not only would this relieve some of the pressures that presently impinge on the police, but it would also result in better services.[6]

Unfortunately, this view overlooks a centrally important factor. While it is true that policemen often aid sick and troubled people because physicians and social workers are unable or unwilling to take their services where they are needed, this is not the only or even the main reason for police involvement. In fact, physicians and social workers themselves quite often "call the cops," for not unlike the case of the administration of justice, on the periphery of the rationally ordered procedures of medical and social work practice lurk exigencies that call for the exercise of coercion. Since neither physicians nor social workers are authorized or equipped to use force to attain desirable objectives, the total disengagement of the police would mean allowing many a problem to move unhampered in the direction of disaster. But the non-law-enforcement activities of the police are by no means confined to matters that are wholly or even mainly within the purview of some other institutionalized remedial specialty. Many, perhaps most, consist of addressing situations in which people simply do not seem to be able to manage their own lives adequately. Nor is it to be taken for granted that these situations invariably call for the use, or the threat of the use, of force. It is enough if there is need for immediate and unquestioned intervention that must not be allowed to be defeated by possible resistance. And where there is a possibility of great harm, the intervention would appear to be justified even if the risk is, in statistical terms, quite remote. Take, for instance the presence of mentally ill persons in the community. Though it is well known that most live quiet and unobtrusive lives, they are perceived as occasionally constituting a serious hazard to themselves and others. Thus, it is not surprising that the police are always prepared to deal with these persons at the slightest indication of a possible emergency. Similarly, though very few family quarrels lead to serious consequences, the fact that most homicides occur among quarreling kin leads to the preparedness to intervene at the incipient stages of problems.

In sum, the role of the police is to address all sorts of human problems when and insofar as their solutions do or may possibly require the use of force at the point of their occurrence. This lends homogeneity to such diverse procedures as catching a criminal, driving the mayor to the airport, evicting a drunken person from a bar, directing traffic, crowd control, taking care of lost children, administering medical first aid, and separating fighting relatives.

---

[6]The authors of the *Task Force Report: Police* note that little has been done to make these alternative resources available as substitutes for police intervention. President's Commission on Law Enforcement and the Administration of Justice (Washington, D. C.: U.S. Government Printing Office, 1967).

There is no exaggeration in saying that there is topical unity in this very incomplete list of lines of police work. Perhaps it is true that the common practice of assigning policemen to chauffeur mayors is based on the desire to give the appearance of thrift in the urban fisc. But note, if one wanted to make as far as possible certain that nothing would ever impede His Honor's freedom of movement, he would certainly put someone into the driver's seat of the auto who has the authority and the capacity to overcome all unforeseeable human obstacles. Similarly, it is perhaps not too farfetched to assume that desk sergeants feed ice cream to lost children because they like children. But if the treat does not achieve the purpose of keeping the youngster in the station house until his parents arrive to redeem him, the sergeant would have to resort to other means of keeping him there.

We must now attempt to pull together the several parts of the foregoing discussion in order to show how they bring into relief the main problems of adjusting police function to life in modern society, and in order to elaborate constructively certain consequences that result from the assumption of the role definitions we have proposed.

At the beginning we observed that the police appear to be burdened by an opprobrium that did not seem to lessen proportionately to the acknowledged improvements in their practices. To explain this puzzling fact we drew attention to three perceived features of the police that appear to be substantially independent of particular work methods. First, a stigma attaches to police work because of its connection with evil, crime, perversity, and disorder. Though it may not be reasonable, it is common that those who fight the dreadful end up being dreaded themselves. Second, because the police must act quickly and often on mere intuition, their interventions are lacking in those aspects of moral sophistication which only a more extended and more scrupulous consideration can afford. Hence their methods are comparatively crude. Third, because it is commonly assumed that the risks of the kinds of breakdowns that require police action are much more heavily concentrated in the lower classes than in other segments of society, police surveillance is inherently discriminatory. That is, all things being equal, some persons feel the sting of police scrutiny merely because of their station in life. In so far as this is felt, police work has divisive effects in society.

Next, we argued that one cannot understand how the police "found themselves" in this unenviable position without taking into consideration that one of the cultural trends of roughly the past century-and-a-half was the sustained aspiration to install peace as a stable condition of everyday life. Though no one can fail being impressed by the many ways the attainment of this ideal has been frustrated, it is possible to find some evidence of partially effective efforts. Many aspects of mundane existence in our cities have become more pacific than they have been in past epochs of history. More importantly for our purposes, in the domain of internal statecraft, the distance between those who govern and those who are governed has grown and the gap has been filled with bureaucratically symbolized communication. Where earlier compliance was secured by physical presence and armed might, it now rests mainly on peaceful persuasion and rational compliance. We found the trend toward the pacification in governing most strongly demonstrated in the administration of justice. The banishment of all forms of violence from the criminal process, as administered by the courts, has as a corollary the legalization of judicial proceedings. The latter reflects a movement away from peremptory and oracular judgment to a method in which all decisions are based on exhaustively rational grounds involving the use of explicit legal norms. Most important among those norms are the ones that limit the powers of authority and specify the rights of defendants. The legalization and pacification of the criminal process was achieved by, among other things, expelling from its purview those processes that set it into motion. Since in the initial steps, where suspicions are formed and arrests are made, force and intuition cannot be eliminated entirely, purity can be maintained by not taking notice of them. This situation is, however, paradoxical if we are to take seriously the idea that the police is a law enforcement agency in the strict sense of legality. The recognition of this paradox became unavoidable as early as in 1914, in the landmark decision of *Weeks* v. *U.S.* In the following decades the United States Supreme Court issued a series of rulings affecting police procedure which foster the impression that the judiciary exercises control over the police. But this impression is misleading, for the rulings do not set forth binding norms for police work but merely provide that *if* the police propose to set the criminal process into motion, *then* they must proceed in certain legally restricted ways. These restrictions are, therefore, conditional, specifying as it were the terms of delivery and acceptance of a service and nothing more. Outside of this arrangement the judges have no direct concerns with police work and will take notice of its illegality, if it is illegal, only when offended citizens seek civil redress.

Because only a small part of the activity of the police is dedicated to law enforcement and because they deal with the majority of their problems without invoking the law, a broader definition of their role was proposed. After reviewing briefly what the public appears to expect of the police, the range of activities police actually engage in, and the theme that unifies all these activities, it was suggested that *the role of the police is best understood as a mechanism for the distribution of non-negotiably coercive force employed in accordance with the dictates of an intuitive grasp of situational exigencies*.

It is, of course, not surprising that a society committed to the establishment of peace by pacific means and to the abolishment of all forms of violence from the fabric of its social relations, at least as a matter of official morality and policy, would establish a corps of specially deputized officials endowed with the exclusive monopoly of using force contingently where limitations of foresight fail to provide alternatives. That is, given the melancholy appreciation of the fact that the total abolition of force is not attainable, the closest approximation to the ideal is to limit it as a special and exclusive trust. If it is the case, however, that the mandate of the police is organized around their capacity and authority to use force, i.e., if this is what the institution's existence makes available to society, then the evaluation of that institution's performance must focus on it. While it is quite true that policemen will have to be judged on other dimensions of competence, too—for example, the exercise of force against criminal suspects requires some knowledge about crime and criminal law—their methods as society's agents of coercion will have to be considered central to the overall judgment.

The proposed definition of the police role entails a difficult moral problem. How can we arrive at a favorable or even accepting judgment about an activity which is, in its very conception, opposed to the ethos of the polity that authorizes it? Is it not well nigh inevitable that this mandate be concealed in circumlocution? While solving puzzles of moral philosophy is beyond the scope of this analysis, we will have to address this question in a somewhat more mundane formulation: namely, on what terms can a society dedicated to peace institutionalize the exercise of force?

It appears that in our society two answers to this question are acceptable. One defines the targets of legitimate force as enemies and the coercive advance against them as warfare. Those who wage this war are expected to be possessed by the military virtues of valor, obedience and *esprit de corps*. The enterprise as a whole is justified as a sacrificial and glorious mission in which the warrior's duty is "not to reason why." The other answer involves an altogether different imagery. The targets of force are conceived as practical objectives and their attainment a matter of practical expediency. The process involves prudence, economy, and considered judgment, from case to case. The enterprise as a whole is conceived as a public trust, the exercise of which is vested in individual practitioners who are personally responsible for their decisions and actions.

Reflection suggests that the two patterns are profoundly incompatible. Remarkably, however, our police departments have not been deterred from attempting the reconciliation of the irreconcilable. Thus, our policemen are exposed to the demand of a conflicting nature in that their actions are supposed to reflect military prowess and professional acumen.

In the following, we will review certain well-known aspects of police organization and practice in an attempt to show that the adherence to the quasi-military model by our police forces is largely a self-defeating pretense. Its sole effect is to create obstacles in the development of a professional police system. On the basis of this review we will attempt to formulate an outline of a model of the police role in modern society that is recognizably in accord with existing practices but which contains safeguards against the existence and proliferation of those aspects of police work that are generally regarded as deplorable. In other words, the proposed suggestions will be innovative only in the sense that they will accent already existing strength and excise impeding ballasts.

II. THE QUASI-MILITARY ORGANIZATION OF THE POLICE

The conception of the police as a quasi-military institution with a war-like mission plays an important part in the structuring of police work in modern American departments. The merits of this conception have never been demonstrated or even argued explicitly. Instead, most authors who make reference to it take it for granted or are critical only of those aspects of it, especially its punitive orientation, that are subject of aspersion even in the military establishment itself.[7] The treatment the topic receives in the Task Force Report on the Police of the President's Commission on Law Enforcement and Administration of Justice is representative of this approach. The authors note that "like all military and semi-military organizations, a police agency is governed in its internal management by a large number of standard operating procedures."[8] This observation is accompanied by remarks indicating that the existence of elaborate codes governing the conduct of policemen relative to intradepartmental demands stands in stark contrast to the virtual absence of formulated directives concerning the handling of police problems in the community. The imbalance between proliferation of internal regulation and the neglect of regulations relative to procedures employed in the field leads to the inference that the existing codes must be supplemented by substantive instructions and standards in the latter area. The question whether such an expansion of regulation might not result in a code consisting of incompatible elements is not considered. Instead, it is implicitly assumed that policemen can be instructed how to deal with citizens by regulations that will not affect the existing system of internal disciplinary control.

The lack of appreciation for the possibility that the developments of professional discretionary methods for crime control and peacekeeping may conflict with the enforcement of bureaucratic-military regulations is not merely a naive oversight; more likely, it represents an instance of wishful thinking. For the military model is immensely attractive to police planners, and not without reason. In the first place, there exist some apparent analogies between the military and the police and it does not seem to be wholly unwarranted to expect methods of internal organization that work in one context to work also in the other. Both institutions are instruments of force and for both institutions the occasions for using force are unpredictably distributed. Thus, the personnel in each must be kept in a highly disciplined state of alert preparedness. The formalism that characterizes military organization, the insistence on rules and regulations, on spit and polish, on obedience to superiors, and so on, constitute a permanent rehearsal for "the real thing." What sorts of rules and regulations exist in such a setting are in some ways less important than that there be plenty of them and the personnel be continually aware that they can be harshly called to account for disobeying them.[9] Second, American police departments have been, for the greater part of their history, the football of local politics, and became tainted with sloth and corruption at least partly for this

---

[7]Recently some authors have expressed doubts about the merits of organizing the police along military lines. Wilson takes issue with Smith's assertion that the police have "disciplinary requirements of a quasi-military body." *Op. cit. supra,* note 16 at p. 79, n. 24. Similarly, A. J. Reiss and D. J. Bordua have questioned the adequacy of the idea of the police as a military organization; see "Environment and Organization: A Perspective on the Police," in Bordua, ed., *The Police,* (New York: John Wiley & Sons, 1967).

[8]*Task Force Report: Police,* President's Crime Commission (Washington, D.C.: U.S. Government Printing Office, 1967).

[9]The tendency of police departments to adopt outward military rigidities has been frequently emphasized; see *Task Force Report: Police, ibid.;* J. D. Lohman and G. E. Misler, *The Police and the Community,* A Report Prepared for the President's Commission

reason. Police reform was literally forced to resort to formidable means of internal discipline to dislodge undesirable attitudes and influences, and the military model seemed to serve such purposes admirably. In fact, it is no exaggeration to say that through the 1950's and 1960's the movement to "professionalize" the police concentrated almost exclusively on efforts to eliminate political and venal corruption by means of introducing traits of military discipline. And it must be acknowledged that some American police chiefs, notably the late William Parker of Los Angeles, have achieved truly remarkable results in this respect. The leading aspiration of this reform was to place the tragicomic figure of the "flatfoot cop on the take" by cadres of personally incorruptible snappy operatives working under the command of bureaucrats-in-uniform. There is little doubt that these reforms succeeded in bringing some semblance of order into many chaotic departments and that in these departments "going by the book" acquired some real meaning.

Finally, the police adopted the military method because they could not avail themselves of any other options to secure internal discipline. For all its effectiveness, the military method is organizationally primitive. At least, the standard part of the method can be well enough approximated with a modicum of administrative sophistication. Moreover, since most of the men who go into police work have some military experience, they need not go to outside resources to obtain help in building a quasi-military order. This is important because a century of experience taught American police forces that outside intervention into their affairs—known as the "shake-up"—was almost always politically inspired. Because the suspicion of high-level chicanery is still very much alive, and not without reasons, the police is the only large scale institution in our society that has not benefited from advances in management science. In the absence of lateral recruitment into supervisory positions and developed technical staff skills, changes had to be achieved mainly by means of rigid enforcement of regulations of internal procedure and by emphasizing external trappings of discipline. In a situation where something had to be done, with little to do it with, this was no mean accomplishment.[10]

Acknowledging that the introduction of methods of military-bureaucratic discipline was not without some justification, and conceding that it helped in eliminating certain gross inadequacies, does not mean, however, that the approach was beneficial in larger and longer range terms. Even where the cure succeeded in suppressing many of the diseases of earlier times, it brought forth obstacles of its own to the development of a model of a professional police role,

---

on Law Enforcement and Administration of Justice. (Washington, D.C.: U.S. Government Printing Office, 1966), Vol. I, p. 152, Vol. II, p. 196; Banton reports that American police chiefs admire Scottish officers who "bore themselves well, and were smartly and uniformly dressed." *Policeman in The Community,* (New York: Basic Books, 1964).

[10]In addition to the rigors of outward discipline, military establishments also rely on "command charisma," a feature observed in American police departments by D. J. Bordua and A. J. Reiss: see their "Command, Control and Charisma: Reflections on Police Bureaucracy," *American Journal of Sociology,* 72 (1966), 68—76. The term indicates a leadership principle in which subordinates are moved to obedience by a high regard for, and trust in, the person in command.

if by professional role is meant that practice must involve technical skill and fiduciary trust in the practitioner's exercise of discretion. The reason for this is simple. While in early police departments there existed virtually no standards of correct procedure at all and no inducement to do well—since rewards were scant and distributed along lines of personal favoritism—one can now distinguish between good and bad officers, and engaging in what is now defined as correct conduct does carry significant rewards. But since the established standards and the rewards for good behavior relate almost entirely to matters connected with internal discipline, the judgments that are passed have virtually nothing to do with the work of the policeman in the community, with one significant exception. That is, the claims for recognition that have always been denied to the policeman are now respected, but recognition is given for doing well *in* the department, not *outside* where all the real duties are located.

The maintenance of organizational stability and staff morale require that praise and reward, as well as condemnation and punishment, be distributed methodically, i.e., predictably in accordance with explicit rules. Correspondingly, it is exceedingly difficult to assign debits and credits for performances that are not regulated by rule. Because the real work of the policeman is not set forth in the regulations, it does not furnish his superior a basis for judging him. At the same time, there are no strongly compelling reasons for the policeman to do well in ways that do not count in terms of official occupational criteria of value. The greater the weight placed on compliance with internal departmental regulation, the less free is the superior in censoring unregulated work practices he disapproves of, and in rewarding those he admires, for fear that he might jeopardize the loyalty of officers who do well on all scores that officially count—that is, those who present a neat appearance, who conform punctually to bureaucratic routine, who are visibly on the place of their assignment, and so on. In short, those who make life easier for the superior, who in turn is restricted to supervising just those things. In fact, the practical economy of supervisory control requires that the proliferation of intradepartmental restriction be accompanied by increases in license in areas of behavior in unregulated areas. Thus, one who is judged to be a good officer in terms of internal, military-bureaucratic codes will not even be questioned about his conduct outside of it. The message is quite plain: the development of resolutely careful work methods in the community may be nice, but it gets you nowhere!

There is one important exception to the priority of intradepartmental quasi-military discipline in the judging of the performances of policemen. Police departments have to produce visible results of their work. The most visible results are arrested persons who keep the courts busy. This demand naturally devolves on individual officers. The question about the expected contribution of individual policemen to the statistical total of crimes cleared, summonses delivered, and arrests made is a matter of heated controversy. The problem is usually addressed as to whether or not there exist quotas officers must meet. Of course, the question can always be so framed that one can answer it truthfully either way. But more fundamentally it is quite clear that individual policemen must contribute to the sum total of visible results, unless they have some special excuse, such as being assigned to a desk job. Moreover, how could any police superior under present conditions of supervision ever know whether the men assigned to the traffic division or to the vice squad are on the job at all, if they did not produce their normal share of citations or arrests?

Clearly, therefore, there is added to the occupational relevance of the military-bureaucratic discipline the demand to produce results.[11] While the emphasis on stringent internal regulation, taken alone, merely discourages the elaboration of careful approaches to work tasks, it exercises in combination with production demands a truly pernicious influence on the nature of police work. There are several reasons for this but the most important is based on the following consideration. Though the explicit departmental regulations contain little more than pious sermonizing about police dealings with citizens, whether they be offenders, an unruly crowd, quarreling spouses, accident victims, or what not, it is possible that a policeman could, despite his discretionary freedom, act in some such way as to actually come into conflict with some stated rule, even though the rule is not topically relevant to the situation at hand. Since he knows that his conduct will be judged solely with respect to this point he must be attuned to it, avoiding the violation even if that involves choosing a course of action that is specifically wrong with respect to the realities of the problem. For example, it is far from unusual that officers decide whether to make an arrest or not on the basis of their desire to live within departmental regulation rather than on the merits of the case at hand. In these situations the military-bureaucratic discipline regulates procedure speciously; it does not provide that in such-and-such a situation such-and-such a course of action is indicated. On the contrary, the regulations are typically silent about such matters; but in insisting on specific ways for officers to keep their noses clean they limit the possibilities of desirable intervention and they encourage transgression. Thus, it has been reported that in the New York Police Department, known for its stringently punitive discipline, officers who violate some official rules of deportment while dealing with citizens simply arrest potential complainants, knowing the complaints of persons charged with crimes are given no credence. Incongruously, while in New York the Police Department is much more likely to discipline an officer for brutalizing a citizen than elsewhere, it in fact rarely gets a chance to do it. For whenever there is a situation in which it is possible that an officer could have an infraction entered in his record, an infraction against an explicit regulation, he will redefine it into an instance of police work that is not regulated. Thus, while citizens everywhere run the risk of receiving a beating when they anger a policeman, in New York they run the added risk of being charged with a crime they did not commit simply because its officers must keep their records clean.[12]

---

[11]The most illuminating and extensive discussion of pressures to produce is contained in Skolnick, *Justice without Trial*, (New York: John Wiley & Sons, 1966), pp. 164–181.

[12]Paul Chevigny explains that New York policemen sometimes rebut allegations of brutality by maintaining that they are obviously fabrications since the complainant

As long as there are two forms of accounting, one that is explicit and continually audited (internal discipline), and another that is devoid of rules and rarely looked into (dealings with citizens), it must be expected that keeping a positive balance in the first might encourage playing loose with the second. The likelihood of this increases proportionately to pressures to produce. Since it is not enough that policemen be obedient soldier-bureaucrats, but must, to insure favorable consideration for advancement, contribute to the arrest total, they will naturally try to meet this demand in ways that will keep them out of trouble. Thus, to secure the promotion from the uniformed patrol to the detective bureau, which is highly valued and not determined by civil service examinations, officers feel impelled to engage in actions that furnish opportunities for conspicuous display of aggressiveness. John McNamara illustrates this tactic by quoting a dramatic expression of cynicism, "If you want to get 'out of the bag' into the 'bureau' shoot somebody."[13] Leaving the exaggeration aside, there is little doubt that emphasis on military-bureaucratic control rewards the appearance of staying out of troubles as far as internal regulations are concerned, combined with strenuous efforts to make "good pinches," i.e., arrests that contain, or can be managed to appear to contain, elements of physical danger. Every officer knows that he will never receive a citation for avoiding a fight but only for prevailing in a fight at the risk of his own safety. Perhaps there is nothing wrong with that rule. But there is surely something wrong with a system in which the combined demands for strict compliance with departmental regulation and for vigorously productive law enforcement can be met simultaneously by displacing the onus of the operatives' own misconduct on citizens. This tends to be the case in departments characterized by strong militaristic-bureaucratic discipline where officers do not merely transgress to make "good pinches," but make "good pinches" to conceal their transgressions.[14]

No matter how elaborate and no matter how stringently enforced codes of internal regulations are, they do not impinge on all segments of police depart-

---

would have been arrested had the officer laid hands on him. Chevigny reports numerous instances of arrests following altercations with citizens which were ineptly or deviously provoked by policemen, and he comments, "Many lawyers think it a triumph for a felony to be reduced to a mere offence, but the truth is that it requires only two simple ingredients: guiltless clients and infinite patience." *Police Power: Police Abuses in New York City,* (New York: Pantheon Books, 1969), p. 167.

[13]J. H. McNamara at p. 189 of his "Uncertainties in Police Work: The Relevance of Police Recruits' Background and Training," in Bordua, ed., *op. cit. supra,* Note 7, pp. 193–252.

[14]McNamara cites the following case at p. 171, *ibid.:* "a patrolman directing traffic in the middle of an intersection . . . fired his revolver and hit an automobile whose driver had not heeded the officer's hand signals. The driver immediately pulled over to the side of the street and stopped the car. The officer realized the inappropriateness of his action and began to wonder what he might offer as an explanation to his supervisor and to the citizen. The patrolman reported that his anxiety was dissipated shortly upon finding that the driver of the car was a person convicted of a number of crimes. The reader should understand that departmental policy did not specify that any person convicted of crimes in New York City thereby became a target for police pistol practice." Nevertheless, as the officer's feeling of relief indicates, the transgression was apparently construable as an instance of aggressive crime control.

ments with equal force. By and large the highly visible uniformed patrol is exposed to far greater disciplinary pressures than personnel in the detective bureaus, which Arthur Niederhoffer aptly described as "mock bureaucracies."[15] While this situation is viewed as unavoidable, because the conduct of detectives cannot be as closely scrutinized as the conduct of patrolmen, and necessary because detectives need more freedom than patrolmen,[16] it tends to demean uniformed assignments. Because patrolmen perceive military discipline as degrading, ornery, and unjust, the only motive they have for doing well—which, of course, involves, among others, the devious practices we have just described—is to get out of the uniformed assignments.[17] Thus, the uniformed patrol suffers from a constant drain of ambitious and enterprising men, leaving it generally understaffed and, incidentally, overstaffed with men who are regarded as unsuitable for more demanding tasks. Though by no means all competent personnel take advantage of opportunities to leave the patrol for the detective bureaus, those who remain are dispirited by the conditions under which they are obliged to work and by the invidiously low level of prestige connected with their performance.[18] In consequence the outwardly snappy appearance of the patrol hides a great deal of discontent, demoralization, and marginal work quality.

Another complex of mischievous consequences arising out of the military bureaucracy relates to the paradoxical fact that while this kind of discipline ordinarily strengthens command authority it has the opposite effect in police departments. This effect is insidious rather than apparent. Because police superiors do not direct the activity of officers in any important sense they are perceived as mere disciplinarians.[19] Not only are they not actually available to give help, advice, and direction in the handling of difficult work problems, but such a role cannot even be projected for them. Contrary to the army officer who is expected to lead his men into battle—even though he may never have a chance to do it—the analogously ranked police official is someone who can only do a great deal *to* his subordinates and very little *for* them. For this reason

---

[15]Niederhoffer, *Behind the Shield,* (New York: Doubleday, 1967), p. 85.

[16]Wilson notes, however, that this view is probably mistaken. The patrolman deals with matters that are ill defined and ambiguously emergent, while detectives deal with more precisely defined crimes and only after they have been committed. *Varieties of Police Behavior,* (Cambridge, Mass.: Harvard University Press, 1968), pp. 8–9.

[17]"A high arrest record reinforces the cynicism that inspired it in the first place, while often establishing a policeman's reputation for initiative and efficiency. His superiors recommend him for assignment to the detective division. This route to promotion appeals to many young policemen who have little hope of passing a written competitive test for promotion, and impels many of them to adopt cynicism as a rational and functional way to advancement." Niederhoffer, *op. cit., supra,* Note 15, pp. 76–77.

[18]At present the principal rewards are promotion, which takes a patrolman off the street, or reassignment to a detective or specialized unit, which takes him out of order maintenance altogether; not surprisingly, patrolmen wanting more pay or status tend to do those things . . . that will earn them those rewards." Wilson, *op. cit., supra,* Note 16, pp. 292–293.

[19]On the pervasiveness of purely punitive discipline, see McNamara, *op. cit., supra.* Note 83, pp. 178–183. Wilson reports that regulations are so framed that they do not instruct but "give the brass plenty of rope with which to hang us."

supervisory personnel are often viewed by the line personnel with distrust and even contempt.[20] It must be understood that this character of command in police departments is not due solely to its administrative incompetence. It is exceedingly rare that a ranking police officer can take positive charge of police action, and even in the cases where this is possible, his power to determine the course of action is limited to giving the most general kinds of directions.[21] But like all superiors, police superiors, do depend on the good will of the subordinates, if only to protect their own employee interests within the institution. Thus, they are forced to resort to the only means available to insure a modicum of loyalty, namely, covering mistakes. The more blatantly an officer's transgression violates an explicit departmental regulation the less likely it is that his superior will be able to conceal it. Therefore, to be helpful, as they must try to be, superiors must confine themselves to whitewashing bad practices involving relatively unregulated conduct that is, those dealings with citizens that lead up to arrests. In other words, to gain compliance with explicit regulations, where failings could be acutely embarrassing, command must yield in unregulated or little regulated areas of practice. It is almost as if patrolmen were told, "Don't let anyone catch you sleeping on the job; if they do I'll get it in the neck and you will too. So, please, keep walking; in return I'll cover for you if you make a false arrest." Superiors, needless to say, do not speak in such terms. They probably do not even communicate the message covertly. Indeed, it is quite likely that most police officials would honestly view the suggestion with contempt. But this is the way things work out and the more a department is organized along military-bureaucratic lines the more likely it is that they will work out this way. Naturally, the situation is not conducive to the development of relations of genuine trust, respect, and loyalty.

Finally, emphasis on elaborate codes of internal regulation of a military kind tends to subvert police training, at least wherever this training is administered in departments, as is commonly the case. In the very best existing training programs instruction consists of three parts. There are some lectures concerning criminology, criminal law, human relations, mental health, etc., given by visiting social scientists and lawyers. The second part consists largely of homilies about the social importance and dignity of police work, which emphasize that the occupation makes the highest demands on integrity, wisdom, and courage. The third part, to which the bulk of instructional time is devoted, relates to the teaching of departmental regulation. Since this is the only practical part of the course of instruction, it is abundantly clear that the overall purpose of the training is to turn tyros into compliant soldier-bureaucrats rather than competent practitioners of the craft of peacekeeping and crime

---

[20]McNamara, *op. cit.*, pp. 187–188, reports attitudes of patrolmen towards their superiors and concludes, "Regardless of their accuracy, these assertions strongly support the feeling that the 'bosses' of the department do not deserve the respect which the organization requires or demands."

[21]Banton views the absence of instructions and supervision as a main characteristic distinguishing American police from their British counterpart, *op. cit.*, at pp. 115–116. The absence of supervision is frequently noted; see McNamara, *op. cit.* at p. 183; and *Task Force Report: The Police, op. cit.*, Note 6, p. 52.

control.[22] But since there exist no direct relation between knowing the regulations and maintaining the appearance of complying with them, the first thing graduates learn on their first assignment is that they must forget everything they have been taught in the academy. The immediate effect of the "reality shock" is a massive increase in the attitude of cynicism among first year policemen, not surprisingly since their introduction to the occupation was not only inadequate as far as their work duties are concerned, but also misleading.[23]

It could be said, of course, that the argument proposed thus far merely shows that efforts to professionalize police work by means of importing traits of outward military discipline is apt to create tendencies to displace misconduct into unregulated areas because the pertinent regulations have not yet been formulated. In time, these areas too will come under the scope of the existing discipline. It is our view that it is exceedingly unlikely that this development will take place. The charting of realistic methods of peacekeeping and crime control is profoundly incompatible with the style of current regulations of internal discipline. One simply cannot bring under the same system of control rules relating to dress and bureaucratic formalities, on the one hand, and norms governing the discretionary process of handling an instance of disorderly conduct on the streets, on the other. Emphasis on the first defeats care for the other. This does not imply that all presently existing regulations must be rescinded to encourage a methodical approach to police work tasks. Quite the contrary, the majority of present expectations will probably retain value in any alternative system of control. But their relevance, mode of presentation, and enforcement will have to be made subsidiary to a system of procedure that charts professionally responsible decisionmaking under conditions of uncertainty. In simplest terms, if policemen can be induced to face problems in the community and to deal with citizens in ways that meet at once criteria of purposeful efficiency and will correspond to the expectations of the kind public trust commonly associated with the exercise of professional expertise, then there will be no need to treat them like soldier-bureaucrats. Correspondingly, as long as policemen will be treated like soldier-bureaucrats, they cannot be expected to develop professional acumen, nor value its possession.

It must be said, however, that the true professionalization of police work, in and of itself, is no weapon against sloth and corruption, no more than in the case of medicine, the ministry, law, teaching, and social work. That is, the professionalization of police work still leaves open the matter of its control. But if we are not willing to settle for having physicians who are merely honest, and

---

[22]McNamara speaks about the dilemma, "whether to emphasize training strategies aimed at the development of self-directed and autonomous personnel or to emphasize strategies aimed at developing personnel over whom the organization can readily exercise control. It appears that the second strategy is the one most often emphasized." *Op. cit., supra,* Note 83, p. 251. Niederhoffer similarly states that, "At the Academy he [the recruit] masters and simultaneously succumbs to, the web of protocol and ceremony that characterizes any quasi-military hierarchy." *Op. cit. supra.* Note 19, p. 45.

[23]Niederhoffer, *ibid.,* speaks about the "reality shock" and documents the rapid rise of cynicism among first year policemen; see especially p. 239.

who would frankly admit that in curing diseases and dealing with patients they have to rely entirely on "playing by ear," it is difficult to see why we would devote all our energies to trying to make the police honest without any concern whatever for whether or not they know, in a technical sense, how to do what they are supposed to do. Some people say it is foolish to demand technical proficiency and professional ethics where none exists. This view is certainly premature and probably wrong. We know far too little about the way police work is actually done to say with assurance that what we desire does not exist. What we know is that policemen have not written any scholarly tracts about it. We also know that presently good and bad work practices are not distinguishable, or, more precisely, are not distinguished. Worst of all, we have good reasons to suspect that if some men are possessed by and act with professional acumen, they might possibly find it wiser to keep it to themselves lest they will be found to be in conflict with some departmental regulation. The pending task, therefore, has less to do with putting external resources of scholarship at the disposal of the *police departments,* than with discovering those good qualities of police work that already exist in the skills of *individual practitioners.* It is not enough to discover them, however, they must be liberated and allowed to take their proper place in the scheme of police organization. By making the possession and use of such skills the controlling consideration in the distribution of rewards, we will have a beginning of a professional system for controlling police practices. The prospect of such control is in strict competition with presently existing methods of military-bureaucratic regulation.[24]

---

[24]The competitive nature of ideals of military discipline and methodical discretion has been noted in a survey of the Boston police department undertaken in 1934: "Too often the military aspect of organization pushes the essentially individual character of police work into the background." Cited in *Task Force Report: Police, op. cit., supra.* Note 6, p. 136.

PART TWO
CONTEXT OF POLICING

One of the most salient aspects of police departments in the United States is their local character. Departments vary greatly from one another. The social science student of policing should resist the rather seductive tendency to over-generalize. Across communities, for example, local politics vary, populations differ, purposes diverge, and histories contrast, all of which can be expected to leave their mark on specific police organizations and practices. As Selznick (1949) and others have noted, any organization over time will come to reflect peculiarities specific to the region in which it is embedded, the choices it has made in the past, the enduring patterns in which these choices have been made, and, more generally, the particular and more or less unique culture which informs individuals as to how they are expected to behave within and sometimes beyond the organization's boundaries. Even within a given law enforcement organization, both large and small, policing the body politic takes on particularistic features according to among other things: certain bounded neighborhoods; the fluctuating temporal patterns linked to the private use of public space; and, of course, the unpredictable periodicity associated with the dramatic events of community life that come to be seen as police problems. And, in addition to the drama of crime waves, savage killings, and unusually troublesome teenagers, the more banal events of the day such as budget crises, reform, chiefs of police, and the ebb and flow of federal funds vary unpredictably, and thus also shape and define the character of the organization at a given time.

Nonetheless, police agencies everywhere are charged with the classification and control of people. They are also expected to insure the public safety of citizens, to minimize the fear, terror, and hostility people may potentially direct toward one another, and to perform a host of social services which other public agencies appear reluctant to do. That the police have an impossible mandate is a point well made in Part I. Here, however, we wish to explore in greater depth just how this mandate is played out structurally in police departments. In other words, what common institutional characteristics are associated with policing as an activity, and how do such characteristics create, distort, reify, or otherwise mystify the reality experienced by the police? We refer to this structural domain as the context of policing.

Several apparently insolvable yet highly general dilemmas facing police are crucial for coming to an understanding of this context. First, and perhaps of most importance, within police agencies obedience to generalized rules and regulations is never categorical but always situational and, therefore, always problematic. Since the police task on the street is primarily interactional and few interactional encounters can ever be the same, the police know that the standardization of their mission is as futile as the labors of

Sisyphus. Furthermore, they know that since their everyday tasks vary widely, the practical rules useful, for instance, in silencing or satisfying the cantankerous neighborhood grouch are far different than those useful when doing perennial battle with the children in a district. Scraping a dead animal out of the gutter is an altogether different job from trying to corner a fleeing robber in a high-speed automobile chase. Given the magnitude of the police task, the limited resources available to do it, the associated low visibility and spatial independence of those members of the organization most often charged with the doing of the task, all organizational rules, codified or not, are then replete with special meanings carved out in different segments of the organization. Indeed, if the same event will be interpreted differently by persons located in various parts of the organization (as all of the authors of the selections in this section suggest), then so too will the rules that supposedly govern the proper police response to the event.

Relatedly, the world in which the police are expected to take action is pregnant with procedural troubles. Not only are people differentially disposed to cooperate with the police but some are downright dangerous to the health and well-being of the police. Incivility, disrespect, hostility, insult, threat, and assault are everyday features of policing. To argue that a role can insulate and protect an individual from the intrusion of anger, alarm, and dread is to suggest that the police must become automatons, a perilous but, thankfully, impossible demand. While reducing the reducible risks on the job may lead to an occupational need to always disbelieve people or to routinize and cut back on as many police tasks as possible, such procedures also limit the potential physical and emotional hazards of the police life. In short, such responses are almost functional conditions for the continuing performance of the police job.

Structurally, the police are also surrounded by conflicting expectations of what they are to do. Different social groups vary in their power over, and expectations of, both individual officers and the police as an organization. What in one section of the town represents the decent desires of a normal citizen is, in another part of town, the indecent desires of someone not seen to be a citizen at all. There can be no standardization of much of the behavior the police are presumably out to regulate. And, as if this were not problem enough, the police must continually operate in the absence of criteria applicable to those relatively few areas in which there is more or less public agreement regarding the seriousness, threat, and illegality of certain behavior. Included here would be such crimes as murder, burglary, robbery, rape, and other vicious pokes into the social tissues of the community. Though there may be agreement on these matters, nonetheless we cannot know how citizens would regulate their own conduct in the absence of police watchfulness. Without such knowledge, the success (or failure) of the police at regulating the community can never be demonstrated. Obviously, this situation places the police at a severe disadvantage, for, while they are told and, in fact, believe their work is among the most crucial to social well-being, no one can document how well they are doing at such an enormous task. Nor, we might add, has anyone even attempted to approach this problem of verification in empirical detail. Since the respect, position, and perhaps survival of the organization in the community are at stake when issues concerned with evaluation are raised, the police must always act as if they are doing (or, at least, striving to do) an altogether exemplary job. The work from this vantage point becomes akin to a staged and continuous drama, for an appearance of police success, lawfulness, and earnest commitment to the task must be maintained at all cost lest the citizenry become hopelessly disenchanted with the ability of the police to sustain what is called law and order and take matters into their own hands.

Finally, the police, in the interest of achieving broad coverage at the street level, have organized themselves virtually everywhere into a bottom-heavy horizontal work structure wherein advancement up the ranks is a distinct possibility for only a few. Sealed off at the low level, enclosed within a given territory, and interacting primarily only with fellow members of the organization who are working one's shift and squad, the patrolman's career is conspicuous by its unique but rather limited satisfactions. While the patrol subculture may be rich, filled with colleagual good humor and tales of personal courage and high (and "low") adventure, it offers one few tangible rewards beyond collective wage increases, the possibility of obtaining greater freedom from supervision, or an assignment which carries with it reduced burdens. Such is the structural confinement of the patrolman's lot.

All of the readings that follow deal in various ways with each of these structural conditions. But what flows from this brief examination of the context of policing is a recognition that structurally the police are neither bureaucrats nor professionals despite many loud claims to the contrary. To be sure, any occupation possesses what Hughes (1958) called a bundle of tasks, and this bundle is no doubt organizationally stratified by a division of labor wherein some members may behave more or less as functionaries and others as autonomous practitioners relatively free to follow the impersonal dicta of a studied task. And, certainly, even a given task may possess different attributes which can be pursued in various ways. Street-level policing, from this standpoint, then, represents a tradition-bound curiosity, for it stands operationally in a horde of paradoxical and often conflicting demands. The patrolman can be both bureaucrat or professional depending upon what he is up to at any given moment.

James Q. Wilson, in the first section of this part, considers the tangle of contrary tendencies embedded within police agencies and concludes that police work itself resembles a craftlike occupation wherein individual solutions to common problems are likely to persist forever. This sharp but gloomy argument mocks those who urge massive alterations in police practices through such means as enlightened management, increased resource allocations, intensified "professionalism," or any other of a host of traditional or trendy exhortations. Indeed, as Wilson suggests, the essential and intractable dilemma of policing lies in the inherent inability of those in the organization (or, for that matter, anyone else) to specify the root causes of crime. Like mental hospitals, police departments cannot succeed in a role that asks them to solve problems for which no solutions presently exist. Borrowing from Banton's (1964) astute earlier analysis of the police, Wilson's remarks on the split and discordant responsibilities of the police to both enforce the law *and* keep the peace are classic and suggest that the consequential locus of discretion in police departments does not lie with the administrator but resides fundamentally with the working patrolman. It is also interesting to note that most, if not all, of the potential reforms alluded to by Wilson in this article (which is now nearly ten years old) have come to pass in many police agencies. And, just as the author predicted, these reforms have not changed the face of law enforcement in any substantial fashion.

Some of the deep reasons behind this rather remarkable tenacity of the patterns of police conduct to persevere are taken up in the next selection. Peter K. Manning addresses what is perhaps the essential and elementary internal division in police organizations, the sometimes far-reaching gap separating the concerns of police administrators from those of their charges. Using the latent but practical rules that emerge socially around the use of, and exceptions to, codified disciplinary procedures, Manning displays the problematic nature of the relationships that exist across divergent segments of police organizations. Following Wilson's lead, administrators in the British constabulary examined here are engaged, like their American counterparts, in the continual struggle to maintain at least the appearance of discipline and control. The picture of policing that emerges from this study is one of an activity organized, not around internal solidarity, but around basic cleavages in the values and interests of the diverse membership. Such an organization, as Manning goes about detailing, is knit together at certain places and in certain times by patterns of accommodation and collusion. In Geertz's (1973) term, the members of the organization are "jointed" together. And such jointing takes place through interaction patterns frequently marked by strategic evasiveness, duplicity, and conspiratorial shadings by which common ends are manufactured by members who might otherwise disagree on the means to these ends were they to be articulated. That these collaborative tactics represent a structural feature of police organizations whereby different segments of the organization pursue different objectives under different circumstances is a central theme of Manning's essay.

Moving to another linkage on the hierarchical ladder, Larry L. Tifft also finds that these not-so-conjoint interactional patterns between different levels typify policy agencies. In particular, he finds that the various tasks engaged in by the police promote divergent local control structures. Examining five "functional" areas of police work—traffic, patrol, detective work in vice and in robbery, and the tactical squad—Tifft notes that supervisors in each area have at their disposal quite different resources with which to exercise power and control over their men. Each operational area in effect presents a separate and distinct working environment—apparently complete with its own mysteries and superstitions—which diminishes, amplifies, and, in general, constrains the official command responsibilities of those closest to the everyday operations of the police—the sergeants. Citing what are essentially structural bases of control, Tifft shows how a sergeant's power to influence the performance of underlings is, for instance, tied to the technological characteristics of the task, the routine or lack of routine that can be created to help carry out the task, and the subcultural norms that develop in response to the problematic features of the task.

Patrol work is dissected by activities and by time in the following selection by John A. Webster. Utilizing departmental records, Webster lifts what he calls the "opaque veil" shielding much of the patrol function from public view and discovers just how little clock time is accounted for by the police when it comes to their favored activity—crook-catching. In what has come to be a hallmark time-and-motion study of the police, we learn that patrolling city streets is dominated by service and administrative duties. While such a portrait hardly mirrors the crime-fighting image cultivated with some zeal by many police administrators, Webster's study goes some distance toward informing us about what the patrolman does when he is policing (as opposed to what he would *like* to do, or have others *believe* he is doing).

Of course, performing the more mundane role of service worker or order taker hardly compliments the patrolman's image of his occupational self. Indeed not, for, as John Van Maanen's essay demonstrates, patrolmen have rather firm notions accompanying what they take to be their "real work." From a street cop's perspective, even though the long hours of a shift may elapse slowly with little or nothing to do, the patrolman knows that he may be called upon at any moment to risk his life. Whether apprehending someone he believes to have violated a law, ejecting an enraged and rowdy patron from a local saloon, or standing between two earnest combatants in a family squabble, the patrolman is fully aware that his is a risky business. Such danger gives meaning to his existence and sets him off from others who follow gentler ways of life. As the police often claim, their work is not for the squeamish. Yet such an occupational perspective requires continual renewal, for, as all serious observers of the police have suggested, everyday patrol work does not fit the images of it promoted by many of the men in blue. Van Maanen attempts to clarify this seeming paradox between the appearance and the reality of policing by linking the occupational perspectives of the police to various structural characteristics of their work. While he notes that the police brotherhood is far from a harmonious and trusting one, certain unavoidable task demands and organizational features of the work promote a strong mutual concern among patrolmen. Too often police attitudes are displayed by social scientists as if they were somehow lifted straight from a Martian landscape with little or no apparent reason for their social contours. Van Maanen's view of these attitudes, however, locates them squarely within the day-to-day working milieu of the patrolman.

This part on the context of policing closes with Jonathan Rubenstein's dense description of the kinds of information sought by patrolmen on the street in Philadelphia. Here we learn something about the structural constitution of the policeman's curiosity. Critically, we learn of its contingent, concrete, and highly particularistic nature. Furthermore, few others in the organization care about what the streetwise patrolman may know; therefore, information within the organization belongs to its possessor and is guarded rather jealously. Vice information, in particular, holds a central and continuing interest of the patrolmen studied by Rubenstein because vice arrests were scrutinized closely by superior officers in the department and used by them as indices of patrolman "performance and success," thus sensitizing the men on the street to vice-relevant information (often to the exclusion of other information available to patrolmen of possible police concern). This pattern of concern for vice may or may not be true of patrolmen working for other police departments in urban America. However, regardless of content, the contextual limitations surrounding the gathering of information by patrolmen are depicted clearly in this section. As a feature of this informational domain, Rubenstein also highlights one of the most vexing and universal dilemmas faced by police: the longer a street patrolman remains in a given territory, the better working knowledge he develops of the people and their activities in his sector. Yet, at the same time, the patrolman is necessarily drawn into a swarm of interpersonal relationships and exchanges in the course of seeking, encountering, and accepting certain information which makes the *use* of his cultivated knowledge increasingly problematic in both personal and tactical ways. While Whyte (1943) was the first to notice this structural dilemma, Rubenstein's account of how it is managed by some patrolmen remains altogether illuminating. And, most appropriately, this concern for the strategies of policing takes us directly to the issues raised in the next part of the book.

Dilemmas of Police Administration

James Q. Wilson

Policy making for the police is complicated by the fact that, at least in large cities, the police department is an organization with at least two objectives, one of which produces conflict and the other of which cannot be attained.[1] The dilemmas facing police administrators arise out of their inability to obtain agreement on what constitutes satisfactory performance of the first objective, and their difficulty in finding a strategy which would permit the realization of the (agreed-upon) second objective. (There are, of course, additional objectives which a police department serves—providing certain nonpolice services and handling large-scale disorders, for example.)

OBJECTIVES

The first objective I call *order maintenance*—the handling of disputes, or behavior which threatens to produce disputes, among persons who disagree over what ought to be right or seemly conduct or over the assignment of blame for what is agreed to be wrong or unseemly conduct. A family quarrel, a noisy drunk, a tavern brawl, a street disturbance by teenagers, the congregation on the sidewalk of idle young men (especially in eccentric clothes or displaying an unconventional demeanor)—all these are cases in which citizens disagree as whether or how the police should intervene. If the police do intervene, one party or another is likely to feel harassed, outraged, or neglected. Though a law may have been broken, as with an assault inflicted by a husband on his wife, the police do not perceive their responsibilities as involving simply the comparing of a particular behavior to a clear legal standard and making an arrest if the standard has been violated. For one thing, the legal rule is, in many order-maintenance cases, ambiguous. A "breach of the peace" implies a prior definition of "peace," and this is a matter on which persons commonly disagree. For another thing, even when the legal standard is clear enough—as with an assault—the "victim" is often not innocent (indeed, he may have called for the police because he was losing a fight he started) and thus the question of *blame* may be to the participants more important than the question of "guilt" and they will expect the officer to take this into account. Finally, most order-maintenance situations do not result in an arrest—the parties involved wish the officer to "do something" that will "settle things," but they often do not wish to see that settlement entail an arrest. And in any case the infraction is likely to be a misdemeanor and thus, in many states, the officer cannot make a valid arrest unless the illegality was committed in his presence or unless the

---

[1]This article is in part adapted from material [that appears] in my book-length study of the police, *Varieties of Police Behavior* (Cambridge, Mass.: Harvard University Press, 1968).

REPRINTED FROM: *Public Administration Review*, 28, 5, 1968 (407–417).

victim is willing to sign a complaint. As a result, the officer cannot expect a judge to dispose of the case; the former must devise a substantive solution for a disorderly event which the latter will never hear of.

The second objective is *law enforcement*—the application of legal sanctions, usually by means of an arrest, to persons who injure or deprive innocent victims. A burglary, purse snatch, mugging, robbery, or auto theft are usually crimes committed by strangers on persons who did not provoke the attack. Though there is, in these matters, a problem of finding the guilty party, once guilt is established there is no question of blame. For almost all such law-enforcement situations, the officer is expected to either make an arrest or act so as to prevent the violation from occurring in the first place. His task is the seemingly ministerial and technical act of either apprehending or deterring the criminal. The difficulty is that the officer lacks the means—the information, primarily—to apprehend or deter more than a very small fraction of all criminals. Leaving aside murder, rape, and aggravated assault—in which a high proportion of suspects are known or even related to their victims—few major crimes such as burglary and robbery that are of primary concern to the citizen are "cleared by arrest." In 1965 only 38 per cent of all *known* robberies and 25 per cent of all *known* burglaries were cleared by arrest, and even that figure is artificially high. The household victimization study done by the National Opinion Research Center for the President's Commission on Law Enforcement and Administration of Justice[2] showed that in 1965 there were over three times as many burglaries and 50 per cent more robberies than were reported to and recorded by the police; thus, the adjusted clearance rates are only about 8 per cent for burglary and 24 per cent for robbery. But even those figures may be too high, for, as Skolnick points out, there are often strong organizational pressures leading detectives to induce arrested burglars and robbers to "cop out" to as many offenses as possible in order to boost the clearance rate.[3]

There is, of course, no way to measure the number of crimes prevented by police activity, but the number is not likely to be large. Crimes of passion that occur in private places (many, if not most, murders, rapes, and serious assaults are in this category) probably happen at a rate independent of the nature or intensity of police activity. Crimes of stealth, such as burglary and many forms of larceny, may in unknown ways be affected by police activity, but the effect is probably not great—no city, whatever its police strategy, has been able to show any dramatic reversal in the rising rates of reported thefts. There is some evidence that certain kinds of street crimes—muggings, purse snatches, holdups of taxi and bus drivers, and the like—can be reduced by very intensive police patrol, the use of officers disguised as cabbies or lady shoppers, the formation of citizen auxiliaries, and the like. But even with these crimes, which surely

---

[2]Philip H. Ennis, *Criminal Victimization in the United States,* a report to the President's Commission on Law Enforcement and Administration of Justice (Washington, D.C.: U.S. Government Printing Office, 1967), p. 13.

[3]See Jerome H. Skolnick, *Justice Without Trial* (New York: John Wiley & Sons, 1966), pp. 167–181.

are the ones most disturbing to the average person, two problems exist. First, no one is confident that what appears to be a reduction is not in fact a displacement of crime (to other places or to other forms of crime), or that if a reduction genuinely occurs it will persist over time.[4] And second, the kinds of police activities apparently best adapted to suppressing street crime—intensive patrols, close surveillance of "suspicious" persons, frequent street stops of pedestrians and motorists, and so on—are precisely those most likely to place the police in conflict with important segments of the community—primarily with persons who because of their age, race, or social class are regarded (and, as far as the evidence goes, correctly regarded) as most likely to commit criminal acts. In short, in the one aspect of law enforcement where there may be opportunities for substantial deterrence, the police are obliged to act in a way which, like their actions in order-maintenance situations, is most likely to bring them into conflict with the citizen.

The dilemmas of police administration arise out of the difficulty confronting a chief who seeks policies which can guide his men in performing the order-maintenance function and a technique which will prove efficacious in serving the law-enforcement function. The conflict over how the police should behave in order-maintenance cases results from differing expectations as to the appropriate level of public or private order and differing judgments over what constitutes a just resolution of a given dispute. In a homogeneous community, where widely shared norms define both the meaning of order and the standards of justice (who is equal to whom and in what sense), the police role is comparatively simple. But where the community, usually because of differences of class or race, has no common normative framework, the police have no reliable guides to action and efforts to devise such guides will either be half-hearted or sources of important public controversy. The conflict that arises over the performance of the law-enforcement function, on the other hand, arises out of the lack of any technique by which crime can be reduced significantly and without incurring high costs in terms of other values—privacy, freedom, and so forth. The dispute about the law-enforcement function is, unlike the dispute over order maintenance, not over ends but over means.

CRITICISMS

Organizations to which society gives tasks that cannot be performed to the satisfaction of society suffer not only certain frustrations but some fundamental administrative problems as well. The criticisms directed at the police are

---

[4] A "get-tough" policy by the police in Miami was reported to have led to a drop in street crimes, at least in one area of the city (*New York Times,* February 19, 1968). When off-duty police officers began to work as taxi drivers in New York City, there was a drop in the number of robberies and assaults against cabbies (*New York Times,* February 20, 1968). After the stories appeared, however, it was reported that these street crimes had begun to show an increase, though they had not yet risen to the level they attained before the counter-measures were adopted. We know very little about how great a reduction in crime is the result of criminal perceptions of police intent and how much the result of the direct consequences of police actions, nor have we tried (except in a very few cases) to measure the persistence of such improvement as does occur.

well known and often sound, but conditions giving rise to these criticisms are frequently not well understood by the critic. For example, police departments are frequently charged with hiring unqualified personnel, suppressing or manipulating crime reports, condoning the use of improper or illegal procedures, using patrol techniques that create tensions and irritation among the citizens, and either over-reacting (using too much force too quickly) or under-reacting (ignoring dangerous situations until it is too late) in the face of incipient disorder. All of these criticisms are true to some extent, though the extent of the deficiencies is often exaggerated. But let us concede for the moment that they are all true. Why are they true?

Explanations vary, but commonly they are some variation on the "bad men" theme. Unqualified, unintelligent, rude, brutal, intolerant, or insensitive men, so this theory goes, find their way (or are selectively recruited into) police work where they express their prejudices and crudeness under color of the law. Though a few of the commanding officers of the department may try to improve matters, on the whole they are ineffective. At best they invent paper palliatives—empty departmental directives, superficial community relations programs, one-sided internal disciplinary units—which do little more than offer a chance for issuing favorable, but misleading, publicity statements about the "new look." And at worst, the theory continues, such administrators exacerbate tensions by encouraging, in the name of efficiency or anti-crime strategies, various techniques, such as aggressive preventive patrol, that lead to the harassment of innocent citizens. The solution for these problems is, clearly, to hire "better men"—college graduates, Negroes, men who can pass tests that weed out "authoritarian" personalities, and the like. And those on the force should attend universities, go through sensitivity training, and apply for grants to develop "meaningful" community relations programs.[5]

Some critics go even further. Not only do the police fail to do the right thing, they systematically do the wrong thing. Not only do the police fail to prevent crime, *the police actually cause crime*. Not only do the police fail to handle riots properly, *the police cause riots*. Presumably, things might improve if we had no police at all, but since even the strongest critics usually recognize the need for the police under some circumstances, they are willing to permit the police to function provided that they are under "community control"—controlled, that is, by the neighborhoods (especially Negro neighborhoods) where they operate. If police departments are at best a necessary evil, filled with inept or intolerant men exploiting the fact that they are necessary, then the solution to the problem of abuse is to put the police under the strictest and closest control of those whose activities they are supposed to regulate.

The view taken in this paper is quite different from at least the more extreme of these arguments. If all big-city police departments were filled tomorrow with Negro college graduates and placed under the control of the

---

[5]Various proposals for changing police practices are reported in the President's Commission on Law Enforcement and Administration of Justice *Task Force Report: The Police* (Washington, D.C.: U.S. Government Printing Office, 1967), p. xi, and the National Advisory Commission on Civil Disorders *Report* (Washington, D.C.: U.S. Government Printing Office, 1968), chap. 11.

neighborhoods they are supposed to control, most of the problems that exist today would continue to exist and some in fact might get worse. The crime rate would not go down; indeed, owing to police timidity about making arrests among people who have a voice in their management, it might go up marginally. Police involvement in conflict and disorder would have no happier outcomes, because most disorder—family or neighbor quarrels—does not involve the community nor would the community necessarily have any better idea how to resolve it than do the police now. Perceived police abuse and harassment might decline in the neighborhood, but since each neighborhood would have its own police, the amount of abuse and harassment perceived by a person from one neighborhood entering a different neighborhood (say a Negro entering a white area, or vice versa) might increase. The conflict between neighborhood residents who want more police protection (small businessmen, home-owners, older people) and those who want less (teenagers, transients, young men hanging on street corners) would remain and the police would tend, in the eyes of one group, to serve the standards of the other.

There would, of course, be some improvements. The police might have better information about the neighborhood if they were controlled by it and thus, in the event of large-scale disorders, be able to distinguish more accurately between solid citizens and trouble makers. They might also be more alert to the customs of the area and thus prepared to tolerate behavior (street-corner gatherings, loud noises) which the neighborhood tolerates, even though in other places such behavior might be regarded as breaches of the peace. And college-educated men might display more civility in routine encounters, handling incidents more impersonally and people more politely.

But it is difficult to say that such gains would be more than marginal. Some police departments (such as those on the West Coast) already have large numbers of men with some college training, but these departments (Oakland and Los Angeles, for example) are frequently criticized by Negroes for being "too tough," "too impersonal," "gung ho," and the like. (There may be no causal relation between police education and Negro criticism, but it is possible that while college men are more civil, they also have a stronger sense of duty.) It is not clear that departments with large numbers of Negroes patrolling Negro areas have experienced less community tension than departments with few Negroes, or that in any given encounter a Negro officer behaves much differently from a white one. This is not an argument against hiring Negro police officers; on the contrary, there are in my view compelling reasons for having as many as possible patrolling Negro areas. But their value would, in my opinion, be primarily symbolic (no less important for that!) and their presence would not make substantially easier the policy-making or administrative problems of the police. Nor are the consequences of different patrol and community relations policies clear. Some departments (San Francisco, Chicago) have made a major community relations effort, but they seem to fare no better than those (such as Philadelphia or Albany) with a "get tough" policy. Departments which use aggressive preventive patrol and have strict traffic enforcement policies (such as Los Angeles) produce criticism and experience disorders, but so do departments (such as Boston) which are less aggressive or strict. Though there are these differences in police practices,[6] it is not clear how they affect the management of order, the enforcement of laws, or the maintenance of good community relations.

NATURE OF POLICE FUNCTION

The difficulty in managing the police arises, in my view, less from the quality of men recruited or the level at which authority is exercised and more from the nature of the police function. Mental hospitals provide a useful comparison to the police in this regard. Like the police, they are regarded as essential; like the police, they are routinely and repeatedly condemned for failures and inadequacies. The indictment of such institutions found, for example, in Ivan Belknap's book, has become commonplace.[7] The appalling conditions to be found in hospital wards, the apparent callousness and brutality of the staff, the denial of rights and privileges, the shortage of qualified psychiatric and medical staff, and (equally important) the inability of such professional staff as exists to control the practices of the hospital—all these circumstances have been described, and the accounts are no doubt in large measure correct. Repeated efforts at reform have been made. Budgets have been increased, hospitals have been reorganized, better-qualified personnel have been sought, staff services have been increased, and volumes of research have been published. And yet each decade sees essentially the same lamentable conditions exposed and the same indignation unleashed. With the failure of successive reform efforts, the prescriptions have become more radical. At first the need was thought to be for "better men" and "more money." Then the attack shifted to the professional staff itself—doctors and others were charged with "causing" mental illness, or at least retarding its elimination. The hospital was administration-centered; it should become patient-centered.[8]

In an incisive review of the literature on mental hospitals, Perrow concludes that the reason for the failure of reform has not been bad men or low budgets or improper organization or incompetent management (though all of those things may exist); the central problem is that we do not know how to cure mental illness. The problem is not one of ideology, but of technology. The hospitals are given a task they cannot perform, yet they must try to perform it, for

---

[6]Differences in patrol styles or strategies are described and to some degree explained in Wilson, *op. cit.,* chaps. 4–7.

[7]Ivan Belknap, *Human Problems of a State Mental Hospital* (New York: McGraw-Hill, 1956). It is striking to note the similarities between Belknap's description of mental hospital attendants and my description of patrolmen in large cities—see especially Belknap, pp. 115, 116, 138, 152, 154, and 170.

[8]See the excellent analysis in Charles Perrow's, "Hospitals: Technology, Structure, and Goals," in James G. March's, ed., *Handbook of Organizations* (Chicago: Rand McNally, 1965), pp. 916–946, and the accounts of certain "elite" hospitals practicing "milieu therapy" in W. Caudill's *The Psychiatric Hospital as a Small Society* (Cambridge, Mass.: Harvard University Press, 1958), R. N. Rapoport et al., *Community as Doctor* (London: Tavistock, 1960), and A. H. Stanton and M. S. Schwartz's *The Mental Hospital* (New York: Basic Books, 1954).

the alternative (doing nothing) seems even worse.[9] The most important recent improvement in mental hospital care was the result of an advance in medical technology—the development of tranquilizer drugs. Changes in organization, leadership, and in the men recruited to hospital tasks have rarely produced significant or lasting results from the patient's point of view. To be sure, some hospitals manage to treat the inmates humanely—these are often small, heavily staffed hospitals with patients who can afford the high costs of such facilities. Bestial practices can be eliminated, but it costs a lot of money and requires large concentrations of scarce talent. But even in these circumstances, the improvement in the mental health of the patient does not seem to be much greater than whatever improvement occurs in less intensive (and less expensive) programs.[10]

The parallel with the police is striking. Abusive practices or indifference to citizen needs can be eliminated, but it typically requires a community that (like the intensive-treatment hospital) is small, expensive, and cooperative. In short, it requires a middle- or upper-middle class suburb. Some advocates of community control over the police argue that it is the close supervision of the police by the suburban community that accounts for the good relations between police and citizens to be found there; if one duplicates those political conditions in the central city—if one, in short, "suburbanizes" the central-city neighborhoods—comparable inprovements in police-citizen relations will occur. My research suggests that it is not the degree or kind of control that produces this effect in the suburbs, it is the class composition of the community. In a homogeneous, middle-class suburb there is relatively little public disorder; consequently the police rarely need intervene in situations of high conflict, and thus rarely need become parties to conflict. When the chief law enforcement problem involves crimes of stealth (burglary and larceny) rather than street crimes (assaults, robberies, muggings), the police need not practice aggressive preventive patrol or otherwise keep persons on the streets under close surveillance; accordingly, it is rare for a suburban resident walking the streets at night to feel he is being "harrassed." Finally, a socially homogeneous middle-class area provides the police with relative unambiguous cues as to who should be regarded as a "suspicious person" and thus who should be made the object of police attention. Teenagers hanging around a suburban ice-cream parlor late at night or a Negro in the back alley of an all-white residential community would be viewed suspiciously by the police and citizenry alike. Though this suspicion may be, in the particular case, unjust to the teenagers or the Negro, acting on the basis of it does not bring the police into conflict with the community. (But though an affluent suburb may provide the conditions that reduce the likelihood of police-citizen conflict or of police abuses of their authority, it does not provide the conditions that make the management of such disorder as exists or the prevention of such crimes as occur any easier. In short, high-status communities permit the police to solve their ideological but not their technological problems.)

---

[9]See Perrow, *op. cit.*, pp. 925, 926, 930, 934.

[10]Rapoport et al., *op. cit.*, p. 208.

The policy implications of this argument are clear, though gloomy. Substantial and lasting improvements in police-community relations are not likely until and unless there is a substantial and lasting change in the class composition of the central city population—i.e., until the street-crime rate and the incidence of public disorder in the central cities becomes closer to that in the middle-class suburbs. Only then will it be possible to reduce substantially the police-community tension generated by practices like aggressive preventive patrol and the use of gross indicators such as race and apparent class as clues to criminal potential.

RACIAL COMPLICATION

Race complicates the issue, of course, and renders it more explosive. A black person is more likely to be regarded as lower class or otherwise suspicious than a white person, and thus a law-abiding and peaceful Negro is more likely to be treated as if he were potentially lawless and disorderly than an equivalent white person. Innocent Negroes so treated will naturally feel a deep sense of injustice. It is sometimes argued that this would not happen if police officers were not prejudiced. No doubt many officers are prejudiced (indeed, one study indicates that the vast majority are) and this prejudice may make matters worse.[11] But the crucial point is that large numbers of innocent Negroes would still be treated in (to them) unjust ways even if all policemen were entirely free of race prejudice so long as a disproportionate number of Negroes are lower class. Violent crime and disorder are predominantly (though not exclusively) lower-class phenomena;[12] Negroes are disproportionally (though far from exclusively) lower class; a black skin, therefore, will continue to be a statistically defensible (though individually unjust) cue that triggers an officer's suspicion.

---

[11]Donald J. Black and Albert J. Reiss, Jr., "Patterns in Police and Citizen Transactions," in *Studies of Crime and Law Enforcement in Major Metropolitan Areas,* a report to the President's Commission on Law Enforcement and Administration of Justice (Washington, D.C.: U.S. Government Printing Office, 1967), Vol. II, Section I, pp. 132–139. Observers working under the direction of Black and Reiss in Boston, Chicago, and Washington, D.C., reported that 72 per cent of all white officers and 28 per cent of all Negro officers volunteered "highly prejudiced" or "prejudiced" comments about Negroes. There was, however, no clear relationship between attitude and behavior: "A recurring theme in the observer's reports was the great disparity between the verbalized attitudes of officers in the privacy of the patrol car, and the public conduct of officers in encounters with Negroes and members of other minority groups" (p. 138). After observing police behavior, Black and Reiss conclude that "Policemen generally do not disproportionately behave aggressively or negatively toward Negroes," though they do "disproportionately behave amiably or positively toward white citizens" (p. 56).

[12]A good summary of the evidence on the disproportionately lower-class origin of assaultive crime is Marvin E. Wolfgang's *Crimes of Violence,* a report to the President's Commission on Law Enforcement and Administration of Justice (1967), pp. 166–169. Additional evidence based on direct observation can be found in Walter B. Miller's "Violent Crimes in City Gangs," *Annals,* 364 (March 1966), 96–112, and "Theft Behavior in City Gangs," in Malcolm W. Klein's *Juvenile Gangs in Context* (Englewood Cliffs, N.J.: Prentice-Hall, 1967), p. 34.

Among the consequences of this generalization will be continued police suspicion of blacks and continued Negro antagonism toward the police.

The point is perhaps more easily understood if we examine other cues to which police respond and other forms of prejudice which they may have. Young people commit a disproportionate share of many kinds of crime, especially crimes against property. Being young is therefore a statistically useful cue to an officer who is scanning a population in search of persons more likely than others to commit, or to have committed, a crime. In addition, it is quite possible that the police have "youth prejudice"—that is, they may impute to young people even more criminality than in fact they possess, just as officers having race prejudice impute to Negroes more criminality than in fact they display. But if all officers were cured of "youth prejudice," young people would still be singled out for special attention and suspicion. The difference, of course, is that young people outgrow their youth, while Negroes cannot outgrow their blackness.

The best evidence that race prejudice is not the crucial factor can be found in the behavior of Negro police officers. There has been no systematic study of such men, but my observations suggest that black policemen are as suspicious and tough in black neighborhoods as white officers. Indeed, in the long run Negroes have an advantage over youth. It may be possible to improve the class position of Negroes so that the crime rates found among them will be no higher (and perhaps even lower) than the rates found among whites. Then there will be no reason, other than prejudice, why an officer would treat a Negro differently from a white. By contrast, there is probably no way even in principle to reduce greatly the crimogenic properties of youth and therefore no way even in principle to make the police less suspicious of young people.

If the fundamental problem is one of class (admittedly greatly complicated by the problem of race), what can a police administrator do in the short run while he waits for society somehow to solve the class problem? If the point of view presented here is correct, not a great deal. But since even marginal gains are desirable when conditions are (or are widely thought to be) deplorable, it is worth considering palliatives however slight may be their benefits.

First, the police should recognize clearly that order maintenance is their central function—central both in the demands it makes on time and resources and in the opportunities it affords for making a difference in the lives of the citizens. Hunting criminals both occupies less time (at least for the patrolmen) and provides fewer chances for decisive action. How well disputes are settled may depend crucially on how competent, knowledgeable, and sensitive the police are; how fast the crime rate mounts is much less dependent on the level and nature of police activity. (As will be argued below, other than by reducing the size of the lower class the best way society can affect the crime rate may be through the court and correctional systems rather than through the police.)

ORDER-MAINTENANCE FUNCTION

A police department that places order maintenance uppermost in its priorities will judge patrolmen less by their arrest records and more by their ability to keep the peace on their beat. This will require, in turn, that sergeants and other supervisory personnel concern themselves more with how the patrolmen function in family fights, teenage disturbances, street corner brawls, and civil disorders, and less with how well they take reports at the scene of burglary or how many traffic tickets they issue during a tour of duty. Order maintenance also requires that the police have available a wider range of options for handling disorder than is afforded by the choice between making an arrest and doing nothing. Detoxification centers should be available as an alternative to jail for drunks. Family-service units should be formed which can immediately assist patrolmen handling domestic quarrels. Community-service officers should be available to provide information, answer complaints, and deal with neighborhood tensions and rumors.

Patrolmen who are given the order-maintenance function will obviously require a great deal of information about their beats—more than can be obtained by riding around in a patrol car or rotating frequently among several beats. Obtaining this knowledge will be made easier by the decentralization of the patrol function so that local commanders deal with local conditions subject to general policy guidelines from the police administrator. This decentralization need not always take the form of proliferating precinct station houses— these facilities, as traditionally used for mustering the watch, jailing prisoners, and keeping records, are expensive. Many of them, indeed, were built in a period when patrolmen, like firemen, slept in when they had night duty. Smaller, less elaborate, and more numerous "store-front" police offices scattered throughout central-city neighborhoods might prove more effective and less expensive. Officers assigned to a particular neighborhood ought to remain in that area for long periods of time, rather than experience frequent rotation among neighborhoods. An even more radical experiment might be to assess the value of having patrolmen actually live in certain key areas. For example, some officers might be encouraged, on a volunteer basis, to live in public housing projects. To make such an assignment more attractive and to increase the pay of the officer, he could be given the apartment rent-free or at a substantial discount.

Such decentralization of function requires the strengthening of the command system if it is not to produce inconsistent behavior, political intervention, and corruption. Supervisory officers, especially watch commanders, ought to have more authority to assign, direct, and evaluate their officers. Mechanical, fixed assignments and evaluation solely by written examinations decrease the possibility of inducing patrolmen to take seriously their order-maintenance function and lead them instead to emphasize following the safe routine, memorizing the penal code and departmental rule book, and "pushing paper"—filing reports, writing tickets, and so forth.

At the same time, if patrolmen are expected to devote themselves primarily to the most conflict-laden, unpleasant parts of their task, there must be rewards available that are commensurate with the burdens. At present, the major rewards open to the patrolman—promotion, higher pay, specialized duty—all take him out of the patrol force and place him in supervisory posts, criminal investigation, or headquarters staff units. If the patrol function is the most important and difficult job in the department, the best men ought to be rewarded for doing it well in ways that leave them *in* the patrol force and on the street. It should be possible to obtain substantial pay increases while remaining a patrolman, just as it is now possible to win higher salaries in the Federal Bureau of Investigation while remaining a special agent.

Getting good men to serve, not only in the police department, but in those police roles that are the most demanding, may produce only a marginal gain, but we are largely ignorant of how to achieve even that. Almost no systematic research has been done to define and measure those qualities characteristic of officers best able to keep the peace. Entrance examination in many states and cities may not measure any relevant quality other than (perhaps) general literacy, familiarity with a police handbook, or some knowledge of current events. Indeed, there is hardly any evidence that they measure even these traits very accurately. How—or indeed, whether—such tests can be more useful is a matter on which we know very little, and perhaps a modest amount of research would be in order (though I would not be surprised if such research turned out to be inconclusive).

POLICY STATEMENTS

If able men are found and assigned to neighborhood patrol forces under conditions that will facilitate their understanding of neighborhood conditions and personalities and if they are rewarded for successful performance of the peace-keeping function, what in concrete terms will these men actually do? How, in short, does one keep the peace? Some have argued that police departments ought to develop and issue policy statements that will give some guidance to officers who must necessarily exercise wide discretion with respect to matters where legal codes contain few applicable rules.[13] To the extent this is possible, of course it should be done, and it is not being done at all in many departments. But it would be a mistake to assume that policies can be found that will provide meaningful guides to action in most situations of real or potential disorder. The most feasible rules perhaps are those which tell the patrolman what *not* to do—don't use racial epithets, don't hit a man except in self-defense, don't grasp a man's arm or shoulder unless it is necessary to complete an arrest or prevent violence, and so forth. But relatively few rules can be devised that tell a patrolman what he *should* do with quarrelling lovers, angry neighbors, or disputatious drunks. This is not because the police have had little experience with such matters (on the contrary!) or even because they do know in a given case what to do (they may), but because so much depends on the particular circumstances of time, place, event, and personality. No psychiatrist would attempt to produce, much less use, a "how-to-do-it" manual for these cases, and he has the advantage of dealing with people at his leisure, over long periods of time, and in moments of relative calm. The best that can be done is

---

[13]See President's Commission on Law Enforcement and Administration of Justice, *Task Force Report: The Police* (Washington, D.C.: U.S. Government Printing Office, 1967), pp. 21–27.

to list "factors to be taken into account," but in the concrete case everything depends on *how* they are taken into account.

In the broadest terms, the patrolman in performing his order-maintenance function is neither a bureaucrat nor a professional, and thus neither increased bureaucratization nor increased professionalism will be of much value. He is not a bureaucrat in that he does not and cannot apply general rules to specific cases—there are no general rules, and thus his discretion is wide. (In performing his law-enforcement function, by contrast, he can act more nearly like a bureaucrat—the legal rules defining a crime are relatively unambiguous and the officer's discretion, especially if it is a serious crime, is narrow.) On the other hand, the patrolman is not a professional—there is no organized group of practitioners (as there is with doctors or physicists) who can impart to him by education certain information and equip him by apprenticeship with certain arts and skills that will make him competent to serve a "client" when the latter cannot be the sole judge of the quality of the service he receives. Nor do such external reference groups (professional societies) exist to certify that the patrolman is competent or to make him subject to a code of ethics and a sense of duty.

The patrolman is neither a bureaucrat nor a professional, but a member of a *craft*. As with more crafts, there is no generalized, written body of special knowledge; learning is by apprenticeship, but the apprenticeship takes place on the job rather than in an academy; the primary reference group from which the apprentice wins (or fails to win) respect are his colleagues on the job, not fellow members of his discipline wherever they may be; and the members, conscious of having a special skill or task, think of themselves as set apart from society and in need of restrictions on entry. But unlike other members of a craft—carpenters, for example, or journalists—the police work in an environment that is usually apprehensive and often hostile, and they produce no product (like a finished house or a well-written newspaper) the value of which is evident and easily judged.

An attempt to change a craft into a bureaucracy will be perceived by the members as a failure of confidence and a withdrawal of support and thus strongly resisted; efforts to change them into a profession will be seen as irrelevant and thus in great part ignored. Such gains as can be made in the way the police handle citizens are not likely to come primarily from either proliferating rules (i.e., bureaucratizing the police) or sending officers to colleges, special training programs, or human relations institutes (i.e., "professionalizing" the police). Instead, the most significant changes will be in organization and leadership in order to increase the officer's familiarity with and sensitivity to the neighborhood he patrols and rewarding him for doing what is judged (necessarily after the fact) to be the right thing rather than simply the "efficient" thing.

LAW-ENFORCEMENT FUNCTION

These recommendations leave out of account the law-enforcement function of the police. This has been deliberate, partly because the crook-catching, crime-stopping function is so often exaggerated. But obviously there is a law-enforcement function, and it is in any given case hard to separate from the order-maintenance function. Law enforcement ideally should be organized differently from order maintenance, however. It is, for example, more suitably managed through centralized command structures, the issuance of explicit rules, and the specialization of tasks (burglary details, homicide details, traffic enforcement divisions, and so forth). Perhaps a police department should make the two functions even more separate than they are now. For example, there is some impressionistic evidence that such tactics worsen police-community relations.[14] Perhaps the roving patrol force should be composed of men different from those in the neighborhood patrol force, so that the tensions created by the former could be directed away from the role performed by the latter. Or perhaps intensive street patrol in a particular area could be done under the guidance of and on the basis of tactical intelligence furnished by neighborhood patrol officers who are best able to distinguish between innocent and suspicious behavior and between decent citizens and "bad actors."

But in crime prevention not too much should be expected of the police. I doubt that any deployment, any strategy, or any organizational principles will permit the police to make more than a slight or temporary reduction in the rate of most common crimes. As the police themselves are fond of saying, "we don't cause crime," and, as I would like to see them add, "we can't stop crime." They can and should make arrests and they can and should investigate suspicious circumstances. But I know of no police administrator who is optimistic that they can make more than marginal gains, however they behave. It would be well, therefore, not to "over-sell" proposed improvements in police manpower, organization, training, equipment, or tactics. Already too many citizens share the rather dangerous view that if only we "unleashed" the police we could "stop crime"—dangerous because if we act on that assumption we are likely to produce only frustrated expectations and deeper passions.

Indeed, it might be well if we shifted the focus of our legitimate concern to the behavior of those institutions that dispose of criminals once arrested—the courts and the correctional and probation systems. For all offenses other than the most trivial, the vast majority of the persons processed by these institutions are repeaters. According to one estimate, 87.5 per cent of all persons arrested for nontraffic offenses have been arrested before.[15] The average person arrested will be arrested 7.6 times in his lifetime.[16] The problem of recidivism is obviously of the greatest importance—if we fail to induce a person after his first arrest to avoid crime, there is a strong chance we will have to arrest him six or seven more times; how many more times we *should* arrest him for crimes

---

[14]*Report* of the National Advisory Commission on Civil Disorders (1968), chap. 11.

[15]Ronald Christensen, "Projected Percentage of U.S. Population With Criminal Arrest and Conviction Records," in President's Commission on Law Enforcement and Administration of Justice, *Task Force Report: Science and Technology* (Washington, D.C.: U.S. Government Printing Office, 1967), Appendix J, p. 220.

[16]*Ibid.*, p. 227.

we do not learn of is anyone's guess. In the simplest cost-effective terms, a dollar invested in the right correctional program is likely to have a higher marginal product than a dollar invested in the right police program.

But what is the "right program"? Do we have a correctional technology capable of significantly reducing the recidivism rate? I am not sure we do, or that we ever will, but I suspect that we have not tried very hard to find out. There have been some promising experiments with community-based, heavily staffed programs in California, Utah, and New Jersey, but there appears to be little organized effort to repeat these experiments elsewhere, or if they are repeated to evaluate them rigorously, or if they are evaluated to institutionalize what we learn from them.[17] In our preoccupation with the crime problem, we have come to identify it either as wholly a "social" problem (which can only be solved in three or four generations by programs which might—no one quite seems to be sure how—eliminate the lower classes) or as a "police" problem which can be solved only by taking the "handcuffs" off the police and "cracking down." I am certainly not opposed to ameliorating social problems or to increasing public support for the police, but I would like to see at least an equivalent amount of attention given to improving the way existing institutions now manage the offenders who have already shown by their actions that antipoverty programs are yet to have a therapeutic effect, and by their appearance in court that they have not managed to escape the police.

---

[17]President's Commission on Law Enforcement and Administration of Justice, *Task Force Report: Corrections* (Washington, D.C.: U.S. Government Printing Office, 1967), chap. 4, especially pp. 38–39, 41–42.

Rules, Colleagues, and Situationally Justified Actions*

Peter K. Manning

INTRODUCTION

Formal organizations attempt to systematically reward participants who adhere to some set of stipulated goals or objectives; the organizations also use a public official imagery of their operations to both constrain members and to obtain deference from external audiences. However, organizations vary in their internal compliance structures and external environment.[1] Organizations operating in highly problematic environments (environments that engender public deference and expectations of diverse but effective intervention; e.g., the police, military, and to a lesser degree fire, ambulance, and emergency services of all types), have historically tended to develop rigid and quasi-military internal structures (McNamara, and Reiss and Bordua, in Bordua,

*Research funded by a General Research Support Grant from the College of Human Medicine and All University Research of Michigan State University. The data were gathered during my tenure as Visiting Research Scholar at University of London, Goldsmiths' College, London, 1972–73. I gratefully acknowledge the assistance provided by Chief Superintendent Stephen O'Brien, Chief Superintendent Benjamin Plunkett, Superintendent Angus Pattison and the many men who so willingly gave of their time and energy to facilitate my inquiries. Mike Chatterton and Maureen Cain were very helpful throughout my investigations. None of them is responsible for my conclusions.

[1]Structural features of the police *mandate* in Anglo-American society, i.e., the virtual monopoly on the legitimate use of violence and the authority to intervene in private affairs, create socially patterned demands for maintaining viable means of controlling the politicality of police actions, insuring the use of legal means for coercing the civilian populace, and guaranteeing an approximation of universal criteria in application of the law. The police, however, do not possess what they consider to be adequate public confirmation of their *mandate*, and are subject to socially structured (e.g., class, race, age, and situational) variations in public definitions of acceptable modes and frequency of legal intervention (Reiss, 1971:2). [See the writings of Banton (1964); J. O. Wilson (1968); the essays in Bordua, ed. (1967); and Manning (1971).] Because they do not enjoy the solidity of mandate required to establish the necessary degree of autonomy from their environment, police organizations have accommodated to their threatening situation by developing strategies and tactics by which they expect to maximize (dramatize) the appearance of their own efficacy. In what follows I am deliberately avoiding the issue of cross-cultural comparison, i.e., the issue of generality of my findings. The emphasis upon scientific policing and the police theory is less pronounced in England than in the United States, but it appears to dominate the public statements of police administrators in both societies. To that extent, then, criticism based on actual functioning of police departments in either nation should bear on the relevance of police theory to everyday reality in either society. I believe that the basic problems of policing in Anglo-American society are endemic and structural, and that the present paper contains themes and data that could be generalized to American police departments. I am not making the claim here. At present, I am engaged in an organizational study in a medium-sized police department in the American Midwest that should provide data bearing on these questions.

REPRINTED FROM: R. Blankenship (ed.) *Colleagues in Organizations*. New York: Wiley, 1976 (263–289).

ed., 1967, and Bittner, 1970). In such organizations, although the degree of dependency of lower participants on higher participants may fluctuate around the midpoint among organizations (Stinchcombe, 1965: 180–185), rules, especially disciplinary rules, are the primordial nexus around which colleague relationships are negotiated. The types of dependency and exchange that result are fundamentally different from organizations typically called "professional" or even those with a high degree of flexibility and innovative potential. (Scott, 1966 and Wilensky, 1960). The aim of this paper is to explore some of the commonsense or assumed grounds of organizational integration (Manning, 1970). An English police organization serves as a context or background against which to analyze the perspectives of the two principal organizational segments. Those perspectives become most visible through a study of the place of rules and rule-enforcement upon colleagueship within this organization. The results of such a study have important consequences for the participants' view of the organization as an acting unit and the boundaries of organizational reality.[2]

METHOD AND SETTING

The study from which these data are drawn was undertaken in July and August 1973 in one of three subdivisional headquarters within one of the 23 divisions of the London Metropolitan police. Interviews, observation, and records were gathered.[3]

The subdivision studied ("Thameside") was bordered on one side by the Thames, on one side by one of the "home counties," and on the other sides by metropolitan London. Once a lively industrial and military center, the area declined in size following the end of World War II and is now a quiet lower middle and middle class community that includes riverside, docks, several large commons, numerous public housing developments, and residential dwellings.

---

[2]I draw here on writings of Burns (1958); Crozier (1964, 1971); Bittner (1965); Silverman (1971); and Blankenship (1973). See also Manning (1970, 1973, 1973a).

[3]Observational and focused interview techniques were employed. I took field notes while making home beats, while riding in area and panda cars, while sitting in the reserve room (the main information room of the station), canteen, in the office of the Criminal Investigation Division (CID or "Detectives") and in the office of the chief superintendent. I also gathered statistics and assisted reserve officers by collating phone and teleprinter messages received at the station. The hours of observation were spent as follows:

TABLE 1
Hours of Observation on "Thameside"
Subdivision June 13 through August 13, 1973[a]

"Early Turn" 6 A.M.–2 P.M.	"Late Turn" 2 P.M.–11 P.M.	"Nights" 11 P.M.– 6 A.M.	
74 hours	89 hours	21 hours	
	Total hours		184

Police work on the subdivision is varied, but tends toward "order maintenance" (Banton, 1964). The clearance rate for crime allegations is considered to be one of the highest in the London metropolitan police area. The chief superintendent sets the style of law enforcement to a considerable degree and is "community minded" rather than "crime minded," an emphasis compatible with the career concerns and age of the men on the station. The average age is 38.5, and it has been 4 1/2 years since a new probationer reported to this subdivision. The age and experience of the men, with this policy emphasis, contributes to the general feeling of satisfaction and high morale that characterizes the station.

THE COMMONSENSE REALITY OF POLICING

Policemen on this subdivision are bound by a set of implicit and unexplicated understandings that might be called the "commonsense reality of policing"— what everyone knows and takes for granted—and the skills that a policeman must acquire in order to be viewed as a competent member of the force. Three aspects of this organizational reality are the shared assumptions about the nature of police work, the occupational culture, and task dependency.

All London policemen share a *base-line of experience* as a lower participant because they enter the organization at the same point. Practical experience forms the basis for a conviction that policing is to a certain extent, situationally justified ("You can't police by the book") and lacks certainty and clarity ("You never know what to expect next"—"A policeman has seen everything"). Although this experiential foundation of police work is seldom discussed as a basis of agreement, it is implicitly accepted and recognized as essential to occupational competence. Policemen understand that people (especially "civvies," i.e., the public) who lack this work experience cannot understand "what it is like being a policeman." Further, it is understood that: (1) all decisions, whether "on the ground" (on patrol), or in the station, whether by patrolmen or senior officers, are made situationally, are based on commonsense and require

---

[a]Since the research problem did not require comparison of functions or differences in work load, crime reporting or the like, the distribution of time spent at the station, walking, or on patrol, is relatively unimportant. However, by varying the times at the station and the days of the week, I satisfied myself that there were regularities in behavior and attitude that were not specific to given reliefs or turns (men work in reliefs that are rotated through turns on a 5-week basis). The outlines of the English urban policing system are well described in Cain, 1973: chap. 3. Although she studied a Midlands city, her description of the fundamental organization of policing is also accurate for "Thameside."

Focused interviews were conducted with 33 men [10 officers above the rank of sergeant; 9 sergeants and 14 police constables (PCs)] in an attempt to gather information on concepts of success and competence as well as acceptable work performance (the level and direction of effort and terms for variation from "acceptable normal behavior"). Eliciting techniques were used with 26 men (4 officers, 8 sergeants, 14 PCs) to generate data relevant to the latter issues. Five group interviews with officers were held in the officers' dining room of the subdivisional headquarters.

discretion. They cannot be made on the basis of an abstract theory of policing, the law, or police regulations. (2) That both internal and external sources offer competing definitions of rules is a reality of police work. Ample collective experience supports the belief that different segments of the public make different demands on the police. Senior officers and men can recall having used more than one interpretation of a law, depending on the situation. They have seen courts reverse previous positions and make illegal what was once legal. Policemen have argued, often in self-defense, over the meanings of many disciplinary rules and legal statutes.

At the center of the occupational culture of policing (Manning, 1971; 1972) are features of the role considered to be *core skills, cognitions*, and *affect*. They collectively serve as the defining characteristics of the "good practitioner" and "good police work." Among the uniformed English policemen who were interviewed, administrative policemen (above the rank of sergeant) and others agreed that the following were aspects of "good police work":[4] a cool emotional tone, properly executed tactics (in order to obtain and maintain control over interaction), properly applied skills, and a fair and open-minded view of given encounters with the public. If these conditions obtain, then policemen feel that they can bring off a clear closure or termination based on agreement or at least minimal dissensus, and they remain able to control the level and direction of effort. That is, they feel able to exercise a level of conscientious withdrawal of efficiency if need be to protect a definition of good police work derived from the implicit rules of the occupational culture.

A third basis for collective action as well as tension and misunderstanding is a set of ties growing from *task dependence*. The extensive nature of this web of solidarity binding together police constables (PCs) and senior officers, intermediate and immediate supervisors, is well documented. With regard to the constable's dependency on senior officers, matters of formal discipline, promotion and evaluation of performance, transfers, accommodation, general welfare, and other informal and formal rewards are most important. Constables also depend on their intermediate and immediate superiors (sergeants and inspectors) for support in extralegal situations (e.g., domestic disputes), good progress reports, recommendations for formal rewards, congenial working conditions, and backing in disputes with senior officers. Senior officers depend on the men below them for information, restraint and discretion in "easing" behavior (drinking, sleeping on the job, accepting favors), legal infringements, and for striving for a level of work efficiency (Cain, 1973: 181). Although situational and problematic, these exchange networks that channel information,

---

[4]"Real police work" as a concept has parallels in other occupations. To the policeman, these are considered the "core skills" of the occupation and the "characteristic professional acts." These concepts are found, respectively, in Harvey L. Smith, "Contingencies of Professional Differentiation," *American Journal of Sociology,* 63 (January 1958), 410–414; and Rue Bucher and Anselm Strauss, "Professions in Process," *American Journal of Sociology,* 66 (January 1961), 325–334. For an application of these concepts to medicine, especially in regard to associated political attitudes, see Peter K. Manning, "Occupational Types and Organized Medicine: Physicians' Attitudes Toward the American Medical Association," unpublished Ph.D. dissertation, Duke University, 1966, especially chap. 3.

gifts, nonverbal affirmations, and written data between organizational segments constitute an important determinant of the internal morphology of the organization.

ORGANIZATIONAL SEGMENTS

These potentially binding funds of shared experience (assumptions, occupational culture, and task dependence) are simultaneously a basis of organizational integration *and* a source of shared misunderstandings. The ambiguous basis for organizational action and the means by which it is accomplished (rules) creates the context within which the two principal organizational segments interact. One's perspective on these shared assumptions derives directly from one's position in the organizational structure.

Senior officers (ranks above sergeant, including in this subdivision inspectors, chief inspectors, superintendent, and chief superintendent), see their connection to the organization through the ideology of scientific police administration. This view justifies their life style, mobility aspirations, and, most importantly, their identification with the respectable and propertied middle classes whom they define as their target audience. Their world is organized from a seemingly natural acceptance of the legitimacy of their position within the organization, a justification of this position through an identification with the traditions of upholding the law and providing protection for British citizens, and a perceived consensus on their role provided from their target audience. Positing a *consensual other* seems to be a significant part of the police ideology articulated by the administrative strata:

> Policemen need to believe in a largely consensual populace whose values and standards they represent and enforce. It is by reference to this that they legitimate their activities. They are intermediaries who bring forth for punishment whom 'most people' deem to deserve it. (Cain, 1973:69)

Since senior officers are not required to appear in court, deal with face-to-face problems of justice, or to do "real police work," they are paradoxically insulated against the stigma of policing while they are denied a degree of credibility from those they supervise. That is, once senior officers accept administrative posts they are deprived of direct contact with social groups and persons who are seen as representatives of evil and are thus permitted to move symbolically closer to the socially sacred and traditional values of English society. On the other hand, senior officers are deprived of the legitimacy within the organization that is granted by constables to officers who maintain even an intermittent contact with the men and with activities defined by policemen as containing the essence of the entire enterprise.

Police constables cannot draw upon a formalized ideology of policing. For them, the legitimacy of police authority is unquestioned and assumed rather than discussed; obedience to senior officers is, however, contextual rather than entirely categorical. Constables simultaneously hold a view of senior officers as incompetent to serve in the positions they hold (e.g., "when you join a rat race, as you move up, there are fewer contenders. . .") and an envious under-

standing that "somebody has to do it." The *ambivalence* of constables is manifest in two ways. There is a common belief that Chatterton (personal communication) has called "the myth of protecting the higher ups." Constables,
recognizing there are no concrete rules governing policing, believe that it is
"down to them" to prevent senior officers from embarrassing themselves. This
is done in part by avoiding blatant displays of skyving or easing behavior,[5] by
informally sanctioning policemen who are considered to be excessively lazy or
self-serving, and by informally providing information to senior officers. (Since
channels are rarely used "up the line" by patrolmen except in their written report of incidents, senior officers are quite dependent on sergeants to fill them
in on "what's happening downstairs" and to discreetly avoid telling other
things.)

The other manifestation of ambivalence bears on the conception of higher
officers. They see senior officers as equivalent on "human terms" insofar as
both constables and other ranks "are fathers and heads of families, property
owners, and members of the community." Other named features of sergeants'
role, for example, such as "more pay," "a little more knowledge of the law,"
were considered as embroidery upon the basic fact that they could "do the job"
(the constables' job—real police work) but were "the same on other grounds."
"One does not respect them [officers] because of rank only." If PCs view those
above them in this way, they reason, then the men above should view PCs as
individuals as well as policemen. Solidarity of policemen is seemingly required
vis-à-vis outside groups where policeman and person are not separated; within
the organization, however, it is not possible to respect an officer who does not
see one as a person.[6]

It is quite possible the *stability and continuity of the authority of the organization required a reification of higher authority while personal face-to-face
contacts made individualistic and situational judgments necessary.* Even in the

---

[5]The policeman, not unlike members of other occupations, may elect to control the
extent of effort applied in the course of work. Argot terms, such as skyving and easing, give
evidence that what is expected in the way of effort on-the-job is an open question. Easing
behavior, for example, may allow one to hold back effort, but still be prepared to deal with
problems which may arise. Skyving goes further. Skyving implies actual avoidance of
situations calling for effort. To park one's patrol car alongside the river, with the radio left
on, is easing behavior. To do the same with the radio turned off is skyving behavior. The
subject is treated more fully in Cain (1973).

[6]I do not fully understand the implications of this argument. Perhaps the symbolization of rank, which is displayed by the use of titles while in organizational role (which
occurs always when addressing a person of higher rank in the presence of a member of the
public or of another person of higher rank), projects the constraints of the classification of
relationships as hierarchically ordered, impersonal, and categorical. On the other hand,
senior officers including sergeants, often address those below them, especially constables,
by first name. Superiors can individualize "rank inferiors," while at least in face-to-face
address, inferiors can only symbolize linguistically categorical and hierarchical relationships. Behind their backs, the men will refer to senior officers by nicknames or by
affectionate corruptions of their names, thus providing the undertone of individualization
and egalitarianism that draws attention to the fundamental equality of policemen, and to
those who have been constables. The same pattern of asymmetrical exchange takes place
in the lending of money.

absence of a general theory of policing, it was agreed that the administration was held responsible and publicly accountable for policy and operations. Policemen of all ranks see police work as logically requiring personalistic and particularistic decisions. However, the police mandate in the context of the British political system required them to act collectively *as if* there were indeed a clear abstract legal and social mandate from which they derived goals and purposes.

DILEMMAS OF ORGANIZATIONAL ACTION

Given these very different commitments, or social anchorages, within the organization, the dilemmas of organizational action are very real. Given the two segments and their perspectives on organizational action, and the structural features of police work (to be discussed), *rules can only function as resources for organizing and rationalizing a given contingency.* This characteristic of the work exercises important influences on the nature of colleagual relationships within the police organization. There are four fundamental reasons why police work is essentially situationally justified action. Let us explore these four structural conditions of police work.

First, knowledge is *asymmetrical:* all senior officers have served at least two years "on the ground" as constables, but with very few exceptions (none on this subdivision) constables have not served as senior officers. Senior officers continue to believe that they "understand" their men, and they are encouraged in this belief by exercising their legitimate capacity to reverse decisions taken by men on the street. Constables, on the other hand, deny this understanding, seeing most of their senior officers as out of touch, careerist, preoccupied with paper work, trivialities, and public relations. Second, the work is defined and justified "clinically" or tactically, rather than theoretically or even organizationally. *Police work is seen as individualistic, entrepreneurial, practical, face-to-face activity involving particular people and their problems.* As a consequence, only the everyday activities of the constable even approach the form and functions of "real police work." Paper work, court appearances, administrative tasks, or report writing (even routinely required occurrence booklets) are considered *ex post facto* glosses upon the real work on the ground. "Let's face it," one PC said to another as he gestured grandly out the window, "real policework is out there." Third, administrative tasks rarely permit dispensing of work within a clear, encapsulated episode, meeting the public directly in a law-enforcement capacity, or performing activities defined in line with "on the ground" standards of adequacy, competence, and level of effort. Since administrators do not and often cannot publicly define the decision-making rules by which police work should be carried out, and since the degree of discretion that is required is admittedly high, the administrator from the patrolman's perspective appears to be an accessory after the fact. From the administrator's point of view, on the other hand, the execution of policy, the efficient achievement of organization goals, and the maintenance of hierarchy and discipline are both required and a source of prestige and satisfaction. Fourth, although critical personal concerns, such as the nature of the work and the progress of an individual career, are located within the context of exchange between and mutual dependency of the ranks, implicit meanings are provided by the frames of *separate* experiences and individual biographies.

Conflicts between organizational segments over fundamental issues of policy and the degree of control of the organization over its members is *publicly* resolved in terms of the ideology of the higher strata. This rhetoric serves the important symbolic functions of defining publicly the limits of organizational action and providing terms of reference within which the outer boundaries of the organization's control over its participants are discussed. However, definitions implicit in the social world of lower participants (e.g., informally sanctioned discretionary practices and understandings) constantly *modify* and make *problematic* the imagery of bureaucratic authority displayed by the higher strata. In an important sense, the negotiation of organizational authority takes place *internally* rather than externally, particularly in the context of rules about the infraction of rules.

NEGOTIATION AND THE MEANING OF RULES

The principal arena in which the relationships between organizational segments are patterned is the domain of the enforcement of internal or *disciplinary rules* (Gouldner, 1954a, 1954b, and McNamara, in Bordua, ed. 1967).[7] Although rules can clarify particular procedures, they also provide for areas of discussion, negotiation, and uncertainty; each rule contains an indexical or contextual quality that makes it *defeasible* (Bittner, 1970:4).

Wilson writes: "The absence of agreed-upon standards for how the police should behave makes it hard for the patrolman in his opinion, to do his job properly; the presence of many procedural rules makes it easy to penalize him for doing it, in somebody's opinion, improperly." (Wilson, 1968:75) Only one aspect of rules will be discussed here. Uncertainties in the enforcement, interpretation, and consequences of disciplinary rules bearing primarily on the behavior of lower participants lead to forms of association which in turn modify the impact, and thus display the limits, of the power and authority of the administrative segment.

The seemingly inherent *uncertainties* manifest in the actual process of internal discipline within the subdivision reflect the tenuous multiplex rela-

---

[7]Invoking of rules as a means of social control clearly is related to a number of structural properties of types of organizations. Cf. Rushing's useful paper, "Organizational Rules and Surveillance: Propositions in Comparative Organizational Analysis" *Administrative Science Quarterly,* 10 (March 1966), 423–443. In this subdivision, the ratio of sergeants to police constables was 6–7 to one; and there was an additional sergeant supervising the three subdivisions under the command of the subdivisional headquarters. Conflict within the organization was low; it was relatively small, the degree of differentiation of task was relatively low (criminal investigation division members, dog men, and traffic patrol were supervised by divisional command which in part overlapped with the chief superintendent of the subdivision), and the organization had been characterized for years by a low turnover rate. This sort of stable organization in a relatively "quiet" area perhaps makes this a limiting case for studies of police work. In the United States police organizations are large, the supervisory ratio is high, conflict is typical, and conflict with the public is the norm.

tionships that obtain between senior officers and constables. First, and most importantly, there is a general feeling among PCs that one cannot predict when one will be sanctioned for a violation. The view is that there are so many regulations, covering so many aspects of the job, that routine work will intrinsically require violation of one or more of the rules listed in the 10,000-paragraph *General Orders*. It is considered purely a matter of chance or luck whether a rule will be invoked at a given time. One sergeant explained that the *General Orders* contained

> 140 years of fuck-ups. Every time something goes wrong, they make a rule about it. All the directions in the force flow from someone's mistake. You can't go 8 hours on the job without breaking the disciplinary code. For example, you have to sign [in CID] the duty book which places you specifically when you leave the station. Perhaps you return to the station at 3:00, but you chat, or have a cup of tea, and forget to book back in until 3:45 or 4. Then you forget what time you returned when you make out your weekly personal diary [a record of activities, expenses and evidence that must be turned in weekly to the Detective Inspector], and maybe put down 3 or 4, but in any case don't remember what time you actually appeared, when you signed the duty book, or what time you entered when you did. But, no one cares until something goes wrong. The job goes wild on trivialities.

Two PCs and Sergeant A were discussing the use of disciplinary reports by a notorious station sergeant, Sergeant B:

> A PC has been investigating a traffic accident and at a time when discipline was very strict, and where a specific refreshment time was assigned to each constable, and fairly carefully observed. He arrived after other constables on his relief had left the canteen. As he sat down for tea, the Sergeant entered and put him on report for exceeding his refreshment time. He did not ask the PC for details of the circumstances of his being there. The Sergeant asked for his book, entered the report, and made a note in his own book. It was later revealed when the Sergeant talked with the Chief Superintendent that he was in error. The incident was dropped. On another occasion Sergeant A [when a PC] was in the canteen and was asked for his book by Sergeant B who was going to put him on report for excessive refreshment time. Sergeant B didn't have a pen, used the PCs pen to write a report with an incorrect date and time. In this case, the charge was never carried to an investigation because of the error in the book.

Sergeant B was said "to put you on report and ask questions afterward." However, uncertainty also undercuts the authority of sergeants' disciplinary reports. A perception of dependent uncertainty among sergeants and PCs is heightened by the ways in which many apparently major violations of the disciplinary code reported to seniors by sergeants are handled:

> One PC could not be raised on the personal radio while on patrol; his supervisor could not locate him for over two hours. Finally, the sergeant set out and found him drunk in his car parked on a side street. He put him on report. The chief superintendent called in the man charged and merely cautioned him, did not fine him or ask for further disciplinary ac-

tion. Two weeks later, the same PC was on a small traffic patrol motorcycle [a "noddy"], and was shooting a .22. He thought he saw a rabbit walking on the sidewalk, took out his gun and shot the pet terrier of a citizen taking an evening stroll. Again, he was put on report and the chief superintendent cautioned him.

In this case, the expectations of the sergeant and the chief superintendent were not in conjunction; and as in many cases of disciplinary action, it could be said that the intention of the chief superintendent to give the man a second chance, and to "prove himself" was not well-understood by the sergeant in the case. (This is assuming that the sergeant did in fact desire to carry out the orders of the senior officer.) These kinds of situations demonstrate the importance of the *assumptions* in which orders are embedded, assumptions that to an important degree are rooted in the organizational position of the persons involved.[8] Orders from senior officers to sergeants with regard to the enforcement of laws or the disciplinary code are like the orders given from senior

---

[8]The following story illustrates what can happen when the unexplicated and nonverbal understandings which embed instructions are *not properly* or "accurately" read by a subordinate receiving orders from a senior officer:

A Chief Inspector was asked to go to the home of an Inspector who was just coming off duty and return him to the station. He suspected that it was because the man had been drinking on duty and the Superintendent wanted to have him on report. The C.I. went to his house and asked him to come to the station for a breathalyzer (used to determine the amount of alcohol in the blood; a test must be made initially to ascertain whether there is possible evidence for a blood sample to be drawn by the divisional surgeon and further analysis done). The C.I. administered the breathalyzer at the man's house and then took him in. The indication that a blood sample was needed was a green tinge in the sample vial. The vial of fluid was bright green. When the Chief Inspector took in the evidence, the Superintendent looked at it, said, "Well, that's all that's necessary," and had the C.I. take the Inspector home. No disciplinary charges were filed. The C.I. said the Superintendent "didn't want to know," i.e., he was unwilling to consider the evidence, and made the entire process into a ritual. (Presumably, either no report was written, or it was written stating that the investigation had been made and the Superintendent was satisfied that the man was not drunk on duty.)

Mike Chatterton, who has done extensive work in a large Midlands police department has commented extremely insightfully on this anecdote, and his remarks reveal what I take to be the *essence* of the problem of cross-rank communication, even though it occurred between members of the higher strata. Chatterton writes (personal communication): "In this particular case it could be argued (and this would increase the degree of uncertainty and support your point as it reveals the problem which men have in knowing what the bosses expect and in inferring what is at the back of their instructions) that the Chief Inspector *ought* to have known that the Superintendent would deal with the case in this way. As it was, he (the Chief Inspector) had not realized that it was not the Superintendent's intention to collect evidence to have the man charged with an offence. Had he correctly read the boss orders as intended to frighten the Inspector, give him a second chance, he would have furnished the Superintendent with evidence which would not have required him to make the embarrassing and, indeed, potentially incriminating decision he did."

My point here and in the above text is that the context of rule announcement and rule enforcement is one of implicit understanding; to the degree that one does not share this context, one is likely to see the actions and feelings of others as "random," "arbitrary," "capricious," or "stupid."

officers to patrolmen in the form of general advisements, suggestions, or policy statements written in the parade book (a book containing useful information—e.g., "prisoner escaped; work to be done on Barclays' bank this weekend; child runaway from home on the section"—which officers are required to read when they come on duty.) The following appeared in the parade book: "The number of stops has increased, but I cannot believe there are not more to be made on this section" signed, Chief Inspector D. This note followed by a week an earlier "suggestion" written in the parade book asking PCs to increase the number of "stops" they made for investigatory purposes (odd-looking cars, persons on the street late at night). The first note had not been taken "seriously enough"; that is, it was not understood by constables. Since they turn in stops at the end of each duty turn, it is quite easy to check on their production rates. The second note was written in more threatening language in an attempt to decrease discretion. Similar dynamics of threat and then excess in applying negative sanctions occur when "disciplinary crackdowns" are mobilized by sergeants. From the point of view of the chief superintendent and superintendent, the enforcement of disciplinary rules by sergeants is always lax. When sergeants do periodically respond to ambiguous instructions from command officers (similar to the instructions regarding "stops"), for example, actually routinely enforce the disciplinary code, their actions are perceived by constables as unpredictable harsh, capricious and arbitrary. Thus, to *make sense of instructions*, one has to understand what "lies behind" instructions and to anticipate "what is really meant" by the person setting the task. To the degree that PCs are *unable* to make an "accurate" reading of formal or informal instructions they receive, they perceive themselves to be subject to enormous variations in enforcement practice. Stories concerning failure to understand the intentions of instructions are often told, and these "failures" as well as one's own delicts may be told in mixed groups of officers and constables by inspectors and sergeants who supervise the very men to whom they are talking.

Secondly, if a complaint is filed with the chief superintendent and an investigation initiated, there is uncertainty concerning the "side" that the investigatory officer will take—the "public's side" or the "policeman's side.[9] One CID man said, "the present state of mind in the force is roughly like that of the Jews in Nazi Germany in the late 'thirties. We fear knocks at the door at night and the like, and it has happened." An incident on the subdivision gave substance to the remark:

> Three policemen were sent to a fire in a local chemists' shop to supervise the protection of possible damaged goods, etc. After the fire, it was discovered that a large 25–30 cup tea boiler had "gone missing." The policemen suspected members of the fire brigade because they were not watched and moved freely in and out of the shop while attending the fire.

---

[9]The internal investigatory division of the Metropolitan Police, A-10, is feared within the force, and has grown in size and authority over the years, especially since the tenure of the present commissioner who is known as a "crusader" and "reformer." In late 1973, the commissioner was publicly advocating the institutionalization of a public procedure for the investigation of public complaints against the police.

The policemen, on the other hand, were under constant observation: two were outside, while one policeman was inside accompanying the owner. Subsequently, the three policemen were subject to an inconclusive investigation, and their homes were searched by other officers at the order of the chief superintendent. It was said that since one was usually given a pack of cigarettes or something anyway, taking goods was "more than the job was worth."

Another set of incidents illustrates the uncertainty with which police constables view the support of their senior officers. Police regulations state that no unauthorized passengers shall ride in police vehicles. In practical terms, this permits only prisoners or those under the authority of the policemen to ride. On the other hand, the public expects a wide range of generally willingly provided services from the police. Doing such services often leads to friendly thanks, a cup of tea, or sense of having accomplished a good piece of work (i.e., all the ends are tied up and the episode is closed). When a citizen requests a ride, the policeman feels that whether he refuses or offers a ride, he "cannot win."

While driving a panda car, B encountered two girls standing on a street corner about 2 a.m. He stopped and asked if he could help (a polite way of asking them what they were doing out at this time of night. Virtually everyone out after 12 or 1, depending on the area of London, is stopped and questioned). One of the girls explained that they had been at a party and that she had been subject to unwanted advances from a young man. They were afraid that he might make further advances, so they left the party on foot. The patrolman decided to give them a ride home. One girl saw her Dad on the corner; he asked if they were in trouble and the PC explained he was taking them home. He left the girls with the father. Three days after, correspondence was received from the father of one of the girls thanking the policeman for bringing his daughter home. The PC was called to the chief superintendent's office and given a lecture on the importance of following departmental regulations and it was suggested that the only thing which prevented a disciplinary action (2 or 3 days' pay lost) against the PC was the fact that the girls made the allegation of rude and annoying behavior on the part of the boys at the party. The PC involved alleged that if he hadn't picked up the girls, and something happened to them, someone could ask, "Why didn't you take them home?"

On another occasion, the same policeman was involved in an accident investigation. The driver of one car was not injured, but could not drive home. The PC was asked to drive him home, but refused explaining that it was against departmental regulations. A letter was received from this driver complaining that the police did not provide a minimal public service in the form of transport home for a hapless accident victim. Since all correspondence must be shown to have been dealt with, the PC was again called into the chief superintendent's office and the matter was discussed.

Thirdly, PCs consider that there is a further set of uncertainties surrounding the *meaning of any given violation*. I asked one chief inspector what the ribbons on his tunic indicated. He pointed out that the last one was a police good conduct ribbon (or the equivalent) for "14 years of keeping out of trouble." PCs nearby said it was for "14 years of covering up mistakes or blaming them on someone else." The C.I. replied that "if you don't have any complaints after 14 years, you're in trouble! If they [a promotion board] look at a man with 14 years and he's got no 7's (investigations of complaints against him), they wonder what he's been doing." At a lunch with three detective inspectors and a chief inspector, one of the senior detectives on the division, the chief inspector, laughed at one point and said, "The public expects you to police by the book, the guys (administration) expect you to police by the book; but it can't be done. Given the fact you can't police by the book, if a bloke hasn't got a few investigations in his file, he's probably not doing his job." The implication here is that if you are active as a policeman, you will have complaints against you. Another chief inspector, now nearing retirement, said that when he served on promotion boards some members would inspect a man's dossier, see a "black mark" against him (a complaint), and conclude "as you would about any person with a criminal file (convicted or not), that he's "bent" (a criminal). The existence of such marks, he explained, affects promotion possibilities when names are sifted for a "short list" group [those included in the final group sent before a promotion board]. He further explained that a man's file can include items of which he is unaware, for example, a traffic patrolman's file can include complaint letters written to the Yard without his knowledge. Complaints are filed and listed anonymously, and it was said that they are sometimes sent in by one's colleagues at a station (a "poison pen" letter). These anecdotes suggest at least that a constable can reasonably suspect that items in his file are held against him, and this knowledge may be a source of a degree of realistic "paranoia." However, even if one is aware of the complaint, its investigation, and the outcome, one can never be precisely certain what it means. Other policemen are also warned, everyone talks about the complaint experience, the air is full of tales of mistaken and erroneous complaints, and "policing by the book" is not seen as a guaranteed means for obtaining a "clean record." *It all depends, they feel, on whether the "guys" will support you when questions are raised.*

RULES, INDETERMINACY, AND COLLEAGUESHIP

What is most significant about police regulations is that they are soon stripped of moral coating. People in general are viewed as stupid, fallible, greedy, lustful, immoral, and hypocritical—such views provide policemen with resources for hours of stories and jokes. Man is seen as a translucent Machiavelli, easily uncovered by insightful probing or police action. Fellow policemen are viewed in much the same fashion. Rules and written records become for the most part a *tactical* means of defending oneself against accusation, and a basis for counterattack if necessary. In relations with the public, the police, sensitive to the needs and demands of the more powerful members of the community (Black, 1968; 1970), are virtually forced to adopt a strategic moral position in order to ritualize the appearance of consensus (Burns, 1953:660). Since rules are resources by which a number of outcomes can be rationalized, policemen are often caught between these demand conditions and personal morality.[10] Sometimes PCs must manipulate the paper reality—what the record shows—in order to achieve desired outcomes, and sometimes they must conspire with others in the same situation to alter the dynamics in a way that makes a given outcome highly probable. The reality of police work, given this high component of uncertainty, is at times defined as writing the proper paper (what Goffman, 1961, calls "paper reality") in order to construct the appearances (what one wants to show to superiors in order to protect himself), and at other times, it is seen as managing problematic interactions such that analogous outcomes are generated.

There are thus two types of situations in which relationships based on norms not shared by those in the dominant group are displayed or in which ambiguity of the superivsion of the senior officers leads to collusion. Two types of colleague relationships emerge: a *vertical/situational clique* based on the need to manipulate a face-to-face situation involving both PCs and senior officers (including in this case sergeants); and *horizontal/situational cliques* based on PC relationships.[11]

Vertical situational cliques result because situations are presented repeatedly that, if they were solved by the book, would be time-consuming, potentially embarrassing, and explosive for all concerned. These cliques most commonly were observed in the reserve room with a sergeant present with a complement of PCs. An efficacious solution required trust between the persons involved. When one manipulates the situation rather than the written record, one enters into a collusion with others present. For example, an act of Parliament stipulates that all phone messages received at a station must be logged in writing. In practice, the enormous volume of calls could not possibly be completely logged.

---

[10]Conflict between personal morality and the demands of social groups can be illustrated by two examples from fieldnotes. In both situations, the personal morality of the policemen involved differed from the actual outcomes of the case, and in each case the outcome favored the interests of the higher or more powerful classes. (The temporary refusal of the police to prosecute for petty theft was a pyrrhic victory because such cases were subsequently accepted from the factory by CID.)

CID officers on a station in the subdivision were frequently asked to a toy factory to arrest and charge (as was the company policy) employees caught stealing the little cast metal scale model autos (the 50¢ Corgi/Matchbox type) the company manufactured. This was a fairly regular occurrence, and the young DCs were eager for an arrest and charge so cleanly and simply accomplished. These arrests were, however, a source of some discussion among the DCs, since the value of the item was small and the crime insignificant. They felt it a bit extreme to routinely arrest people for such a petty crime. However, they rationalized the practice as helping their careers, saying it "looked good on your record to have frequent arrests and convictions." A call was received by CID asking officers to come to the board room of the same factory to make an arrest. The officers learned that it was alleged that one of the managers had altered the production instructions in the plant, substituting inferior materials and selling the high quality metal specified for the casting of the cars. By so doing, he had accumulated and sold some 20,000 Pounds ($50,000) worth of metal. The Board of Directors of the company was meeting to decide whether to file a legal charge against this manager. The CID, as they sifted the facts, were

The manager of a local department store calls to report to the police that he is turning over to them the fact that a woman had her purse stolen in the store. He reports that she does not want to report it to the police (but he wants to protect himself against a later claim by her against him or the store). The sergeant volunteers to enter it in the lost property book (therefore it is not a crime, and will not require investigation or clearance). The call is not shown in the message book.

Calls out are not logged unless they close an episode ("keyholder notified and went to the scene"). Errors in calls to area cars, duplications in messages to a panda and an area car are not recorded. Inter-police calls are not logged.

Once a man wanted a car which was left on his lot investigated as stolen property. He tried to hand the key to the sergeant on duty. The sergeant refused it (policemen cannot accept gifts nor property without a written reason or justification). He suggested that, "if the key were left, and if they looked around later, it might be found and then they might try some cars in the area to ascertain if any of them belonged to the key." The lot attendant blinked, left the key, and walked out. A PC immediately said in a false tone of surprise: "Hey, Sarge, someone left a car key on the counter! What should we do?" None of this was recorded.

In acting as they did in these incidents, policemen were violating laws requiring a written record to be kept of all police communications and of police handling of property. They were acting in collusion not only against "the public interest," but by handling the matter informally, they prevent senior officers from monitoring performance by means of written records. Thus informal control substitutes for formal controls and cliques become an active force in procedural matters. A similar pattern is revealed in the conversations between

---

convinced of his guilt. They waited outside the board room, were served dinner and drinks, but were finally informed by the Chairman of the Board that the company had decided not to prosecute. It was suspected by the police that since the manager held stock in the company, they had decided to drop the case to avoid public embarrassment and possible financial loss. Soon thereafter, the same company called to have an arrest made for stealing one of the 50¢ model cars, and they were informed they would have to proceed in the matter by private summons. That is, the police did not wish to take legal action, although the company could utilize its private resources to bring the matter to adjudication.

[11]A brief overview is provided by Miller and Form (1964:252–262). My discussion of cliques draws on Dalton's ideas (1959:57–67), but places these matters more in the context of situational adjustments rather than crisis management or of orientations toward mobility or success. See the elegant formulations of Burns (1953, 1955, 1958, 1960). Wilson (1968) writes: "One reason for the oft-noted tendency of patrolmen to form cliques, factions and fraternal associations is not so much to celebrate the virtues of ethnic solidarity, though the organizations be among ethnic lines, but to defend officers against what is to them arbitrary authority and "outside influence." The power of the administrator is to be checked because the administrator, if he is a strong man, is "out to get us," and, if he is a weak one, is "giving way before outside pressure." (73). This is a very insightful analysis, although in urban American departments race and ethnicity are apparently a more critical basis for cliques than in the department studied. Although there were a number of officers of Scottish descent, they did not form a clique, partially because they were spread out throughout the rank hierarchy of the subdivisional headquarters.

sergeants and constables prior to writing a charge in the charge book. Various laws are discussed as covering the event, and related charges are discussed; procedural questions; especially with juveniles (there have been a number of recent changes in the juvenile rules), are discussed and a final polished version is entered. This informal conference makes the eventual countersigning by the sergeant a ritual affirmation rather than a formal means of social control. It is these discussions, the understandings that the men draw on when they engage in such negotiations as well as their typifications of "crimes like this one" (Sudnow's "normal crimes" concept), that permit another policeman to "see" or understand what has happened prior to the written record. Understandings of the meanings of written records that emerge from situational negotiation with sergeants or inspectors are frequently made possible by direct personal knowledge of the sergeants on the shift at the time.

There was one sergeant on the station who was not trusted by the men because he was said to be the chief superintendent's man ("his toady"). He was assigned paper work duties in the station and had little contact with the daily affairs in the reserve room. But other sergeants, because there was an excess of sergeants on the subdivision, were often looking for something to do and would take out the reserve area car on patrol. One sergeant became well known for obtaining this duty and became closely associated with men on this turn. On nights and weekends, especially Sundays, sergeants and at least two of the inspectors on the station would play pool in the basement or cards in the charge room with the men. Thus, when problematic cases of rule-violation occurred, these sergeants "didn't want to know," and were particularly critical of the station sergeant (Sergeant B in the above anecdotes) who was known for harsh and unquestioning punishment.

If, however, one manipulates the written record to protect himself against superiors and sergeants, one typically must have the trust of a horizontal clique [what is sometimes called the "occupational subculture"; (Westley, 1970)]. Since rules are surrounded by uncertainty, when disciplinary action is taken it is always viewed as arbitrary; cynicism is expressed about all forms of supervision on the subdivision. "Supervisors do not enforce what they want to enforce, but what they are told to enforce." (One ranking member of Scotland Yard, when asked what he was doing at the moment said, "I'm doing what I'm told to do.") "It isn't the conviction or detection rate they are worried about any more," one sergeant told me.

> I work more and more to cover the trivialities. I'm all right provided I appear to be doing something, provided it all looks all right, and that all the squares are filled so that supervisors could come around and say, "You did something right yesterday." So you only do as much as necessary to have others conclude that you're doing something. Provided that you give the impression that your doing something no one can know differently. Carrying a piece of paper indicates work.

One virtually always manipulates the written record to protect oneself. As one detective sergeant put it, "We work against when one might go wrong. It comes down like a rocket" [is returned with a note from the legal department at the Yard]. Thus, when one manipulates the written record in a case, one has to have specific knowledge and *trust* of the others involved.

The manipulation of the rules that takes place among horizontal cliques, typically partners in an area car, crew in the reserve room, or a team of people working plain clothes, allows lower participants to decrease the uncertainty in rule-enforcement and to protect themselves so that things don't come back. Young policemen must learn these guiles, lest they be as vulnerable as one very successful detective inspector who was asked to do a favor for his "Skip" (supervising sergeant) while working as a TDC (Temporary Detective Constable):

> Because there was no transport available at the time on the station, he took his own car and was subsequently involved in a traffic accident. He was bustled back to a uniform and lost 5 days' pay. He pointed out that it was stupid, he should have covered himself. [How?] "I should have asked someone to book me off, or book myself off when I got back to the station so that I would be covered, i.e., be off duty (detectives have to write in the duty book where they are at any time they leave the station, what they are investigating, and the purpose of the visit, e.g., Manning, to 121 Blackhearth Park S.E. 3, in Re: Smith to obtain statements).

However, these collusions and situational clique formations did not seem to create major rifts within the organization, perhaps because "success" and competition for success, either in the occupational milieu or outside, was not a ubiquitous concern, and the segments of the organization were more often divided by rank than by orientations to success. Had the success milieu obtained, as Burns (1955) has described, it is likely that the growth of corruption, the conscientious withdrawal of efficiency, and attempts to alter the legal and social constraints on policing might have been commonly observed among these policemen.

COMMENT

The quasi-military structure of police organizations creates the potential for capricious authority to be employed to define proper and adequate work. This seems to flow from the uncertain organizational environment in which Anglo-American police organizations operate: the relationships between the publics served by the organization and organizationally tied actors are open, ambiguous, and problematic. Rules, in the context of police work, are also areas in which negotiations will typically occur (e.g., if arrests and charges are more highly valued than community order-maintenance, then greater uncertainty will surround questions of a "good pinch"—an arrest that will stick. Rules legitimate punishment and provide rationalizations for administrative action. The rules stipulate universal minimal performance (grounds for dismissal, acceptable days of leave). The most significant source of power, or, conversely, the area of perhaps least dependence of lower participants upon senior officers, is that which devolves from variations in the enforcement practices themselves, what Weber has called "the conscientious withdrawal of efficiency." This is seen in the common American phenomena of "Blue Flu" (calling in sick in large numbers), waves of ticket enforcements, or refusal to enforce laws against some kinds of victimless crimes especially gambling, prostitution, and after-hours drinking. In English police departments, these actions are unknown. Nevertheless, rules stipulate an *area of autonomy* for lower participants. The very proliferation of rules within a police organization permits lower participants to virtually always "work to rule." That is, they always have some rule as a resource and protection insofar as certain stipulated areas are those within which rules operate.

What might be investigated in future analyses of police organizations is the extent to which *rules* are not stipulated solely for the use of administrators in line with the ideology of scientific police theory, but set a bargaining ground for organizational strata, bring them into contact to negotiate the meanings of events, and thus to produce the basis for *justifications* of organizational action that draws together segments into *acting units*.[12] The acquiescence of lower participants to the rule negotiation process is itself an important and significant indication of their acceptance of the legitimacy of the organization. The ways in which these rules are negotiated are a most significant indicator of the limits of the organizational situation. That is, rules set out the limits of the organization's power over its various publics (a phenomenon, which as Hughes has pointed out, expands and contracts over time) and its power over its members. The degree to which a person is submerged within an organization (Burns, 1961; Goffman, 1961) is at least in part a function not only of rules, but the ways in which they are applied to particular persons and situations.

The application of these rules in turn creates a set of perhaps temporary collusions, or flexible alliances that are a form of colleagueship well suited to negate some of the more potentially repressive and destructive consequences of highly elaborated, codified system of rules and rules about rules. As McNamara notes, "police work does not consist of a standardized product or service. . . . Given that the individual problems presented to officers are unique and given the existence of a bureaucratic structure, then one should expect to find that officers face many of the problems generally faced by professionals who are

---

[12]Ethnomethodologists (Cf. Manning, Wieder, Zimmerman, and Zimmerman and Wieder chapters in Douglas, ed., 1970) have argued that rules are a means by which social settings and situations are made accountable and coherent for participants, "The work of making and accepting such descriptions of conduct makes social settings appear as orderly for the participants and it is this *sense and appearance* of order that rules in use, in fact, provide . . . " (Zimmerman and Wieder, p. 292). It is clear that greater emphasis must be placed upon the underlying and assumed organizational reality to which the rules are "referred" (what it takes to properly understand what is meant by an instruction or by the invocation of a rule) rather than to rules themselves as providing order. What is well captured in the above quotation is a necessary but not sufficient feature required for competent functioning and understanding within organizations. That is, people must be able to indicate to each that they "understand" by means of rules or other formal blueprints of action, but without the ability to understand what "lies behind" a rule and to communicate that understanding to others, the appearance of order is just that. It should be recalled that misunderstandings are so central a feature of everyday life that a sense of order may be "false," i.e., it may isolate a person outside the bounds of others' experience, and the invocation of rules is itself an indexical and therefore defeasible process.

employed by large organizations." (McNamara, in Bordua, ed., 1967:185) "Professional" in this context does not refer to elaborated codes, abstracted theories, or formalized training procedures, but rather to the form of problem faced. In the absence of the public affirmation of a mandate, and the structural dilemmas of police work, cliques and flexible informal groups may have both the potential for corruption and malfeasance and for enabling a degree of coping with relatively unpredictable events in a routine fashion.

REFERENCES

Banton, M., (1964) The Policeman in the Community. New York: Basic Books.

Black, D. J., (1970) "The production of crime rates." American Sociological Review 35 (August): 733–748. (1968) "Police encounters and social organization." Unpublished Ph.D. dissertation, Department of Sociology, University of Michigan.

Bittner, E., (1970) The Functions of the Police in Modern Society. Washington, D.C.: United States Government Printing Office. (1965) "The concept of organization." Social Research 32 (Winter): 230–255.

Blankenship, R., (1973) "Organizational careers." Sociological Quarterly 14 (Winter): 88–98.

Burns, T., (1961) "Micropolitics: mechanisms of institutional change." Administrative Science Quarterly 6 (December): 257–281. (1958) "Forms of conduct." American Journal of Sociology 64 (September): 137–151. (1955) "The Reference of conduct in small groups." Human Relations VIII (November): 467–486. (1953) "Friends, enemies, and the polite fiction." American Sociological Review 18 (December): 654–662.

Cain, M., (1973) Society and the Policeman's Role. London: Routledge, Kegan Paul.

Crozier, M., (1971) The World of the Office Worker. Chicago: University of Chicago Press. (1964) The Bureaucratic Phenomenon. Chicago: University of Chicago Press.

Dalton, M., (1959) Men Who Manage. New York: John Wiley and Sons.

Goffman, E., (1961) Asylums. Chicago: Aldine.

Gouldner, A. W., (1954a) Patterns of Industrial Bureaucracy. Glencoe: Free Press. (1954b) Wildcat Strike. Yellow Springs, Ohio: Antioch Press.

Manning, Peter K., (1973a) "Dramatic aspects of policing: selected propositions." Unpublished paper. (1973) "Existential sociology." Sociological Quarterly 14 (Spring): 200–225. (1972) "Observing the police: deviants, respectables and the law." In J. D. Douglas (ed.), Research on Deviance. New York: Random House. (1971) "The police: mandate, strategies and tactics." In J. D. Douglas (ed.), Crime and Justice in American Society. Indianapolis, Indiana: Bobbs-Merrill. (1970) "Taking and becoming: a perspective on organizational socialization." In J. D. Douglas (ed.), Understanding Everyday Life. Chicago: Aldine.

McNamara, J., (1967) "Uncertainties in police work: the relevance of police recruits' backgrounds and training." In D. J. Bordua (ed.), The Police. New York: John Wiley and Sons.

Miller, D. C., and W. H. Form, (1964) Industrial Sociology. 2nd ed. New York: Harper and Row.

Reiss, A., and D. Bordua, (1967) "Environment and organization: a perspective on the police." In D. J. Bordua (ed.), The Police. New York: John Wiley and Sons.

Reiss, A. J., Jr., (1971) The Police and the Public. New Haven: Yale University Press.

Scott, R. W., (1966) "Professionals in bureaucratic organizations: areas of conflict." In H. Vollmer and D. Mills (eds.), Professionalization. Englewood Cliffs, N.J.: Prentice-Hall.

Silverman, D., (1971) The Theory of Organizations. New York: Basic Books.

Stinchcombe, A., (1965) "Social structure and organizations." In J. March (ed.), Handbook of Organizations. Chicago: Rand McNally.

Westley, W., (1970) Violence and the Police. Cambridge: MIT Press.

Wilensky, H. L., (1960) "Work, careers and social integration." International Social Science Journal 12 (No. 4): 543–560.

Wilson, J. Q., (1968) Varieties of Police Behavior. Cambridge: Harvard University Press.

Zimmerman, Don H., and D. Lawrence Wieder, (1970) "Ethnomethodology and the problem of order: Comment on Denzin." In Jack D. Douglas (ed.), Understanding Everyday Life. Chicago: Aldine.

Control Systems, Social Bases of Power and Power Exercise in Police Organizations*[1]

Larry L. Tifft

This paper analyzes (1) the structural conditions which affect the location of social bases of power in an organizational position; (2) the structural conditions affecting the exercise of power; (3) the necessity of altering these structural conditions if one wishes to increase the power-control of the organization over its boundary-spanning members; and (4) the consequences these organizational structures have on persons handled by the organization's personnel.

The analysis was accomplished through studying and comparing the control systems of five street-contact units of one major city police department. The analysis is intended to provide a strategy for recognizing certain organizational problems, locating their sources, and suggesting organizational changes.

An understanding of control structures, structurally determined power bases, and the exercise of power from these bases is especially critical in organizations wherein highly discretionary activity is required of lower level employees. In many organizations the lower level employees of the organiza-

*An earlier draft of this paper was presented at the Midwest Sociological Association Meetings, April 1973, Milwaukee, Wisconsin. The author wishes to thank Professors Dennis Sullivan and Bernard Dolnick for their helpful comments on the earlier draft.

[1] Research support was provided under the Law Enforcement Assistance Act of 1965 by the U.S. Dept. of Justice, Office of Law Enforcement Assistance Grant #385-266-5215: David J. Bordua, Project Director; Larry L. Tifft, Research Associate; Robert Ford and Ivan Kitzmiller, Research Assistants. As to the methodolgy involved, see Tifft, "*Comparative Police Supervision Systems:* An Organizational Analysis," unpublished doctoral dissertation, University of Illinois, Urbana, 1970; Tifft and Bordua, "Police Organization and Future Research," *Research in Crime and Delinquency,* 6(2) (1969), 167–176; Bordua and Tifft, "Citizen Interviews, Organizational Feedback, and Police-Community Relations Decisions," *Law and Society Rev.,* 6(2) (1971), 155–182.

REPRINTED FROM: *Journal of Police Science and Administration.* 3, 1, *1975* (66–76).

tion have considerable power and critically determine the organization's efficacy.[2] Consequently, influencing the behavior of policemen, sales personnel, nurses and aides, teachers, guards, welfare workers and government service workers, in their interaction with citizens (victims, suspects), customers, patients, students, inmates, welfare recipients, and clients, is critical to the goals of their organizations.

Much of the organizational literature assumes that supervisors are in a position to influence the interaction or the behavior of their subordinates. What has not been adequately studied, however, is the structural contingencies and constraints which differentially affect the location of power bases in an organization and consequently the potential and actual exercise of power or influence by supervisors.[3]

BACKGROUND AND LITERATURE

Power can be described as "O has power over P to the extent that O can influence P to do something O wants P to do."[4] Raven and French[5] describe five bases of power which O can exert over P: (1) *reward power*, based on P's perception that O has the ability to mediate rewards for him; (2) *coercive power*, based on P's perception that O has the ability to mediate punishments for him: (3) *legitimate power*, based on the perception by P that O has a legitimate right to prescribe behavior for him; (4) *preferent power*, based on P's identification with O; and (5) *expert power*, based on the perception that O has some special knowledge or expertise.[6] These bases of power require perception or cognition on the part of P.[7] Thus, this definition of the concept of power is a perceptual and relational one. Power is in this sense meaningless unless it is exercised. Mose researchers have consequently measured the bases of supervisory power

---

[2]Wilson, "Police Morale, Reform, and Citizen Respect: The Chicago Case," in Bordua ed., *The Police: Six Sociological Essays* (1967) 137–162; Homans, *Social Behavior: Its Elementary Forms* (1961), 336–352; Wager, "Leadership Style. Hierarchial Influence, and Supervisor Role Obligations," *Administrative Science Quarterly,* 9 (1965), 391–420; "Mechanic, Sources of Power of Lower Participants in Complex Organization," *Administrative Science Quarterly,* 7 (1962), 349–364.

[3]Tannenbaum and Bachman. "Structural Versus Individual Effects," 69 (1964), 585–595; Tannenbaum and Smith, "Effects of Member Influence in an Organization: Phenomenology versus Organizational Structure," in Tannenbaum, ed., *Control in Organizations*, (1968), 199–211.

[4]Hall, *Organizations: Structure and Process* (1972), chap. 7.

[5]French and Raven, "The Bases of Social Power," in Cartwright and Zander, eds., *Group Dynamics* (1960).

[6]For similar formulations, see Weber, *Theory of Social and Economic Organization* (1947), 324–328; Etzioni, *A Comparative Analysis of Complex Organizations* (1961).

[7]Bachman, Bowers, and Marcus, "Bases of Supervisory Power: A Comparative Study in Five Organizational Settings," in Tannenbaum, ed., *Control in Organizations*, (1968), 229–238.

[8]Bachman, Smith and Slesinger, "Control, Performance, and Satisfaction: An Analysis of Structural and Individual Effects," in Tannenbaum, *op. cit.* pp. 213–229; Bachman, Bowers, and Marcus, in Tannenbaum, *op. cit.*; Warren, "Power, Visibility, and Conformity in Formal Organizations," *American Sociology Review,* 33, (1968), 951–970.

by asking subordinates why they comply,[8] what type of compliance is elicited via different types of power,[9] or different combinations of power,[10] and which structural constraints[11] are associated with these different power bases.

Studies have indicated (1) that there are numerous types of power,[12] (2) that the type of power system critically affects the way in which people are linked to the organization;[13] (3) that organizations and positions within organizations consist of combinations of types of power;[14] (4) that power is not something that is available in a fixed amount;[15] (5) that compliance, satisfaction, performance and effectiveness are linked to the social bases of power;[16] (6) that the nature of the work required, the training and beliefs of the personnel, and the nature of the clients contacted may affect the social base and/or exercise of power;[17] and (7) that more than one base of power may be located in an organization but not necessarily in the same position.[18] However, these research findings and the general approach tend to assume that superiors have the power base to affect P and exercise it.

Much of the supervision literature suggests that lower level supervisors are the backbone of their organizations, or are, at the very least, in a position of high potential for influencing the subordinate and determining his morale.[19] Police administrators often see sergeants as the backbone of their organizations. In some organizational contexts it is more probable that clients, depending on the degree of client orientation, significantly affect the morale of the

[9]Warren, *op. cit.*, 954.

[10]Warren, *op. cit.*; Bachman, Bowers, and Marcus, *op. cit.* Bachman, Smith, and Slesinger, *op. cit.*

[11]Warren, *op. cit.*

[12]Weber, *op. cit.*; Etzioni, *op. cit.* in Tannenbaum; Warren, *op. cit.*

[13]Etzioni, *op. cit.*

[14]Bachman, Smith, and Slesinger, in Tannenbaum, *op. cit.*; Bachman, Bowers, and Marcus, in Tannenbaum, *op. cit.*

[15]Hall, *op. cit.*; Perrow, "A Framework for the Comparative Analysis of Organizations," *American Sociological Review*, 32 (2) (1967), 194–208; Perrow, *Organizational Analysis: A Sociological View* (1970).

[16]Bachman, Smith, and Slesinger, in Tannenbaum, *op. cit.*; Evan and Zelditch, "A Laboratory Experiment on Bureaucratic Authority," *American Sociological Review*, 26 (6), 883–893.

[17]Perrow, *American Sociological Review*, 32; Perrow, *Organizational Analysis: A Sociological View* (1970); Warren, *op. cit.*; Blau and Scott, *Formal Organizations: A Comparative Approach* (1962).

[18]Hall, *op. cit.*

[19]Wilson, *op. cit.* It is pointed out by Ohlin *et al.*, in "Major Dilemmas of the Social Worker in Probation and Parole," *National Probation and Parole Journal*, 2 (1956), 219, and by Scott, "Reactions to Supervision in a Heterogenous Professional Organization," *Administrative Science Quarterly*, 10 (1965), 65–81, that in heteronomous professional organizations the role of the supervisor is that of an educator rather than an administrative authoritative superior. This would seem to be directly applicable to the police. Wilson, *op. cit.* also points out that factors such as morale are not determined solely by police management but by such factors as the status and honor of the occupation, the opinions of clients, and by the other organizations in the criminal justice system, especially the courts, who process the products of the police department. Not feeling backed up by the courts is a typical syndrome decreasing morale among policemen.

operative employee.[20] Thus, one could argue that students rather than an assistant principal affect teachers' morale; that the parolees rather than the parole officers' supervisor affect the parole officers' morale; and that the citizens, victims, complainants, and suspects, rather than the patrol sergeant, affect the patrolmen's morale.

Whichever the stronger influence on morale, the quality and dynamics of police-citizen interactions are very highly dependent upon, and are products of, an intricate and complex set of variables and structures both within and outside a police organization.

In recent years police administrators have felt increasing pressure to control the discretionary behavior of policemen and have often turned to consultants and advisors in the police organization and management field. These consultants have often responded by suggesting such personalistic reforms as better selection of officers, longer training, etc. More frequently, however, they have suggested better and closer supervision, or management human relations programs. Basing their advice on the bulk of the supervision literature,[21] their

---

[20]March and Simon, *Organizations* (1958), 89; Etzioni, *op. cit.*; Blau and Scott, *Formal Organizations: A Comparative Approach* (1962), 77. Note that recently there is an attempt at some community control of police departments and schools, student attempts to organize to influence universities, and welfare recipients forming unions, all to gain a position of more than an "object" of these extended bureaucracies. For other references see Black and Reiss, "Patterns of Behavior in Police-Citizen Transactions," *Studies in Crime and Law Enforcement in Major Metropolitan Areas*, Field Surveys III, 2, sec. 1 (1967); Thomas, "Role Conceptions and Organization Size," *American Sociological Review*, 24 (1959), 30–37; Reissman, "A Study of Role Conceptions in Bureaucracy," *Social Forces*, 27 (1949), 305–310; Parsons, "Suggestions for a Sociological Approach to the Theory of Organizations," in Etzioni, *op. cit.*, 39–46; Janowitz and Delany, "The Bureaucrat and the Public: A Study of Informational Perspectives," *Administrative Science Quarterly*, 2 (1957), 141–162; Clark, "Organizational Adaptation and Precarious Values," *American Sociological Review*, 21 (1956), 327–336, and Clark, *The Open Door College* (1960). Also see Carlson, "Environmental and Organizational Consequences in the Public School and Its Clients," in *Chicago National Society for the Study of Education, Behavioral Science and Educational Administration* (1964). Carlson demonstrates that schools, like police departments, have little or no control over selection of clientele and likewise the clientele lack options to these organizations. This is especially true in the ghetto where most of the social agencies have been abandoned or do not operate hours other than 9–5. The police are thus called to perform many services and enter many encounters which they feel "are not police work." Bredemeir, "The Socially Handicapped and Their Agencies: A Market Analysis," in Reissman et. al., ed., *Mental Health of the Poor* (1964), 88–109: Lefton, and Rosengren, "Organizations and Clients: Lateral and Longitudinal Dimension," *American Sociological Review*, 31 (1966), 802–810; Tifft, *op. cit. op. cit.*

[21]For a review and bibliography regarding this literature, see Tifft, *op. cit.* Basically these studies can be divided into three different categories: those showing the importance of psychological and relationship factors of supervisors affecting organizational effectiveness; those stressing factors other than the relations between people and situations (as well as the first category) and their effects on organizational effectiveness; and those demonstrating the necessity of exploring the larger system of control in order to assess organizational effectiveness. The first group of studies conclude that productivity, morale, and other effectiveness criteria or variables are dependent on many factors and conditions. Under rather specific conditions productivity and morale can both be high. Yet, morale is dependent, for example, on the experience of the group members and varies with the size of the group. Therefore, large work groups generally have more difficulty identifying with their units and bosses. According to these authors, supervisors are regarded as having an

remedies make the faulty assumption that supervisors have great power potential, yet varyingly exercise this power to influence their subordinates.

THE STUDY

The information presented in this study was collected by an observational analysis exploring comparative control structures. The research demonstrated the necessity of distinguishing among the specialized organizational units within a police department. In significant ways each organizational unit contained different work roles, control structures, task environment, and clients.[22]

The research focused on observing police-citizen encounters as a means of assessing the efficacy of police behavior under alternate control systems and in different police units. Observation was focused upon officers' everyday "normal" work. Observers systematically recorded information detailing the content and process of police officer encounters with citizens and with supervisors. In addition, observers wrote final reports summarizing their observations on each unit.

---

important effect. The second group of studies conclude that the human relations analysts and other psychologists have neglected the complexity of management and dealt, to the exclusion of important factors, with relationship, inferring that organizational effectiveness is a matter of good interpersonal relations and only secondarily a matter of technical skill. These authors found that factors such as planning, discipline, organizing, pressure for production, and not pride in the work group, sympathy, communication, lack of arbitrariness, helpfullness, etc. were significant variables differentiating high and low effective supervisors. The third group of studies conclude that there is a need for exploration of organization effectiveness deeper: (1) than supervisor-subordinate relations; (2) than supervisor traits, manner, and abilities; and (3) than the position of the supervisor and his relationships within the role set, to study different work groups within an organization, between organizations, work groups of white vs. blue collar groups, different sized groups, and groups under differing organizational structures.

[22]Tifft, op. cit.

[23]Perrow, in American Sociological Review, 15; Perrow, Organizational Analysis.

[24]Goldthorpe, "Technical Organization as a Factor in Supervisor-Worker Conflict," British Journal of Sociology, 10 (1958), 213–230; Scott, "Reactions to Supervision in a Heteronomous Professional Organization," Administrative Science Quarterly, 10 (1965), 65–81; Thurley and Hamblin, "The Supervisor and His Job," The Problems of Progress in Industry, no. 13 (1963); Perrow, in American Sociological Review, 15; 194–208; Litwak, "Models of Organization Which Permit Conflict," American Journal of Sociology, 67 (1961), 177–184; Thompson and Bates, "Technology, Organization and Administration," Administrative Science Quarterly, 2 (1957), 325–343; Gouldner, Patterns of Industrial Bureaucracy (1954); Stinchcombe, "Bureaucratic and Craft Administration of Production: A Comparative Study," Administrative Science Quarterly, 4 (1959), 168–187; Stinchcombe, "Comment on Technical and Institutional Factors in Production Organizations," American Journal of Sociology, 67 (1961), 225–259; Bell, "Formality Versus Flexibility in Complex Organizations," 97–108, in Bell, ed., Organization and Human Behavior (1967).

[25]Strauss, Schatzmen, Bucher, Ehrlich, and Sabshin, Psychiatric Ideologies and Institutions (1964).

[26]See Note 20. Piliavin and Briar, "Police Encounters with Juveniles," American Journal of Sociology, 70 (1964), 206–214.

[27]Thompson, Organizations in Action (1967), 70.

To analyze the control and power structure of a large differentiated police department and suggest structural changes, it is first necessary to describe the control structures, their environments, and the relative weight and importance of different tasks,[23] technologies,[24] ideologies,[25] and publics.[26] Secondly, it is necessary to determine the effects which these elements have on the control structures and on the performances of task specific policemen.[27] However, this approach, while focusing on each task specific organizational unit, deemphasizes critical control and power relations between organizational units.[28]

The premise of this study was that the social bases of power of a supervisory position are dependent upon the nature of the work being supervised, including the technology involved,[29] where it is done,[30] the occupational cultural norms of subordinates,[31] the type of work group structure,[32] the phase of the organizational unit's history, and the culture or environment in which the organization operates.[33] Furthermore, the social bases of power located in a specific supervisory position may be the result of the use of other, alternate mechanisms of control. Past research has indicated that supervision (surveil-

---

[28]Hall, op. cit.; Perrow, op. cit.; Perrow, "Departmental Power and Perspective in Industrial Firms," in Zald, ed., Power in Organizations (1970), 59–89.

[29]Goldthorpe, op. cit.; Woodward, "Management and Technology," Problems of Progress in Industry, no. 3 (1958); Thurley and Hamblin, op. cit.; Litwak, op. cit.; Perrow, footnote 15; Selznick, "Foundation of the Theory of Organization," American Sociological Review, 13 (1948), 25–35; "Role Specializations in Supervisors," University of Michigan, microfilms (1957).

[30]Stinchcombe, footnote 24; Gouldner, op. cit., Goldthorpe, op. cit.

[31]Gouldner, op. cit.; Patchen, "Supervisory Methods and Group Performance Norms," Administrative Science Quarterly, 7 (1962), 275–294.

[32]Whyte, "Small Groups in Large Organizations," in Rohrer and Sharit, eds., Social Psychology at the Crossroads (1951), 303–304: "We have tended to think of effective supervision as being a product of a relationship between a good leader and a group on the assumption that the group of subordinates was a constant. In fact, variations in the effectiveness of supervision may be as much due to inherent differences in the group itself as to the leadership or supervisor's practices exemplified by the supervisor."

[33]National Institute of Industrial Psychology, The Foreman: A Study of Supervisors in British Industry (1952). The influencing factors of the social, economic, and political milieu in which the organization operates is very important. The supervision of leadership needed in a young struggling organization is different from that needed in an established organization. The organization's market position is crucial as well as its phase of history and organizational form. Thus we consider leadership or effective supervision as not a property of individuals but a set of complex relationships among numerous variables listed in the previous footnotes. Also see Goldthorpe, op. cit.; Stinchcombe, "Social Structure and Organizations," in March, ed., Handbook of Organizations (1965), 142–169; "Foundations of the Theory of Organization," American Sociological Review, 13 (1948), 25–35; Selznick, Leadership in Administration (1957); Selznick, TVA and the Grass Roots (1949); Dill, "An Analysis of Task Environment and Personal Autonomy," unpublished Ph.D. Dissertation (1957); Dill, "Desegregation or Integration? Comment about Contemporary Research on Organizations," in Cooper, Leavett, and Shelly II, eds., New Perspectives in Organization Research (1964); Evan, "The Organization Set: Toward a Theory of Interorganizational Relations," in Thompson, ed., Approaches to Organizational Design (1966); Forehand and von Haller, Environmental Variation in Studies of Organizational Behavior," Psychological Bulletin, 62 (1964), 361–382. Also see Clark, "Isolation of the Police: A Comparison of British and American Situations," Journal of Criminal Law, Criminology and Police Science, 56 (3) (1965), 307–319.

lance) is important and utilized in some organizational contexts, and relatively unutilized and unimportant in other organizational contexts.[34]

Drawing on the research of Bell,[35] Perrow,[36] and Thompson,[37] we hypothesized that the most crucial factor affecting the amount of discretion employed by a specific organizational member is the predictability of the work demands faced by that person. The degree of predictability of the work demands is determined by:

1. the perceived extent (range and magnitude) of unexpected events or unpredictable situational demands (dynamic task environment);

2. the degree to which the nature of the task problems are perceived as analyzable; and

3. the perceived degree of uniformness and understandability of the persons (raw material) handled.

We hypothesized that within this highly differentiated police department, in the organizational units where the work demands were highly predictable, we would find:

1. that the discretionary power of the working or processing organization member (subordinate) would be low;

2. that the social bases of power of the supervisor would be relatively few;

3. that the exercise of power or influence by the supervisor would be highly constrained and not significantly affected by style;

4. that the use of other mechanisms of organizational control would be high;

5. that the tasks would be preplanned; and

6. that peer (subordinate) interaction and communication would be centered about the issues of job security, pay, and arbitrary power.

Conversely, in the organizational units where the work demands were highly unpredictable, we hypothesized that we would find:

1. that the discretionary power of the working or processing organization member would be high;

2. that the social bases of power of the supervisor would be relatively numerous;

3. that the exercise of power or influence by the supervisor would be highly interpersonal, contingent, and dependent on style;

4. that the use of other mechanisms of organizational control would be highly problematical, though a peer or professional mechanism might develop;

---

[34]Rushing, "Organizational Rules and Surveillance: Propositions in Comparative Organizational Analysis," *Administrative Science Quarterly*, 10 (1966), 423–433; Warren, *op. cit.*, Tifft, *op. cit.*

[35]Bell, *op. cit.*

[36]Perrow, *American Sociological Review*, 32; Perrow, *Organizational Analysis* (1970).

[37]Thompson, *Organizations in Action, op. cit.*

5. that the tasks would not be preplanned; and

6. that much of the peer interaction and communication would be based on discussions of the work mission, the character of the organization, competency, and the issue of police "professionalization."

FINDINGS

Each of the analyzed organizational units was found to vary considerably with respect to the nature of the work performed by the policeman at the operating level, the nature of the citizens with whom the police officer came into contact, and the variability of the work demands. These elements, as well as other contextual elements, create pressures both in defining the nature of the work (role) expected of a police sergeant in each of the organizational units in determining the structural, social bases of power located in that particular position. These elements consequently had considerable effect on the potential exercise of power by an incumbent of these positions. If the bases of power were not structurally located in the position, the incumbent could not exercise this form of power.

An analysis of the five police units—patrol, traffic, tactical force, detective, and vice—discloses the factors which affect the distribution of the social bases of power in a supervisory position, the factors affecting the exercise of power, the consequences of these conditions, and some suggestions and cautions regarding organizational change.

Patrol: Social Bases of Power

Utilizing the concepts of Raven and French, the sergeant in patrol had some coercive power (the ability to mediate punishments) and some legitimate power (the right to prescribe behavior by virtue of holding the position). Yet he had little reward power (the ability to mediate rewards), expert power (special knowledge or expertise), and few opportunities to develop referent power (influence based on the subordinates' identification with the supervisor). Assessing these bases of power, the patrol sergeant was in a structurally weak position to exercise significant influence on his subordinates.

The first of many elements constructing this weak power position is the nature of the work supervised and its spatial distribution. The patrolman handles a large variety of incidents. These incidents or encounters are likely to range from issuing traffic citations to handling domestic disturbances, suspicious persons, sick persons, kids playing ball, thefts, landlord-tenant problems, and burglaries. In the course of these situations the patrolmen are likely to receive a wide variety of conflicting demands from the persons involved, whether they are "victims," "complainants," "offenders," or "ballplayers". Moreover, these encounters vary in the actions they demand for resolution from the extreme routine of crime case report writing to the complex dynamics of family conflict. Patrolmen are disproportionately required to deal with service, order maintenance, and disturbance situations, regarding which there are few departmental discretionary guidelines. For some patrolmen, these "jobs" are outside their definition of police work; for others, the legitimacy of the demands of the persons involved is highly questionable. Others have no clear ends toward which they act, or see that only "temporary resolutions" are possible.

The nature of the task and consequent task demands are such that without departmental or professional guidelines the patrolmen must generally rely on their own judgment, past experiences, and definitions of the persons involved. Resolutions or actions taken in these situations are thus determined by the interaction of the patrolmen's and citizens' perceptions and definitions. Differences, especially cultural differences, in these sets of perceptions and definitions, are at the core of numerous police-citizen conflicts.

In patrol work there is rarely a need for coordination of the officers, since there is little division of labor among the patrolmen in different cars. They are generally dispatched by radio or respond on-view to an event, and there is generally no need to increase the number of policemen handling most calls. Therefore, there is generally little contact among the patrolmen. They are not visible to supervision (surveillance) because they are mobilized in cars and because they interact with citizens in the private space of the citizens' homes or apartments.

The control mechanism of radio dispatch generally yields immediate service, but it precludes the close supervision of actual patrolman-citizen interaction, and controls only the extent of availability and the number of calls handled. This control mechanism has no effect in inducing patrolmen to make uniform, or unique, decisions. It also has no effect on the approach made toward citizens, definitions of situations, missions, or domains. Additionally, the nature of many of these situations often involves the need for instant decision-making and prompt action, making the patrolman's job the most vital, difficult, and dangerous.

The patrol sergeant was expected to enter major crime scenes, to see that the patrolmen made out the correct reports, and to spot-check to see that patrolmen responded to their calls in an acceptable amount of time. In the actual work process of most work situations, the supervisor could be of little assistance to the men. If the sergeant entered a situation involving highly discretionary, "non-crime," disturbance-type encounters, his intrusion was generally resented, as he was believed to have less knowledge or at least less recent experience in handling these situations. Contributing to this situation is the fact that the few available rewards for patrolmen (assignment of beat, shift, partner) were distributed by supervisors in organizational positions above sergeant. This consequently reinforced the very strong tendency for patrolmen to see the sergeant as a potential source of trouble rather than a potential source of help. The men tended to avoid and resent contact and communication with the sergeant. We found very few supervisory intrusions into the less clearly defined situations.

The patrol sergeant additionally had few opportunities to get to know the patrolmen both because of the spatial distribution of patrolmen and the fact that sergeants rotated shifts (hours worked) every month and often rotated supervisory beats, while patrolmen generally worked the same hours and beats. Supervisor-subordinate relations were consequently highly impermanent, preventing the contact base necessary for the development of referent power.

Essentially, the patrol supervisor's position had few and weak social bases of power. He was forced out of a significantly influential basis for extracting compliance from his subordinates through the complex interaction of (1) the nature of the work supervised, (2) the impermanence of sergeant-patrolman relations, (3) the environmental "high crime" task demands, (4) the nature of manpower deployment decisions, (5) the lack of executive policy guidelines for handling non-crime incidents, (6) the pressures of subordinates and (7) the nature of his superiors' task expectations.

Those administrators seriously desiring to increase the weight of the organizations' influence over the discretionary behavior of patrolmen via the mechanism of supervision must alter the social bases of power of this position by altering the elements which determine these bases of power. However, only some of the aforementioned elements are amenable to structural manipulation. Reducing supervisor-patrolmen impermanence, restructuring rigid manpower and spatial deployment providing knowledge-based discretionary guidelines, and increasing reward structures could have the effect of increasing the power base in the lower-level supervisory position. This does not mean that all lower-level supervisors would or could develop these power bases, nor does it mean that the persons placed in these positions would have the perceived expertise, charisma, or legitimacy to exercise their power potential. Furthermore, the particular uses and the ends of the behavior which this greater organizational power would take must be carefully examined. Finally, changing the bases of power in one organizational position could result in a renegotiation of power-based relations in other organizational positions, both within the patrol unit and in other organizational units. Increasing the power bases of one position does not necessarily mean a reduction in the power bases of other positions.

Traffic: Social Bases of Power

In the traffic unit the position of the sergeant in the organization was quite similar to the sergeants' position in the patrol unit. The sergeants' power/influence bases were significantly affected and constrained by the nature of the work supervised, departmental task demands, command role conceptions and expectations, impermanence of sergeant-traffic officer relations, the deployment of traffic cars to very large, spatially distanced posts, and the rules and regulations regarding the handling of traffic accidents. As in patrol, the exercise of power was further constrained by the pressures from subordinates not to interfere in their work.

Unlike the patrolman, the traffic man had a constricted area of discretionary action, handling the investigation of accidents and issuing moving traffic violation citations. The radio directed him to accidents, and elaborate procedures, rules, and regulations governed his investigations and reports. The issuing of traffic citations was generally the only other type of encounter entered by these specialized officers. Because of this very limited work activity, the work demands of the traffic man were much less dynamic and varying, and the demands of the citizens involved were more routine and understandable than those experienced by patrolmen. Consequently, the traffic officer was much more tightly controlled via a network of indirect, non-surveillance control mechanisms. Radio dispatch, regularized procedures, highly scrutinized reports, a centralized citation accounting system, and the required issuance of a quota of moving traffic violation citations are examples of these mechanisms.

This work situation seems to produce an organizational structure, similar to many well-controlled industrial production units, in which the first line supervisor lacks the structural social bases for influencing his subordinates. The traffic unit, like these industrial production units, had quite rigid hierarchical lines of authority, minimal vertical communication, and minimal normative supervisor control.

As in patrol, the traffic sergeant had some legitimate power and some, though generally minimal, coercive power, depending on the delegation of this from his immediate superior. He had minimal reward power, as there were relatively few rewards to be distributed to this highly "punishment oriented bureaucracy." Furthermore, minimal expert power was possible in the sense that little investigatory expertise was necessary for handling most accidents. As a consequence of the lack of an expert power base, wide spatial distribution and rotation-impermanency, a minimal referent power base developed in spite of the greater interaction of the men and the brass in these relatively small traffic units.

The contact necessary for the development of a referent power base was observed in one traffic unit, wherein the command personnel were intent on mediating the punishment-inspection-surveillance orientation of the division's centralized superiors. However, the development of this potential power base in this case was drained off into the social sphere, rather than critically affecting trafficman-citizen interactions. This suggests that size, intraorganizational conflict, and ideology may also affect the structural bases of power.

Tactical Force: Social Bases of Power

The sergeants and men in the tactical force worked in two very different work situations. The men and sergeants were organized into squads of 10–16 men on a permanent basis, so that the permanency of the sergeant-officer relationship was generally high. In work situations in which the squad worked as a whole—handling crowds, demonstrations, marches, and school walkouts—the sergeant was thrust into a situation demanding coordination, direction, and strategic knowledge or experience. In these situations the compliance of subordinates is critical and the bases of power which yield attitudinal compliance are most significant. Referent, legitimate, and expert power bases are thus most important, and structurally possible through the squad system. Reward and coercive power have extremely low salience in the heat, confusion, and threat or actuality of danger inherent in these highly unpredictable work situations.

Tactical force officers and district patrolmen were subject to the same rules and regulations. However, these formal rules were applicable to a limited range of the tactical force men's tasks, and specifically operable only with regard to crime and arrest procedures. When the squad members were not working as a squad, but were working on tactical, aggressive preventive patrol (stop and frisk) missions, they were not radio controlled and they were spatially dispersed in two-men cars. Consequently, they were quite invisible to the sergeant.

While these men were generally required to stop and search a specified number of persons per tour, and expected to make a certain number of arrests (points), only in some squads were they affected by the squad sergeant. The sergeant was thus thrust into conflicting work situations regarding the development of power bases and the exercise of power. Consequently, the power base of the sergeant was structurally affected by the proportion of time spent in crowd control squad activities versus aggressive-preventive patrol activities. In our observation, the bulk of tactical force activity was concentrated on the latter work situation. Only in a few instances did this mix of squad work experience place the sergeant in a position in which he directly affected the aggressive-preventive patrol operations of the tactical officers. Few sergeants affected the tactical force officers' definition of mission, type of stimuli responded to, type of stop made, manner of handling these encounters, morale, and commitment to the work. Previous work experience, especially the weak power-based patrol experience, seemed to deter the exercise of power or the development of referent power in this structurally conflicting position. Personal style significantly affected power exercise. Sergeants were in a position to have high reward and coercive power, since they determined who stayed in the squad, who worked together, where they worked, and what type of assignments were worked. They had as much legitimate power as any other sergeant by virtue of an assessment of the promotional system. They had varying opportunities to develop high contact and potential referent based power; and they had some expert power, based on squad-type activity.

Unlike the position of the sergeant in either patrol or traffic, in the tactical force unit development and exercise of socially based power was highly dependent upon whether the sergeant made use of the potential influence opportunities located in his position. Critical for the organization, of course, is how this power is used (if used); and if it is not used, then it is critical for the organization to recognize that these proactive, or crowd-controlling, officers, are virtually uncontrolled by organizational control mechanisms. When the sergeant does not exercise his power, the behavior of the tactical force officer becomes dependent upon his own attitudes and definition of mission, the norms of his coworkers, and possibly upon the attitudes and behavior of the citizens with whom he interacts.

This suggests that supervisors placed into these positions must recognize the dependence of the organization on the exercise of their influence. There must be a careful selection of persons who will fill these positions, and superiors must come to grips with discretionary decisions regarding the ends of crowd control or "preventive patrol." They must guide and direct the types of stops made, the tactics and approaches used, and the handling of persons in these encounters. Special education in the nature of, and control of, mass behavior, social movements, and street psychology is necessary. In crowd control situations, the potential consequences of not developing these social bases of power are the occurrence of uncontrolled police responses, overreactions, and "police riots." In the preventive patrol situation, the consequences are potentially severe citizen hostility, harassment, and abuse.

Detective: Social Bases of Power

In the detective units, the sergeants' and detectives' positions were affected by a combination and interaction of numerous constraints. The type of crime investigated, the type of "offender," the type of work pressures and conditions, case load demands, and the cooperation perceived and received within the specific community, all interact to affect the detective, his definition of mission, commitment, approach, attitudes toward citizens and "productivity." Sergeants were affected by these elements and by organizational task demands such as the number of men assigned to the unit and the volume of administrative tasks required. The position of the sergeant was also greatly affected by the need for field coordination. Because of the seriousness of the offense, possible media coverage, and coordination of investigation demands, sergeants in the robbery or homicide-sex-assault units were required to develop a much more active position than detective sergeants placed in other less serious, politically visible, coordinational units.

Administrative demands were critical in determining the power bases of these different detective sergeant positions. As indicated in the foregoing comparisons, robbery and homicide-sex-assault sergeants had a greater opportunity to develop and exercise referent and expert power than did their rank-similars in other detective units. In many detective units the sergeant is required to stay in the office, handle paperwork, review investigation reports, distribute case assignments, and make sure that cases are investigated and reports returned on time. In this position, he could potentially be a consultant, helper, or service coordinator of information for the detectives. He also could function as a decision-maker for the members of the patrol unit, who are required to notify the detective units on cases they think might warrant an immediate investigatory follow-up.

Detectives were rarely controlled by surveillance or by rules and regulations except as they applied to investigative requirements. Rather, they were influenced by production-evaluation controls regarding their "success" in arrest and case-clearance activity. This, of course, was a significant control, in that the detective (not performing) could be transferred back to district patrol with the consequent loss of numerous benefits (money, prestige, soft clothes and other desirable working conditions). The importance of this production-evaluation assessment criterion can be seen when it combines with such organizational elements as minor offenses and great volume to cause the practice of rationing, by which attention was focused on those cases which appeared likely to be resolved successfully, quickly, and with a clearance of some type.

Detective sergeants supervised all of the men in their unit rather than some specified subset. This was a consequence of the administrative constraints affecting the sergeant's task demands, and the relative smallness of the specific operating units. The detective sergeant thus had some legitimate power, some reward and coercive power, and differential opportunity for the development of referent power and expert power depending on the unit, its task specialization, and consequent demands. The degree of influence the sergeant in the detective units had was largely dependent on contact (work potential), coordination tasks, and the specific knowledge-skill the detective sergeant possessed as an individual. This latter influence-source is, of course, not located in the position other than in the opportunity for knowledge to be displayed.

The degree of influence or control by the sergeant in the detective units was largely dependent on his knowledge as an expert. If the sergeant was respected for his knowledge of burglars/burglary or robbers/robbery, then he could potentially be used as a consultant, or he could coordinate the detectives into a cooperative group working on their specific crime problem. The significance of this knowledge power source was seen and reflected in our comparison of burglary and general assignments units. Specialized knowledge was generally nonexistent in the general assignments units, as they did not specialize in any specific crime, but rather were catch-all, unsegmented units. There was, thus, no reason for the detective in the general assignments unit to interact with the sergeant. The general assignments detective was much more concerned with getting his cases followed up and turned in on time. The general assignments sergeant was well out of the influence system. Contrastingly burglary sergeants were at least potentially more influential than the general assignments sergeants because of the greater need for coordination, and the possibility of specialized knowledge.

Since knowledge is one of the most crucial variables determining whether or not the detective sergeant will be highly involved in the communication-consultation network of his men, it should be a requisite that detective sergeants be assigned who have had previous detective experience and/or knowledge. Further it is critical that they structure communication between the detectives in their unit regarding suspects, modus operandi, crime patterns, etc. If these bases of power/influence are not developed, the detective is actually quite uncontrolled in his behavior by the organization. On the other hand, extraorganizational sources of control, namely citizens as victims, complainants and witnesses, have considerable control potential, because the detective must, in essence, trade his social skills (civility, politeness, and concern) for information, cooperation, and investigatory leads.

Vice-Gambling: Social Bases of Power

In the gambling unit, the sergeant, because of the potential development of multiple social bases of power, was perhaps located in the most potentially powerful position of any of the sergeants' positions studied. The sergeant in this unit was generally assigned to work with and supervise three or four vice men. This meant that direct supervision (surveillance) was designed to be a significant control mechanism. Most significant among the structure-power base defining constraints in this unit were the nature of the work and the potentially disastrous consequences for the department's public image and its leaders' security which might result from corruption or poor discretionary judgment on the part of gambling unit officers. The sergeant, generally thrust into a co-working position, was constrained in exercising power by such factors as his knowledge of gambling operations relative to that of his crew members and interpersonal constraints upon the manner of his control. The sergeant was positioned as legitimately responsible for the actions of his crew members and their productivity, which all tended to make him an active working sergeant and gave him high reward-coercive power. The crew co-working arrangement also provided the opportunity for significant development of referent power. However, this social base of power depended on the sergeant's assignment to one specific crew rather than to the position of a coordinator of several crews. When the sergeant was administratively required to coordinate the work of two or more crews, his potential referent power base decreased, as did his contact in general.

When the sergeant position was one of coordinator rather than co-working leader, we witnessed the creation, within the crew, of a "substitute sergeant" team-leader, replacing the non-street working sergeant. This clearly attests to the work demands for direction, coordination of activity (i.e., the planning of raids), control over discretionary decisions on the street, and the consequent demand for responsible leadership. Someone was needed to call the shots, to be responsible, to plan the coordinated actions of the members of the crew and also to prevent the ever-present corrupting environment from "getting to" these men. In this position (sergeant or team-leader), knowledge of the operation was crucial. Close contact made personalities significant and referent power was potentially high, out of loyalty if not out of expert knowledge. Other mechanisms of control were virtually nonexistent, though moderate productivity pressures, good working conditions, prestige, and the nature of the work, which encompassed the total range of the police function, made the men highly susceptible to the sergeant's high coercive, reward, and referent power bases.

SUMMARY AND CONCLUSIONS

In summary, supervision is but one of a number of alternate control mechanisms which vary in their relative power or controlling influence over the men as functions of the interaction of numerous constraints defining the context of the sergeant's position and its social bases of power. The nature of the work supervised, including the technology involved, the nature of the enforcement pattern, the spatial context in which it is carried out, the occupational culture norms of the subordinates, the type of group structure involved, environmental constraints affecting the definition of the crime, the constraints of the definition of legitimate intrusion as defined by subordinates, the nature of the citizens in contact and their specific roles, the uniqueness of discretion involved in the work, and the task demands and superior expectations demanded, all interact to constrain and define the position of the sergeant in each specific organizational context vis-à-vis other, alternate, organizational control mechanisms. The environmental-structural context of the position of the sergeant in each specific organizational unit largely determines whether or not supervisors can even potentially have significant influence on the working ideology, orientation, or performance of the operative policeman in that unit. Consequently, we have seen that only under specific, exacting organizational-environmental-structural conditions which affect the social bases of power located in the position of supervisor has the style of the sergeant had a significant effect on the performance of his subordinates.

It is sincerely hoped that, through the analysis of the complexities of control structure, the alternate use of mechanisms of control, the contextual determinants of these alternate mechanisms, and the social bases of power located in the position of the lower-level supervisor, we have contributed both to the knowledge of complex organizational analysis and to the analysis of elements which affect organizational strategies for change, greater organizational control or influence over member behavior, and greater "effectiveness" of the specific segregated organizational units, especially in their effects on the citizens in contact with these organization members.

The analysis is limited in dealing with a highly differentiated police organization and we caution the reader about the generalizability of our structure-power analysis. Rather, we hope that persons anticipating special programs designed to improve the effectiveness of their employees via greater organizational influence will analyze the nature of the work performed, the task environment, and the social bases of power located in the "influencing" positions within the organization. Our analysis, while limited in the realm of interorganizational consequences and relationships, suggests that each unit within an organization has quite different organizational control problems and solutions. There are no panaceas and no programs applicable to whole organizations (police departments), and often the solutions create new problems.

Police Task and Time Study

John A. Webster

... This study has probed one area of police activity—the patrol division. The police department of a city, we will call Baywood, with a population of nearly 400,000 citizens was the object of this study. It was immediately learned that the patrol division comprised only 43 percent of the 900 authorized sworn and civilian personnel strength and only 41 percent of the police department budget. Data processing and computer science were the tools that made it possible to account for and catalog every assignment to which patrolmen were dispatched over a 54 week period. There were a total of 599,211 assignments for the period. Primary assignments amounted to 540,481. There were 58,730 cover assignments.

REPRINTED FROM: *Journal of Criminal Law, Criminology and Police Science.* 61, 1, *1970* (94 –100).

The time consumed on each individual assignment was also recorded. The primary dispatches consumed 277,475 hours and the cover assignments used 23,652 hours. The total consumed time was 301,127 hours.

Each assignment to which a patrolman was dispatched was coded, such as homicide, assault, stolen car, abandoned vehicle, burglary, a barking dog, or a rest break. Through the process of data reduction the nearly 600,000 assignments were reduced to 109 types of events.

The 109 types of events were grouped into six categories labeled: Crimes Against Persons, Crimes Against Property, Traffic, On-View, Social Services, and Administration. A new perspective on police activity resulted from this analysis. For example, the frequency and consumed time of assignments pertaining to Crimes Against Persons amounted to only 2.82 percent and 2.96 percent respectively of the total assignments. The percent of frequency of assignments and consumed time for all categories is found in Table 1.

TABLE 1

	Frequency	Consumed Time
Crimes Against Persons	2.82%	2.96%
Crimes Against Property	13.76%	14.82%
Traffic	7.16%	9.20%
On-View	19.68%	9.10%
Social Services	17.27%	13.70%
Administration	39.28%	50.19%

The functional aspects of most of the 109 types of events were also examined and an effort was made to more accurately describe, along with the statistical accounting, the reality of police activity.

The practical application of this study is to assist the police administrator to formulate a realistic mission and to provide him with information so that he can better allocate his manpower and material resources. A police job description can be formalized enabling the administrator to measure a patrolman's effectiveness. Training programs can be more intelligently designed to meet the policeman's needs so that he can better serve his community.

CRIMES AGAINST PERSONS

The first of the six categories of events into which this study was organized pertains in general to offenses against the person. The events included in this category are criminal homicide, rape, kidnapping, battery, robbery, assault with intent to commit murder, etc.

As previously mentioned, Crimes Against Persons constituted only 2.82 percent of the total assignments and 2.96 percent of the total time consumed on all assignments.

Murder and Non-Negligent Manslaughter. Patrolmen were dispatched to 46 reported murders and non-negligent manslaughter cases. These 46 homicides represented only .01 percent of the total events and required only 67.67 hours of their time.

Baywood, like other urban police departments which are entrusted with the prevention and control of criminal homicide, finds the task impossible. A California Bureau of Criminal Statistics Study showed that most criminal homicides occur in places such as homes, automobiles, and other locations where surveillance as a measure of prevention or control would not be feasible.

The major contributing factor to homicides in America—both accidental and criminal—is the extremely easy availability of guns. According to Carl Bakal in his book *The Right to Bear Arms* 60 percent of our criminal homicides are caused by guns, knives 23 percent. It is inevitable that an argument that might end with a bloody nose in Ireland ends with a murder in Atlanta. It seems quite obvious that it would be easy to reduce the number of murders if rational and effective gun laws were invoked.

Rapes. The Baywood Communications Section recorded 330 rapes. Dispatches for rape constituted .02 percent of the total assignments.

There is a great deal of skepticism among the police of Baywood regarding the offense of rape, and an effort was made through interviews with police personnel to learn the basis of this skepticism. When the subject of rape was mentioned, one lieutenant stated, "They are mostly whores." The explanation was that prostitutes use the police to help them collect their business fees. The police are also used by women other than prostitutes to remove unwanted boyfriends. Not all of the forcible rapes are consummated acts. Over half are attempted rapes.

Statutory rape is the other category of rape. Statutory rapes are referred to in the Baywood Police Department as "welfare rapes," since most statutory rape offenses come to the attention of the police through the County Welfare Department.

Rapes, according to the President's Crime Commission, are much like criminal homicides. They occur most frequently between friends and associates and in places where prevention and control by police surveillance is not possible.

Assault and Battery. The police, during interviews, dismissed a large portion of assault and battery cases as "those West Baywood Batteries." West Baywood is a ghetto section of predominantly Negro residents.

The police comment does seem valid however. Under the classification of assaults, white citizens were arrested 513 times, while there were 1,540 arrests of non-whites for this offense. Although one-third of the Baywood population is non-white, the assault arrests of this group were three times as many as the assault arrests for whites.

Robbery. Patrolmen were dispatched to 2,917 reported robberies. This represented one-half of one percent (.51%) of the total number of events to which they were dispatched.

Baywood policemen arrested 449 persons for robbery in 1967 and reported 1,421 actual robbery offenses. This official reported statistic is half the number of events to which the Communications Section dispatched patrolmen as robberies. Police, when interviewed, have stated that the reporting citizen does not distinguish among larcenies, burglaries, and robberies.

Police rarely, if ever, come upon a robbery in progress. The most that can be expected of the police is that they will respond quickly enough to interview witnesses who may have seen the robbery take place and conduct a successful investigation from the evidence they obtain.

CRIMES AGAINST PROPERTY

Crimes against property accounted for 12.24 percent of the total number of events and 14.82 percent of consumed time to which patrol units were dispatched in the period this investigation covered. Dispatches in the categories of Administration, Social Service, and Patrolman Initiated-Events all exceeded the category of Crimes Against Property in frequency.

The role of the patrolman comes into focus with an analysis of the complaints pertaining to Crimes Against Property.

Space limitation will restrict my comments to the most significant findings of this research.

Burglary and Burglary Alarms. The Communications Section dispatched patrol units 28,164 times to complaints of burglary and burglary alarms. These dispatches accounted for more than three times the 9,122 "actual offenses" reported in the Baywood Annual Report.

Many of the burglary alarms are false and the complaints of burglary turn out to be a lesser offense such as larceny or trespassing or in fact no burglary at all. The conclusion to draw is that the police are literally spending a great deal of their effort on other than actual offenses.

Burglar Alarms. Correspondence from the Los Angeles Police Department to the Baywood Department included this paragraph. "A recent departmental survey indicated that in excess of 90% of all alarm calls are false and that automatic dialing units have a slightly higher false alarm factor."

Richmond, California, a city of about 80,000 population, had a similar experience with false alarms. This small community averaged almost five (4.8) false burglary alarms every day. The total for 1967 was 1,784 false alarms.

Baywood police have made several surveys of false alarms. However, their data was obtained from the commercial alarm companies in two of the three surveys, and it may be biased toward fewer false alarms.

a. One alarm company stated that over a three month period, from July 1 to October 10, 1966 there were 628 alarms and that 574, or 91 percent, were false alarms.

b. During the month of September 1966, another company reported 22 of 27 alarms, or 82 percent, were false.

c. The Baywood Police Communications Section surveyed 123 alarms during the period of March 2 to March 13, 1966. Their findings for this 12 day period included 2 valid alarms, 121 false alarms, and one arrest. This amounts to 98 percent false alarms as surveyed by the police.

The President's Commission on Law Enforcement and the Administration of Justice reported that in Washington, D.C. in 1965, 4,450 alarms were directed to the police, and 98 percent of these were false. "Since answering each false alarm takes about 30 minutes, these alarms consume about 2,100 car-hours each year."

The frequency of primary dispatches for burglary alarms in Baywood was 8,632 with a back-up frequency of 6,520. This totals 15,152. The total number of patrol unit hours consumed is 4,704.49 hours. If 95 percent, and this appears to be a reasonable figure, of these alarms are false, then 14,394 dispatches of patrolmen, including the cost of man hours, equipment, and hazards in responding to an emergency are open to serious re-evaluation.

The possibility that an average of almost 40 emergency vehicles are dispatched every 24 hour period in response to false alarms is an emergency in itself. A survey may show that a relatively small group of alarm locations may be contributing to a large percentage of false alarms.

Auto Theft. Patrolmen were dispatched to 5,401 reported stolen car cases during the 54 week study period which is .94 percent of total assignments. Total patrol unit time amounted to 3,694 hours and averaged 39 minutes per dispatch. There is a disparity of more than 2,000 auto theft cases between dispatches by the Communications Section and the 2,737 "actual offenses."

Many of the reported auto thefts are solved at the scene by the patrolman who asks the complainant three questions.

1. Could the car have been repossessed because of nonpayment of car payments?

2. Was the car loaned to anyone?

3. Could a relative or a friend have taken it and failed to notify you?

A patrol lieutenant said that citizens often "lose" their cars because they forget where they parked them, members of the family or friends have borrowed the car, or they will report a car missing after work only to remember later that they did not drive their car to work.

Petty Theft. Shoplifting is the major petty theft offense to which the police are dispatched. An event termed "citizen holding a prisoner" also refers to shoplifting. Patrols were dispatched 13,983 times to complaints of petty theft and 534 times to "citizen holding prisoner." 9,637 patrol hours were spent on these events.

Major department stores employ private police. The procedure is for the private policemen to watch a suspected shoplifter leave the store without paying for merchandise in his possession. The private policeman then apprehends the suspect and takes one of two courses of action. Either he holds the individual under a citizen's arrest until the arrival of the Baywood patrol, or else he releases the suspect after the suspect surrenders the merchandise and signs a statement relieving the store of all charges of false arrest.

During a six week period from November 21, 1966 to January 1, 1967 there were 391 shoplifting arrests made. The police accounted for only 69 of these arrests. Store detectives and private police arrested the other 322 suspects. Shoplifting arrests greatly improve the police "clearance rate" since almost all complaints made to the police result in clearance by arrest.

Defrauding a Cab Driver, Defrauding an Inn Keeper. On the average of about once a night, the Communications Section receives a complaint from a cab driver saying that someone is trying to defraud him. About half as often a complaint is received from a hotel, motel, restaurant, or flophouse because someone refuses to pay his bill. These two relatively minor offenses occurred a total of 491 times and consumed 253.27 hours of patrol time. The calls averaged about 30 minutes each.

Malicious Mischief. The police receive a large number of calls complaining of malicious mischief. Generally, they are not serious and consist of anything from kicking over a garbage can to breaking a window.

Patrols were dispatched 7,150 times on complaints of malicious mischief.

The public schools, street lights, and transit systems are major targets of vandalism in Baywood. Private property is also damaged by vandals. There is no reliable information available regarding the suspects, but young people are believed to be mainly responsible. There are very few arrests made for malicious mischief.

Suspicious Persons. "The police are as close as your telephone," the Baywood citizens are told. As a result, the police received 7,331 complaints about prowlers, suspicious persons, "someone breaking in," etc. How many of these complaints are valid is hard to judge. Was the prowler frightened off by the telephone call or the arrival of the police? Were the suspicious occupants of a car merely a young neighbor and her boyfriend saying goodnight? Was the report of someone breaking in actually the report of a tree branch striking the house?

The police have a heavy sense of obligation to the citizen on this type of complaint. It is one of the few opportunities that the police have to provide a beneficial service "of a police nature" to the citizen. The policeman is not citing, arresting, directing, or questioning the citizen, and it is police work, not social work in this case. The policeman knows that if he handles the complaint well, the citizen will hold him in high esteem. Over half of these dispatches have assist or back-up patrols, but they are of shorter duration than most other dispatches.

Bad Checks. Patrolmen were dispatched 2,007 times for forgery and counterfeiting, and this essentially means bad checks. Each event averaged about 48 minutes. Although bad checks constitute only .13 percent of the total consumed time dealt with in this study, the 1,159 hours nevertheless account for 144 eight-hour days.

The victim's interest is in financial recovery alone, and he uses the police as a collection agency, as a threat to effect reimbursement or cause embarrassment.

The citizen could be saved millions of dollars annually in police costs by shifting to the banks, grocers, and other merchants the responsibility for the bad check problem. The banking and retail industries should explore ways and means of taking this problem away from the police and returning it to the private sector, where it properly belongs in a free-enterprise system.

The Institute for the Study of Crime and Delinquency claims the cost of bad check offenses in California to business and government combined is prob-

ably over 200 million dollars per year, and nearly 2 1/2 billion dollars nation-
ally. Most fraudulent check violations are committed by check writers with
"not sufficient funds." A California survey revealed that false signature checks
comprised only $8,000 of $112,076 fraudulent checks.

Even more significant is the fact that about nine percent of California's
prison population is made up of bad check offenders. A large but unknown
number of inmates in the County and City jails are bad check offenders.

TRAFFIC

The most frequent traffic assignments for Baywood patrolmen are responding
to complaints from citizens that their driveway is blocked or someone is parking on their property, automobile accidents and abandoned motor vehicles.

Almost 9,000 assignments were made to patrol units to remove illegally
parked cars from driveways or private property as compared to 46 homicide
assignments. The 10,935 abandoned vehicle assignments are more than twice
as many as the robbery dispatches. The primary and cover dispatches for automobile accidents total 18,112—this is more than three times the 5,234 assignments made for assault and battery.

Traffic assignments amounted to 7.16 percent of the total and 9.20 percent
of the consumed time.

Accidents. Patrols are dispatched on an average of 50 times a day to investigate automobile accidents. The policy of the Baywood Police Department is
that all reported traffic accidents occurring on public streets within the city
shall be investigated and recorded on the prescribed report forms.

Accident investigations are time-consuming events. Accidents alone account for more than 5 percent of the total consumed time of all patrol activities.

Abandoned Vehicles. The efficiency of the abandoned car program is accomplished at the expense of the other patrol operations. It is essentially an
administrative function that consumed 2,339.59 hours of patrol dispatch time.
There were 10,935 occasions when a patrol car was dispatched for this event,
and the number of abandoned vehicles involved was probably less than half
that number.

PATROLMAN-INITIATED ASSIGNMENTS

The patrolmen mobilized themselves 117,853 times, or 20.6 percent of the total
599,211 events. Citizens or police headquarters initiated the rest of the patrol
dispatches. This, of course, does not include patrolman-initiated events such as
meals, rest stops, and reporting to headquarters which are included under the
section on Administration Activities. Only 9.37 percent of the total consumed
time of all dispatches was spent on these patrolman-initiated events.
Patrolman-initiated time totaled 27,400 hours out of a total of 292,420 consumed hours.

Black and Reiss have written an exceptionally clear description of
"mobilization of police" and their conclusions are strongly supported by the
findings made in this study. When they state that the police are actually

mobilized more often by the action of private citizens and police headquarters than by patrol initiative, they are correct.

There is a dilemma in Baywood between citizens' demands for service and the police-initiated or preventive patrols. For several years the police have been telling the citizen about the rise in crime and encouraging the citizens to call for police service.

The result is that the citizen, by taking the police too literally, imposes such a workload on the patrols that police-initiated or preventive patrols are reduced. The patrol personnel complain because they do not have enough time for patrolman-initiated activity. They claim that the demand for service by the citizen is so great that they are too restricted to perform what they call preventive patrol.

A patrol sergeant said the police are "order takers." He arrived at this term simply on the basis that the police spend almost all of their time, according to him, responding to service calls, writing their reports, and submitting their reports to police headquarters.

The patrolman has much more discretion in self-initiated activity than he has in events initiated by the citizens or headquarters. The officer is monitored when he is dispatched in response to a citizen's complaint, both by the citizen and by his superiors through a report. Self-mobilized events, such as on-view situations, have low visibility, and the officer has obviously greater latitude in his actions. He can choose the event, and if it is contact with a citizen, he can choose the citizen with whom he will make contact. Arrests and reporting are also discretionary elements in the police-initiated type of event.

The Baywood patrolman takes the initiative in mobilizing himself for six different types of events, which are:

1. On-View. This code includes those violations of law and other acts which the patrolman observes and which he decides he must investigate or act upon.

2. Walk stop. The stopping and questioning of individuals on foot who arouse the suspicions of the patrolman by their dress, appearance, or actions.

3. Car stop. This includes parked vehicles, both occupied and unattended as well as moving vehicles. Vehicles and passengers that arouse any suspicion by their appearance or actions are checked by the patrolman.

4. Security check. The patrolman checks a commercial establishment to make certain it is secure.

5. Autostatis (Automated Statewide Auto Theft Inquiry System). In Baywood it is known as a "rolling stop" and is a check of vehicle registration against a statewide file of stolen and suspicious vehicles.

6. Warrant check through a Police Information Network. This involves the stopping of a vehicle in hope of apprehending individuals with outstanding warrants. The warrant information is computerized and contains outstanding warrant data from a six county area.

These activities except for the security check do the least good for the community and produce tremendous hostility.

SOCIAL SERVICES

Social services is a natural category into which more than 17 percent of the total dispatches—both primary and cover could comfortably be accommodated. Over 13 percent of the total time consumed by all primary and cover dispatches was spent on events in the social services category.

Events that did not meet the general criteria of crimes against persons, crimes against property, patrolmen-initiated activity, traffic, or administration were considered for the social service group.

Social service includes family crisis, incidents involving drunkenness, suicide, and mental illness, ambulance service, and public nuisances, etc.

Family Crisis. "Social surgery" is the term James M. Slavin, former Chief of Police of Denver, Colorado used in reference to the police role in family crisis. He claimed that "65 percent of all aggravated assaults, which occur more frequently than murder, rape, and robbery combined take place in the privacy of the home."

Drunkenness. Baywood police made 15,590 arrests for drunkenness in 1967. Total arrests for all offenses other than traffic were 34,362. Drunkenness constituted 45.3 percent of all arrests. There was an average of 42 persons arrested every day in Baywood for being drunk.

Startling as these figures are, a special study revealed that two-thirds (66.4) of the arrests for drunkenness involved citizens who were arrested two or more times for that offense. Specifically, 2,537 individuals accounted for 10,361 of the arrests for drunkenness.

Mental Illness. The 1,676 calls for police assistance in handling mental illness cases was 255 more than the 1,421 actual robbery offenses.

The author of a recently published book on the subject of Community Relations and Riot Prevention states, "One might ask why the policeman should be concerned, for the primary responsibilities of the police do not include the solving of sociological problems." This is consistent with the general theme of most police officers which is, "We're not social workers, we're law enforcement officers."

It is unfortunate for the country that the police are imbued with this totally wrong perception of themselves. The police do perform social work. In fact, they perform more social work than they perform law enforcement. Regretfully, as social workers, most police are poorly trained and incompetent.

ADMINISTRATION ACTIVITIES

"What do patrolmen do?" The answer to this question is that they spend more than 50 percent of their time on administrative tasks. Traffic, police-initiated events, social service, and crimes against property account for about 47 percent of their time. Less than three (3) percent of the Baywood patrolman's time is spent on dispatches concerning crimes against persons.

The events that have been classified under the heading of administration include such items as coffee breaks, meals, community relations, taking reports, running errands, attending court, serving warrants, and performing as police technicians.

There are several other time-consuming tasks that were assigned to other categories that could very easily be placed in the category of administration. For example, in crimes against persons and crimes against property, the patrolman functions as an "order taker." It is very seldom that a patrolman will be dispatched and arrive at the crime scene while the crime is in progress.

In some cases such as larceny and burglary and even in some crimes against persons such as assault, the citizen may not notify the police for several hours or days after the event. Bad check cases may be 45 days old before the citizen requests a patrolman to write up the complaint. The spotting and towing away of abandoned vehicles is an excellent example of a purely administrative task.

SUMMARY

Police departments are about the most poorly managed organizations in our society. No business—government or private—could survive very long without knowledge of the functions it performs. The only record of activities most departments maintain is the FBI Uniform Crime Report of the seven index crimes, and the police come to perceive themselves as crime fighters when in fact the police are more social worker and administrator than crime fighter . . .

Kinsmen in Repose:
Occupational Perspectives
of Patrolmen

John Van Maanen

The people on the street would miss us if we weren't there. I mean they expect us out there and we're part of the whole scene too. That's what everybody seems to miss. We've got a say in what goes on in the streets. You just can't give an honest picture of what happens in society without talking about what the cop on the street does.

A patrolman[1]

INTRODUCTION

In the midst of derogatory epithets, laudatory salutations and apathetic silent-American acquiescence, the "man" acts out a curious societal role. To some, a policeman is a "fucking pig," a mindless brute working for a morally bankrupt institution. To others, a policeman is a courageous public servant, a defender of life and property, regulating city life along democratic lines. To most, a policeman is merely an everyday cultural stimulus, tolerated, avoided and ignored unless non-routine situational circumstances deem otherwise. Yet, virtually all persons in this society can recognize a policeman, have some conception of what it is he does, and, if asked, can share a few "cop stories" with an interested listener.

Fundamentally, a police officer represents the most visible aspect of the body politic and is that aspect most likely to intervene directly in the daily lives of the citizenry. If one considers the President to be the "head" of the political system, then the patrolman on the street must be considered the "tail." The critical and symbolic nature of the police role in society is perhaps best illustrated by a number of child socialization studies indicating that it is the head *and* tail of a political system which are its most salient aspects—the features most likely to be learned first as a child develops an awareness of his surrounding environment (Hyman, 1959; Almond and Verba, 1963; Easton and Dennis, 1969, 1967).

Given this rather visible position in society, it is somewhat surprising that social scientists have, until recently, largely ignored the police. In particular, little research has been devoted to the everyday standards of police behavior. The few studies we do have tend to confirm an occupational stereotype of the police as a conservative, defiled, isolated and homogenous grouping of men bound together perceptually through a common mission (Rubenstein, 1973;

---

[1]All police quotes unless otherwise stated are taken from my field study in Union City (see Epilogue for a full account of the methods followed—eds.). Following a research agreement, Union City is a pseudonym for a sprawling metropolitan area populated by well over a million persons. The police department employs more than 1,500 uniformed officers, has a traditional training program, and provides a salary above the national average (footnotes renumbered—eds.).

REPRINTED FROM: John Van Maanen, Working the Street: A Developmental View of Police Behavior. In H. Jacob (ed.) *The Potential for Reform of Criminal Justice* Volume III, Sage Criminal Justice System Annuals. Beverly Hills, California: Sage, 1974 (83–84, 87, 100–110).

Reiss, 1971; Wilson, 1969; Neiderhoffer, 1967; Skolnick, 1966). . . . Yet, what is of interest here is the recognition by the police of the implied differences between themselves and the rest of society. According to one knowledgeable observer, a former Chief of Police:

> The day the new recruit walks through the doors of the police academy he leaves society behind to enter a profession that does more than give him a job, it defines who he is. For all the years he remains, closed into the sphere of its rituals . . . he will be a cop. (Ahern, 1972:3)

Policemen generally view themselves as performing society's dirty work. Consequently, a gap is created between the police and the public. Today's patrolman feels cut off from the mainstream culture and stigmatized unfairly. In the percussive words of one young patrolman:

> I'll tell ya, as long as we're the only sonfabitches that have to handle ripe bodies that have been dead for nine days in a ninety degree room or handle skid row drunks who've been crapping in their pants for 24 hours or try to stop some prick from jump'en off the Liberty Bridge or have to grease some societal misfit who's trying to blow your goddamn head off, then we'll never be like anyone else . . . as far as I can see, no one else is ever gonna want to do that shit. But somebody's gotta do it and I guess it'll always be the police. But hell, this is the only profession where ya gotta wash your hands before you take a piss!

In short, when a policeman dons his uniform, he enters a distinct subculture governed by norms and values designed to manage the strains created by his unique role in the community. From the public point of view, a policeman is usually treated as a faceless, nameless "Rorschach-in-blue" with persons responding either favorably or unfavorably according to ideological predisposition or situational imperative. Yet, a policeman's response to the cornucopia of civilian manners and mores follows a somewhat more orderly and acquired pattern. Thus, policemen learn—in particular, patrolmen—characteristic ways of conducting themselves on the street, devices for organizing work routines about their perceived areas of responsibility, and methods of managing their own careers vis-à-vis the police department. . . .

OCCUPATIONAL PERSPECTIVES

Workers in all occupations develop ways and means by which they manage certain structural strains, contradictions and anomalies of their prescribed role and task. In police work, with danger, drudgery and dogma as prime occupational characteristics, these tensions are extreme. Correspondingly, the pressure on new members to bow to group standards is intense. Few, if any, pass through the socialization cycle without being persuaded—through their own experiences and the sage-like wisdom passed from generation to generation of policemen—to accept the occupational accepted frame-of-reference (see Part V—eds.). This frame-of-reference includes, of course, both broad axioms related to police work in general (role) and the more specific corollaries which provide the ground rules of the workaday world (operations). In this paper, the label "occupational perspectives" is affixed to the former. It is intended merely to imply that my concern is with the wider, institutional view of policing shared by patrolmen rather than explicit "how-to" work prescriptions. . . . Thus, the focus is upon the characteristic view patrolmen eventually come to hold regarding their organizational and occupational milieu—using a dramaturgic metaphor, the "backstage" views of police. Occupational perspectives represent the solution to what Schein (1961) has suggested is the critical problem of organizational socialization, namely, "coping with the emotional reality of the job." In the police world, these perspectives provide the perceptual filter through which a patrolman views his work life. In a sense, they provide him with something akin to an occupational ideology. Such an ideology—rooted in common experience and knowledge—serves to support and maintain the codes, agreements and habits existing in the work place.

Two distinct occupational perspectives are crucial for our understanding of patrolmen. Together' they form a definitive credo which shapes the personal identity of policemen and regulates the pace, style, and direction of "on-the-street" police behavior. The first perspective grows from the patrolman's unique role in the social world and concerns his "outsider" position in the community. The second perspective develops from the nature of the patrolman's task requirements and deals with the survival dictums of his occupation.

THE OUTSIDER: SEPARATE AND APART

A young patrolman soon learns that in uniform he is a very special sort of person. Not only does he have a low visibility vis-à-vis his superiors, but he has a monopolistic grip on the legal application of force. Amplifying this societal trust is the awesome responsibility of deciding virtually on his own and in sometimes terrible situations when to and when not to exercise this force. This feature alone places him in a solitary and somber position compared to the rest of society. Certainly there are legal and administrative guidelines set up which presumably govern his actions. Yet, in by far the majority of cases in which his right to force and violence may be utilized, the decision must be made in the emotional fever of fear or anger, the immediacy of danger, and in the flicker of an instant. In these powerful and dark moments there is not time to ponder the alternatives. Such is the ultimate responsibility of a patrolman.[2]

Of course, situations of the extreme are rare. Some officers progress through their entire career without once having to draw their weapons or physically subdue an obstinate suspect. But among those who spend their days on the street, they are few. Uncommon indeed are those officers who have not come within a hairbreadth of "squeezing-off-a-round" or who have not been

---

[2]One of the standing jokes among police officers is that they were taught at the academy—from the department's point of view—that they had little discretion on the street. According to their classroom instructors hard and fast guidelines cover all police actions. Yet, as they discovered quickly on the street—indeed knew instinctively at the academy—police rules and regulations offer few solutions to the intricate, dynamic, and specific situations in which patrolmen become involved.

through the bruising give-and-take of street battle. For most, these experiences are the defining characteristics of their occupation and it distinguishes them from other gentler ways of life.

While it would be a mistake to view police work from this danger aspect only, the symbolic importance of this feature cannot be underestimated. In large measure, these experiences (and their not infrequent retelling) set the tone for patrol work. As one young patrolman who had been on the street for several years explained:

> Most of the time this job is boring as can be. You just sit behind the wheel and go where they tell you. When you're not bullshitting with your partner, your mind kinda wanders and some nights it's a bitch to stay awake. . . . But somehow you never forget that the next call you get or car you stop might be your last. Mentally that's hard to accept but it's real. . . . You know there's one hell of a lotta people out there who'd love to off a cop. I've gotten over that pretty much by now because you just gotta live with it. If anybody wants to kill you, there's no way you could ever stop 'em. . . . But what really gets you is that whoever it was probably wouldn't even know your name, he'd just be out to kill some cop. To the people out there we're just faceless blue suits. You sure begin to wonder what kind of crazy bastard you are for getting into this job in the first place.

The danger inherent in police work is part of the centripetal force pulling patrolmen together as well as contributing to their role as strangers to the general public. Importantly, however, the risks of policing also provide real psychological satisfaction to men who spend most of their time performing activities of the more mundane or routine variety (for example, report taking, service calls, preventive patrolling, and so on). Without danger as an omnipresent quality of the work setting, patrolmen would have little of the visceral pleasures that contribute to their evaluation of performing difficult, important, and challenging (if unappreciated) tasks.

The "outsider" perspective arises as well from the unforgettably indifferent or antagonistic manner in which he is treated by the public. The rookie painfully discovers that wherever he is to go, his presence is bound to generate anxiety. People stare at him and scrutinize his movements. While driving through his sector, he finds that a major problem is avoiding accidents caused from the almost neurotic fashion in which other drivers react to his perceptually nefarious squad car. Soon he appreciates the relatively few places where he receives a warm and friendly welcome. All-night diners, hospitals, fire stations, certain niches in the courthouse, the precinct locker room, and even a private recess where a patrolman may park his squad car unnoticed become havens from his totem-like existence, providing him an opportunity to relax (Rubenstein, 1973).

In general, there is little to link patrolmen to the private citizen in terms of establishing a socially satisfying relationship. Small businessmen have perhaps something to gain in terms of the protection a rapid response might provide. However, businessmen know that there is little likelihood that the patrolman they are friendly with today will respond to a call for help tomorrow.

Similarly, patrolmen recognize accurately that few civilians are likely to return favors. For mutual concern and friendship to develop, some sort of exchange relationship must be sustained—the *quid pro quo* of Homans (1950). In the police world, patrolmen rarely see the same people twice unless the contact is of the adversary variety. And such encounters are not apt to prove rewarding to the patrolman regarding the development of friendships.[3]

Thus, it is a lonely, largely friendless world the patrolman faces. The only assistance and understanding he can expect comes solely from his brother officers who, as the police enjoy saying, have "been there." In light of his public receptivity, it should not be surprising that policemen in general have assumed many of the characteristics of other stigmatized groupings.[4]

I have suggested elsewhere that the rules and regulations of police work are so numerous and immobilizing that from the patrolman's point of view, no one could ever obey all of them (Van Maanen, 1973). In effect, this implies that police officers, to be protected from their own infractions, must protect others. While rule violations run from the trivial to the serious, no officer is free from the knowledge that in his past (and no doubt in his future) are certain acts which, if reported, could cost him his job and perhaps even his freedom. From a failure to clear with his dispatcher for lunch to perjury on the witness stand, police must live each day with the knowledge that it is the support of their brother officers that insures their continuance on the job. Thus, it is his colleagues who represent the only group to whom the patrolman can relate. As one patrol veteran suggested:

> How the fuck can I tell anyone who ain't a cop that I lie a little in court or that sometimes I won't do shit on the street 'cause I'm tired or that I made some asshole 'cause he was just all out wrong. If I told people that they'd think that I'm nothing but a turd in uniform. The only people that can understand are people who've had to pull the same shit . . . and there just ain't nobody in this department, from the Chief on down, who hasn't pulled some tricks in their time on the street.

When this officer speaks of "tricks" there are, of course, important matters of degree involved. Nevertheless, the point remains that all officers are indebted heavily to their patrol colleagues. In the last analysis, it is this two-way obligation which forms the basis of a relationship which can never be approximated with persons from the non-police world.

These features along with the more salient aspects of the occupation—the

---

[3]Whyte (1943) first noted the dilemma in which street officers are caught. If the officer takes a formal, no-discretion, duty-only position in his sector, he cuts himself off from the personal relationships necessary to receive information or settle disputes in the area. On the other hand, if he becomes close and involved in the personal affairs of his sector, he must necessarily utilize much discretion and is unable to act vigorously in situations which may demand such action. While the use of the automobile for patrol purposes has sealed off most officers in a sort of urban spaceship (with few contacts in their sectors), it is clear that discretion still occupies a central place in the day-to-day environment of patrolmen and cannot be kept in the *sub rosa* position of being a simple management control issue.

[4]See Goffman (1963) for a theoretical treatment of stigmatization.

shift work, the uniform, the 24-hour nature of occupational responsibility, and so on—provide a perspective on the world which will last for as long as the patrolman remains with the department.[5] Behaviorally, all outsider groupings tend toward isolationism, secrecy, strong in-group loyalties, sacred symbols, common language, and a profound sense of estrangement from the larger society. It is these subcultural properties which underpin the common understanding among police that they are different.

The cynicism popularly attributed to police officers can, in part, be located in the unique and peculiar role police are required to play. Treated shabbily, hated, or feared by many of the contacts they have, police are asked frequently to arbitrate messy and uncertain citizen disputes. In such disputes, all concerned generally construct a particular account which exonerates them from blame. After a few years on the street, there are few accounts patrolmen have not heard. Hence, whether a claim is outrageous or plausible, police react by believing nothing and distrusting everything at the same time. Only one's colleagues can understand and appreciate such skepticism.

The hardness commonly thought to be the mask of many policemen arises to fend off the perceived curse of doing society's dirty work. To be a sponge, absorbing the misery and degradation that pass daily through a patrolman's life, is an untenable position which would soon drive one from the police midst were it accepted. Therefore the proverbial "shell" is constructed, which protects the patrolman from the effects of nasty encounters which would leave most persons visibly shaken. But in the patrol world such coldness becomes almost a legendary personal property. To wit, one inexperienced patrolman related the following story:

> Man that Sergeant Kelly is something. . . . Remember the night that David Squad nailed that shithead coming out of Mission Liquor Store? Blew him up with a couple of rifle slugs and the guy's brains were splattered all over the sidewalk. You couldn't even tell if the dude was white or black 'cause of blood he was swimming in. Anyway we're standing there waiting for the coroner to show, when Sergeant Kelly decides it's time to eat. So what does he do? He goes back to his unit, grabs his brown bag and proceeds to come back and start chowing down on an egg sandwich. Jesus! You shoulda seen the face on the kid working in the liquor store.

Only the police could understand the hardness implied in such stories. While many sordid tales are no doubt organizational fictions, they serve to denote the peculiar attributes of the police occupational code and also serve to detach patrolmen from the more polite social world of their origin.

In essence, the "outsider" perspective crystallizes the patrolman's occupational identity. It sets him off from others and provides an anchor to which he

---

[5]Police officers are legally bound to take action off-duty in the presence of a felony offense and can, in fact, be fired for a failure to do so. Few patrolmen go anywhere off-duty without first arming themselves—whether it be to the corner market, out "on-the-town," or to play golf. While the "off-duty" gun is more symbolic than functional, it is but another factor isolating patrolmen from the mainstream of social life.

attaches his interpersonal relationships. Since the private interests and concerns of one are the interests and concerns of most others in the patrol setting (for example, avoiding injury and disciplinary action, displaying the proper amount of commitment and aggressiveness on the street, developing "pat" testimony for courtroom use, and so on), they form a common source of appeal and support. This can be summarized neatly by referring to a bond of sympathetic understanding existing among the police.[6] As one officer remarked succinctly:

> To most people we seem to be inhuman, somehow separate and apart. Almost like another species. Maybe they're right but I'll tell you, I'd trust even my worst enemy in this department before I'd trust the people out there.

SURVIVAL: LAY LOW AND AVOID TROUBLE

Although police know that the unanticipated and nonroutine event may occur at any moment, they nonetheless have firm expectations about what work will consist of on any given shift.[7] An experienced officer establishes therefore his own tempo and style of work. Like any occupation, patrol work falls into set patterns: take a burglary report, meet complainant, interview victim, investigate open door, direct traffic, and so on. The discovery of certain organizing devices by which to categorize the myriad of work duties is a major task for young officers and—as with the perspective developed in response to their perceived déclassé social position—follows the socialization paradigm as one learns what it is like to work the streets.

Importantly, the young officer learns that there is a subtle but critical difference between "real" police work and most of what he does on patrol. "Real" police work is, in essence, his *raison d'être*. It is that part of his job that comes closest to the romantic notions of police work he possessed before attending the Police Academy. In short, "real" police work calls for a patrolman to exercise his perceived occupational expertise: to make an arrest, save a life, quell a dispute, prevent a robbery, catch a felon, stop a suspicious person, disarm a suspect, and so on. "Real" police work involves the "hot" call, the unusual "on view" felony situation, or the potentially dangerous "back-up" predicament in which an officer may have to assist a threatened colleague.[8] During such en-

---

[6]Certainly this bond is strongest among members of a particular squad. But it exists to some degree among all police officers. To wit, the unwritten code of never ticketing or arresting another police officer regardless of where he may be from unless the offense is very serious indeed.

[7]Officers soon learn that there are quiet Sundays, busy Fridays, and crazy Saturdays. There are those days when welfare or unemployment checks are distributed and certain sectors seem to be considerably faster than usual—drunk and disorderly calls, family fights, muggings, and so on. Of course, there are also those ubiquitous evenings of the full moon when, as one officer put it, "those demons wreck havoc until the sun rises." Whether or not such perceptions are backed by statistical evidence does not matter for most officers nonetheless have firm expectations of public conduct fixed in their minds. And, to paraphrase W. I. Thomas's famous dictum, a man's actions are attributable to his perceptions of reality and not to reality *per se*.

counters all the contradictions and humiliations that accompany most of what the patrolman does evaporate as he, for example, pursues someone he believes to have committed a crime or defends his fellow-officers (and himself) in the chaos of a tavern brawl. Yet, because of this narrow definition of police work, little of his time on the street provides the opportunity to accomplish much of what he considers to be his primary function. Thus, "real" police work to the patrolman is paradoxical; a source of satisfaction and frustration.[9]

At another level, one can divide the patrolman's dispatched (radio) calls into a rush, non-rush dichotomy. Rush calls are those involving "real" police work. Statistically, however, non-rush calls are much more common.[10] The decision to rush is, of course, a learned one, developed as a patrolman learns his territory and gains knowledge of the patrol lexicon. There is not a universal code for rush calls. They are dependent upon the dispatcher's choice of words, the time, the place, the particular unit receiving the call, and perhaps even the mood of the officer. For example, to some officers a 220 (in Union City, a so-called "dangerous mental case") represents a call demanding lightning speed; to others it is treated simply as a "normal" call and handled without undue rush or concern. Only those situations calling for "real" police work are treated seriously by all officers.

The "back-up" responsibilities of patrolmen present an interesting amendment to the limited definition of "real" police work. Back-ups are those situations—dispatched or not—in which one patrol unit will proceed to a particular sector location to assist, if necessary, the patrol unit which has been assigned to the call. Certainly, most of the time back-ups amount to simply sitting in the squad car waiting to be waived off by the other unit; yet, the symbolic importance of back-ups cannot be dismissed.

There are several classes of dispatched calls which almost automatically guarantee the presence of a back-up, providing the sector work distribution at the moment is not overloaded. For example, the "help the officer" call is treated most seriously. Almost always such calls result in the rapid appearance of all officers in the district. In another class, less critical yet nonetheless sure to receive at least one back-up, are calls such as the felony-in-progress or man-with-gun. Other calls, such as the bar disturbance or the family fight in the ghetto neighborhood, also generate *pro forma* back-up units. To a large degree these back-up situations help young officers establish their street creden-

---

[8]In most ways the popular notion of "street crime" is a misnomer. The vast majority of crime takes place inside buildings, in entranceways, in alleys, in the dark and silent public parks, in living rooms of private homes, and so on. Policemen know this and their expectations of catching a criminal "in-the-act" are consequently quite low. Thus, they wait patiently for the serendipitous "on-view" situation to arise if, in fact, it ever will.

[9]It is interesting to note that I rode with many officers who claimed—when relaxing after a busy shift answering some ten calls or so, handling several traffic stops, assisting a few citizens and driving fifty to seventy miles in and out of their respective sectors—that the night had been a "total waste" since they had not accomplished any "real" police work.

[10]See Webster (1970) and Reiss (1971).

tials as squad members in good standing. Patrolmen note the presence (or absence) of their peers as well as the speed with which they arrived. Such behavior demonstrates to all present the mutual concern and loyalty police feel they must have for one another. It is also the measure of one's commitment and motivation to share the risks involved in working the street. In the police world, such behavior is not overlooked. One officer suggested pointedly:

> I'll put up with a hell of a lot from guys working this sector. I don't care if they're on the take, mean or just don't do anymore than they have to. . . . But if some sonfabitch isn't around on a help-the-officer call or shows up after everybody else in the city has already been there, I don't want him working around me. Those cops are dangerous.

In Union City, as in all large city departments, the work of patrolmen is difficult, if not impossible, to evaluate. There are the required annual patrolman performance ratings submitted by the sergeants, but these are essentially hollow paper exercises in which few men receive low marks. The real task of evaluating patrolmen falls on the squad sergeant, and he is most concerned with the "activity" of his men.[11] However, activity is judged differently by sergeants. The same activity that is appreciated and perhaps demanded by one sergeant is treated indifferently by another sergeant. For example, one patrolman who had worked the same sector under several sergeants noted:

> Now you take Sergeant Johnson. He was a drunk hunter. That guy wanted all the drunks off the street and you knew that if you brought in a couple of drunks in a week, you and he would get along just fine. Sergeant Moss now is a different cat. He don't give a rat's ass about drunks. What he wants are those vice pinches. Sergeant Gordon wanted tickets and he'd hound your ass for a ticket a night. So you see it all depends on who you're working for, each guy is a little different.

To patrolmen, such idiosyncratic policies, while sometimes difficult to understand, provide a margin of safety in what can be a very uncertain work environment. By satisfying the sergeant's rather unambiguous demands (tickets, drunks, vice, juveniles, field investigation reports, and so on) a man can insure a harmonious relationship with the department.[12] If he provides the activity his sergeant desires, he will be left alone to do his work. If not, he may

---

[11]I am indebted to Rubenstein (1973) for coining the term "activity." However, in Philadelphia, where Rubenstein's work was done, activity had a specific referent in that it applied to the number of vice arrests a patrolman made. In Union City, no such departmentwide focus existed. Each sergeant was more or less free to emphasize whatever activity he individually felt important, hence, activity is used here in a much broader fashion.

[12]These demands are probably most important when a man is new to the squad. If the man responds, the sergeant will slack off, only occasionally suggesting activity to the man. Usually, a casual remark by the sergeant is enough to promote action among the newcomers. The ease or difficulty with which veteran officers respond to a sergeant's wishes is, however, another matter and considerably more complicated and problematic (to the sergeant).

find himself working his days off or transferred to another, less desirable sector. To the men, these activity guidelines are received with some grumbling. But, in the main, they are acknowledged as simply a fact of work life. Furthermore, they are, to some degree, valued as the lodestar of their day-to-day work activities. Patrolmen realize, of course, that these activity measures have little to do with "real" police work. Yet, when one's patrol log contains evidence of activity for the sergeant, a patrolman is provided with a certain degree of comfort as well as the gratification that follows a job completed successfully.

It is important to recognize, however, that providing one's sergeant with his required activity can be done with relative ease. Whether it is tickets, car stops, drunks, or vice, patrolmen have little trouble and spend little time accomplishing the required task. In fact, most officers in Union City would simply remark sometime during a shift something to the effect of, "well-let's-go-do-our-bit-for-the-sergeant," and proceed to casually make whatever the quota might be. One FTO explained his particular job requirement to his recruit partner in the following manner:

> Here's our little duck pond (a busy but poorly marked intersection in Union City). Just sit here for five minutes and you can write all the tickets Sergeant McCallion wants. Just bag five of those illegal left turners and you're done for the week. Keeps him off your back.

Aside from producing activity for the sergeant and the infrequent opportunities to perform "real" police work, most of the patrolman's work time is dominated by what officers call "staying-out-of trouble." Essentially, this means that the officer will do what is assigned to him and little more. The novice patrolman soon learns that there are few incentives to work hard. He also discovers that the most satisfactory solution to the labyrinth of hierarchy, the red tape, the myriad of rules and regulations, the risks of street work, and unpleasantness which characterize the occupation is to adopt the group standard, stressing a "lay-low-and-don't-make-waves" work ethic. And the best way in which he can stay out of trouble is to minimize the amount of work he pursues.[13]

to leave had just gone back into the house. One patrolman said to the other, "Did you see all those bottles?" The other nodded, the light of recognition in his eyes. He said they has just blown a speak. They knocked on the door again, but it was not reopened. They had three alternatives: to call their sergeant, to break down the door illegally, or to leave without mentioning their error. They left.

---

[13]An example of the distain patrolmen feel toward the "rate-buster" is provided by Whittemore's (1973) romantic account of Batman and Robin, the so-called "supercops" in New York City. These officers met their biggest problem inside, not outside, the department. Most often, this pressure came from their fellow patrolmen who actively resented their aggressive approach. At various points in their early career, both officers were told point blank to "stop making waves and just do what you're supposed to do." Another similar account is found in Maas's (1973) superior biography of Serpico, a New York officer who—aside from his violation of the police code of secrecy in front of the Knapp Commission—was distrusted by his colleagues for his "working ways."

increases the number of citizen contacts an officer may have and, therefore, represents an opportunity to make both serious and banal mistakes. Citizen contacts are always delicate when an officer is on uncertain or merely suspicious grounds. Such encounters are strained interpersonally, troublesome legally, and almost always invite disrespect. In other words, aggressive patrol tactics are bothersome. Since working hard offers few occupational rewards, the logical solution for the patrolman is to organize his activities in such a fashion as to minimize the likelihood of being sanctioned by any of his audiences. The low visibility of the patrolman's role vis-à-vis the department (that is, his sergeant) allows for such a response. Thus the pervasive adjustment is epitomized in the "hang-loose-and-lie-low" advice frequently heard in the Union City department.

Rookies were always accused of what was referred to as a "gung-ho" attitude (rushing to calls and pushing eagerly for action). They were quickly taught, however, the appropriate perspective toward their work.[14] For example, the aggressive patrolman who constantly was seeking out tasks to perform was the butt of community jokes. In fact, many police expressed the sentiment that it was wise to spend as much time off the street as possible for, as they claimed, "you-can-get-in-trouble-out-there." One experienced officer noted:

> Those goddamn rookies are dangerous. I worked with one guy who was so gung ho that every time I got in the car with him I figured I was gonna get killed. This ass used to drive like a bat outta hell just to go to lunch . . . he wanted to always be looking for stolens or stopping everybody on the street. He settled down eventually when he found out that he wasn't getting anything done except make the other cops in the squad laugh.

While staying out of trouble occupies a great deal of the patrolman's working hours, it is to be distinguished sharply from what Rubenstein (1973) calls "loafing." While one may or may not work hard on any given shift, he is always to do his share by covering his district and answering his dispatched calls. Taking a call in another man's sector is occasionally acceptable. However, to do so consistently is personally insulting and considered by all policemen to be unjust. To the squad, answering a call for another indicates that the neglectful officer no longer cares or is committed to his "team," for he will not pull his fair share of the work. Relatedly, an officer who regularly fails to appear as a back-up on a call or arrives well after the potential danger has passed is considered to be either fearful or loafing and will, if possible, be expelled from the squad. The definition of loafing is therefore quite specific. . . .

During a newcomer's first few months on the street he is self-conscious and truly in need of guidelines as to his actions. A whole folklore of tales, myths,

---

[14]This "gung-ho" attitude was a real source of irritation to most veteran officers in Union City. The "gung-ho" patrolmen were thought to be overly aggressive. In police argot, they wore "big-badges." It was felt that their presence in a squad created difficult situations in which other officers would have to assume needless risk untangling. Thus, most officers did not follow a "work-hard" rule. As noted, most learned to sit back and patiently answer their calls, rarely venturing from their squad car unless otherwise directed.

and legends surrounding the department is communicated to the novice by his fellow-officers, conspicuously by his FTO. Through these anecdotes—dealing largely with "mistakes" or "flubs" made by policemen—the recruit begins to adopt the perspectives of his more experienced colleagues. He becomes aware that "nobody's perfect," and the only way in which one can be protected from his own mistakes is to protect others. Among members of a particular squad, this "no rat" rule has deep and meaningful roots. Violations of the rule are met with swift (albeit informal) disapproval.[15] Since all officers have at sometime in their career broken a rule or regulation, the conspiracy-like network of support remains intact. The tacit norm is to never do something which might embarrass another officer. To draw critical attention to a colleague is strictly taboo in the police world. On the other hand, it is acceptable—and often demanded—that one cover for the mistake of another. While citizen complaints are felt to be unavoidable occupational hazards, fellow officers go to great lengths to insure such complaints against one of their squad members will be ruled unfounded.[16] The sergeant plays a critical role in this regard for he screens all reports written by his men. If an account on, for example, an arrest report contains an ambiguous phrase which could possibly be interpreted negatively by the court, or the report fails to mention a detail (factual, or otherwise) which might keep an officer (and, by implication, the squad and the sergeant) out of trouble, he will have the man rewrite the report until it is flawless in his eyes. Let me quote a passage from my field notes for illustrative purposes:

> When Blazier was placed under guard in the hospital (after a rather brutal encounter in which Blazier, a black homosexual, was severely beaten in the back of a patrol wagon), we returned to the precinct station to handle the paperwork. Officer Barns filled out the many reports involved in the incident and passed them to his sergeant for approval. The sergeant carefully read each report and then returned the "paper" to Barns saying that he better claim he was kicked in the face *before* he entered the patrol wagon or Barns would get a heavy brutality complaint for sure. He also told Barns to change the charge on Blazier to felony assault from refusal-to-obey and add drunk-in-public to the disturbing-

---

[15]See Westley (1951) for a more extensive account of just how deep this code runs in police circles.

[16]Complaints, as well as commendations in the police world are viewed somewhat sardonically. To patrolmen, a complaint is more a sign of where an officer works than his particular policing style. For example, if an officer works a central city, black, lower-class sector, complaints are felt to be simply a taken-for-granted feature of life in the area. Reciprocally, citizen letters of commendation will be extremely rare. On the other hand, if a man works a suburban, white middle-class sector commendations will be more frequent and complaints relatively few. Patrolmen know this and therefore assign little importance to either of the two categories. Apparently, the only exception to this rule of unimportance are those extreme cases where an officer may be under investigation as a result of a serious complaint (e.g., a shooting, extreme brutality, a felony, etc.). In such cases, patrolmen, if they are allowed to remain on the street, will act discreetly until the department resolves the complaint. As patrolmen say, "they go hide because they have a big one hanging."

the-peace charge Barns had originally thought appropriate. According to the sergeant, the heavier charges were necessary to protect Barns from IID (Internal Investigation Division). Finally, after some discussion and two re-writes, Barns finished a report which the sergeant said "covered their asses" (February 1973).

This "cover your ass" perspective pervades all of patrol work. In a sense, it represents a sort of bureaucratic paranoia which is all but rampant in police circles. Again, the best way for patrolmen to "cover their ass" is to watch carefully the kind of activities in which they engage. It is best therefore to not take the initiative on the street but rather react primarily to departmental direction. In this way, one seldom becomes involved in those potentially explosive situations which might result in disciplinary action for the patrolman.

The "lay low" occupational perspective also develops as officers gradually discover that the external rewards of a police career are more or less fixed. The patrolman knows for example that he will be at top salary within three years after joining the department. Advancement through the hierarchical network is a realistic expectation to only a few. In Union City, almost eighty percent of the men remain at the patrolman level for the extent of their careers.

At times, patrolmen feel as if the department goes out of its way to make things uncomfortable for them. For instance, Union City patrolmen are not provided parking spaces for their private automobiles and must spend considerable time locating spots on the busy and crowded city streets. Locker room facilities are dirty, cramped, and new officers often wait a year or so before they are assigned a space. The administrative detail in checking certain records or requesting information from one of the detective bureaus is almost prohibitive. An officer must also dig into his own pockets to cover many occupational expenses, such as having his uniforms cleaned or replaced after a duty-related accident. Critically, patrolmen discover that the department answers very few of their requests; for example, assignment shifts, new equipment, car repairs, expense reimbursements, and so on. And when the organization does act, it is usually after a long delay.

In response to their situation, patrolmen assume a "don't-expect-much" stance. They begin to realize that it is the rewards of camaraderie and small favors granted to them by their sergeant that makes their daily task either pleasant or intolerable. A few extra days off, a good partner, enjoyable squad parties, an agreeable assignment, or an extra long lunch become important rewards offered by a police career. It would appear consequently that the following advice given me by an older street veteran in Union City represents a very astute analysis of the patrolman's work role. He suggested cryptically:

> . . . You gotta learn to take it easy. The department don't care about you and the public sure as hell ain't gonna cry over the fact that the patrolman always gets the shit end of the stick. The only people who do care are your brother officers. So just lay back and take it easy out here. Makes things a lot smoother for us as well as yourself.

The survival perspective is strengthened finally by the fact that patrol work prepares one for very few other occupations in this society. The knowledge and skill involved in working the street (and these are considerable) have meaning and value only in the police world. Thus, the only alternative a man has to his patrolman position is to return to the work he did before joining the department. To most this would be unthinkable, for patrol work remains, in the last analysis, far more interesting and stimulating than most occupations open to young men in the police environment. Even after an officer discovers that the work is much duller than he had imagined before his initiation into the occupation, the simple pleasures of warm fellowship and working in the heterogeneous, unpredictable world of city streets is enough to bind most men to their careers. As one officer remarked:

> If I ever quit, the only thing I guess I could do would be to go back to the market where I used to work. But the thought of stacking Del Monte tomato cans on aisle six at exactly ten o'clock every morning would drive me nuts. This job may be slow most of the time, but at least the routine doesn't get you down. Besides, once police work gets into your blood, that's it! You can never really go back out there again as a civilian.

REFERENCES

Ahern, James F. (1972) *Police in Trouble*. New York: Hawthorn Books, Inc.
Almond, Gabriel A. and Verba, S. (1963) *The Civic Culture*. Princeton, New Jersey: Princeton University Press.
Easton, David and Dennis, J. (1967) "The Child's Acquisition of Regional Norms: Political Efficacy" 61, *American Political Science Review*, 25–38. (1969) *Children in the Political System: Origins of Political Legitimacy*. New York: McGraw-Hill, Inc.
Goffman, Erving (1963) *Stigma*. New York: Doubleday.
Homans, George C. (1950) *The Human Group*. New York: Harcourt, Brace and World, Inc.
Hyman, Herbert (1959) *Political Socialization*. New York: The Free Press.
Maas, Peter (1973) *Serpico*. New York: The Viking Press.
Neiderhoffer, Arthur (1967) *Behind the Shield*. Garden City, New York: Doubleday and Co.
Reiss, Albert J. (1971) *The Police and the Public*. New Haven: Yale University Press.
Rubenstein, Jonathan (1973) *City Police*. New York: Farrar, Straus and Giroux.
Schein (1961) "Management development as a process of influence," 2, *Industrial Management Review*, 9–77.
Skolnick, Jerome (1966) *Justice Without Trial: Law Enforcement in a Democratic Society*. New York: John Wiley and Sons.
Van Maanen, John (1973) "Observations on the Making of Policemen," 32, *Human Organizations*, 407–418.
Webster, J. A. (1970) "Police Task and Time Study," 61, *Journal of Criminal Law, Criminology and Police Science*, 94–100.
Westley, William A. (1951) "The Police: A Sociological Study of Law, Custom and Morality." Ph.D. Dissertation at University of Chicago.
Whittemore, L. H. (1973) *The Super Cops*. New York: Stein and Day.
Whyte, William H. (1943) *Street Corner Society*. Chicago: University of Chicago Press.
Wilson, James Q. (1968) *Varieties of Police Behavior*. Cambridge, Massachusetts: Harvard University Press, 1968.

Private Information

Jonathan Rubenstein

"See that guy? If I knew what he does about the people here I'd be the best cop in the district. I been here twelve years and I don't know what he knows. And I know more than most. Goin' in their houses every day, seein' what kinda mail they get, checks and stuff," a patrolman mused, watching a mailman making his deliveries.

The only formal incentive to collect information is the advancement in his platoon that "vice activity" assures the patrolman. Anything else he learns about the nature of his territory and the habits of its people is a private matter reflecting his personal involvement in his work. There is no pressure on him to know anything. He is not asked to share what he knows with anyone else, nor does he confer formally with the men from other squads who also police his sector. Each of them acquires information independently. When a man finishes his tour of duty each day, nobody asks him if he learned anything of value to the department or to the squad that follows his onto the street. He may share something he has learned with another patrolman or a detective in exchange for a favor. The police, like many of the people from whom they get information, use it as an exchange commodity to pay debts among themselves and encourage preferential treatment. But this is not a systematic activity, and if a patrolman's sergeant finds out that he is giving information to men outside their platoon, the man risks punishment and retaliation. The only information the patrolman is required to share with the department is what is known by the people he arrests who are turned over to the detectives for interrogation prior to booking. But this is a by-product of his work; the information he obtains directly is his own.

The children on the streets are the most fertile source of information about the geography and the street behavior in a sector, but the patrolman makes little effort to exploit them. When he has a specific problem—looking for some youths drinking beer, pursuing someone down an alley, trying to find out about a person seen committing a burglary—he does not hesitate to question the children standing about. They are willing to talk to him and display very little solidarity with their peers. Frequently they offer him information which he ignores because he does not care about the problem. Many local fires are caused by juvenile arsonists, and it is common to see little children being shooed away by the patrolman whom they are trying to inform. He does not want to know about the fire, he is just watching the crowd. It is not his problem. But if he arrests a juvenile for some crime, he will listen carefully to any offered information on other criminal activity. He is willing to credit their veracity in situations where he is extorting information from them, but not otherwise.

REPRINTED FROM: Jonathan Rubenstein, *City Police*. New York: Farrar, Straus and Giroux, *1973* (200–217).

Children are also willing to tell him things about their neighborhoods which he would otherwise not know, but often they have to force this information on him. He does not stop to ask the children to help him out but accepts the information in the context of a working situation where he sees it as having specific connections to the job at hand. If it has a longer-term value, that is incidental.

Two patrolmen were investigating a call of males in a building and could not find a way into the place. As they were checking, a boy approached and showed them a concealed door leading to the basement which he said "they all use." He offered to show them what went on inside, leading them through a building that had been converted into a clubhouse, a shooting gallery for addicts, and a love nest. The officers did not ask him who used the place or whether there were any other places in the neighborhood being similarly used. They had been past the place hundreds of times without knowing how extensively it had been exploited by neighborhood youths. Without their voluntary informant, the patrolmen would have remained in the dark.

Several officers were searching a railroad trestle on a males-with-rifles call in an unsuccessful effort to locate the boys, who they thought were trapped. There were police at both ends, and the officers could not figure out how the boys had eluded capture. Several teenagers—about fifteen years old—were watching the police conduct their fruitless search and, when the officers were about to leave, approached. "They didn't have no guns," one said. "They were just up there huffin'. They always huff up in the yard." In response to several questions, the children willingly conducted the patrolmen on a tour of the freight yard, showing them where the boys hid merchandise stolen from the boxcars, when and where they hid while glue-sniffing, and, finally, how they got on and off the trestle. "Nuthin' to it," one boy exclaimed, eager to display his expertise. He shimmied up the twenty-foot iron support column, using the bolts as foot rests. After he had shown them how easy it was to slide up through the railroad ties to the top, he quickly climbed down the other side. The patrolmen just shook their heads as the boy said, "Everybody around here can do it. Even she can," nodding to the girl standing nearby. The policemen did not share this information with anyone, but incorporated it into their personal conception of the area and used it to make a number of arrests during the summer.

The patrolman's disinclination to exploit children for information is all the more curious when it is understood how limited are his other voluntary sources. In high-crime areas adults are willing to call the police in moments of extreme danger or if their anonymity can be assured, but they are very reluctant to do anything that will disclose them as informers. Some patrolmen are angered by this attitude, but most sector men accept the fact that people fear reprisal. The patrolman knows he cannot protect anyone all of the time, and their fear is seen as a legitimate reason for keeping quiet.

Two patrolmen went to the house of a woman whose windows had been broken by a gang of teenagers, but she refused to identify them. She wanted the police to come, which would put an end to the attack, but she did not want to be marked as a person receiving special treatment. Anyone might have called them. When one officer offered to accompany her to the local grocery store after she mentioned that she had no food in the house, she looked dumfounded and quickly refused. The patrolman was angry, until his partner explained that if she were seen on the street with the police, people would identify her as someone who sought the protection of the police. He said this could provoke attacks on her, unless the officer wanted to move in and protect her around the clock.

Frequently people who willingly call the police simply deny their participation if they are required to reveal themselves as the source of information. Two patrolmen were investigating a disturbance. A man standing on the street said he had seen three men go inside a taproom after pushing some construction equipment into an excavation. The patrolmen walked to the bar and looked inside. There was only one threesome, and they were ordered outside and taken to where the man was standing. They were followed by several men from the bar. As the group approached, the man said, "What are you comin' to me for? I didn't see nuthin'." The patrolmen smiled, shook their heads, and allowed the three men to go.

In moments of agitation, people often give the patrolman information which they would normally withhold and conceal. The experienced sector man is used to being informed in this way, and he allows people to yell and shout at each other in his presence. His first inclination is to put a stop to any possible violence, but he learns to be in no great hurry to quiet them when he is in a position to listen. These situations occur frequently in disturbance-house calls, when people are agitated and begin accusing each other of being number writers, speakeasy operators, or junkies. "He's just a fuckin' junkie. I'm so tired of his stealin' all my stuff. Get him outta here. I've been . . ." The woman was cut off in mid-sentence. "Is he carrying?" the patrolman asked. "No. He shot up before you came. I came back and found my radio gone and he was shootin' up. Get him outta here, please." The patrolman turned to his partner and said, "There's no point in taking him now. He's noddin' out. Take a good look at him and we'll stop him on the street when we see him."

The patrolman is approached on the street by people who offer him information that they hope will increase their own security and well-being. People come to him with tales of abandoned houses being used, juveniles breaking into stores, or burglaries they have seen committed. His interest in any of this is very limited, unless it is specific information about a person or a place that is being used at certain times. General information has little value to him since he cannot do anything with it. The department is not interested, and it does not help him to make an arrest. He cannot sit and watch a place, and unless he knows when people are going to be there, the information is useless. So he passes it off.

Businessmen, storekeepers, cabdrivers, hospital and personnel are good sources of casual information for the patrolman. They occasionally are in-

terested in telling him things about what is going on. Frequently this information is exchanged for personal attention. In a poor black area of the city, where
cabs were scarce, an informal and illegal taxi service was organized. There
were regular stops, unmarked but well known to local people. The police allowed it to operate because the drivers gave them "tips." These sources are irregular, as people must be careful about whom they tell and how they convey
the information. For example, one drugstore had been held up so many times
the police decided to put men inside the store to wait for the robbers to strike
again. In six months' time the place was robbed four more times, each time a
few hours after the police had left their stakeout. Presumably one of the employees or a policeman was informing the bandits, who timed their holdup so
as to evade the trap.[1]

The alert and skillful patrolman supplements his knowledge without aid
from others by exploiting the opportunities his work provides. In areas where
speakeasies are common, for instance, he casually scrutinizes liquor bottles for
tax stamps. This is something he learns to do, and those who do not are dismissed as not "vice-wise." Two rookies answered a disturbance-house call that
was quickly settled. The people of the house had not called and were anxious
for them to leave. The patrolmen had been admitted because there was too
much noise for the occupants to deny that something was amiss. It was Sunday
morning and they could not claim they were just having a party. Ten or fifteen
bottles were on a table, but the patrolmen did not take much notice of them. As
they left, one officer noticed that a person who had been inside and had asked
to leave had just gone back into the house. One patrolman said to the other,
"Did you see all those bottles?" The other nodded, the light of recognition in his
eyes. He said they had just blown a speak. They knocked on the door again, but
it was not reopened. They had three alternatives: to call their sergeant, to
break down the door illegally, or to leave without mentioning their error. They
left.

There was a call of "shooting and a hospital case" at a bar; the lieutenant
drove quickly to get there. When he arrived, he was pleased to see several cars
already at the scene. The call was unfounded, and he stood on the sidewalk
looking at the people. When the sergeant arrived, he called him over and said,
"Do you see all the juveniles in there? I want you to hit this place later."

Two patrolmen took a call to "investigate an open property." They arrived
at a well-maintained house, the front door of which stood open. A man approached and said that he had called. He lived across the street and knew the
owner was not at home during the day. He noticed the open door, rang the bell,
and then called the police when he received no answer. The three men entered.
It was empty, the thieves having left in a hurry from the appearance of the

---

[1]On businessmen and the police in relation to criminal information, see Albert M.
Reiss, Jr., *Studies in Crime and Law Enforcement in Major Metropolitan Areas,* Vol. I
(Research Study of the President's Commission on Law Enforcement and Criminal Justice, Washington, D.C., 1967), Sec. 2, pp. 10 ff. Much of this information is channeled directly to detectives and other units bypassing the district men and even the captain
(footnotes renumbered—eds.).

living room. There were several appliances, a record player, and three television sets sitting in the middle of the floor, waiting to be moved. "Either he scared 'em off or they found somethin' else they wanted more," the older officer said, while he was checking the bathroom window through which the burglars had come. "I've never been here in all the years in the district," he said, as he began to look around. "Talk to that old man and see what you can find out." A few moments later the officer called down from the second floor, "Hey, Ruby, come up here a minute."

The upstairs had been ransacked: drawers pulled out, books thrown on the floor, and cabinets overturned. "Lookin' for cash. That's all them junkies want." He pointed to the bed and peeled back the mattress to reveal two fully loaded pistols. "They found money and stopped lookin'. These are worth thirty or forty apiece. They'd a taken 'em for sure if they'd seen 'em." The .25 and .32 automatics were in holsters, and the patrolman commented, "Maybe he owns three. Anyway, he sleeps prepared." He rolled the mattress back in place, leaving the guns where they were. He did not take their serial numbers, unless he had done that before calling his partner.

After questioning the friendly neighbor about the owner, the patrolmen continued to look around the house, and then locked it. They asked the neighbor to tell the owner to call when he came home, since only he could inform them of what had been taken. "I wonder what that dude looks like," the older officer mused. "I'm gonna make a point of meetin' him. Three TV's in his house." He did not intend to tell anyone what he had found. He had violated department regulations by investigating the house without calling his sergeant, but with fifteen years in the business, he was beyond these technicalities. Anyway, if he had called, he might not have learned something.

Later in the day the owner came into the district to report the burglary. The patrolmen were called in to take the information. He thanked them for coming to his house and said that $125 in cash and some jewelry had been stolen. When he was leaving, one officer said, with his friendly smile, "I'll be seein' you around." Later he commented, "It could have been a lot more. Around here you don't want people to know how much money you got in your house. You might get broken into again real soon. Next time I see him on the street, I think I'm gonna make me an illegal car stop." He chuckled.

The experienced patrolman does not expect to learn the things he is interested in voluntarily. He gradually learns about other methods of obtaining information from watching colleagues, and he must decide whether he will use them. Most illegal activity in any area is carried on discreetly. The illicit activities an inexperienced or new man learns about are usually operated under some kind of informal (and illegal) police protection and are therefore of no value to him. Most of the people who have information are not interested in giving it to the police, and when they are, they are usually in a position to give it to someone with more influence than a patrolman. Even on his own sector, there are people with good information whom he cannot really exploit. Bartenders, pool-hall owners, and anyone whose business is linked to the police licensing power gives his information to a sergeant or lieutenant, unless the sector man is known to be closely linked to his supervisors. This restricts the opportunities available to the patrolman who wants to make vice activity and advance his career.

His steadiest source of information is what he collects as rent for allowing people to operate without arresting them. "Prostitutes and faggots are good. If you treat 'em right, they will give you what you want. They don't want to get locked up, and you can trade that off for information. If you rap 'em around," a very skilled patrolman said, "the way some guys used to, or lock 'em up, you don't get nothing." At a lunch counter another officer said, looking at the waitress who was getting his order, "She thinks I don't know she's hustlin' the truck drivers. She'll find out tomorrow. I don't care if she makes a few bucks on her back, but she is gonna tell me what I want to know." People who are arrested often try to get better treatment in exchange for information. Inexperienced patrolmen are willing to "cut someone some slack," but they often do not know how to go about it and frequently are unwittingly introduced to the ins and outs by people who are a lot more cop-wise than they are.

Two officers answered a call of "male breaking into an auto." The dispatcher gave a good description of the suspect, and when they arrived, the recorder spotted him immediately, partly concealed by a car. When they stopped, the man came forward with his arms spread out, to show he was not armed. "Did you want to talk to me?" he said. The patrolman had not seen him do anything, and they had no reason to hold him. He said that he had not broken into any cars, but a woman leaned out of a window and said, "That's him, the junkie motherfucker." He had not been accused by anyone whose property had been disturbed and therefore could not be charged with any offense. The patrolman asked him what he was doing, and he said he was a pool hustler. When he told them where he lived, he was asked, "What are you doin' here, my man, so far from your place?" It was several blocks away.

"I was goin' to my girl friend's to pick up some money, but she wasn't home."

"How many bags a day you usin'?"

"Honest, I ain't shootin' no more."

"Let's see your arms. Take off your coat."

"Sure I got tracks, but I ain't usin' no more. Don't lock me up. I don't want to go in. I got no money, nobody to take care of me. I'll get all fucked up inside." His hands shook and there were tears in his eyes. The patrolmen had no reason to hold the man, and they were on the verge of releasing him when he said, "If you treat me good, I'll give you good information on some pushers."

They put him in the car and took him to the district. They knew little about narcotics and needed someone who could corroborate what he told them. They got the corporal to call another man in off the street.

The three patrolmen and the informant stood in a tight circle, while other policemen came and went. Nobody stopped to chat or lingered in their vicinity. Even the lieutenant, who had come into the station, walked past without acknowledging their existence. The informant, displaying his experience, asked,

"What area ya interested in? I don't want to give you nuthin' you don't care about."

"Just give us everything below Beacon Avenue," one officer commanded.

"Hey, man, I don't know any of their names or nothin'. Just where they push the stuff." He mentioned several places, bars and hotels, where heroin was sold. The third officer said, "Come on, pal, get it up. Everybody knows those places." They stared at each other for a moment, and then the informant mentioned a place where heroin was being bagged and an apartment where a man driving a Cadillac "with a phone in it is droppin' twenty bundles [fifty bags to a bundle] twice a week. Look, I don't know no more. I give you good information. They'd kill me, man. That's all I know. What's gonna happen to me?" The patrolmen exchanged glances, and after the third man nodded, the older of the arresting officers said, "I pronounce you guilty and sentence you to six months' probation. Go on, beat it." He said nothing, turned on his heels, and walked quickly from the station.

The information was obtained on the last tour of daywork. When the squad returned to work, it would be last out, a bad time for narcotics raids, since most heroin is sold by early evening. This meant that the patrolmen could not use their information for at least ten days, when they would be going on the four-to-twelve shift. Although they knew that narcotics information is notoriously short-lived, because operators keep shifting around to evade capture, the men had no intention of sharing what they had learned, just as they had no interest in obtaining information about places outside their district. The arresting patrolmen told the third officer that they didn't want anything to be done with the information until they went on the nightwork shift. "I don't want the sergeant to know about this until we're ready to get warrants. He's got to know then, but not before," one man said, and the third patrolman replied, "Oh, come on, he wouldn't fuck with narcotics." "Oh yeah? I don't want him to know nuthin'." They agreed.

The men had another problem that had to be resolved before they could use their information. After agreeing not to do anything for the next ten days, they had to decide how to bring the patrolmen who worked the sectors which they were going to raid into their operation. "The way they're pushin' for vice, they wouldn't care if we made one in another district," one quipped, "but we still can't go tearing up another guy's sector."

The patrolmen said nothing until they were ready to apply for their warrants. "I think he's O.K., but there's no point in telling a guy too much or too soon. This guy don't understand that I was on that sector before he come to the district. He don't own it yet," the man said. But when he made application for the warrants, he had to tell the sector man. While cruising one night, he saw the man drive by and hailed him over. The patrolman mentioned that he was going to hit a place with a warrant and wanted him to come along. He did not mention the address. The man asked where it was and, after he was told, said that he would like to know if there were more. "The reason I'm askin' is I don't want to duplicate the work. There's a couple of places I'm lookin' into and I don't want them ruined on me," he said. The first officer replied, "I seen you in the project yesterday. Don't worry, the things I'm lookin' at ain't in there." He had lied and had no idea if the other man knew or would find out. The previous day he had been ordered by the lieutenant not to request a warrant on an apartment in the project because one had just been approved. A few hours prior to their conversation, the sector man and the lieutenant, along with a wagon crew, had made a successful raid and the patrolman who had once "owned" the sector wanted to conceal his disappointment. But he let the man know when he got his warrants and shared the credit with him for the arrests that were made.

The district patrolman is not loath occasionally to pay money for vice information if he finds it necessary. One Sunday morning a sergeant watched an elderly black man stumble in the street. He halted his car and watched the man regain his feet, then called him to the car. "Hey, pop, where did you make your load?" The man grinned and offered to give the sergeant a speak if he would put up the money for a bottle. The sergeant smiled affably and called for his favorite wagon crew. When they arrived, he drove the man to the location mentioned. He gave him enough money to buy two bottles, one for evidence and one for drinking, and told him to come out soon after he had made the purchase. The old man asked the sergeant not to let on that he knew him. "If that bitch knows I ratted, she'll get me killed. No shit, you gotta treat me rough. I'll put up a stink, too." The sergeant laughed and agreed. He watched the man go around the corner and knock on a door.

The police waited, sitting in a side street but not concealed. The wagon was parked so that the driver could observe anyone coming from the house. When the man stumbled out about a half hour later, the wagon crew grabbed him. The sergeant took him, and the two officers knocked on the door and went directly in without waiting. A few minutes later they came out with a woman. She looked at the old man, who was jumping up and down, shouting at the sergeant and calling him names. The wagon men handcuffed the woman and put her into the wagon. Then they smacked the old man across the face and handcuffed him. The woman was arrested for illegal sales. In the station the sergeant put a false name down on the arrest book for the informer. "When they call him for court, they won't find him. It will be dismissed, but we got our vice pinch. Anyway, they would kill him if he testified." The old man was quickly released and allowed to take one bottle with him. He thanked the sergeant and the wagon crew for holding up their end of the bargain and offered to come by any time they had the price of a bottle and give them another speak.

The interest of the police in vice crime, particularly gambling and drinking, as well as prostitution, must be satisfied by information supplied to them by their own undercover agents or by informers. Even in neighborhoods where some people oppose drinking and gambling, they are loath to inform the police because they fear reprisal and banishment by their neighbors. The police know this better than anyone else and they pursue their information covertly. Most uniformed men who make vice arrests achieve their successes by luck, when they stumble on something in the course of looking into an unrelated matter, or by getting occasional information from someone who has access to the action. Some men who have been in a district for a few years come to recognize and know people who are involved in the rackets. They have seen colleagues bring in persons charged with writing numbers; they know which bars and clubs are associated with gambling activities. Whenever they see one of these people around during daywork, they make an effort to follow him. "Well, well, there goes my old friend," a patrolman chirped, as he spotted an ancient car, driven by an elderly man, pulling out ahead. "Take down his plate number and we'll check it out later. I think we will just take a little ride and see where he goes this morning."

Men who have any experience with vice work are alert to the appearance of any new people on the streets during the morning hours. "I just don't know that old guy. The one going into the restaurant. I don't know where he lives yet, but the way he keeps floating around, he's gotta be a writer. He turned up a couple of weeks ago and I only see him on daywork. I don't know anybody who knows him yet, but I'll get him," the patrolman said.

The vice-wise policeman is constantly on the alert for any behavior that may indicate gambling. Nothing is too innocent to be overlooked and checked out. "Oh ho, what do we have here? Don't turn around when I pull up at the corner. Did you see those two guys talkin' on your side when we went by? Did you see how they moved together when they spotted the car? You stay here while I go into the store. Watch where they go and we'll check 'em out." When the sergeant returned with his newspaper, he was told which building the men entered and noted the address as they drove past. The police car did not slow down, nor did the men look at the buildings as they drove past, but they calculated the address by counting the number of houses to the corner. When they were off the block, the sergeant asked the dispatcher to send a wagon crew to meet with him. He gave these reliable men the address of the suspected house and told them to make inquiries about who lived in it.

Not all informers are paid, although many of them are. Sometimes the police will use their station-house characters, paying them by the pinch for the information they provide. In some districts there are people who give the police information because they genuinely support what they believe the police are doing. "You know, Jack's father lives in the district and he gives us good information. That's why he ain't going on this raid. The old man lives around the corner and it could be embarrassing if his son took the door." Occasionally, local pensioners who sit around their neighborhoods all day give the police information. Some of these people may be number writers who are trying to protect themselves by clearing their areas of junkies and others who threaten their own businesses. There are also paid informers, "rats," who are treated on a stringently commercial basis. They are not protected and they get paid for what they produce.[2]

An officer was cruising an area looking for a man. "There he is, my chief rat." The man was called to the police car, but the officer did not get out. The

---

[2] In common law an informer was eligible for protection and payments, which were scaled according to the crimes on which he gave his information. The legal status of the informer was not revoked in England until 1951. A very useful account of an informer system used by narcotics detectives in an American police force is in Jerome H. Skolnick, *Justice Without Trial* (New York: Wiley, 1966), pp. 112–38.

man said hello and then asked for his money. "You'll get paid when I get the right information. You gave me the wrong address. I can't hit her where she works. It's a fuckin' church. Get me her home address and I'll see you later in the day."

If the policeman is seriously interested in maintaining his informant, he is stringently careful about when he meets him and where he acknowledges recognition. One night after work several officers were having a few drinks in a district bar that they frequented. A man known to them walked in but passed by without any recognition. He stopped at the other end of the bar, where he met several people. The policemen did not comment on his arrival. After a few hours the bar had mostly emptied and the bartender was introducing the remaining customers to each other, indicating to all that the three men at the far end were police officers. They all shook hands with the man who had been at the other end. "Nice to meet you, Lieutenant," he said. He was the lieutenant's rat and nothing was done to threaten his role.

Some patrolmen never develop any interest or skill in vice work. It is almost impossible for a white officer, for example, working in a black area, to develop sources of information that are not rooted in some form of compulsion. Many men do not have the stomach for this kind of work, and even when they stumble across a speakeasy, they will let it pass if it is small and informal. Others who do develop skills feel obliged to limit their activities because they know that their connections to the local people can be damaged if they press their vice work vigorously. Ethnic connections frequently create links for an astute policeman to exploit, but he must be cautious. In some residential areas a patrolman who has worked the same place for a long time may decline to make any vice arrests. "Look at Norton," a sergeant said. "He's the best vice man in the platoon, in the squad, but he won't lock anybody up on his sector. He told me when I took over that it was embarrassing for him and that people would stop talking to him. So we made a deal. He gets me the information and the wagon makes the pinch. But he offered to make a grab on another sector for someone else."

Although it cannot be known exactly, it is reasonable to ask how much information is denied the patrolman about criminal matters in areas where vice activity is widespread because of people's reluctance to call policemen into their homes. No matter what he is called for, the patrolman is always keeping an eye out for an illegal bottle or a number slip, or listening for some loose talk about a game or a party. Since vice is usually found in the same places where street crime is most common and the demand for police services greatest, it is interesting to speculate whether the patrolman does not lose more than he is able to squeeze out.

The patrolman's sector is not exclusively his, but what he learns on it is his own. His colleagues—the wagon men and other patrolmen—cannot come into his sector for any reason without informing him, unless they want to risk his wrath. But others may penetrate his territory regularly without prior consultation. His sergeant and lieutenant do not have to tell him what they are doing, and an astute sector man often spends some of his time trying to find out what his superiors are doing in his sector. Plainclothesmen, headquarters units, and detectives may operate without his knowledge. There are also two wagon crews and two other patrolmen who work his territory each day besides himself, and he knows little of their activity. They may tell him some things, and he can learn more from people who live and work in the sector, but these men have no obligation to tell him anything. Less frequently, but with great discretion, his sector is visited by agents from the district attorney's office, state police agents, military policemen seeking deserters, F.B.I. agents, federal treasury, narcotics, and alcohol agents; insurance investigators and private detectives, too, operate without his knowledge. He has no control over any of these men, but he is usually not concerned about what they are doing unless he is involved in some kind of illicit or illegal actions. But his own colleagues do interest him and he does have a measure of control over them. He fortifies his control by denying them the information he accumulates and sharing it with them only when he feels it is to his benefit.

Much of what he knows is not of any particular interest to them, since they do not work his area, but the other men who do work the same area do not get much information from him. His sergeant and lieutenant may share some information with other squad supervisors when they are pressed by their captain, but this is infrequent. It is only in very rare circumstances that the department makes any effort to get the men who know more than anybody about what is going on in the streets to share their knowledge with each other.

It was two days after a patrolman had been murdered in the district. A rookie had been gunned down by three young men as he stepped from his car to speak with them. His gun had been found snapped in its holster. Detectives from homicide had come to daywork roll call to speak with the men. They looked tired, probably because they had been up most of the night. One man said, "Fellas, you know why we're here. We need information. We ain't askin' any questions. If you saw anything that night, anything at all, put it on a 48 and send it to us. If you were some place you shouldn'ta been, we don't care. You don't have to sign it, just send it downtown. Anything you can do will help. You know some people, you got sources of information. Squeeze 'em. We need it. It's for all of us. It could be any one of us next time."

Each man is obliged to learn his own territory and acquire the informal notions of public behavior he uses to evaluate what he sees about him. He gets no systematic help from anyone. How many more people would he know on his sector if he pooled his information with the other men who work his territory? How much time and how many errors might he be spared if he were cooperatively introduced into the lore of his area? Most of the people he sees on his sector are not known to him personally. He is obliged to rely on his notions of local behavior and of the legitimate use of public places and on the behavioral cues people give him when they come into his presence in making judgments of what they are doing.

Because he cannot know a good deal of what is going on, and since much of what is going on people do not want him to know, he is frequently obliged to rely on suspicion to guide him into actions. This will probably always be so, but it is far from clear that it is not possible to improve his personal knowledge. If he is obliged to do certain kinds of work, he will certainly have to continue using the techniques that the police have always employed to get information from unwilling participants. But these practices are not going to encourage any group of people to support actively, not simply decline to oppose, the men they are told to depend on to protect them from violence and depredations, the men who are supposed to shield us all from ourselves in our most violent and disordered moments.

The longer a patrolman is in a district, the more he knows about its people and their lives. His sources of information increase, as does his knowledge of how to exploit them for activity as well as for personal gain. A patrolman needs a solid knowledge of geography and people to do his work with confidence. The more he knows about the manners and habits of the people he polices, the less likely is he to become involved in misunderstandings and fights which arise from a misreading of what he sees. The more people he comes to know, however, the more likely he is to develop private and even intimate connections with some of them. This involves the police in an insoluble dilemma.

If the experienced patrolman is not allowed to remain where he is, the private stock of information and knowledge he accumulates will be dissipated. But if he remains in a district for many years, his inclinations to ignore many illegal things may increase. His personal involvements with some people may influence him to ignore their violations of the law. He may exploit his knowledge of gambling and illegal drinking to cash in on some of the easy money that is around and being collected by some plainclothesmen and, he suspects, by men even higher up in the organization. But even if he is not corrupted, he may become lazy and difficult to control. The more he knows about vice, the more valuable he becomes to his sergeant and lieutenant; if he provides them with activity, they will not supervise him too closely or demand of him the work they require of others. He can exploit his position to increase his personal freedom. At the same time, this relationship provides a model of success to younger patrolmen that undercuts the department's efforts to promote "professional" goals and attitudes in its men. The men who work the street see clearly who gets rewarded informally and for what. The department does not approve of this situation, but it has not changed much in the last century and a half.

PART THREE
STRATEGIES OF POLICING

In this part, we are concerned with the various means by which the police attempt to accomplish their self-stated goals of crime reduction and control. Although the police do not often use the term "strategies," our use of it here is at least consistent with the police symbolization of their organization as a paramilitary one and with their use of the omnipresent war-on-crime metaphor employed so frequently to describe their activities. Strategies, then, refer to the means by which the police hope to achieve certain objectives.

Strategies can be defined in one of two ways when looking at the police. First, as illustrated in the preceding section, strategies can refer to some general forms of presenting the police mission and mandate. These can be considered *presentational* strategies—rhetorics which symbolize, rationalize, and otherwise attempt to make sensible the overall efforts of the organization. For example, a popular presentational strategy is the use of a professionalism vocabulary that describes the police as a group of prestigious, neutral, effective, and responsible public servants whose education, training, skills, and importance in the scheme of things calls out an aura associated with such honored occupations as law, medicine, and the priesthood. However, strategies can also be defined as specific means of allocating efforts to achieve given ends. These can be considered *operational* strategies. Take, for instance, a series of strikes against massage parlors or pornographic bookstores, saturation patrols by two- and three-man units in selected high-crime locales, or the use of undercover agents in narcotics law enforcement. All are means of allocating police resources with an intended effect and hence can be described as operational strategies.

Both sets of strategies represent the ways in which the police aim to channel cases into the legal system, to serve their own ends, to forestall criticism, to isolate and harass a particular group in the community, and so forth. As such, strategies can be both offensive and defensive in intent, and, like all forms of rational action, they can yield anticipated as well as unanticipated consequences. Specifically, operational strategies are at least theoretically subject to some sort of evaluation as to their success in achieving a desired purpose. Presentational strategies are perhaps less subject to evaluation, although it is conceivable that some criteria surrounding their authenticity or suasive power might be developed. Typically, however, police departments, like most governmental bodies, worry very little about and devote few resources toward evaluating either operational or presentational strategies.

As Peter K. Manning and Lawrence J. Redlinger point out in the first essay of this part, there are a variety of internal pressures felt by police agents to achieve success in terms familiar to the department (especially the arrest and charge statistics). Thus, the strategies surrounding such activities as narcotics enforcement tend to build up a momentum of their own. That is, any given strategy followed by the police, since it is rarely, if ever, judged as to its effectiveness, tends over time to become both taken for granted and self-justifying. Individuals are, of course, evaluated as to their ability to make use of the strategy, but, as Manning and Redlinger show, this too leads to a further rationalization of the strategy itself. It is as if police strategies represent the grounds upon which the figures of police action move; and, like the proverbial iceberg, these grounds remain beneath the surface and are examined, questioned, and discussed only occasionally.

Relatedly, organizational units within a police department vary in the sorts of strategies they employ. In particular, they vary with respect to the extent to which a specific operational strategy depends upon the citizenry for information, cooperation, and complaints to mobilize the legal system. Donald Black's concise and provocative article, which is the second reading in this part, addresses precisely this connection between the private system of social relations and the legal system. Black is concerned essentially with the types of constraints that exist upon different types of policing. From this standpoint, patrol work rests almost exclusively upon citizen complaints; and most investigative work, by the same logic, is equally dependent upon citizen-supplied intelligence, since detectives must rely on cases brought to their attention by the patrol division. However, vice-enforcement units, concerned with gambling, drugs, organized crime, and the like, must rely almost entirely on information they can gather and assemble through their own efforts, through paid or volunteer informants, or, in large departments, through information generated and supplied them by elite surveillance units. Black also discusses the organizational capacity to know crime by virtue of the discretion that inheres in policing and the availability of the law to citizens, meaning the degree to which particular cases can be brought to legal attention. Such an analysis suggests the variable capacity of policing to effect events, something that is only hinted at by the police themselves when they employ certain presentational strategies such as the quixotic but popular rhetoric of the "war on crime."

At a most general level, if we examine operational strategies, they fall into three generic types. There are *preventive* strategies by which the police seek to discourage the commission of crime by such means as increasing the visibility of the uniformed force on the street or by encouraging citizens to make use of various protective devices such as "burglar-proof" locks or robbery alarm systems. There are also *proactive* strategies by which the police seek to discover crime as it is being accomplished. Here are perhaps the most controversial of all police strategies, for through such activities as soliciting propositions from prostitutes or through purchasing stolen goods by means of a police fence, the agents of a law enforcement agency can be accused of actually provoking the very crimes they wish to suppress. Finally, *reactive* strategies are the most commonly employed by the police and represent perhaps the most popular and conventional view of policing held by the public at large. Reactive strategies are concerned with establishing a set of "facts" such that the perpetrator of a given crime can be brought to account. Table 1 summarizes these strategies and directs our attention to certain important features which discriminate among them.

Examining Table 1, we see with regard to time, preventive strategies occur prior to a criminal act. These strategies are considerably more popular in Western European communities than in the United States where the understanding and application of preventive strategies tend to be low. Proactive policing focuses either on prior conditions, such as the knowledge of the location of certain criminal activities, or, on the observation of a crime as it is being committed, such as a vice officer making a buy from a drug dealer. Reactive strategies, as the name implies, deals with crime after the fact—crimes that are brought to the attention of the police by citizen complaint. The point of intervention for a preventive strategy like a community block organization for crime reduction or a publicity campaign to increase citizen awareness of criminal opportunities is, clearly, the community's social system. Proactive strategies, as we have noted, work by requiring police agents to "make crime happen." Reactive strategies handle certain complaints received by the police department from citizens as allegations that must first be established or founded prior to their being considered in the category of "crimes known to the police." Thus, reactive strategies require the investigator to work "backward" from the facts of the crime to the criminal. In preventive strategies, citizens are central and their activities are the crucial factors in determining the degree of success of the strategy. Proactive strategies are least dependent upon citizens and their wishes, while reactive strategies fall somewhere between (they are, by definition, at least initiated by citizens, though the police must decide what is to be done, if anything). While clearance rates, along with arrests and charge data, can be used to ascertain the activities and relative success of reactive policing, they cannot be so used in preventive or proactive police work. Assessing the success of preventive strategies is the least developed, though where it is used it often inverts the conventional indices of police success by seeking reductions, not gains, in the numbers of known street or property crimes. Proactive strategies are evaluated upon very crude indices of effect such as seizures made, or, more commonly, of number of arrests made and cases brought to court. In fact, because the police have emphasized reactive strategies more so than either preventive or proactive strategies, they have converted this concern into various measures of internal functioning. It is a curious world the police have created for themselves, for if we take, say, the popular measure of police functioning known as the "clearance rate," we learn nothing about the effectiveness of the police to control crime but learn only of their capacity to process what they already know about crime. Similarly, arrests are often used, mistakenly, to indicate the success of a particular police activity, yet arrests are relevant only, of course, after the fact of a criminal occurrence.

TABLE 1. Types of Police Operational Strategies

	Preventive	Proactive	Reactive
TIME	Prior to crime commission	Prior to, or simultaneously with, crime commission	After crime comes to the attention of the police
AIM	Crime is to be prevented, fore-stalled or deterred.	Crime must be "created" and made court rele-vant; a case must be presented	Crime must be founded— facts established and a perpetrator brought to task if possible
PLACE OF AGENT	Police-citizen obligations similar (cooperative)	Agents ecologically removed from crime commission; Agents rely on informants or own information; Crime often a pri-vate transaction involving officer as complainant; Selection of targets (groups, persons, locales) is discretionary	Agents stand in variable relation to commis-sion of crime; Agents rely almost exclusively on citizens information and complaints
MEASURE OF EFFECT	Measured by the reduction, absence, or shift in the pattern or level of crime (defined as crimes known)	Measured by arrests and charges, seizures, or warrants served	Arrests and clearance rates
INTERNAL MEASURES	Not developed	Clearance rates cannot be used because the base number of cases is unknown	Clearance rates can measure extent of effect on founded crime

In the readings to follow, each of these strategies is discussed at some length. Manning and Redlinger illustrate some of the problems associated with proactive policing, especially those that come to be labeled "corrupt." Like Black in the second article of this section, Manning and Redlinger see proactive police actions as patterned by social constraints and embedded in something akin to a political economy. Unlike reactive policing, where the relationship between the private moral system and the law permits citizens to mobilize the law in their own personal interests, proactive policing reflects more the police private interests than any other.

Reactive policing is the focus of the third paper in this part. Harvey Sacks directs our attention to a police officer's capacity as an individual to know crime, to handle or manage its features, and to bring a case more or less to closure. Sacks illustrates in analytic detail the problems police face when initiating action on the basis of a citizen complaint, or, in those rare instances, on the basis of a police-detected crime in progress. In short, Sacks's astute arguments demonstrate, at a very fundamental level, the kinds of resources commanded by a street-level police officer as well as the kinds of operational strategies he has available in which to utilize these resources.

The last selection presented here is an essay by James Q. Wilson. This article provides a very useful summary of the research attempting to assess the effect of the various police strategies. Surveying a number of important quasi-experiments in the area, Wilson concludes tentatively that routine patrol has little effect on crime. Although he implies that saturation patrol strategies (i.e., preventive strategies) have some impact in a given area, they may also displace crime to other areas. Furthermore, he notes that such strategies are quite expensive and are perhaps even incompatible with the concern in some segments of the community upon the protection of citizen rights. Community crime-prevention strategies present a somewhat mixed picture but do not seem to produce unambiguous increases in reported public satisfaction with the police. It is likely, as Wilson warns, that the citizenry has overestimated the effects that the police can and do have on crime. Indeed, he is cautious about drawing any firm conclusions on the potential of the police to fulfill any of their professed objectives.

When considering proactive strategies, can we assess the success of the police in accomplishing their mission? Again, this is unlikely because, as Wilson suggests, there are no standards or indices that can unequivocally detect either reduced amounts or increased amounts of crime. Nor are there means available to calculate such figures independent of the police tactics themselves. Furthermore, how does one go about measuring a crime that did not happen? Should one rely on citizen reports which provide various reasons as to why the citizen might be dissatisfied with certain police services and hence not report crime? What about victimization surveys which are developed independent of citizen complaints and crime reports? Each has been used, sometimes in concert, but there is no agreement about which is the more useful in evaluating police efforts.

In summary, a close and detailed evaluation of virtually any police strategy has not been attempted often—as the recent House Select Committee investigations and Senate Hearings on police functioning discovered. Certainly there is growing interest in trying to assess how well the police are going about their job. One crucial reason that makes this issue so visible and topical is that by requiring of the police some sort of evaluation for their operational strategies, a certain amount of public accountability can be obtained from the police. Needless to say, such accountability has been sorely lacking in most American police agencies.

Invitational Edges of Corruption:
Some Consequences of
Narcotic Law Enforcement[1]

Peter K. Manning and Lawrence J. Redlinger

Prior to the early years of this century, the nonmedical use of narcotics was largely unregulated and distribution and sales were routinely handled by physicians and pharmacists. However, sparked by international obligations and fervent moral crusaders, a series of legislative acts and court decisions were enacted and enforced. The enforcement of the laws resulted in marked changes in the population of users and drove the trafficking of narcotics underground.[2] Since the early twenties, then, federal, state and local agents have been engaged in enforcing the law and attempting to eradicate the illicit trafficker and his activities. Even though it can be demonstrated by official statistics that large numbers of users and dealers are arrested and prosecuted each year, narcotic law enforcement problems continue to generate considerable governmental and public concern. Our purposes in this essay are to examine the dominant or operative mode of enforcement, to point out the particular problems associated with it, and to indicate how these problems are not unique to narcotics enforcement.

The enforcers of the narcotics laws stand on the invitational edge of corruption, and the problems they encounter while regulating and attempting to eradicate illicit trafficking of drugs reveal similarities to regulation of other markets. Study of their problems and of the corruption that can, and does occur, will lead to insight into the structural problems of regulation, and to an

---

[1]Manning is Professor of Sociology and Psychiatry at Michigan State University and is currently on leave as a Law Enforcement Assistance Administration Fellow. Redlinger, Assistant Professor of Sociology at University of Michigan, is currently completing a book on illicit drug markets as a Fellow at the Drug Abuse Council. This chapter is one of a series of collaborative efforts dealing with Social Control and Social Regulation.

[2]Extensive research on the early years has been done by several scholars, and the reader interested in how the drug problem was socially constructed, how legislation was passed, and how initial attempts at regulation gave way to the enforcement mode, should look at such works as Brecher, *et al.* (1972 pt. 1); Lindesmith (1965); Musto (1972); and King (1972). One result, however, deserves mentioning primarily because it set up the now accepted linkage between urban crime, poverty, and narcotics addiction. Whereas, prior to criminalization, narcotics users were mostly women who self-administered the drug for a variety of medicinal reasons, after criminalization males became the primary users. In addition, the social class of the user steadily declined so that in contrast to the late 1800's when use was spread throughout the class structure and even concentrated more in the middle and upper classes, the majority of users are today from the lower classes (this does not, of course, include physician addicts who obtain their drugs in other manners). In addition, prior to criminalization, the average age of a user was between 40 and 50 years of age, whereas today, the user is more likely to be under thirty. Thus, resulting from criminalization and the enforcement of the laws, the patterns of addiction and use changed remarkably. Today addiction is most often associated with poor, young, urban males, usually from one of the other "minorities."

REPRINTED FROM: Paul Rock (ed.) *Drugs and Politics.* Rutgers, New Jersey: Society/Transaction Books—E. P. Dutton, *1977* (279–310).

understanding of the stress or tension points in regulatory apparatuses of the government.

As Robert Merton has noted, there are many similarities between legitimate and illegitimate businesses. *"Both are in some degree concerned with the provision of goods and services for which there is an economic demand"* (his italics) (Merton, 1957:79). Thomas Schelling (1967) has noted that there must be many commonalities between illicit and licit markets, and Redlinger (1969) analyzing heroin markets demonstrated their remarkable correspondence to licit markets. Likewise, Moore's analysis (1970) indicates that the economics of heroin distribution have comparable shapes to those of other consumer products. So the question is, then, what are the similarities and differences, and how do these effect variations in the regulation of the market?

Licit and illicit markets share several structural properties in common.[3] Both involve willing buyers and sellers. The buyers make demands for goods and services, and the sellers provide those for some reimbursement. In both licit and illicit markets, the sellers have in mind the making of a profit, and ideally maximizing that profit. Both types of markets are regulated by agencies whose mission is to do so, and both types of markets have sellers within them who seek effective control over the manner and type of regulations that will be applied to them. However, there are some differences and these stem from the moral intention of the regulatory statutes, the loyalties of those applying the regulations, and the nature in which they are applied.

The moral intention of regulatory statutes either legitimizes particular behaviors, goods and services, or it jades them. Some goods and services (e.g., the production, distribution, and possession of alcoholic beverages) become morally transformed; first they are defined one way, and then another. The nature of the definition structures the manner in which regulation is to be accomplished. Where products are determined to have "legitimacy" those who buy and sell them often are *licensed*. The license is part of the regulatory process and identifies dealers. These dealers in turn are regulated by a set of standards that are set by the various jurisdictions: for example, federal, state and local. Consumers are assured, in so far as sellers adhere to the standards, that products are of sufficient quality. The moral intention of the regulation, then, is to insure the adequate *delivery* of goods and services and to insure the delivery of *adequate* goods and services. This is not the case for markets that

---

[3]The literature on "legitimate" versus "illegitimate" markets and their associated regulatory activity is growing. Sociologists have long recognized that police control crime rather than eliminating it. For example, Hughes (1971) has written on "bastard institutions" which provide desired products not otherwise available, and Schur (1966) analyzed some of the consequences of making illegal certain consumatory patterns. N. Davis (1973) has provided an intensive and detailed analysis of the changing patterns of regulation associated with abortion, and sociologist Gusfield (1963) and political scientists such as Lowi (1969) and Edelman (1962) have examined the symbolic fictions of regulation. In a sense, all regulation is an additional price or value-added cost, and while the cost of regulation is passed onto both the seller and buyer, more often than not the seller is able to transfer his costs to the buyer. Thus, the buyer becomes the taxpayer. Corruption is a variant on the cost coming as it does, directly as one resultant of the enterprise of morality regulation.

have been morally transformed into "deviant" markets. Demand for products that are defined as illicit places a stigmata on the consumer; selling such products places the dealer in a criminal and highly sanctionable position; the regulation seeks to collapse distribution channels, reduce supplies, and effectively reduce demand. Markets which are defined as immoral become "legally suppressed" and the regulatory functions become "enforcement" functions rather than compliance functions. Strictly speaking, there is no difference between compliance functions of regulations and enforcement functions because both seek to persuade and coerce sellers to "comply" with the regulations. The difference between the two arises out of the intent of the statute. In legal markets, the actions of distribution, production and consumption are not illegal in themselves, and the persons doing this activity are not subject to criminalization. The regulation seeks to insure the channels of distribution and seeks to insure the quality of the product. Licensing of dealers performs this function, and in addition secures revenue for the licensing agent who in this case is the State.[4] The revenue provides resources for the licensing and compliance agents to continue their performances. This is not the case with illicit markets. Regulations do not insure product adequacy, cannot provide revenue intake and thus cannot generate their own resources. Finally, the regulations seek "compliance" only in the sense that they wish *no one* to engage in the activity.

In a similar manner, the loyalties of licit market regulators are focused in a different manner than those agents regulating illicit markets. Very often, the regulators of licit markets are products of those markets. The staffing of regulatory agencies is accomplished by using industry executives who are "experts" in the field. Thus, the loyalties of the people as agents is not wholly to the regulation process. They have an "insider's" view of the marketing structure and are able to consider both the regulations and their effects on the sellers. Obviously, this type of interpenetration between regulators and sellers is not extant for illicit markets. The regulators are never drawn from the ranks of sellers,[5] and one can imagine why. The sellers of illicit products are typically viewed as unwholesome characters, and the aim of the regulations is to put them permanently out of business.

The ways in which the regulations of licit markets are applied vary considerably from the manner in which illicit markets are regulated. Compliance sections of regulatory agencies frequently warn the seller to correct his prac-

---

[4]Associations, such as the American Sociological Association and the American Medical Association also license practitioners, and collect revenues for their agents. The agents through their certification attest to the credibility of the licensed persons' claims to be what they are and to be selling what they claim to be selling.

[5]This can be seen through our later analysis to not always be the case. Numerous examples from nations other than the United States will indicate complicity between those who seek to suppress the illicit marketing of products and the sellers of those products. Given the extremely lucrative nature of illicit narcotics, unscrupulous entrepreneurs and power-driven people, whether in legitimate occupations or illegitimate ones, will be tempted. In a society where money is equated with social respectability and power, lucrative ways to make money become extremely attractive, and constraining themes in morality can be neutralized.

TABLE 1. A Comparison of Selected Aspects of Legally Regulated
Versus Legally Suppressed Markets

Legally Regulated Markets	Legally Suppressed Markets
1. Willing buyers and willing sellers	1. Willing buyers and willing sellers
2. Sellers seek to maximize profits	2. Sellers seek to maximize profits
3. Intent of law to set and maintain standards of goods and services	3. Intent of law to suppress all activity
4. Law licenses and legitimates dealers	4. Law stigmatizes and illegitimates dealers
5. Law legitimates use	5. Law stigmatizes use
6. Agents of regulation often drawn from sellers' ranks	6. Regulators never drawn from sellers' ranks
7. Agents seek compliance and seek maintenance of market at established levels	7. Agents seek eradication of market
8. Buyer quality protected	8. Buyer quality unprotected

tices, or at best take him to court where the process of advocacy litigation is applied. The seller when convicted is often fined or reprimanded. Since the regulators are often drawn from the industries they regulate and since the regulations legitimate, albeit regulate, the market, the same moral stigmata is not applied to violators. Indeed, the violators may not view themselves as having committed a violation (see Sutherland, 1949, on this point). Suppressive enforcement has some similarities, but is ultimately geared toward bringing about virtual *cessation* of activity. Agents may warn a seller of narcotics whom they cannot arrest, but in general, they seek to catch him in the act (although these patterns vary by size of city and patterns of seller's activities). Once caught, they seek to remove him from the market or immobilize him, since removal and immobilization are the only manners in which he can be forced to comply with regulatory standards. Some of the differences we have been discussing between legally regulated and legally suppressed markets and their relationships to regulatory agencies can be summarized in Table 1.

Variation in moral intention, reflected in legal definition, creates differences in the kinds and types of influence sellers have on regulators and regulations. As we noted earlier, sellers of a product will seek to maximize their profits and will seek to have effective control over market conditions. Legally regulated markets offer the seller more opportunities for influence than do illicit ones. One reason we have already noted; in licit markets very often the regulators are drawn from the ranks of sellers, and often return to those ranks when they leave the regulatory agency. Secondly, in legally regulated markets, sellers have available other means for political influence. Because their activities are defined as credulous, they can utilize legislative means to attempt effective control. That is, they can attempt to have regulations set, sustained or altered in line with their wishes rather than the wishes of other partisans in the market (e.g., agents and consumers). They can "lobby" and thus attempt to influence the legislative process, and they can appear before congressional committees as "expert witnessess." When they appear, they can produce market data to support their position, and their legal staffs can actively seek changes in the law through aggressive court action. They can engage in negotiation with regulatory agents and attempt to mitigate the regulatory effects, or have them apply only after a certain period that will allow for industry "adjustment." They can engage in reactive challenging of regulations; that is, when they are charged formally and brought into court, they can initiate challenges to the law. They can band together into Associations on the basis of common interests and utilize these associations to voice their collective position. Finally, they can resort to bribery, blackmail, extortion, payoffs, and a variety of other corrupting measures in pursuit of their goal of effective control. These corrupting attempts can be made both at higher official levels (since they have access to the personnel at this level of the regulatory process), and at agent enforcement levels. Thus, legally regulated sellers have *both* licit and illicit means of influence available to them.

Sellers operating in illicit markets do not possess the same credibility of licit sellers and consequently, they do not have the same types of access to influence over their market.[6] Regulators usually view the sellers as morally reprehensible, and take a hostile position vis-à-vis their activities. As a result of the moral intention of the regulations, then, illicit sellers have limited capacity for legitimate political influence. They do not engage in lobbying in a traditional sense, and they do not actively and voluntarily come forth as "expert witnesses" during drug law hearings. They do not engage legal staffs to construct alternatives to present regulations and to initiate active resistance to present statutes through litigation. To challenge regulations, they usually must wait until the regulation is applied to them, and thus, their posture is defensive. They cannot band together and have an Association represent them and their collective views. Presumably, in the United States, their access to officials higher up in the regulatory apparatus and other government agencies is severely limited, and thus, they have minimal opportunities to corrupt upper echelons of regulatory agencies. *Thus, for sellers in illicit markets, their focal points for effective control of their market must be enforcement agents.* Retail

---

[6]The foregoing analysis operates with the assumption that illicit sellers of narcotics do not sell licit goods and services. This assumption is, of course, not totally warranted. Licit sellers may be engaged in selling illicit goods, and in fact, at higher dealing echelons, this may be a rule rather than an exception. Thus, licit sellers of one set of goods, may be able to indirectly use their political influence through these channels to effect the regulations surrounding their "other business." What the nature and extent of effects seller interpenetration may have is difficult to measure due to the relative paucity of data. However, there are several suggestive remarks one can make. In instances where the interpenetration is political in nature, illicit sellers may have direct and enduring influence in the enforcement of regulations and the nature of these regulations. Where mayors or governors, for example, are also sellers of illicit goods and services through illicit organizations or act as middlemen between illicit producers and regulators, the types and kinds of police enforcement capacity are often affected. In some countries other than the United States, the interpenetration between licit and illicit markets and control may be greater. Percentages of the take may be typically allotted to the political structure so that influence will be exerted and the seller can maintain effective market control. Recent cases in this country of government corruption accent the possibility of greater seller interpenetration than heretofore might have been thought.

TABLE 2. Indicators of Degree of Access to and influence Upon Sources of
Legitimate Authority for Sellers in Legally Regulated
Versus Legally Suppressed Markets

Legally Regulated Markets	Legally Suppressed Markets
1. Sellers have potential political influence	1. Sellers have limited potential for political influence
2. Sellers can engage in lobbying to change and to maintain laws	2. Sellers cannot, do not lobby
3. Sellers can testify as expert witnesses	3. Sellers do not testify
4. Sellers can engage legal services to actively challenge existing law and to create alternatives	4. Sellers do not actively challenge laws
5. Sellers can engage in negotiation on regulations with officials	5. Sellers cannot engage in negotiation
6. Sellers can engage in reactive challenges to charges under regulations	6. Sellers can engage in reactive challenges to charges under regulations
7. Sellers can form visible voluntary associations that can take collective positions	7. Sellers cannot form visible voluntary associations
8. Sellers can engage in the corruption of officials	8. Sellers cannot engage in corruption of officials
9. Sellers can engage in the corruption of compliance agents	9. Sellers can engage in the corruption of enforcement agents

sellers in licit markets, to be sure, concentrate at this level since their span of control and resources warrants attempted intervention only at this level. However, wholesalers and producers are able to intervene successfully at higher levels. In legally suppressed markets, even wholesalers must focus on enforcement levels since influence at higher levels is denied them.[7]

The *structural constraints* of legally suppressed markets expose the agent to an accumulation of attempted influence. Because sellers want effective control over their markets, they must find ways to neutralize enforcement agents. If they cannot avoid at least arrest and charge, and it is probably that eventually they cannot, then they must attempt to gain favorable influence with agents. The differences between legally regulated and legally suppressed markets is summarized in Table 2.

We want to point out that we are not attempting to explain why individual enforcement officials become corruptible and corrupted, nor are we making

---

[7]Evidence suggests that in America, there are no producers of heroin *per se* (it is smuggled in in a refined form). However, even in cases of producers of other illicit substances, the producers rarely have recourse to influence a higher echelon official unless as noted in an earlier footnote, this official has "interpenetration" with the illicit market.

comparisons between corrupted agents and those who are credulous. Further-more, we are not arguing that all enforcement is corrupt or that a sizeable number of agents are corrupt. We are specifying the structural conditions which focus pressure and tension on agents, antecedent to the actual day-to-day occasions of enforcement. Each department of agents makes varying adjustments to these conditions: the department may be cognizant of the pressures, demand high agent accountability, and thus be relatively immune to seller influence; or, individual agents within a department may be either "clean" or "on the take" and the problem is isolatable to individuals; or, the entire department can be involved in aiding seller control of the market; or, finally, the department itself can, or agents within the department can be selling in the market resulting in interpenetration of seller and regulator.[8]

There are additional structural constraints on agents that promote infractions of other laws in the performance of their assigned duties. Because the narcotics market involves willing buyers and sellers, agents must find ways of obtaining information that are not "victim" centered. That is, agents do not have a victim willing to give information. Thus, they must buy information or attempt to gain information from others within or near to the sellers. Moreover, having once obtained access to information about seller activity, agents must find ways of keeping their channels of information open. The manner in which they do so may involve them in infractions of other laws. As we shall detail later, there are structural pressures on enforcement agents that promote both infractions in enforcement of regulations, and that promote obstructing legal proceedings. All of these considerations gradually lead to a corruption of regulations and negotiated law enforcement practices.[9]

The focus of strain upon the agent points up a structural problem of regulation in general, and specifically the regulation of lucrative illicit markets. By looking at some of the enduring patterns of corruption, we may be able to

---

[8]It is not our argument that these are the sole features conducive to the patterns of corruption we describe below. There may be others. However, these are the most important. Insofar as the market features distinguishing the legitimate from the illegitimate markets for illicit substances obtain, and the differences in patterns of regulation obtain, we would expect to find analogous patterns of corruption, i.e., agent-focused. Many Anglo-American societies follow the regulatory model we have described, and would be expected to possess similar corruption patterns. For example, Gabor (1973) reports that Melbourne, Australia narcotics squads utilized blank search warrants. The warrants are signed *en masse* by a judge and agents could then search the premises of anyone they chose. During or after the search, a name is placed on the warrant. The practice came to light when "following a raid carried out in the usual manner, drug squad officers left behind a folder of papers. On examination the folder was found to contain, among other things, four blank search warrants—but with the signature of a Melbourne JP already attached" (Gabor, 1973:20). Other features of a society, e.g., high levels of violence such as occur in Latin American countries, obviously contribute to the likelihood of discovering violence in drug enforcement operations.

[9]Sykes, in *Society of Captives* (1958), makes a similar argument concerning prison guards. Caught in the bind of being accountable for maintaining order, yet having to rely on the inmates to maintain order, the guard must make "trade-offs" with the inmates. Redlinger (1970) offers a similar explanation for the negotiation of order in homes for emotionally disturbed children.

locate and sensitize ourselves to more general problems of the structuring of regulation. There is little irony in the generalization made by the Knapp Commission, in their report on police corruption when it states that ". . . a corrupt police officer does not necessarily have to be an ineffective one" (1972:55). Agent corruption is a product of the requirements of narcotic law enforcement and a theme found in the history of the enforcement enterprise.[10] The structural nature of narcotic law enforcement has historically created the problem of agent corruption,[11] and is reflected by the social organization of enforcement agencies.

ORGANIZATIONAL ASPECTS OF DRUG ENFORCEMENT AGENCIES

Narcotics squads, whether specialized sections within police departments, or subsegments of Vice divisions, are characterized by internally and externally generated pressures to produce visible evidence of their activity and achievements. Because the "products" of such organizations are essentially ineffable and difficult to measure, agencies *reify* specific measures of performance. These measures then become powerful inducements to organizational conformity, for in order to show adequate performance, agents must produce data in conformity with the established measures (Manning, forthcoming). The pressures to produce, and the implied sanctions for failing to produce are the structural mechanisms by which policies of agencies become agent conduct.[12]

---

[10]It may be too, that certain individuals are channeled into being agents and that these individuals are more corruptible than some hypothetical average; this we doubt. For one thing, many police departments work their men on a rotation basis and thus narcotics agents are policemen transferred into and out of sections. Secondly, given the nature of regulation, other officers have the opportunity for bribe-taking, extortion, etc. as is amply documented in the literature on police corruption (Sherman, ed., 1974). Assessment on this proposition would require data most difficult to gather. Among other things one would need detailed life histories of agents that would indicate any and all prior involvement in corruption, and these would necessarily have to be matched against a comparable sample of non-agents. Another way of approaching the problem would be to follow a cohort of "clean" agents through their tenure as police officers noting along the way the temptations to corruption. In either case, the officers, especially those who have something to hide, are not likely to voluntarily subject themselves to close scrutiny.

[11]King (1972) reports that in 1917, two years after the passage of the Harrison Act criminalizing nonmedical use, "the first narcotic agent was caught and convicted for taking a large bribe." In that same year, Treasury agents, who were held responsible for enforcing the regulations, began seizure activities (previous to this time, agents did not seize large amounts of drugs). As King notes, agents even in 1917, needed a way to show they were doing their job, and one way they did and do is to account for their activity in terms of the dollar value that can be attached to what they have acquired:

> By 1917 increasing numbers of civic leaders and responsible citizens were calling for federal intervention and strict federal controls to stop the drug traffic. In that year the first caches of illegal drugs were seized by Treasury agents. The Treasury then started the deceptive practice, continued ever since by drug-law enforcers, of announcing each seizure in terms of how many millions of dollars the contraband substances might have been worth if they had been sold at maximum prices in the illegal market. (1972:25)

Internal pressures can be analytically separated from those external to the agency. In addition, we can separate pressures in terms of their impact. Some pressures induce agents to violate laws to enforce the narcotics law, while others induce agents to obstruct justice. The translation of pressure is very indirect; "varying efforts to enforce these (vice laws) undermine the possibilities for strict supervision because the work obliges the men to engage in illegal and often degrading practices that must be concealed from the public" (Rubenstein, 1973:375). Furthermore, the application of successful techniques on the street (discussed below) produces a continuing ambivalence to law-abiding conduct. As Rubenstein (1973) notes, no department ". . . had found ways of fulfilling its obligation to regulate public morality without resorting to methods that constantly provide policemen with temptation and encourage ambiguous attitudes toward official standards of conduct." That is, narcotic law enforcement is virtually always secretive, duplicitous and quasi-legal, and is extremely difficult to effectively regulate.[13] Greater pressures lead to, at least, greater encounters with problematic situations containing opportunities for corruption. The more pressure there is to enforce the law, the less opportunity for close supervision, and the greater the opportunities for corruption. Ironically, increasing the effectiveness in vice enforcement brings with it the increasing likelihood of corruption.

Internal pressures for excessive enforcement are created by: (1) aspirations for promotion, salary and "easy numbers" within the unit; (2) quotas for ar-

---

[12]Regulatory agencies of all kinds reside and act in a competitive symbolic domain that includes other agencies sharing similar goals and clientele. Drug agencies seek not only to control their clientele (dealers and users) but also to maintain an *image* of control *vis à vis* their public. The public includes not only the tax payers external to the government but other agencies and members within the government. Within all organizations, there are pressures to survive as an organization and to satisfy the needs (economic, social, etc.) of the members (Clark and Wilson, 1961). At least one formal defining characteristic of organizations is their public obeisance to a set of formal goals (as associative pressures to achieve at least a semblance of these goals) and mechanisms to systematically evaluate organizational achievements.

[13]Modes of supervision and control of narcotics agents tend to replicate the dissembling, duplicity, lying and threat used by officers *against* drug offenders. The Knapp Commission, for example, "turned" four patrolmen to spy on fellow officers, often leading to massive misunderstandings (because the other Knapp agents were not known to them). Of the four, three had been essentially blackmailed into working for the Commission (arrests for corruption-type offenses led to their being invited to work undercover) and were given consideration for this work in their own charges. Further, the borders of entrapment were always skirted, if not violated (Wainwright, 1972; reprinted in Sherman, ed., 1974; Whittemore, 1973:364–383). This mode of undercover and secretive enforcement of disciplinary rules is typical in large police departments, and it creates an ambiance of doubt and suspicion of colleagues. It is always possible that a fellow officer is working for internal affairs, or will inform to them. This condition furthers the already suspicious frame of mind of the officer, and sets him against the administrative strata in a very profound fashion. Consequently, when the agent wishes to resist the control of superiors, resistance takes the form of either complicity with the targets of control (in this case, users and dealers in narcotics), or work slowdowns (see Manning, *Police Work*, chapter six, forthcoming, for a further discussion of the question of internal rule enforcement and its organizational consequences).

rests or stops insofar as these are tied to notions of success and enforced on agents;[14] (3) directives from administrators either in conjunction with "dope drives" (departmental efforts to round up users and pushers) or individual officers' attempts; (4) self-esteem maintenance produced by attempts to achieve success in terms of the conventional markers of arrests and buys; (5) moral-ideological commitments by officers to "protecting the kids" by "locking up the junkies and pushers" and thus, "winning the war against dope" and achieving a final E.N.D. ("Eradicate Narcotics Dealers"—a recent Detroit campaign against dealers).

Pressures to obstruct justice flow from similar sources to those mentioned above insofar as to be successful one must: (1) protect informants who constitute the agent's vital link to the underworld; (2) create informants through threats of prosecution on pending cases if cooperation is not forthcoming, and when they do cooperate persuade officials to drop charges against them; and (3) suppress information on cases pursued by other officers (for example, where one's informant is also responsible for a burglary). The last category of obstruction also occurs when there is interagency competition and federal agents, for example, will suppress their information about the case so that other agents (e.g., State agents) will be unable to "break" the case before them, or even with them and get "credit."

Internal pressures are complemented by external pressures to enforce the law and to obstruct justice. Law enforcement, shading into excess, is facilitated by: (1) political pressures from formally elected or appointed political officials translated through the chain of command to agents; (2) media pressures in the form of editorials, feature stories, comments on the rising crime rate (*cf.* Davis, 1952; Cohen, 1973); (3) grand jury, prosecutor's office and judicial pressure (which can work in a "negative direction" as in Washington, D.C. where District Prosecutor Silvert urged officers not to bring to him cases of personal possession of marijuana to prosecute); (4) *ad hoc* community groups and community associations; (5) external funding agencies such as ODALE, DOJ and LEAA which provide money and additional manpower (in the form of strike forces or tactical units).

The obstruction of justice occurs as a result of pressures generated by: (1) bribes to agents from users or dealers either to protect their operations or to avoid a charge once arrested; (2) competition and cooperation between and among agents and agencies (this is especially crucial when informants are needed in cases where both state and federal agents are involved, *cf.* Daley, 1975); (3) grand juries that encourage the development of "big busts" or big cases to show the public that "something is being done," also encourage the protection of snitches in order to have them work bigger cases, and to protect them in the interim from prosecution on other pending charges.

---

[14]In one department the informal quota rules were summarized by a detective in the rhyme: "Two a day keeps the Sarge away." The Knapp Commission (1972) studied the New York City quota system and for many reasons we cite here recommended that it be abandoned, and as a result the system was phased out formally shortly thereafter.

Each of these pressures, it should be emphasized, is not directly translated into the conduct of agents. The point we wish to underscore is that the organizational ambiance of narcotics law enforcement is such that rather than providing inducement to conformity to the law, it is more likely to underscore the virtues of avoidance of the more obvious requirements of law enforcement. It encourages rather more excess in pursuit of the job and modification of procedural rules to maximize arrests and buys. In the course of so doing, one learns to view with only minimal concern somewhat less obvious consequences of systematic obstruction of justice.

PATTERNS OF AGENT CORRUPTION IN NARCOTICS LAW ENFORCEMENT

Corruption, in the sense that we are using the term, refers to departures from correct procedure in exchange for some goods, services or money. That is, the agent modifies what is expected of him by the nature of his employment and thus affects the outcome of enforcement. The corruption of enforcement can occur in seven principal ways:

1. Taking Bribes. If we eliminate for the moment everyday/anyday favors and gratuities, considerations and presents which are exchanged between police officers and the public, bribe-taking is the most common form of corruption (on this point, see Stoddard in Sherman, ed., 1974). In the area of narcotics enforcement, bribe-taking manifests itself in two ways. First, there is a payoff to officers from dealers for advance-warning information concerning raids, or other such warning information. This type of payoff is made on a regular basis. Secondly, there are payoffs made at the time of a raid or arrest. In the first instance, the bribes are made by a single organization or person, whereas in the second, officers accept bribes from a variety of persons; that is, officers accept the bribe from whomever they are arresting. At the time of the arrest, the individual being arrested will make explicit or implicit remarks concerning money or drugs that he may have available. The officers may take the dealer's stash money and then let him go (see Knapp Commission, 1972:94). If the dealer has no money the officers may confiscate his drugs but this case is not as often occurring as the taking of stash money. However, the opportunities for bribery do not end with the making of the arrest, for the agent or agents still has the option of "making the case" badly. That is, the agent can write the case up in such a manner that it will be thrown out of court. And there are other ways:

> . . . [A] police officer who is skillful or experienced enough can write an affidavit which appears to be very strong, but is still open-ended enough to work in favor of a defendant when coupled with appropriate testimony from the arresting officer. For example, an officer could state in his complaint that the suspect threw the evidence to the ground at the approach of the police. Should that officer later testify that he lost sight of the evidence as it fell, the evidence and the case could well be dismissed. The Commission learned that it was not uncommon for defense attorneys in narcotics cases to pay policemen for such favors as lying under oath and

procuring confidential police and judicial records concerning their clients' cases (Knapp Commission, 1972:97).

The Knapp Commission data is substantiated by evidence gathered by other researchers (cf. Sherman, ed., 1974). For example, Sanders (1972) studying the court experiences of middle class drug users, was able to show that police officers, working through defense attorneys, were willing to later drop narcotics charges for a fee. The attorney acted as a middleman in the situation. He would take money from his client, take a percentage for his "service" and pass on the remainder to the officer. The money may buy a change in the charge (e.g., a reduction from a felony to a misdemeanor), but more likely the money was in exchange for "sabotaging" the trial. The officer would make errors such as incompetent testimony or not being able to find evidence (see Sanders, 1972:242–243).[15]

The Knapp Commission also uncovered evidence of bribes in several diverse forms:

> . . . [I]t was quite common for an apprehended suspect to offer to pay his captors for his release and for the right to keep part of his narcotics and cash. This was especially true at higher levels of distribution where the profits to be made and the penalties risked by a dealer were very high. One such case was that of a suspended Narcotics Division detective who was recently indicted in Queens County and charged with taking bribes to overlook narcotics offenses. The indictment alleged that this officer accepted $1,500 on one occasion for not arresting a suspected drug pusher who was apprehended while in possession of $15,000 worth of heroin. There is evidence that on another occasion this detective was paid $4,000 by a different narcotics pusher for agreeing not to confiscate $150,000 worth of heroin. The detective has pleaded guilty to attempting to receive a bribe, and his sentence is pending (1972:96).

2. *Using Drugs.* Agents have been known to use illicit drugs. For example, Harris (1974) interviewing three ex-narcotics agents, reports the smoking of marijuana by agents as they sat "surveillance." In another case witnessed by

---

[15]A vice officer presented these rationales to Sanders concerning the deals that go on behind the scenes:

> I'm sure that there are lawyers who are paying off policemen in some cases. You'll always have this. But this is controlled by the police department because you have the IID (Internal Investigation Division) and the policeman now is making $12,000 a year—he's making good money. I've heard a lot of stories about a lot of policemen and I've learned one thing—if you don't have something good to say about someone don't say anything at all. So I don't carry tales. Some cases are dealt with between the lawyer and the police officer or through other channels, but I think this is really good. I think it is beneficial to the individual that gets busted. If he can pay $300 or $400 to get out of it, good, you're out of it. That's the type of society this is. This is what was built by other people. We are going to have to realize that it is a good point. Sure, there are a lot of policemen making money on it through lawyers. The reason is that it is an easy dollar and the chances of getting caught are slim. I really believe it is good for the citizen. It may sound fascist but it is good to have a way out of something. When you get busted you need a way out. This is the game (Sanders, 1972:235).

one of us, an agent about to participate in a late night raid discussed the fact that he was tired, and promptly produced a nonprescription vial of amphetamines from which he took and swallowed three capsules. Undercover agents, to show their loyalties to the people on whom they are doing surveillance, often must "turn-on" (use drugs) with them. In several observed cases, officers went to parties and carried their own stash as evidence that they were users.

3. *Buying/Selling Narcotics.* Evidence gathered by journalists suggests that many observers believe that dealing in narcotics exists among agents, especially local agents in Los Angeles and New York. *New York Times* reporter David Burnham wrote:

> . . . [S]ome policemen wonder whether the transfer of two hundred plain clothesmen, a highly cynical group of men, to the narcotics beat might not result in a net increase in the flow of narcotics into the city. . . . "The moral jump from making illegal drug deals to get evidence and dealing in drugs to make money is not as big as it might look to an outsider," one experienced narcotics detective said (Burnham, in Sherman, ed., 1974:309–310).

In Gary, Indiana, near Chicago, seven policemen were convicted in February, 1975, of conspiracy to deal in drugs and of drug trafficking (*Washington Post*, February 9, 1975). In 1974, the same group was convicted on trafficking charges. The Knapp Commission discovered in the testimony of two "ex-addicts" that eleven Harlem policemen would supply them with narcotics in exchange for cigarettes, whiskey, power tools, a mini-bike and stereo equipment. The addicts had collected the goods through burglaries (Daley, 1974:339). Several other variations on this pattern occur: the selling of narcotics to informants for resale to other addicts, and the use of narcotics to pay off informants for information useful in making a buy or buy and bust. Narcotics officers also financed heroin buys for others when the aim was not eventual arrest (Knapp Commission, 1972:91–92); they also accept narcotics as bribes, which in turn they sell. In New York, no informant fees were paid officially: narcotics seized in one arrest can be used to pay off informants (Whittemore, 1973:323) (a case of both arrogation of seized property and dealing illegally in narcotics). A more illusive type of corruption is simple conspiracy to deal, such as introducing potential customers to dealers. Since the latter is a requirement of undercover work for informants, it is hardly surprising that agents might introduce, directly or indirectly, clients to a pusher. Without such introductions, the enforcement of most narcotics dealing laws would be impossible.

4. *Arrogation of seized property.* Since the law in most states requires that any property relevant to the crime must be seized until the trial has been held, large amounts of property, typically automobiles, guns, money and drugs are confiscated as evidence. The control of evidence of this type is extremely difficult as well as expensive for large police departments. [Its legal status is

under present review (Technical Papers of National Drug Abuse Commission, Appendix, Vol. III).] A series of scandals in the New York Department in 1973 involved missing or stolen property, including well over one hundred kilos of high quality heroin taken from the Property section of the New York Police Department (Pileggi, 1973a). Further, the arrest situation often involves large amounts of money involved in the exchange that led to the arrest, as well as other monies which may be a part of the dealer's crib or bank. During the Knapp Commission testimony, Patrolman Phillips (one of the corrupt policemen "turned" by the Commission) testified he saw a plainclothesman leaving the scene of a multi-million dollar drug raid with $80,000 confiscated earlier in the raid. In March, 1975, the officer identified by Phillips was indicted, and charged with stealing more than $1,500 in cash and heroin (the minimum amount for a grand larceny charge) (*New York Times,* March 21, 1975). Although the money used in the actual exchange (used by the informant or the agent to buy the drugs) is marked and the serial numbers registered prior to the buy, other confiscated money becomes the responsibility of the agents to collect, record and to insure its safe deposit with the IRS.

  5. Illegal Searches and Seizures. There are several ways in which illegal searches and seizures can be initiated, and each is used at one time or another (see Harris, 1974; Sanders, 1972; Wambaugh, 1973; see also Johnson and Bogomolny, 1973, for a study of reported arrest data). One way illegal searches are conducted is for the narcotics officer to claim there was a "quantity of alleged drugs" in "plain sight" (see Wambaugh, 1973; Sanders, 1972), and then search the house, apartment or vehicle of the person. In the case of a vehicle search, often the outward appearances of the person or the vehicle provide clues to officers that a drug violation *may* be occurring, and in addition, that a "stop" on the vehicle is warranted (Johnson and Bogomolny, 1973, euphemistically refer to these as "ancillary" or "consumption-related" offenses). The officers then stop the vehicle, "see" contraband in plain sight and initiate a search of the vehicle. Another variant on the vehicular search is to claim, as with marijuana, that "smoke could be smelled" and that the search had "probable cause." "Flaking" is a term referring to the act whereby the officer plants illicit drugs on the person (see Knapp Commission, 1972). When an officer has made an illegal search, he may "find" drugs which have been "flaked." Narcotics officers may possess a "sure bust kit" that contains several types of drugs and allows them to select the appropriate contraband that will justify their illegal search. Reiss (personal communication) indicates that a narcotics officer working the Washington, D.C. area told him that he had never made an arrest *without* flaking the person. Still other officers have reported to us that, "If you're gonna' search 'em, it's wise to come up with sumthin'."

  A variation on "flaking" is "dropsey." An officer will report that he came upon the subject just as he was throwing contraband away. The "overt act" of throwing the contraband away allows for the search; however, in the case of "dropsey" the officer actually supplies the contraband. Pileggi (1971) quotes one New York City judge as saying: "Surely, though, not in *every* case was the defendant unlucky enough to drop his narcotics at the feet of a policeman. It follows that in at least some of the cases the police are lying."

"Padding" occurs when the officer adds drugs to the already confiscated evidence either to increase the quality of the substance seized and make the evidence more acceptable in court, or to raise the charge from a misdemeanor to a felony after the arrest had been made (Knapp Commission, 1972:91ff.). In one case, agents seized several ounces of lactose and a dealer, but no narcotics. A Marquis field test was done on the seized lactose and produced negative results. At that point the officers "sweetened" the seizure so that a field test would render it positive. In cases where drugs are added to raise the charge, often the motive is to use the more serious charge as a threat and thereby gain greater leverage over the arrestee. This pressure can be used to "turn" the arrestee into a "confidential informant," or extort money from the arrestee, or to persuade the arrestee to offer bribes or service to the officer (for example, sexual favors).[16]

6. The Protection of Informants. Informants are the heart of the enforcement of narcotics laws. Detectives either pay their "snitches" out of their own pockets, or the department provides a "confidential informant" fund.[17] All major federal enforcement agencies allocate money for payment of information (FBI, DEA, etc.), as do most major police departments. At least four consequences issue from the use of informants in narcotics law enforcement. First agencies may have to compete for information, and informants have the option of accepting the best deal. In one instance, a confidential informant who was "working off cases" found that federal agents were willing to pay more and consequently began working for them. In another instance, local agents were unable to get the prosecuting attorney to drop charges against a potential snitch, so the "confidential informant" went to the federal agency and the charges were

---

[16]One Vermont narc allegedly propositioned a young girl after giving her some cocaine (*Time,* March 10, 1975). When she refused, he busted her two weeks later for selling him drugs. This case of alleged corruption, uncovered in Vermont, was one of some six hundred convictions which resulted in a letter from a County Prosecutor to the Governor asking that all six hundred convictions based on the officer's testimony be pardoned. The officer, in addition to attempted extortion, is suspected of confiscating the drugs he planted on an apparently large number of arrestees, and of converting money assigned for buys to his personal use.

[17]Robert Daley, former Deputy Commissioner of the New York Police Department, describes the present New York system which replaced the previous informal arrangement whereby detectives paid $5 fees to their informants:

> [Informants] are listed with the Police Intelligence Division under a code number and usually a code which they have been obliged to sign onto the equivalent of a bank deposit card. Their verifiable signatures are important, because they must sign receipts for money paid them. Each informant is further classified by speciality, and by the area he knows (Daley, 1975:31).

Of course, as the Knapp Commission pointed out, it is possible to create fictitious informants and for an officer to collect the fees himself.

dropped a short time thereafter. Daley (1975) provides another example: federal agents, in protecting their confidential informant *in cognito* and *in communicado,* inhibited local agents from obtaining necessary information to move on local cases. As noted by Skolnick (1966) and Van Maanen (personal communication), and as we have observed, confidential informants often are protected from prosecution on other charges while they are working. That is, as in one case, the confidential informant was caught breaking and entering a home, but the agents "fixed" the charge with the Prosecuting Attorney's office on the basis that the informant was "one of the best." The officer then added five cases to the informant's caseload. Secondly, informants may be working for several agents or agencies. This occurs more frequently in areas where interagency cooperation is virtually nonexistent. The informant is thus able to receive payment from more than one agency and in addition, perhaps keep more charges off his back. Even in the instance where the informant is working for only one agency, a third consequence results. Most informants are drug users themselves, and the agents provide money or drugs in payment. Thus, the agents become a link in the marketing of narcotics. The fourth consequence we have already briefly noted: informants are oftentimes protected from prosecution. As Skolnick (1966) suggests, informants in effect reverse the hierarchy of criminal penalties in that they are allowed to work off charges, receive no penalty, and may even be paid for their services. In cases where officers hope to reach "Mr. Big," the costs of protection from prosecution spiral. Each level of the dealing chain must be granted some measure of immunity from prosecution, or some consideration for turning state's evidence. For some of those in the dealing chain, charges will never be filed and thus justice will be obstructed in order that someone deemed higher up can be caught.[18]

7. *Violence.* Sometimes the information desired from an informant is not forthcoming and some "physical therapy" is necessary (Redlinger, 1969). the potential for violence in narcotics enforcement is high; often addicts are roughed up in attempts to gain information from them. Moreover, violence can be used to force informants to engage in illegal behavior such as stealing *for narcotics officers* (see Knapp Commission, 1972:92). Agents also have the option of turning the name of the informant over to interested dealers, and can effectively use this threat to gain information. Sometimes, of course, especially on informants who may turn out to be quite unreliable, they do turn the names over. The use of unwarranted violence can also occur during raids. Officers can claim that the dealer "went for his gun" and proceed to blow him away; such a procedure has merits in that the dealer is no longer able to testify otherwise, and in addi-

---

[18]The informant system facilitates extortion, lying, blackmail and violence. Information sold to an officer, or given during questioning, can be used for the officer's own interests. Likewise, the informant can turn the information to his. By informing a dealer that officers are coming, for example, the informant may be able to avenge some affront. Informants often do turn in people they have quarrels or grudges with, and the informant system allows for the turning of the process around. The informant may be able to "set up" an officer much like he sets up dealers. Too, informant information may be used by an officer who is also dealing to effectively eliminate his competition.

tion the officers make a good case and obtain the rewards. Other features of narcotics enforcement make very likely the unfortunate possibility that agents will shoot other agents in the same agency (e.g., in a shoot-out involving an undercover agent who is indistinguishable from the targets of police bullets), or uniformed officers in another agency may shoot narcotics officers (or vice versa) as occurred in Cali, Colombia in February, 1975, and in West Germany in March, 1975. In both of the last cases, U.S. agents killed foreign police officers in "shoot-outs" touched off by raids.

Violence can be used to restore face after agent errors, as happened in Boise, Idaho:

> The narcs hired operatives, at 3 dollars an hour, to make connections with dealers. Near Sun Valley, agents gave one such operative $1,000 and waited outside a bar while he went in, strolled through and left by the back door. Burned on another buy when a dealer passed off powdered aspirin as heroin, agents returned posing as Mafia hoods and retrieved their money at gun point. To support this cover, agents offered to buy guns in the underworld: this sparked a wave of sporting goods-store burglaries around Pocatello. When police figured out what was going and complained, the narcs accused them of being involved in the drug trade (*Newsweek,* January 27, 1975).

COMMENT

Licit and illicit markets have many features in common, but they differ substantially as a result of the moral intention of regulatory statutes, the loyalties of those applying the statutes, and the manner of application. We have noted that sellers in licit markets have both legitimate and illegitimate means to influence regulatory policies and action. Sellers of illicit goods and services (such as narcotics) have recourse only to illicit means, and moreover, because of the nature of their incredulity, they ordinarily must focus their efforts on enforcement agents. Hypothetically, then, if illicit sellers could effect control over their markets through higher, more powerful channels, they would attempt to do so. It is critical to understand that the structural features of society, and in particular regulatory agencies and the activities they regulate, dispose specific elements to be exposed to corruption. Agents, thus, are more often placed upon an invitational edge of corruption, and are a major point of tension in the regulation of legally suppressed markets.[19]

Our discussion should not be taken as limited to the dramatic instances of corruption in the narcotics field, but rather should be viewed as pointing out areas of corruption that one might find in other regulatory agencies. Since the

---

[19]While agents regulating licit markets are located in a similar position, there is not as much focus for effective control upon their position. Licit sellers have other potentially more powerful means for effecting control over their markets. Thus, while the potential for corruption of these agents exists, its return in terms of effective market control is not as great. Agents regulating licit markets have relatively little power to change policy, and licit market sellers have access through both legitimate and not so legitimate channels to persons of greater power.

structural features of both markets and their regulatory-enforcement agencies are similar, evidences of corruption in one should instruct us to look for such features in other agencies and their personnel. The nature of licit markets allows for that corruption to occur at more varying levels than in legally suppressed markets. That is, the same *forms* of corruption occur and exist, but the structural positions where they can occur appear to be more numerous. In addition, because markets and their goods and services are defined as licit, some areas deemed "corruption" in illicit markets are not seen as such in licit ones, and this bifurcation of vision only serves to point out the structuring features of moral intent.[20]

Although some of the similarities are quite obvious, we would like to compare types of corruption found in licit and illicit markets. In both markets, *bribery* is to be found. The history of American politics is punctuated with pay-offs, bribes, gifts and the like forwarded by legitimate businessmen to regulatory agents. The *use of the product* is in many instances obvious, and most often is not seen as a case of corruption. That is, members of regulatory agencies such as the F.A.A. often ride in planes; members of the F.C.C. often watch television; members of the F.D.A. often use drugs. We have already noted that in legally regulated markets, it is quite common for sellers to be asked to accept positions in agencies that regulate the very markets they come from. The interpenetration of regulators, sellers and producers is hardly considered remarkable in this country. There is a circulation of elites through, for example, the Defense Department, military, large armaments, shipbuilding and aircraft manufacturing companies. Furthermore, as Lieberson (1971) indicates, the Senate committees that are supposed to regulate spending and investment in markets are committees composed of senators from the very states that have vested interests in those areas.[21] *Buying and selling of products* one is supposed to regulate occurs in both regulatory and enforcement agencies, as does the *arrogation of seized property*. For example, automobiles seized in raids by drug agencies supply vehicles for many enforcement agents at both lower and higher echelons of the agencies, while such arrogation is a common process in bankruptcy proceedings. The use of wiretaps and bugging, *modes of illegal*

---

[20]Space does not permit the outlining of what might be called a phenomenology of corruption. Suffice it to say that elements in such an outline would be the nature of the *relationship* between the *recipient*, the *donor* and the *object* transmitted. The *definitions* given to such transactions, as well as the *structure* of the exchange (tertiary, secondary or primary exchange; short or long lag systems, *cf.* Blau, 1964 and Levi-Strauss, 1969) would also have to be taken into account. By holding constant *some* of the structural features of regulatory agencies, and examining what is *defined* as corruption, we are suggesting an analytic strategy which we hope to pursue in subsequent analyses.

[21]For example, the House Agriculture Subcommittee on Tobacco is a seven member committee that has six members from the tobacco producing states; the Minerals and Fuels Committee is "loaded with senators from states with relatively large segments of the labor force engaged in these extractive industries" (Lieberson, 1971:579–580). Likewise, the Senate Armed Services Committee has a disproportionately high membership from states that would stand to lose when arms are cut back, and in contrast, "the small Subcommittee on International Organization and Disarmament Affairs is disproportionately composed of senators from states that stand to gain through a military cutback" (Lieberson, 1971:580–581).

entry and/or surveillance is common in virtually all federal agencies; recent headlines have revealed the use of spying and taps by the Internal Revenue Service, Department of Defense and other agencies. Moreover, private industrial concerns have utilized taps to illegally spy on their regulators. *Informants* are an inimicable part of all prosecutorial activity and immunity granted to witnesses is common throughout not only courts but congressional hearings. Watergate is only a most recent example, but policies regarding immunity are also found in the Internal Revenue Service, the F.A.A., the Armed Services, and in the Department of Justice in civil as well as criminal cases.

Finally, *violence* is found more often in the regulation of illicit markets primarily because sellers do not have recourse to contracts and corporate law, but must deal with agents directly as agents must deal with sellers. The independence of the market from conventional conflict-modifying mechanisms produces conditions where violence must be used to settle differences; that is, there is no legitimate or "civilized" locus for the negotiation of disputes and no "dispassionate" third party to resolve them. Moreover, violence may be more common in illicit markets because most sellers operate at low levels of dealing (small clientele and capitalization) and with clientele that are from social classes normally associated with high rates of violence. Put in another manner, most of the narcotics dealer robberies occur at lower levels of the markets *as do robberies of legitimate sellers.* Finally, it is possible that clandestine raids, undercover work and the competition between and among agents and agencies produces greater opportunities for interpersonal violence than does the regulation of, for example, legitimate pharmaceuticals.

We advance these similarities to indicate that there are specific structural reasons why narcotics agents are more often thrown onto the invitational edge of corruption. However, any serious student of social control and regulation should not stop with analysis of enforcement agents, and agencies, but should look farther and ask the very same questions about regulatory agents and agencies. After all, objective analysis of social control should begin by being minimally encumbered by society's morality and its blinders.

REFERENCES

Blau, P. (1964) *Exchange and Power in Social Life.* New York: Wiley.

Brecher, H. W. *et al.*, (1972) *Licit and Illicit Drugs.* Boston: Little, Brown.

Clark, P. and J. Q. Wilson (1961) "Incentive Systems: A Theory of Organizations." *Administrative Science Quarterly* 6 (September):129–166.

Cohen, S. (1973) *Folk Devils and Moral Panics.* London: Palladin.

Daley, R. (1973) *Target Blue.* New York: Dell. (1975) "Inside the Criminal Informant Business." *New York* 8 (March 24): 31–35.

Davis, F. J. (1952) "Crime News in Colorado Newspapers." *American Journal of Sociology* 57 (January):325–330.

Davis, N. J. (1973) "The Abortion Market: Transactions in a Risk Commodity." Unpublished Ph.D. Michigan State University.

Edelman, M. (1962) *The Symbolic Uses of Politics.* Urbana: University of Illinois Press.

Gabor, I. (1973) "Drug Squad Inquiry." *Drugs and Society* 3 (November).

Gusfield J. (1963) *Symbolic Crusade.* Urbana: University of Illinois Press.

Harris, D. (1974) "An Inside Look at Federal Narcotics Enforcement: Three Ex-Agents Tell their Tales." *Rolling Stone* (December 5).

Hughes, E. C. (1971) *The Sociological Eye.* Chicago: Aldine.

Johnson, W. and R. Bogomolny (1973) "Selective Justice: Drug Law Enforcement in Six American Cities." Pp. 498–650 in *Drug Use in America: Problem in Perspective.* Appendix Vol. III. *Technical Papers of the Second Report of the National Commission on Marijuana and Drug Abuse.* Washington, D.C.: U.S. Government Printing Office.

King, R. (1972) *The Drug Hang-up.* New York: W. W. Norton.

Knapp Commission (1972) *Report* [on Police Corruption]. New York: George Braziller.

Levi-Strauss, C. (1969) *The Elementary Structures of Kinship.* Boston: Beacon Press.

Lieberson, S. (1971) "An Empirical Study of Military-Industrial Linkages." *American Journal of Sociology* 74 (January):562–584.

Lindesmith, A. (1965) *The Addict and the Law.* Bloomington: Indiana University Press.

Lowi, T. (1969) *The End of Liberalism.* New York: W. W. Norton.

Manning, P.K. (Forthcoming) *Police Work: Essays on the Social Organization of Policing.*

Merton, R. K. (1958) *Social Theory and Social Structure.* New York: Free Press.

Moore, M. (1970) "Economics of Heroin Distribution in New York City." Hudson Institute Mimeo Report.

Musto, D. F. (1972) *The American Disease.* New Haven: Yale University Press.

Pileggi, N. (1971) "From D.A. to Dope Lawyer." *New York Times Magazine* (May 16): 34 ff. (1973) "How Crooks Buy Their Way Out of Trouble." *New York* (November 19): 45–52. (1973a) "Further Developments in the 'French Connection' Case." *New York* (September 24).

Redlinger, L. J. (1969) "Dealing in Dope." Unpublished Ph.D. Northwestern University. (1970) "Making Them Normal: Notes on Rehabilitating Emotionally Disturbed Children." *American Behavioral Scientist* 14 (December): 237–253.

Rubenstein, J. (1973) *City Police.* New York: Farrar, Straus and Giroux.

Sanders, C. (1972) "The High and the Mighty: Middle Class Drug Users and the Legal System." Unpublished Ph.D. Northwestern University.

Schelling, T. (1967) "Economics Analysis and Organized Crime." In *Task Force Report: Organized Crime.* President's Crime Commission, Washington, D.C.: U.S. Government Printing Office.

Schur, E. (1966) *Crimes Without Victims.* Englewood Cliffs, New Jersey: Prentice-Hall.

Sherman, L. W. (ed.) (1974) *Police Corruption.* New York: Doubleday Anchor Books.

Skolnick, J. (1966) *Justice Without Trial.* New York: Wiley. (1975) *Justice Without Trial* (second edition). New York: Wiley.

Sutherland, E. C. (1949) *White Collar Crime.* New York: Dryden Press.

Sykes, G. (1958) *Society of Captives.* Princeton: Princeton University Press.

Wambaugh, J. (1973) *The Blue Knight.* New York: Dell.

Whittemore, L. W. (1973) *Super-Cops.* New York: Bantam Books.

The Mobilization of Law

*Donald J. Black**

INTRODUCTION

A theory of social control seeks to understand patterns of social control and
their relation to other aspects of social organization. Little theory of this type
can be found in social science, although over the years occasional, self-
conscious efforts in this direction have been made in sociology and social anthropology.[1] Sociological thought about social control has been too broad for
some purposes, too narrow for others. The subject matter has been defined as
the conditions for social order—a subject matter some would give to sociology
as a whole—while the detailed study of social control has centered on how official reactions to deviant behavior affect individual motivation.[2] Focussing thus
upon the relationship between control and individual adaptation, sociology has
neglected the character and integrity of social control as a natural system.[3] In
the anthropological work on social control more emphasis has been placed
upon systems of social control and dispute settlement than upon the influence
of these systems at the level of individual motivation. Unfortunately, however,
anthropologists stress concrete description and have shown little interest in
the development of general theory.[4]

*Assistant Professor of Sociology and Lecturer in Law, Yale University. For com-
ments on an earlier draft the author is grateful to John Griffiths, Jerrold Guben, Robert
Kagan, Richard Lempert, Michael E. Libonati, Maureen Mileski, Albert J. Reiss, Jr.,
David M. Trubek, and Stanton Wheeler. Support was provided by the Russell Sage Pro-
gram in Law and Social Science and by the Law and Modernization Program, both of
Yale Law School.

[1]For examples of the earlier works, see Edward Alsworth Ross, *Social Control: A
Survey of the Foundations of Order* (1901); Bronislaw Malinowski, *Crime and Custom in
Savage Society* (1926); Karl Mannheim, *Man and Society in an Age of Reconstruction:
Studies in Modern Social Structure* (1940); Karl N. Llewellyn and E. Adamson Hoebel,
The Cheyenne Way: Conflict and Case Law in Primitive Jurisprudence (1941); August B.
Hollingshead, "The Concept of Social Control," (notes renumbered—eds.). *American
Sociological Review*, 6 (1941), 217.

[2]E.g., Erving Goffman, *Asylums: Essays on the Social Situation of Mental Patients
and Other Inmates* (1961); Thomas J. Scheff, *Being Mentally Ill: A Sociological Theory*
(1966); Johannes Andenaes, "The General Preventive Effects of Punishment," *University
of Pennsylvania Law Review,* 114 (1966), 949; William J. Chambliss, "Types of Deviance
and the Effectiveness of Legal Sanctions," *Wisconsin Law Review* (1967), 703.

[3]But see, e.g., Richard D. Schwartz, Social Factors in the "Development of Legal
Control: A Case Study of Two Israeli Settlements," 63 *Yale Law Journal* (1954), 471; Irv-
ing Piliavin and Scott Briar, "Police Encounters with Juveniles," American Journal
Sociology, 70 (1964), 206; Donald J. Black, "Production of Crime Rates," American
Sociological Review, 35 (1970), 733; and "The Social Organization of Arrest," *Stanford
Law Review*, 3 (1971), 1087.

[4]But see, e.g., Paul Bohannan, "The Differing Realms of the Law," *American Anthropologist,* Special Publication, 66, no. 6, pt. 2 (Dec. 1965), 33; Leopold Pospisil, *Anthropology of Law: A Comparative Theory* (1971).

REPRINTED FROM: *Journal of Legal Studies,* The University of Chicago Law
School, Volume II(1), *1973* (125–144; 148–149).

The sociology of law is in the long term preliminary to a general theory of social control. Theoretical tools for understanding social control systems of all kinds will undoubtedly be fashioned in the study of law. Although its social characteristics are highly complicated, writ large in law are properties and processes that inhere in all systems of social control but that escape our notice in systems lacking its scale, formalization, and intrusiveness.

Law may be defined, very simply, as *governmental social control*.[5] In this essay I discuss a single dimension of legal systems: the *mobilization of law*,[6] the process by which a legal system acquires its cases.[7] The day-by-day entry of cases into any legal system cannot be taken for granted. Cases of alleged illegality and disputes do not move automatically to legal agencies for disposition or settlement. Without mobilization of the law, a legal control system lies out of touch with the human problems it is designed to oversee. Mobilization is the link between the law and the people served or controlled by the law.

The literature of jurisprudence shows little interest in the problem of mobilization, although here and there an exception is encountered. A century ago, for instance, Jhering appealed to the citizenry to call the law to action in every case of infringement of their legal rights. He argued that without continual mobilization the law would lose its deterrent power and claimed that legal mobilization is the moral obligation of every citizen whose rights are offended.[8] Roscoe Pound, too, warned that the effective power of the law requires

---

[5]Donald J. Black, "The Boundaries of Legal Sociology," *Yale Law Journal* (1972), 1086. My approach to law is uncompromisingly positivist and therefore departs fundamentally from much recent work by sociologists. Cf. Philip Selznick, *Law, Society and Industrial Justice* (1969), and "Sociology and Natural Law," *Natural Law Forum*, 6 (1961), 84; Jerome H. Skolnick, *Justice Without Trial: Law Enforcement in Democratic Society* (1966).

[6]While this use of the word "mobilization" is hardly standard, it is not utterly unknown. For instance, Bronislaw Malinowski speaks of the "juridical machinery" being "mobilized." "A New Instrument for the Interpretation of Law—Especially Primitive," *Yale Law Journal*, 51 (1942), 1237, 1250. Nevertheless, I have misgivings about the appropriateness of the word mobilization in this context. Colleagues have commented that it has a militaristic flavor and that it is too heavy for these purposes. I agree with these criticisms and would add that mobilization is a word ordinarily used in the analysis of larger-scale social phenomena, as in the mobilization of a society for war or the mobilization of dissent for a political movement. Still, I have been unable to find an adequate substitute. "Invocation" is too narrow, for instance, while "activation" seems even more awkward than mobilization. It is to be hoped that someone will eventually improve upon my choice. In the meantime I console myself with the thought that the problem with words reflects the lack of scholarly attention to the analytic problem itself.

[7]Perhaps more specification is required: By "legal system" I mean any governmental organization involved in defining or enforcing normative order. Thus, I speak of a total governmental apparatus as a legal system—the American legal system — but I also refer to a specific legal agency such as the police as a legal system. By "case" I mean any dispute or instance of alleged illegality that enters a legal system. A breach of contract, for example, becomes a case only when a suit is filed; a burglary becomes a case when it is reported to the police. A mobilization of law, then, is a complaint made to or by a legal agency. Mobilization occurs at several stages in some legal processes, e.g., at a detection stage, an evidentiary or prosecutorial stage, and an adjudicatory stage.

[8]Rudolph von Jhering, *The Struggle for Law* (1879).

a citizenry ready and willing to activate the legal process.[9] Pound's point is occasionally repeated by contemporary legal critics and scholars,[10] but the problem of mobilization more often is ignored.

Likewise, legal sociology rarely deals with the problem of mobilization. Usually the study of law as a social control system concerns the process of legal prescription or policy-making, such as legislation, or of legal disposition or dispute settlement, such as we see in judicial decision-making or police encounters. Legal mobilization mediates between the prescriptions of law and the disposition of cases, between rules and their application. Although the usual focus of legal sociology is either rules or their application, a few theoretical references to the problem of mobilization can be found.[11] Also, there is a valuable body of empirical research relevant to a theory of mobilization, revolving primarily around the questions of when and why people go to the law to solve their problems.[12]

In the present discussion I slight the social conditions under which the law is mobilized. My concern is *how* the law is set into motion. I try to show that whether or not the state selects the legal cases it handles makes a critical difference in the character of law as a social control system. I examine the organization of legal mobilization as it relates to other aspects of legal control, including a) legal intelligence, b) the availability of law, c) the organization of discretion, and d) legal change. In so doing, I show how mobilization systems influence diverse aspects of legal life, such as the kinds of cases a legal system handles, the accessibility of the population to the law, the degree of particularism in law enforcement, and the responsiveness of the law to moral change in the citizenry.

THE STRUCTURE OF LEGAL MOBILIZATION

A case can enter a legal system from two possible directions. A citizen may set the legal process in motion by bringing a complaint; or the state may initiate a complaint upon its own authority, with no participation of a citizen complainant. In the first sequence a legal agency reacts to a citizen, so we refer to it as a *reactive* mobilization process. In the second sequence, where a legal offi-

---

[9]"The Limits of Effective Legal Action," *International Journal of Ethics*, 27 (1917), 150.

[10]E.g., Harry W. Jones, *The Efficacy of Law*, 21–26 (1969).

[11]Leon H. Mayhew, *Law and Equal Opportunity: A Study of the Massachusetts Commission Against Discrimination*, 15–16 (1968); Paul Bohannan, *op. cit.;* 4; Vilhelm Aubert, "Courts and Conflict Resolution," Journal of Conflict Resolution, 11 (1967), 40.

[12]E.g., P. H. Gulliver, *Social Control in an African Society: A Study of the Arusha, Agricultural Masai of Northern Tanganyika* (1963); Alan Macfarlane, *Witchcraft in Tudor and Stuart England: A Regional and Comparative Study*, (1970); Stewart Macaulay, "Non-Contractual Relations in Business: A Preliminary Study," *American Sociological Review,* 28 (1963), 55; Laura Nader and Duane Metzger, "Conflict Resolution in Two Mexican Communities," *American Anthropologist,* 65 (1963), 584; Takeyoshi Kawashima, "Dispute Resolution in Contemporary Japan," in *Law in Japan: The Legal Order of a Changing Society*, Arthur Taylor von Mehren, ed., 1963, 41.

cial acts with no prompting from a citizen, we may speak of a *proactive* mobilization process.[13]

Across societies, history, and substantive areas of law there is enormous variability in how the law is mobilized, whether by means of citizens, the state, or both. Some legal processes are organized to allow the government to take action on its own, in others no such route is provided. In the United States, for example, the government has no responsibility for mobilizing what is traditionally called "private law," such as contract law, torts, and property law. There are no government organizations or officers empowered to bring a private-law case on behalf of a private citizen. There are only the courts, where citizens, assisted by attorneys, can make their own claims on their own behalf.[14] American public law presents an entirely different appearance. Here the government is authorized to initiate cases independently of the grievances of private citizens.[15] The major examples are criminal law and the regulatory laws establishing and enforced by federal and local government agencies such as the Federal Trade Commission, the Internal Revenue Service, city health departments, and local licensing agencies. The government is organizationally as well as legally equipped to initiate public law cases since there is a network of government agencies that routinely carry out investigations concerned with detecting illegality. Most visible are the federal, state, county, and city police forces, but numerous government agencies outside the operational jurisdiction of the police are also engaged in proactive enforcement of public law. In the Soviet Union, owing in good part to the office of procurator, considerably more state-initiated legal cases arise than in the United States. The Soviet procu-

---

[13]In psychology the concepts "reactive" and "proactive" have been used to classify individual actions in terms of their origins, the former referring to actions originating in the environment, the latter to those originating within the actor. See Henry A. Murray, "Toward a Classification of Interactions, in Toward a General Theory of Action," in Talcott Parsons and Edward A. Shils, eds., 1951, 434.

Instead of reactive and proactive legal systems we could speak, respectively, of passive and active legal systems. See Philip Selznick, *op. cit.,* 225–228.

[14]Of course, the state can and often does initiate private-law cases on its own behalf as a private party such as when the government is the victim of a breach of contract. The point is that the government cannot bring a private-law case on behalf of a private individual as it does, in effect, in many criminal cases. The participation of a legal-aid lawyer in a private action does not constitute government initiative analogous to a criminal prosecution, since legal aid implies no partisanship on the part of the state itself.

[15]In fact, mobilization provides a useful way to distinguish between public law and private law, although it corresponds only roughly to traditional usage. We can define public law as law that the state is authorized to enforce upon its own initiative, private law as law in which the initiative is granted exclusively to private citizens. By this definition a legal process formally is part of public law whether or not in practice the state acts upon the authority vested in it.

This distinction is very close to one advanced by A. R. Radcliffe-Brown: "In the law of private delicts a dispute between persons or groups of persons is brought before the judicial tribunal for settlement; in the law of public delicts the central authority itself and on its own initiative takes action against an offender." *Structure and Function in Primitive Society* (1965), 219.

racy is the prosecuting arm in criminal cases but also watches over all civil proceedings and may initiate or enter any lawsuit at any stage on either side of the dispute.[16] In earlier historical periods, the proactive capacity of the state in the American system was considerably less than it is now, but never was the American government so passive in the mobilization of law as was, for example, the government of republican Rome, to cite an extreme case where proactive enforcement was almost wholly absent.[17]

But legal agencies with the capacity to initiate cases do not necessarily use that capacity to its limits, if they use it at all. For instance, in legal theory and in the popular mind, American criminal justice is a process in which the government is highly aggressive in ferreting out illegality and bringing actions in court, but in fact the criminal justice system resembles a private-law system far more than is generally recognized. The typical criminal case comes to the attention of the authorities not on account of police initiative but through the initiative of a private citizen acting in the role of complainant.[18] Among the uniformed patrol force of a large police department, where the heaviest part of the police workload is carried, the vast majority of citizen contacts arise at the instigation of citizens who mobilize the police.[19] The police do initiate most cases of vice and narcotics enforcement and are very aggressive in traffic and crowd control. These patterns disproportionately influence the police image in the community, but, again, they are exceptional. Recent studies of other public-law systems, such as antidiscrimination commissions and housing-code enforcement agencies, reveal a similar dependence upon citizen complainants for their influx of cases.[20]

Like any analytic distinction, the reactive-proactive distinction encounters occasional difficulties when it confronts the empirical world. One marginal situation, for example, is when legal cases are brought to court by paid citizen informers. In England the use of common informers who make money from the misdeeds of their fellow citizens has a long history. These informers were a primary source of cases in some areas of English law—notably economic regulation—in the 16th and 17th centuries.[21] Informers also were frequently

---

[16]A description is provided by Harold J. Berman, *Justice in the U.S.S.R.: An Interpretation of Soviet Law* (rev. ed., 1963), 239.

[17]See generally A. W. Lintott, *Violence in Republican Rome* (1968).

[18]See Albert J. Reiss, Jr., and David J. Bordua, "Environment and Organization: A Perspective on the Police," in D. J. Bordua, ed., 1967, *The Police: Six Sociological Essays*, 25, 29–32.

[19]See Donald J. Black, "The Social Organization of Arrest," *Stanford Law Review* (1971), 1090–1092.

[20]Morroe Berger, *Equality by Statute: The Revolution in Civil Rights* (rev. ed., 1967); Leon H. Mayhew, *op. cit.;* Maureen Mileski, "Policing Slum Landlords: An Observation Study of Administrative Control," 1971, unpublished dissertation, Department of Sociology, Yale University, 60–65.

[21]M. W. Beresford, "the Common Informer, the Penal Statutes and Economic Regulation," *Economic History Review*, 10 (2d ser., 1957), 221.

put to use in the early American legal process.[22] They are still widely employed by the police in narcotics work, vice enforcement, and political surveillance. The Internal Revenue Service offers financial incentives to informers against tax evaders. As an actor in the legal control process, the informer mixes the roles of citizen complainant and public official. Another marginal pattern is voluntary surrender and confession by a law-violator. In most areas of early Chinese law a citizen was rewarded with complete immunity if he confessed to an offense before it had been detected.[23] Voluntary confession still holds an important place in Chinese legal practice, and it is by no means unknown or unrewarded in Western legal systems.

I move now to several aspects of law for which the structure of legal mobilization carries significant implications, each being an important topic in its own right in the study of legal control. The first is legal intelligence.

LEGAL INTELLIGENCE

By legal intelligence I mean the knowledge that a legal system has about law violations in its jurisdiction. How the mobilization of law is organized has profound consequences for the discovery of illegality. A reactive system lodges the responsibility for detection of violations in citizens, thereby blinding the control process to whatever law violations citizens are unable to see, fail to notice, or choose to ignore. Thus, private law systems, such as the law of contracts or torts, remain ignorant of that vast number of breaches of law about which the citizenry is silent.[24] On the other hand, a citizen-based system of legal intelligence receives much information about legal cases that would otherwise elude its attention. From a sociological standpoint, however, there is no "proper" or even "effective" system of legal intelligence. The adequacy of any aspect of legal control is not a scientific question.[25]

Access to Cases. The proactive strategy of mobilization often appears in

---

[22]Selden D. Bacon, "The Early Development of American Municipal Police: A Study of the Evolution of Formal Controls in a Changing Society," 1939, unpublished dissertation, Department of Political Science, Yale University.

[23]W. Allyn Rickett, "Voluntary Surrender and Confession in Chinese Law: The Problem of Continuity," *Journal of Asian Studies*, 30 (1971), 797.

[24]Perhaps it is apparent that my concept of illegality is considerably broader than an American lawyer might deem proper. I treat an act as illegal if it falls within a *class* of acts for which there is a *probability* of official sanction, resistance, or redress after the fact of detection. Put another way, an act is illegal if it is *vulnerable* to legal action. A concept of this kind is required if a breach of private law not responded to as such is to be understood as illegality. By contrast, the American lawyer tends to view a breach of private law as illegality only if a complaint is made or if it is defined as such in a court of law. From this legalistic view it is impossible to consider the mobilization of private law as a problem for investigation, since where there is no mobilization there is by definition no illegality. From a sociological standpoint, however, unenforced private law is perfectly analogous to unenforced public law; in both cases the mobilization of law is problematic.

[25]For a critique of studies on legal effectiveness, see Donald J. Black, "The Boundaries of Legal Sociology," *Yale Law Journal* (1972), 81.

legal systems where a reactive strategy would fail to uncover illegality of a particular kind. A reactive strategy would be almost useless in traffic control and impracticable in vice or "morals" control. Frequently those few among the citizens who would make vice complaints do not have access to the violative situations, so they cannot inform the police, and most of those with access do not complain. Detection and enforcement in these cases require a government-initiated mobilization system. Apart from crimes under the authority of the police, numerous forms of illegality, such as income tax evasion and violations of health and safety standards by businesses, are unlikely to be known or recognized by ordinary citizens; enforcement in these cases necessitates a system of inspection carried out by government agencies. To facilitate its enforcement program the government may, for instance, require self-reports from citizens and organizations, as is seen in tax enforcement, antidiscrimination surveys, and price and wage control. Registration and licensing systems similarly assist the government in learning about the population and its activities. Totalitarian regimes employ self-report systems extensively. It might be added that the more differentiated a society becomes, the more illegality tends to arise in specialized domains of social life where the offenders are encapsulated beyond the reach of a citizen detection system. Accordingly, as the process of social differentiation continues, notably in the economic sphere, we see an ever-enlarging battery of administrative agencies involved in proactive enforcement.[26]

The location of law violations is another factor conditioning the access of a legal process to its cases. Most illegality arises in private rather than public settings, making access to much illegality difficult for a government enforcement system. In part this is because of legal restrictions protecting private places from government intrusion.[27] Yet the impact of the law of privacy on legal intelligence can easily be exaggerated. Even if privacy law were totally eliminated, opening every private place to government intrusion at any time, still the sheer unpredictability of illegal behavior would bar the government from knowledge of most illegality. Unless it were to go to the technological lengths fictionalized in George Orwell's 1984, a government could not possibly achieve the surveillance necessary to detect even a minute proportion of all the illegal conduct. This applies to many kinds of law violations. Policemen on patrol in public settings, for instance, rarely discover any but the relatively trivial varieties of criminal behavior. The more serious violations, such as homicide, burglary, and grand larceny, take place behind closed doors. The police therefore depend upon ordinary citizens to provide them with information about crimes that have been committed. Of course much illegality escapes the knowledge of citizens as well. Nevertheless, the latent power of a hostile or alienated citizenry to undermine the capacity of the government to locate violations is undeniable and is amply demonstrated in the history of colonial,

---

[26]See Emile Durkheim, *The Division of Labor in Society*, 221–222, George Simpson trans., 1964.

[27]See Arthur L. Stinchcombe, "Institutions of Privacy in the Determination of Police Administrative Practice," *American Journal of Sociology*, 69 (1963), 150.

revolutionary, and other kinds of authoritarian legal systems.[28] Unpopular law-enforcement programs such as these often use paid informers.

The power of the citizenry is all the greater in private law, where enforcement without the initiative of citizens is impossible. Here the location of illegality is a moot question. People can entirely ignore domestic law or the law of negligence, for example, and the government can do nothing short of redefining these areas as public law. It is popularly believed that laws fall into disuse on account of government indifference or indolence. But in fact the demise of laws is more likely to result from citizens who fail to mobilize courts or other legal agencies. One by one, citizens may lose interest in a law, and, in private, the law may die a slow death.

Limits on Legal Intelligence. Any legal system relying upon the active participation of ordinary citizens must absorb whatever naiveté and ignorance is found among the citizenry. The common man makes occasional errors when he applies what he takes to be legal standards to his everyday life, not only because of his lack of legal training but also because many social situations have a legally ambiguous character. In complex legal systems miscalculations by citizens are continually routed away from the courts by legal gatekeepers of various kinds. In private law, a major gatekeeping burden is carried by the private attorney.[29] In the process of advising their clients, attorneys serve the larger legal process as intelligence agents, sorting through and narrowing the raw input of cases moving toward the courts from day to day. In public law, other gatekeepers screen out the legal dross: government prosecutors, police, and the many enforcement officers attached to administrative agencies, such as health officers, food and drug inspectors, and internal revenue agents. Without these gatekeepers all the intelligence gaps in the citizenry would reappear in the legal system.

Other intelligence losses greatly overshadow those resulting from citizen error. Much illegality is unknown because so many citizens fail to call upon the law when they experience law violations. The reluctance of citizens to mobilize the law is so widespread, indeed, that it may be appropriate to view legal inaction as the dominant pattern in empirical legal life. The number of unknown law violations probably is greater in private law than in public law, although only speculation is possible. The outline of legal inaction is just now beginning to be known through surveys of the citizen population.[30] Other relevant research is afoot. A recent study of dispute settlement in a Swedish fishing village, for instance, indicates that communities can passively absorb an enormous amount of illegal behavior, even when it continues for many years and

---

[28]E.g., Gregory J. Massell, "Law as an Instrument of Revolutionary Change in a Traditional Milieu: the Case of Soviet Central Asia," *Law and Society Review*, 2 (1968), 179.

[29]See Talcott Parsons, "A Sociologist Looks at the Legal Profession," in *Essays in Sociological Theory* (rev. ed., 1964), 370.

[30]See President's Commission on Law Enforcement and Administration of Justice, Crime and Its Impact—An Assessment, (*Task Force Report*, 1967), 17–19.

includes numerous well-defined victimizations.[31] In fact, legal mobilization sometimes is more socially disruptive than the illegal behavior that gives rise to it. Gradually a research literature is collecting around the question of when people mobilize the law, given illegality. The nature of the social relationship enveloping a legal dispute or violation emerges as an especially powerful predictor of legal mobilization. Thus, we know from East African and Japanese materials, among others, that resort to a government court occurs primarily in legal conflicts between relative strangers or persons who live in different communities.[32] Persons in intimate relationships tend to use extralegal mechanisms of dispute settlement when quarrels arise. However, they do not hesitate to call upon the law to settle their disputes when extralegal social control is unavailable in intimate social relationships, a pattern seen, for example, in the loosely structured barrios of Venezuela.[33] Usually, the likelihood that extralegal control will be available in a social relationship is a function of the intimacy of the relationship as measured by such indicators as its duration, the frequency of interaction, the intensity of interaction, the degree of interdependence between the parties, and the number of dimensions along which interaction between the parties occurs. Accordingly, we expect that mobilization of the law will be infrequent in what Gluckman in his classic study of the Barotse of Zambia calls "multiplex" relationships.[34]

Much of this may be summarized in the following proposition: the greater the relational distance between the parties to a dispute, the more likely is law to be used to settle the dispute.[35] With social predictors of this sort we can easily anticipate many empirical patterns, such as the finding that breach of contract rarely leads to a court case when it takes place between businessmen who have a continuing relationship with recurrent transactions.[36] We may observe, then, that a reactive legal system acts to reinforce the tendency of citizens to use law only as a last resort, since it allows citizens to establish their own priorities. Because citizens use the law reluctantly, they help to make the law a conservative enterprise that for the most part leaves the *status quo* to its own designs. Social research on law eventually will reveal the extent and social context of legal inaction in numerous areas of law and across societies, thereby making possible a comprehensive theory of the mobilization of law.[37]

---

[31]Barbara Yngvesson, "Decision-Making and Dispute Settlement in a Swedish Fishing Village: An Ethnography of Law," 1970, unpublished dissertation, Department of Anthropology, University of California, Berkeley.

[32]P. H. Gulliver, *op cit.*, 204, 263–266; Takeyoshi Kawashima, *op. cit.*

[33]Lisa Redfield Peattie, *The View from the Barrio* (1968), 57–59.

[34]Max Gluckman, *The Judicial Process among the Barotse of Northern Rhodesia* (rev. ed., 1967), 18–19.

[35]See Donald J. Black, "Production of Crime Rates," *American Sociological Review*, 35 (1970), 740–742; The Social Organization of Arrest, *Stanford Law Review*, 23 (1971), 1107–1108.

[36]Stewart Macaulay, *op. cit.*

[37]As noted earlier, I make no effort here to survey the social factors that predict the mobilization of law. My discussion of relational distance above is intended only to allude to this issue and to illustrate how it may be approached with general theory. A more

A legal intelligence system resting upon the initiative of citizens involves another kind of limitation, one that occurs regardless of the rate at which citizens mobilize the law. This limitation inheres in the simple fact that reactive systems operate on a case-by-case basis.[38] Cases enter the system one by one, and they are processed one by one. This creates an intelligence gap about the relations among and between cases. It is difficult to link patterns of illegal behavior to single or similar violators and thus to deal with the sources rather than merely the symptoms of these patterns. To discover these patterns a systematic search for factual similarities across cases is needed.

Police systems do some pattern-oriented analysis of the cases coming to their attention through citizen complaints, but most patterns of illegality escape their detection net. One consequence may be a higher chance of survival for professional criminals,[39] although some patterned criminality is uncovered through *modus operandi* files. In other areas where the government does its own investigations, strategies for finding patterns of violation can likewise be used, although illegality varies in its amenability to pattern detection. Proactive enforcement campaigns often originate from single complaints. One case of processed food contamination, for instance, can lead to an inspection effort covering all businesses producing and distributing that particular variety of food. The inspection may expose one business routinely violating health standards or a number of businesses involved in the same category of violative behavior. Frequently one case of illegality by a business enterprise implies a pattern of illegality, since much business activity is by its nature programmed and repetitious. One violation of safety requirements by an automobile manufacturer, for example, usually means that numerous cases are at large in the community, and government inspections may unveil similar violations by other manufacturers. Similarly, in some cities housing-code enforcement officers inspect the whole of an apartment building when they learn, by complaint, of one violation in the building; they assume that the landlord may fail to meet code specifications in all of his units.[40] In the criminal justice system single complaints about narcotics or vice can provide the police with opportunities to penetrate offense networks and markets and discover large numbers of interrelated violations.

The enforcement of private law sharply contrasts with these illustrations

---

comprehensive treatment would include, for example: the seriousness of the dispute or illegality, measured by the nature of the sanction or restitution or by its effects upon the on-going social order; the organization and integration of the community context; the resources required for the mobilization of law; the social status of the parties; the cultural context, including the degree of normative integration between the parties; and the organization of the dispute-settlement process itself, whether adversarial or conciliatory, formal or informal. The concern of this essay—the organization of mobilization—also relates to the probability of mobilization.

[38]Leon H. Mayhew, *op. cit.*, 159.

[39]Egon Bittner and Sheldon L. Messinger, "Some Reflections on the Police and 'Professional Crime' in West City," (Sept. 1966), unpublished paper, Center for the Study of Law and Society, University of California, Berkeley.

[40]Maureen Mileski, *op. cit.*

from public law. A good case in point is contract law, where it is not unusual to find patterns of breach emanating from a single individual or business or from members of a broader category of legal actors, such as real estate agents, mail order businesses, or insurance companies. Apart from patterns involving a recurrent breach, one act by a single business may involve numerous breaches of contract with individuals dispersed in the population, as when a holiday tour or an entertainment event is ended prematurely and the promoters do not make a monetary refund to the many victims. Private-law violations such as these can be remedied through "class actions," single legal suits covering a number of complaints of the same kind, but their frequency is far behind the rate at which patterns of private-law violation apparently occur and would be much greater if the government were involved in enforcement. The government would learn of more patterns of illegality, if only because information about all known violations would pass through one central processing system similar to a police system. At present the only official information on private-law cases is generally to be found in court records. Since no record is made of the private-law cases that do not reach the court, there can be no legal intelligence about them analogous to police records in the criminal realm. And even the court records on file are presently irrelevant to the on-going process of legal control.[41]

Also eluding any case-by-case legal process is the larger pattern by which legal problems are distributed in the population of citizens. Owing to social conditions beyond the reach of any case-oriented mobilization system, legal trouble is differentially visited upon the citizenry. Crimes of violence and interpersonal conflicts of all kinds disproportionately afflict the lower social strata (family-related violence, for example, is particularly common among poor blacks) and property matters often create a need for law among the higher status segments of the population. These structurally embedded patterns cannot be a direct concern of reactive control systems, although case records can be useful to social engineering efforts of other kinds. Because these patterns of misery cannot be confronted by single legal officials dealing with single cases of so many isolated victims and violators, their job is very much a matter of picking up the social debris deposited by larger social forces. Apart from its deterrence effect, the extent of which is unknown, a reactive legal system ever listens to the troubles of the citizenry, while the larger principles and mechanisms by which these troubles come into being escape it. In this sense, a case-oriented legal process always begins too late.[42] While a proactive system also is unable to attack the broader social conditions underlying law violations,

---

[41]I make no effort in this essay to review the extragovernmental controls operating in response to illegal behavior. Some pattern-oriented control of private-law violations, for instance, occurs through credit bureaus and informal reputational networks and black-listing systems.

[42]This is not to deny that a legal agency can respond to pressures built up in a reactive mobilization process. For instance, a high rate of purse-snatching complaints may lead the police to institute patrol or undercover operations to deal more effectively with the problem. In this way, the caseload of a citizen-based mobilization system can be an important source of intelligence to legal administrators and policy-makers.

it does have an ability to intervene in social arrangements that reactive systems lacks. It can, for instance, destroy an illegal business operation, such as a
gambling enterprise or crime syndicate, that may be the source of thousands of
violations a week. Police control of automobile traffic, too, involves prevention
through social engineering of a kind impossible in a legal process relying solely upon citizen complaints.

The proactive system also has the power to prevent illegality in specific
situations. While it cannot reach the many forms of illegality occurring in private places, a proactive system can prevent some violations in public places.
The degree of prevention is difficult to assess, however, and in any case the
forms of illegal behavior subject to situational prevention are likely to be
minor. In a reactive process, prevention of this kind occurs only in the rare case
when a citizen contacts a legal agency concerning an illegal act that is immi-
nent or in progress and the agency intercedes. The heavy reliance of legal systems upon citizens thus assures that prevention will not be a major accomplishment. This is a more concrete sense in which a reactive system begins too
late. To this inherent sluggishness of any citizen-based system, private law
adds the delay involved in gaining a hearing in court. No civil police are available for immediate aid and advice to people involved in private-law problems.
This will probably come with further legal evolution and differentiation, but in
the meantime private-law systems lag far behind in the wake of the problems
they are established to control.

In sum, a mobilization system implies a particular organization of knowledge about law violations. A reactive system places responsibility in the
citizenry and thereby brings law to the private place, with its numerous and
serious forms of illegality. A proactive system can discover violations that citizens are unable or unwilling to report but misses much private illegality. In a
reactive system the kinds and rates of cases are a function of the kinds and
rates of complaints by private citizens. In a proactive system the kinds and
rates of cases result from the distribution of official resources by the control
system itself. Because of the reactive system's reliance upon citizens and its
case-by-case schedule of operation, it involves certain intelligence weaknesses,
such as a near incapacity to identify patterns of illegality necessary to prevention. The proactive system can deal with patterns rather than mere instances
of illegality, which gives it a strong preventive capacity, but it is limited
largely to marginal and minor forms of illegality. The legally more important
problems then, are the responsibility of a mobilization system that cannot prevent them.

THE AVAILABILITY OF LAW

The previous section concerned the access of a legal system to the cases within
its jurisdiction. Now we reverse our viewpoint and consider the access of citizens to the law. We must view legal life from below as well as from above,[43]

---

[43]Laura Nader and Barbara Yngvesson, "On Studying the Ethnography of Law and
Its Consequences, in Handbook of Social and Cultural Anthropology," in John J. Honigmann, ed., forthcoming.

since every instance of legal control is also an instance of legal service. The availability of law to citizens varies markedly across and within legal systems and cannot be taken for granted in a sociological theory of law. Access to law is a function of empirical legal organization.

Two Models of Law. The reactive mobilization system portrays an *entrepreneurial model of law.* It assumes that each citizen will voluntarily and rationally pursue his own interests, with the greatest legal good of the greatest number presumptively arising from the selfish enterprise of the atomized mass. It is the legal analogue of a market economy.

Indeed, it has been argued that the organization of private law as a reactive system is not merely the analogue of a market economy; it is also the legal substructure essential to a market economy. Historically the system of "private rights" in contract, property, and tort law emerged and flourished with capitalism.[44] Here, however, I am suggesting only that a citizen-based system of mobilization—whatever the type of law—operates according to the same behavioral principles as a market system of economic life.[45] In their primordial forms, both are self-help systems. The proactive system, by contrast, is a *social-welfare model of law,* with the legal good of the citizenry being defined and then imposed by government administrators, albeit with some influence by interest groups in the citizen population. In the pure type of the social-welfare model of law, however, no role is provided for members of the citizenry in the determination of legal policy, just as in the pure type of welfare economy the will of the population need not be systematically introduced into the decision process. We might say, then, that a proactive system does not merely make the law available; it imposes the law.

Legal systems that operate with a reactive strategy often employ mechanisms assuring that mobilization will be truly voluntary and entrepreneurial, although this may not be the motive behind their implementation. One American illustration is the prohibition against solicitation by attorneys.

---

[44]David M. Trubek, "Law, Planning, and Economic Development" (1971), 65–70, unpublished paper, Yale Law School.

[45]This claim has also been made for the common law system in general, since, like an economic market, it is highly decentralized, competitive, largely private, and generates strong pressures for efficient performance among individuals. Richard A. Posner, "A Theory of Negligence," *Journal of Legal Studies,* 1, no. 29 (1972), 49. Posner also notes that the mobilization of negligence law is literally an economic market system:

> The motive force of the system is supplied by the economic self-interest of the participants in accidents. If the victim of an accident has a colorable legal claim to damages, it pays him to take steps to investigate the circumstances surrounding the accident; if the investigation suggests liability, to submit a claim to the party who injured him or the party's insurance company; if an amicable settlement cannot be reached, to press his claim in a lawsuit, if necessary to the highest appellate level. The other party has a similar incentive to discover the circumstances of the accident, to attempt a reasonable settlement, and, failing that, to defend the action in court. By creating economic incentives for private individuals and firms to investigate accidents and bring them to the attention of the courts, the system enables society to dispense with the elaborate governmental apparatus that would be necessary for gathering information about the extent and causes of accidents had the parties no incentive to report and investigate them exhaustively. *Supra,* at 48.

Were attorneys authorized to gather legal cases through solicitation, the input of legal business surely would change, since many otherwise passive victims of illegality undoubtedly would be persuaded to mobilize the law.[46] The already great influence that lawyers exert on the input of cases would also be increased. In the American system, where attorneys stand to profit from some cases, the same incentives that entice private citizens to bring suits, such as treble damages in private antitrust actions, might entice attorneys to solicit business. Insofar as attorneys create their own business through solicitation, they in effect become private prosecutors, diluting the purity of the legal market. The legal doctrine of "standing" is another device that buttresses the entrepreneurial organization of law. This doctrine holds that before a party may complain in a lawsuit, he must show that his interests are directly affected in the case at issue. Here it is uninvolved citizens rather than attorneys who are barred from influencing the mobilization of law, again protecting the purity of the legal market.

There are few corresponding mechanisms to accommodate citizens who have occasion to mobilize the law. This is not surprising since, like any entrepreneurial process, a reactive legal system assumes that those wanting to pursue their interests are able to do so.

Limits on Legal Availability. The cost of litigation is a widely recognized limitation on the availability of private law. While services such as legal aid programs and small-claims courts have been established to reduce the financial burden for low-income citizens, the fact remains that the effectiveness with which citizens can pursue their legal interests often is affected by their wealth. In the criminal-law domain, on the other hand, the quality of legal representation does not depend upon a complainant's wealth. This is not to deny that wealthy and socially prominent complainants may receive better service from the public authorities, a form of discrimination in their behalf. But criminal justice is not organized so that wealthy complainants can secure better attorneys in court, since all complainants are represented by a public prosecutor.

A variety of other circumstances can lessen the availability of law, whether public or private, for some segments of the community. Sheer physical proximity to legal institutions can be a highly significant factor in pre-modern legal systems, owing to the meager communication and transportation systems in these societies. In nineteenth century China, for example, the farther a complainant lived from a court, the less likely it was that he could pursue his case. This was especially noticeable in civil matters, but it was also true in

---

[46]It may be useful to distinguish between mere advertising and active solicitation, although both are ethical breaches in the United States. By mere advertising I mean a process by which the legal consumer is simply informed of available legal services, while active soliciting involves an attempt to persuade an already informed consumer. Mere advertising would appear consistent with an entrepreneurial legal process since, unlike solicitation, it does not fly in the face of the assumptions of voluntariness and rationality in the entrepreneurial decision-making model. But then it is also arguable that even active solicitation does not disturb *assumptions* of voluntariness and rationality. Honest advertising and solicitation of all kinds are usually understood as consistent with a market economy.

criminal matters. If the plaintiff resided in a city containing a court, his civil suit would reach a final disposition in 60 percent of the cases, while the corresponding figure was only 20 per cent for plaintiffs living 71 to 80 *li* away (one *li* is about one-third of a mile).[47] Some modernizing nations now employ so-called "popular tribunals" at the neighborhood level, thereby providing law to the common people and, at the same time, a mechanism of social integration important to the modernization process itself. Other pre-modern societies, however, are characterized by a high degree of legal availability. In seventeenth century Massachusetts, for instance, each town had its own court of general jurisdiction, easily accessible to all. In fact, the ease of access to these courts seemingly tempted the citizenry to great litigiousness, resulting in a high rate of trivial, unfounded, and vexatious suits.[48] Back home in England the law had not been nearly so available to the common man. In tribal societies the availability of law also tends to be quite high.

Another force that sometimes interferes with the operation of a reactive legal process is a countervailing normative system. Informal norms among some pockets of the citizenry prohibit citizens from mobilizing the official control system. Generally it seems that people are discouraged from mobilizing social control systems against their status equals. With respect to the police, for instance, some citizens are subject among their peers to norms against "squealing" or "ratting." This morality appears rather clearly in the American black subculture, a factor reducing an already low rate of police mobilization by blacks. We also see strong antimobilization norms in total institutions such as prisons, concentration camps, mental hospitals, and basic training camps in the military. Similarly, these norms appear among the indigenous population in colonial societies, schools and factories. Even in the traditional family, children enforce a rule against "tattling." Antimobilization norms seem to be particularly strong among the rank and file wherever there is a fairly clear split in the authority structure of a social system.[49]

In light of the foregoing, we may propose that whenever there is comparatively open conflict between an authority system and those subject to it, reactive legal systems will tend toward desuetude and there will be pressure for greater use of the proactive control strategy. We should therefore expect to find that governments disproportionately adopt proactive systems of legal

---

[47]David C. Buxbaum, "Some Aspects of Civil Procedure and Practice at the Trial Level in Tanshui and Hsinchu from 1789 to 1895," *Journal of Asian Studies*, 30, (1971), 255, 274–275.

[48]George Lee Haskins, *Law and Authority in Early Massachusetts: A Study in Tradition and Design* (1960), 212–213.

[49]While I am emphasizing here the role of *informal* norms against the mobilization of law, it might be noted that one of the hallmarks of social oppression is a formal incapacity to mobilize the law. For instance, in early medieval England a woman could not bring a felony complaint unless the crime of which she complained was violence to her own person or the slaughter of her husband. Women were excluded from other aspects of the legal process as well, such as jury service, with the result at the time that they were largely unable to give evidence. Frederick Pollock and Frederic William Maitland *The History of English Law: Before the Time of Edward I*, 1, 485, (2d ed., 1968) 484–485.

mobilization when a social control problem primarily involves the bottom of the social-class system. It appears, for instance, that the emergence of a proactive policy in early nineteenth century England reflected the elite's fear of growing class consciousness among the lower orders.[50] In cross-national perspective we see that police authority and political power are generally concentrated at the same points and that every police system is to some extent an instrument of political control. This is especially noticeable in the underdeveloped world; in most of Asia, Africa, and the Middle East the roots of proactive police systems are to be found in earlier colonial policies.[51] Similarly, it appears that proactive control in republican Rome was routinely exercised only upon slaves and that urban throng sometimes known as the "riff-raff."[52] The common forms of legal misconduct in which upper status citizens indulge, such as breach of contract and warranty, civil negligence, and various forms of trust violation and corruption, are usually left to the gentler hand of a reactive mobilization process.

In theory the law is available to all. In fact the availability of law is in every legal system greater for the citizenry of higher social status, while the imposition of law tends to be reserved for those at the bottom. Thus, the mobilization of law, like every legal process reflects and perpetuates systems of social stratification. In contemporary Western society the availability of law is nevertheless greater for the mass of citizens than in any previous historical period, and the trend is toward ever-greater availability. And yet it appears that the scope and depth of legal imposition is also greater than ever before.

THE ORGANIZATION OF DISCRETION

Students of law often comment that legal decision-making inevitably allows the legal agent a margin of freedom or discretion. Sometimes this margin does not much exceed the degree of ambiguity inherent in the meaning of the law, an ambiguity resulting in uncertainty about how the law will be interpreted under variable factual circumstances. Because of this ambiguity and factual variability, a degree of slippage is unavoidable in legal reasoning.[53] Sometimes the decision-maker's margin of freedom is so great, as in much of administrative law, that more of the man than the law determines the decisions made.[54] *Moral Diversity.* The organization of a legal system allocates the discretion to decide when legal intervention is appropriate. A reactive system places this discretion in the ordinary citizen rather than in a legal official. This has far-

---

[50]See Allan Silver, "The Demand for Order in Civil Society: A Review of Some Themes in the History of Urban Crime, Police, and Riot," in David J. Bordua, ed., 1967 *The Police: Six Sociological Essays.*

[51]See David H. Bayley, "The Police and Political Change in Comparative Perspective," *Law and Society Review,* (1971), 91.

[52]A. W. Lintott, *op. cit.,* 102, 106.

[53]Edward H. Levi, *An Introduction to Legal Reasoning* (1948).

[54]See Kenneth Culp Davis, *Discretionary Justice: A Preliminary Inquiry* (1969).

reaching consequences for legal control. It allows the moral standards of the citizenry to affect the input of cases into the legal system. Much of the citizen's power lies in his ability not to invoke the legal process when he is confronted with illegality; this gives him the capacity to participate, however unwittingly, in a pattern of selective law enforcement. Each citizen determines for himself what within his private world is the law's business and what is not; each becomes a kind of legislator beneath the formal surface of legal life.

The anthropoligist Paul Bohannan suggests that law functions to "reinstitutionalize" the customary rules of the various social institutions, such as the family, religion, and the polity.[55] According to this view, law is an auxiliary normative mechanism that comes into play to lend needed support to nonlegal rules. This notion of "double institutionalization" is an extension of the older and simpler view that law enforces the common morality. A conception like this may have serious shortcomings as a way of understanding modern legislative and judicial behavior,[56] but it has some relevance to an analysis of legal mobilization. When citizens call the law to action according to their own moral standards, they in effect use the law as supplementary support for those standards. The functional relationship between the individual and the law is an analogue of the relationship proposed by Bohannan at the level of the total society. But this individual pattern cannot be generalized to the level of the total society, since the moral standards of the citizenry are not homogeneous across social classes, ethnic groups, the races, the sexes, generations, and other such aggregates. On the contrary, the reactive system makes it possible for members of these social segments and enclaves to use the law to enforce the rules of their own moral subcultures. From this standpoint, when the law is reactive it does present a pattern of double institutionalization, but it is a doubling of multiple institutions, as multiple as the moral subcultures we find in society. Thus the law perpetuates the moral diversity in the mass of citizens.[57] This may seem a strange role for some government agencies such as the police and for other predominantly reactive control systems, but the law and morality relationship is very complicated and is bound occasionally to disagree with common sense. In societies characterized by moral heterogeneity, it is only through proactive control that one morality can be imposed on all.[58]

---

[55] Bohannan, *op cit.*, 34–37.

[56] See Stanley Diamond, "The Rule of Law Versus the Order of Custom," in Robert Paul Wolff, ed., 1971, *The Rule of Law*, 115.

[57] For a comment on this pattern in police work, see Donald J. Black, "The Social Organization of Arrest," *Stanford Law Review*, 23 (1971), 1105.

[58] Proactive control sometimes emerges under conditions of moral diversity in a population and serves to integrate the larger system. This same may be said of law itself. See M. Fortas and E. E. Evans-Pritchard, Introduction in (M. Fortas and E. E. Evans-Pritchard, eds., 1940), *African Political Systems*, 9. Proactive law seems particularly likely to arise when moral diversity in a population includes a high degree of normative conflict among the diverse elements, as we see, for instance, among tribal and ethnic groups in new nations. We might go further and suggest that normative conflict is an important predictor of authoritarian law in general.

Discrimination. Discretionary authority often carries with it the possibility of particularistic law enforcement or, more simply, discrimination. From a sociological standpoint, legal discrimination provides an interesting problem in the relation between law and social stratification. The liberal fear of a proactive legal system has long been part of a fear of discriminatory enforcement. But whether a system of mobilization is reactive or proactive does not determine the probability of discriminatory enforcement; rather, it organizes that probability. A reactive system deprives state officials of the opportunity to invoke the law according to their own prejudices, but it creates that opportunity for the average citizen. When a legal system is brought into operation by citizen demands, its direction follows the whims of the unmonitored population, whether they are universalistic or not. Each citizen has the discretionary power to decide which people, of those who are legally vulnerable, deserve official attention. The white citizen has the power to be more lenient toward the white than the black, and vice versa; the bourgeois can discriminate against the bohemian, the older against the younger, the rich against the poor. Even if we assume, *arguendo,* that each citizen does what his conscience dictates, what he thinks is right, the aggregative result of all these individual decisions surely distributes legal jeopardy unequally across the population of law violators, especially when we consider decisions *not* to mobilize the law.[59] The possibilities of government surveillance over this kind of discrimination seem minimal. Reactive mobilization is no more accessible to surveillance than many of the illegal acts in private settings that a reactive system uncovers. The amenability of a proactive legal system to surveillance and control is far greater, if only because a proactive system by its nature involves an organizational base that can be penetrated. Proactive control is itself subject to proactive control while reactive control is dispersed in the citizen mass and is therefore extraordinarily difficult to reach. In short, patterns of legal discrimination in reactive systems, the more democratic form of legal process, are more elusive, and consequently they are more intransigent than are similar patterns in proactive mobilization systems.[60] And yet it remains likely that a government-initiated mobilization system contributes more to the maintenance of the existing forms of social stratification than does a system geared to the demands of the citizenry. Discriminatory decision-making by citizens to a degree cancels itself out in the citizen mass, while discriminatory behavior by legal officials mirrors their own biases, and these are apt to flow in only one direction.

Besides accommodating discrimination by citizens, a reactive legal system permits individuals to appropriate the law for functions that lawmakers may never have anticipated. People may mobilize the law in order to bankrupt or

---

[59] Donald J. Black, "Production of Crime Rates," *American Sociological Review,* 70 (1970), 739.

[60] Just as it organizes the possibility of discrimination and its control, a system of mobilization organizes the possibility of legal corruption. We discover corruption, like discrimination, where it is easier to control, namely, in proactive systems of law enforcement. In police work, for example, we hear about corruption in vice control and traffic control rather than at the level of the citizen complainant, where it is probably most frequent.

destroy the reputations of their competitors,[61] to delay transfers of property or payments of debts,[62] or for revenge.[63] Within the limits imposed by law and legal officials, the discretion accorded to every citizen by a reactive control process, then, lets every citizen do with law what he will, with little concern for the long-range social results.[64] . . .

CONCLUSION

How deviant behavior and disorder come to meet resistance is a problem for investigation, whatever the social context and form of social control. Some societies have managed very well with almost no social control beyond that brought to bear by the complainant and his kinfolk.[65] In others, systems of proactive mobilization emerge and disappear in rhythm with the collectivity's involvement in corporate action; during warfare or a hunt in some earlier societies, proactive control would arise, only to recede during less eventful times.[66] Another pattern occurs in coercive institutions, such as prisons or mental hospitals, where it seems that proactive strategies are used almost exclusively in the everyday maintenance of the official order. At still another extreme are face-to-face encounters among social equals, where social control is more diffuse and there appears a kind of orderly anarchy with no mobilization at all.[67] We see variation expressing the texture of life from one setting to the

---

[61]See, e.g. Bernard S. Cohn, "Some Notes on Law and Change in North India," *Economic Development and Cultural Change,* 8 (1959), 79.

[62]E.g., Daniel S. Lev, "Judicial Institutions and Legal Change in Indonesia," (1971) unpublished paper, Department of Political Science, University of Washington, 64.

[63]E.g., Maureen Mileski, *op. cit.,* 66—68.

[64]The diverse input of requests made upon reactive legal processes can teach much about the internal dynamics of a community. We learn about aspects of male-female interaction, for instance, by looking at who brings whom to court. Laura Nader, "An Analysis of Zapotec Law Cases," *Ethnology,* (1964), 404. Likewise the fact that citizens implicate the police in so many non-criminal disputes suggests that American urban life lacks the battery of extralegal mechanisms of dispute settlement often seen among preliterate peoples. The police find themselves playing conciliatory as well as adversarial roles in dispute settlement. These roles are sometimes wholly differentiated in tribal societies. See, e.g. James L. Gibbs, Jr., "The Kpelle Moot: A Therapeutic Model for the Informal Settlement of Disputes," Africa, 33 (1963), 1.
Like reactive control, systems of proactive mobilization can be put to a variety of uses. These may be public or private. A proactive enforcement campaign, for example, can augment the government treasury through the collection of fines, such as traffic fines, or it can advance or subvert the interests of political figures or political organizations, as is sometimes seen in vice crackdowns and corruption scandals.

[65]E.g., Rafeal Karsten, Blood Revenge, *War, and Victory Feasts among the Jibaro Indians of Eastern Equador,* (1923), 1–32; E. E. Evans-Pritchard. The Xuer: *A Description of the Modes of Livelihood and Political Institutions of a Nilotic People,* (1940). 150–191, (notes renumbered, eds.).

[66]A pattern common among Indian tribes of North America; see Robert H. Lowie, "Some Aspects of Political Organization among the American Aborigines," *Journal of the Royal Anthropology Institute,* 78 (1948), 11.

[67]See Erving Goffman, "Embarrassment and Social Organization," *American Journal of Sociology,* 62, (1956), 264.

next, and it is apparent that law makes visible a process found in every system of social control.

One scientific advance consists in raising the level of generality at which the empirical world is understood. A relationship once seen as unique is shown to be one of a set; that set may in turn be revealed as a member of a still more general class. My observations on the mobilization of law are very general, since they cut across substantive areas of law, societies, and history. This is both the strength and weakness of the observations. Any reader can produce exceptions to my generalizations, and perhaps I made some overgeneralizations, where the number of exceptions will overturn the initial formulations. Yet even with this tentativeness, it is useful to point the direction of a still more general level to which we aspire in legal sociology. We may generalize about all of law, again without regard to substance, place, or time, but now also without regard to a particular dimension of the legal process.

What consequences follow when law is arranged reactively so that ordinary citizens can direct its course? What should we expect if law is proactive, the responsibility of government officials alone? These questions have guided my analysis of legal mobilization. Yet citizen participation in legal life is a problem for study not only in the mobilization of law, but also in other legal processes such as legal prescription and legal disposition. The ultimate issue is: How democratic is the law? Legal rules and policies may arise at the direction of the citizenry, as by plebiscite or by a representative legislature, or at the direction of state officialdom alone, as by dictum or edict. Like the mobilization of law, the degree to which the prescription of law is democratic, then, varies across legal systems. Likewise the disposition of law, or dispute settlement, may be more or less democratic, as is clear when we compare, for instance, the popular tribunals of some socialist countries[68] to the lower courts of the United States with their powerful adjudicatory officials.[69] In modern societies the grand jury and the trial jury are well-known mechanisms by which the citizenry is introduced into legal decision-making. A general theory of law should tell us what difference democratic organization makes.

I close with several examples of propositions about democratic law applicable to a variety of legal situations. Patterns in the mobilization of law suggest these more general propositions. As illustrations, consider the following:

1. *The more democratic a legal system, the more it perpetuates the existing morality of the population.* Democratic law perpetuates moral diversity as well as moral homogeneity among the citizenry.

2. *The more democratic a legal system, the more the citizenry perpetuates the existing system of social stratification.* Where law is democratic, legal discrimination is practiced by citizens more than by government officials and is therefore more difficult to detect and eliminate.

---

[68]E.g., Jesse Berman, "The Cuban Popular Tribunals," *Columbia Law Review,* 69 (1969), 1317.

[69]E.g., Maureen Mileski, "Courtroom Encounters: An Observation Study of a Lower Criminal Court," *Law and Society Review,* 5 (1971), 473.

3. *The more democratic a legal system, the more the law reflects moral and other social change among the citizenry.* Democratic law accommodates social change by historical drift more than planned change.

These propositions about democratic law are preliminary and in need of much refinement. But even primitive propositions give us a necessary starting place. With each unexplained exception comes the possibility of creative reformulation, the heart of theoretical development. With each successful application we have the satisfaction of explanation, even as uncultured as it may presently be. Surely it is worthwhile to build a vocabulary and to make some statements, however haltingly, in a general theory of law.

Notes on Police
Assessment of
Moral Character*

Harvey Sacks

INTRODUCTION

1. For Western societies, at least, being noticeable and being deviant seem intimately related. The notions that one is suspect whose appearance is such that he stands out, and correlatively that the sinner can be seen, have the deepest of foundations. Indeed, in Judeo-Christian mythology, human history *proper* begins with the awareness by Adam and Eve that they are observables.[1] The next

---

*Formerly titled "Methods in Use for the Production of a Social Order: *A Method for Warrantably Inferring Moral Character.*" This paper was written about seven years ago as a paper for one of Erving Goffman's courses at UC Berkeley. It is heavily indebted to a reading of his work and also to materials he presented in lectures, some of which he has since published in his books *Encounters, Stigma, and Behavior in Public Places.* It was also, and equally much indebted to those writings of Harold Garfinkel which were then available, and which have now been collected and published in his volume *Studies in Ethnomethodology.* During the period of its writing I received financial support as a Pre-Doctoral Fellow of the National Institutes of Mental Health, U.S. Public Health Service, and from the Center for the Study of Law and Society, University of California, Berkeley.

[1]By the term "being an observable" I mean having, and being aware of having, an appearance that permits warrantable inferences about one's moral character. This use conforms with a usual use of the term "observable" as the object which an appearance permits inferences about. I might note that the use of the range of terms such as "appearances," "inferences," etc. is not a matter of philosophical or other like election. They are used simply because they seem the most empirically appropriate terms.

REPRINTED FROM: David Sudnow (ed.) *Studies in Social Interaction.* New York: Free Press, 1972 (280–293; 444–446).

bit of social information they thereupon learn is: To be observable is to be embarrassable.[2] The first social technique they learn is: They can by mutual regard achieve privacy.[3] And then they learn the first terrible norm: The retention of privacy is conditioned on *naive* conformity.[4]

1.a If, in American society, it is the case that the inferences as to moral character which particular appearances may warrant is a matter of central concern, then: We expect that there are specialized methods for producing from the appearances persons present such inferences as to the moral character as can warrant the propriety of particular treatments of the persons observed.

1.b It is the case that the relation of observability to deviance is of central concern. In public places persons are required to use the appearances others present as grounds for treating them. Persons using public places are concurrently expected by others to present appearances which can be readily so used, and expect others to treat their own appearances at face value.

1.c When the regulation of inferences (hence of treatments) by reference to appearances determines an elegant means for routinizing casual public interaction, it obviously has characteristic problems. First what is to be done about those persons whose appearance suggests no clear inferences, i.e. whose appearance does not warrant particular treatments?

---

[2]While I shall not focus on the matter in this essay, the central sociological status of the "possibility of embarrassment" is strongly suggested by its prominence in *Genesis*. Not only is it that the first human encounter with God begins with embarrassment, but the treatment of Cain suggests that, if only to avoid embarrassment alone, a conforming life is recommended. He, we recall, is condemned not to death, but to "observability for life."

That these are not merely arcane issues is accentuated by the concerns of modern literature. For example, each of the major works of the great social analyst Franz Kafka begins with, then develops a description of, what life is procedurally like after the transformation of the hero into an observable.

[3]Although, again, I shall not focus on the matter, some remarks on privacy are in order. For the society under consideration, giving a public accounting is about as serious a situation as one can face. Furthermore, given the concern to use the appearances persons present in public as the materials for deciding their proper treatment, privacy is not merely valued, but is enforced. In routine interaction others need not attend to one's actual grounds of conduct. Indeed, within the bulk of legal situations "actual grounds" are enforceably excluded; one enforceably attends only to the typical grounds appearances suggest. See further the author's "The Lawyer's Work," mimeographed.

[4]Conformity is not sufficient. It is the comfort with which one wears conformity that seems critical, as the ensuing (esp. ss.4.) shall suggest. If this is so, it may lead to the development of an explanation for such data as Messinger's *Sociometry*, v. 25, 1962, pp. 98–109, where the trouble ex-mental patients felt was a lack of comfort with their conformity.

The position noted in the text has been expressed most dramatically by Emerson:

Commit a crime, and the earth is made of glass. Commit a crime, and it seems as if a coat of snow fell on the ground, such as reveals in the woods the track of every partridge and fox and squirrel.

Quoted in *Nightsick,* by L. J. Valentine, (N.Y.: Harper & Row, 1947)

Second, what is to be done about those persons whose appearance is projected to take advantage of the enforced inferences others make in order to do the latter ill?

Third, what is to be done about those persons who consistently or blatantly fail to properly read appearances, who consequently produce inappropriate treatments?

Fourth, what is to be done about those persons for whom the problem of properly reading appearances is dramatically tortuous?

In this paper I shall not consider "what is to be done." Rather, I am concerned with how those about whom that question may properly be raised are located.[5]

1.d As the appearances persons present are of central concern, so too are there specialized methods for producing the inferences that appearances warrant.

The concern of this essay is to move towards their description. I shall proceed in this direction by attempting a description of a method used by specialists—the police—for inferring from appearances such a probability of criminality as warrants the treatment of search and arrest.

My grounds for the choice of the police are as follows. First, the police are engaged, with others, in locating persons about whom the question may properly be raised: can they give a legitimate accounting for their appearance?

Second, they are, in contrast to others so engaged, specialized in the locating of candidates on the basis of the appearances presented in public places.

Third, as specialists, certain problems of the relation of the first two and the last two problems of 1.c. above need not be examined. That the police are specialists means that they are accredited for regularly recognizing possible deviants. Since the regular recognition of possible deviants, quite as much as the failure to produce a proper appearance, constitutes evidence for deviance (e.g. paranoia), the professional accreditation of the police provides a quick and easy test as to whether a claimed recognizer of deviants should be given diagnostic examination. The "public-spirited" citizen receives special and ambiva-

---

[5]Let me note, however, that the question "what is to be done" is handled quite widely by requiring of a properly located candidate that he offer an accounting for his appearance. If a person is competent to reasonably answer "why" questions, then that seems to stand as an indicator of his competence to regulate his affairs.

While one might suppose that the term "reasonably" is the sticker here, it does seem to be the case, perhaps curiously so, that even when persons are under interrogation for possibly serious offenses, one for which their lives may be at stake, confessions can be garnered by saying to them that what they have said at some point is inconsistent with what they have said at another point. One might imagine them to say "How can it be inconsistent; I said both those things," or et cetera. A preliminary investigation of the method of interrogations suggests that while in exploration of what goes on in such situation is of great interest, it is by no means to be supposed that persons take lightly the reasonableness, consistency, clarity, and so on, of their answers, and may well be more concerned with preserving their claim to consistency than their claim to innocence.

Persons whose competency is denied, i.e., who are not given the right to state the sense of their actions seem to find the situation of interrogation tremendously frustrating.

lent attention.[6] Since, then, I want only to deal with the location of persons presenting improper appearances, choice of the police avoids in general the question of the possibly symptomatic status of recognizances. Fourth, as specialists their methods ought to be reasonably easy to discover.

1.e Since I am only interested in the police instantially, I shall restrict the investigation to a domain of their work involving a special concern for matters with which persons in general are, albeit less intensively, also concerned. I shall describe a method used for recognizing "suspicious persons," and shall not be concerned with methods used for recognizing either "wanted persons" or those seen in the commission of an offense. While some evidence will be offered that the method the police use for recognizing suspicious persons is in general use,[7] a demonstration of its general use will not be presented in this paper.

A FIRST SIMPLIFIED STATEMENT OF THE POLICEMAN'S PROBLEM

2. Among the Americans, the police are occupational specialists on inferring the probability of criminality from the appearances persons present in public places. Since a mutual orientation to appearances defines a means for producing and accepting the appropriate proprieties by which casual public encounters are routinized, it is important that these means be protected from exploitation. One central role of the police involves protecting the viability of these means. Patrolmen are intensively oriented to the possibly improper appearances persons may present.

2.a The decisional problem faced has the following form: Maximize the likelihood that those who will turn out to be criminals and who pass in view are selected, while minimizing the likelihood that those who would not turn out to be criminals and who pass in view are selected. This problem is faced under the conditions:

---

[6]The public-spirited citizen is not simply someone who responds with moral indignation towards perceived offenses; he is one who adopts an organization of observations— and indeed attends the world—so as to produce and explain with respect to legal system notions, the behavior of his neighbors. Below are some excerpts of what seems to have seemed strange.

... A complaint was received to the effect that neighbors suspected that a woman was a "bookie." The complainant, who remained anonymous, indicated that this woman has been boasting of her winnings on the horse races and has been purchasing clothes and furnishings in excess of what she is capable of purchasing on her husband's earnings as a mail carrier. Neighbors also indicated that a man visited the house each morning and left something in the mailbox. vol. II, p. 61

... Some patrons of a bar reported to the local police that they believed gambling was going on there because two or three other patrons seemed to have quite a bit of money and no visible means of support. p.62.

The above quotes are from pp. 61 and 62 of Vol. II, *The Administration of Criminal Justice in the United States,* Pilot Project Report, American Bar Foundation. This study will hereafter be referred to as ABF.

[7]See ss. 4.g. below.

1. that the persons seen are (differentially, to be sure) oriented to the character of their own appearances as grounds of inference as to probable criminality.[8]
2. that the value of correct and incorrect inferences are neither equal nor uniformly calculable prior to a treatment decision.[9]

2.b. Others—for example, homosexuals while cruising—face a similar problem. For our purposes the latter differ from the police in the following way: The police are concerned to recognize persons concerned to make themselves unrecognizable as criminals. The homosexual is concerned to recognize homosexuals and to inform them of the presence of a colleague; he is also concerned not to be recognized as homosexual by others, particularly by the police. The issue reaches maximal complexity when police seek to have homosexuals recognize them as colleagues for the purpose of having the latter engage in a move that constitutes grounds for arrest.

The police face a similar problem with prostitutes, junkies, and the like, and that class of persons who faces the problem of differentially communicating, by way of their appearances, with potential clients, the public and the police.

THE METHOD IN USE: AN INCONGRUITY PROCEDURE: ITS BASIS

3. The method that the police are trained to employ may be called an "incongruity procedure." In constitutes an attempt to refine a method for observing persons based on the wisdom noted above (1).

3.a It begins with the fact that persons within the society are trained to naively present and naively employ presented appearances as the grounds of treatment of the persons they encounter in public places.

The treatments for which appearances are ordinarily used as grounds of selection vary widely, from, for example, deciding whether "that one" is such a one as one can pass in the street without fear of attack, illegitimate approach, etc., to how it is that one may properly pass, follow, or approach "that one."

3.b Since mutual orientation to appearances determines a means for producing and accepting the appropriate proprieties by which casual public encounters are routinized, it is important for the continuing viability of these means that they be protected from exploitation.[10] The incongruity procedure takes recog-

---

[8]See ss. 4.f. below.

[9]This feature is of course crucial to the problem of bribery. Failures to arrest may have low visibility. The surprise situaion of halting for interrogation prominent citizens and officials, and the generally negative but occasionally positive gains to the policemen are well known. See further ss. 5.d.

[10]It is perhaps because of this orientation of the police that the most dangerous of persons are felt to be the person who uses his appearance as a policeman to cover his crooked acts. The members of the Denver police force who were also thieves used police cars as look-outs. Gosling, in *The Ghost Squad*, 1959, notes that criminals who presented the appearance of detectives were a matter of tremendous concern because of their effect in undermining public certainty about the import of apparent police status.

nizance that the facts of 3.a determine a weapon by which inappropriate treatments may be garnered. Persons may exploit an ability to present appearances to which they are not otherwise entitled.

3.c If a group can be trained to (1) avoid routinely treating appearances at face value, and (2) alternatively to view the persons they see as presenting possibly improper appearances, they can (3) attend to a variety of features, such as the ease with which an appearance is presented, which may (4) warrant empirical investigation of the propriety of the presented appearance. Some comment on these points is appropriate.

First, that a warrant is necessary, i.e. that conditions are restricted under which an empirical investigation may be pursued as to the propriety of a presented appearance, is expectable.[11] The elegance of the use of appearances depends primarily on the fact that appearances in general are not to be questioned.

Second, users of the method do not propose that they are able to state definitively what features they will use to decide that an appearance may be improper, i.e. does warrant investigation. It is perhaps obvious why this should be so. As the police are oriented to using appearances as evidence of criminality, so criminals are oriented to using appearances as fronts, i.e. as hindrances to recognition. Were a definitive list compiled, one to which the police would themselves be bound, it would provide criminals with definitive information on the appearances to avoid in order to assure safe passage across the policeman's line of vision.

Given the latter two points, one central problem of the use of the procedure may be exposed: How is the proper use of the procedure to be decided in any particular case?

While I shall consider this problem further below[12] because of their general relation to the above discussion I note here the general features of its solution. Instead of the proper use of the procedure being decided by reference to the correctness of the inference of probable criminality, the propriety of the inference constitutes the condition for determining whether the persons selected are possibly criminal. And whether the inference was proper is decided in the courts by having the policeman state what it was that aroused his suspicions;

---

[11]While, given the means of routinizing casual public interaction it is expectable that persons need good grounds in order to make the explanations of appearances a project for empirical investigation, this fact that they do need good grounds is by no means of trivial status. The norm "do not investigate, unless a problem is warrantable" may be the practical theorists' correlate of the scientist's norm of elegance. Theorists who warrant their investigations on the grounds that they will have no practical import are perhaps producing a warrant of the sort although there is no good grounds for investigating this, it is investigatable because nothing practical will come of it. If something practical will come of it, then good grounds may be needed. Cf. the emergence of sociology from the study of recognized social problems.

The normative import of knowledge of the world held in common seems such that those who will make of this knowledge a problem must first suggest the troubles we now have with its use.

[12]See ss. 4.g.below.

the judge (or jury) then considers whether an ordinary person would have been roused to suspicion on such grounds. Only if so is the person selected by the policeman convictable.

A PRELIMINARY DISCUSSION OF THE INCONGRUITY PROCEDURE IN USE

4. Given that police ply a route, they must, in order to use the incongruity procedure, learn to treat their beat as a territory of normal appearances. The learned normal appearances are to constitute background expectancies in terms of which the beat is observed during particular patrols. Given these expectancies the patrolman must so sensitize himself as to be arousable by whatsoever slight variations appear which seem to be warrantable bases for making of the explanation of presented appearances a matter for investigation.

4.a The novice policeman is obviously not in position to use the procedure. First he must learn how to see as a patrolman. By having a novice patrol with a mature officer, the former can be shown what it is that one can see by way of the method. The demonstration that may be offered can have a quite considerable charm.[13]

As he walks through his beat with a mature officer, persons who to him appear legit are cast in the light of the illicit activities in which the latter knows they are engaged. The novice is shown that he ought to see persons passing him in terms of the activities in which they are engaged. And the activities in which they are engaged are often more prurient than he might suppose. The lovely young lady alighting from a cab is now observable as a callgirl arriving for a session. The novice is shown how to see the streets as, so to speak, scenes from pornographic films. And what is more, he is able to see the illicitnesses under the conditions that few, if any, who observe him passing through the streets are able to see either that the officer is in such a scene or what it is that he is indeed observing. The policeman, then, has the privacy of the stag show theatre, while parading the streets in full uniform, and, further, there is no noticeable entry or exit at which, if he is seen, embarrassment might be called forth.

4.b Training manuals provide the novice with lists of features constituting good grounds for treating persons who pass in his view.[14] As we have noted,[15] these lists are intendedly not definitive. They have an extremely interesting status. Aside from providing examples of the sorts of features any policeman ought to be attuned to,[16] they operate as records in an expandable history of

---

[13]See R. McAllister, *The Kind of Guy I Am* (New York: McGraw-Hill, 1957).

[14]See e.g., ABF Vol. 5, pp. 1—19 to 1—29, or G. D. Callan *Police Methods for Today and Tomorrow*, (Newark, 1939), chap. 3.

[15]Ss. 3.c. above.

[16]"Milwaukee recruits are instructed that if they observe a young man crossing the street with an overcoat on, collar up, and hat pulled down, in warm weather, they are to suspect that he is a burglar." ABF, Vol. 5, pp. 1–19.

police success and failure. The import of those parts of the lists that consist of "great recognizances" or "great boners" is, to use Moore's term, autotelic.[17] The policeman can attend to his route with an awareness that he can, by making an especially subtle recognizance, take a place within department history. That is to say, he is encouraged to engage, even when patrolling alone, in playing observation games; for example, glance at a store window, note to himself all the items that he can recall within it, then check back to see what he has missed or noted incorrectly. While such games are more readily played when police patrol in pairs, the attended history of recognizances permits the lone patrolman to play the games against the department's historical figures.

The persons on his beat can also reinforce the playing of observation games by expressing their amusement at his awareness when they make slight deviations from their normal habits. Then, too, the fact that one cannot predetermine what information may turn out to be useful encourages the collection of seemingly trivial details because awareness of such details has occasionally paid off with an unexpected arrest which was heavily rewarded.

4.c What is normal for a place is normal for the place at a time. The meaning of an event to the policeman at a place depends on the time it occurs. The time at which it occurs is furthermore a matter of an overlapping and changing group of cycles—that is, the meaning of an event is not merely a matter of the hour, but the day too is involved in deciding its significance; furthermore, the season counts, and then finally "while it didn't used to be that way here," now "such a thing is typical."

While in a sense these facts are obvious, it is obvious as well that sociological theories of deviance are not now constructed to deal with them. Yet even for demographic analysis such facts may be of real importance. For example, given the use of learned normal appearances as the grounds of locating suspect persons, we would expect that territories in transition will have higher crime rates than stabler territories simply because the policeman geared to the normal appearances of a beat may, not adjusting exactly to the rate and character of transition, be ready to see newer arrivals as suspicious for the beat seen as an area in which they are not normal features.[18]

The time-ordered character of normal appearances poses a touchy strategic problem for the police. A patrolman can best be attuned to normal appearances by so scheduling his route such that he appears at places at the same significant time.[19] In doing so he gets the closest awareness of the con-

---

[17] Anderson and Moore, "Autotelic Folk Models," *The Sociological Quarterly*, 1, 203–216.

[18] If one feels that it is strange that the rate of crime vary with the suspiciousness of the police, one probably has in mind crimes of violence or robbery as typical crimes. And these might be expected to be reported by the public. However, such matters as gambling, prostitution, dope selling depend for being listed in statistics on the ability of the police to locate arrestable persons.

[19] By significant time I mean only that "the same time" may not be the same clock time. It may be "closing time" or "dinner time" or the like.

stancies and variances at that time for that place. But if his behavior is so scheduled, it provides criminals with definitive information about where he will be at a particular time, and consequently permits the scheduling of illegal events. In order to reduce the information criminals can gain by observing his course, the policeman is therefore concerned to randomize his path through a beat, i.e. to proceed through different ways each time, to double back occasionally, to take his breaks at different times and in different places. But doing this of course reduces his sensitivity to the normal appearances he uses to detect the presence of something awry or, to avoid that perhaps unfortunate phrasing, reduces his confidence that he can discriminate the peculiar because the range of what he uses as normal becomes more extended.

4.d The police treat the normal ecology of territories as a normative ecology. As sociologists describe them, cities typically consist of discrete ecological areas of socio-economic segregation. Juvenile gangs tend to treat the borders of ecological areas as boundaries. Persons who "don't belong" are seen as foreigners, and are subject to treatment as such. Their safe passage depends on the deference of the local lords. The police too treat ecological borders as of normative import. Persons whose appearance indicates that they are not normal members of an ecological area, e.g. whites in negro areas, the apparently poor in wealthy areas etc., are subject to having a request made for "their papers" and an interrogatory made as to the reason of their presence.[20]

Furthermore, as the police treat territories as a set of normal appearances, so they expect others to treat them.[21]

> . . . Coming to a street intersection, the officers observed a man crossing the intersection who did not appear to know where he was going. The officers alighted from the car, questioned this man, and searched him. He provided the police with full credentials and indicated that this was the first occasion on which he had ever been questioned by a police officer. His answers satisfied the officers that this man was quite "legitimate." They thanked him for his cooperation and sent him on his way.

4.e Two related features of the use of the procedure involve the policeman's appearance.

1. Those who treat the presence of the police as other than normal are seen as other than normal themselves.[22]

> They were in search of "house jumpers"—who are individuals collecting current bet slips and who turn them in at a "drop" station . . . The officers indicate that they can determine who a collector is as a result of their experiences in dealing with these people. As an example, they indicate that if an individual gives them a "double look," they'll check him. By this the officers mean that if an individual sees them in their unmarked car and then turns to look at them once again, chances are the

---

[20] *Ibid.*, pp. 115, 123.

[21] ABF, Vol. 2, p. 118.

[22] *Ibid.*, p. 120; see too Gosling, *op. cit.*, p. 56.

individual has some gambling paraphernalia on his person. In such cases, the officers leave their car and search the person in an attempt to uncover the current bet slips.

2. Conversely, as the police enforce on persons that they treat their presence as normal, so it is enforced on the police that they appear as they are expected to appear, i.e. that if they are present, their presence be apparent.[23]

> An officer attempted to develop an accosting and soliciting case through the use of a private and expensive vehicle. This case was thrown out of court upon the basis that "everyone knows that the police officers use cheap cars," and for a police officer to resort to the use of a Cadillac in order to develop an accosting and soliciting case constitutes entrapment.

> Some time ago a handbook operation was going on in a downtown building. Since the handbook was located near the medical building, doctors dressed in white jackets sometimes frequented the place. An officer therefore disguised himself in a white coat and managed to place a bet. The case was thrown out of court on the ground that entrapment was involved.

4.f Given the orientation of the police to the beat as a territory of normal appearances, a notion of "normal crime" may be constructed. We may talk of the normal crime of an area not in terms of the statistical constancy of certain crimes for time units, but as that crime that is so managed within an area that those so engaged appear while so engaged as features of its normal appearance.

The notion of normal crime has the following import: given the orientation of the police, those routinely engaged in illegal activities will attempt to construct a front such that their routine appearance in a territory will (or can) be treated as a normal appearance of the territory by its patrolmen. Organizers of the numbers racket will, for example, employ those who have a reason for going through a neighborhood several times a day and stopping at a wide range of places. The newspaper deliverers and the mailmen are ideal.

Whether or not the numbers racket has happened to fix the patrolmen, it must adopt a front for its routine collections and dispersals so that (a) public-spirited citizens and (b) various detective groups do not on observing the area interpret their routine presence as "numbers men making pick-ups and deliveries." They must adopt this front not simply to avoid being noticed, but because if by some chance they happen to be noticed, the beat patrolman who has failed to arrest must be able to reasonably claim that they simply appeared to him to be routine features of the territory, i.e. that they gave him no good grounds for an aroused suspicion.

4.g We have noted above (3.c) that it is not the case that the proper use of the method is determined by the demonstrable correctness of the inferences produced.

---

[23]*Ibid.*, pp. 137, 138.

The general warrant of the method is not based on the professional status of the police; its general warrant is that anyone can see its plausibility. Its warrant in particular cases is that the inference made is one which ordinary persons would make. This means that the policeman is not simply concerned to develop his sensitivity. He must balance his sensitivity against his ability to verbalize, i.e. to present descriptions of how he became aroused. And what is more, though he is a specialist on the normal appearances of his beat, his inferences are judged by those who lack both his special knowledge and his developed sense of the unusual.

While the police would like their special skills in observation to constitute grounds of a recognition of their professional status, and their professional status to then operate as a preliminary warrant of their observations, the fact that the warrant of their observations is decided by a test of reasonableness for an ordinary man is not only irking but also places them in a severe bind.

Apart from the fact that they then tend to see the courts as hindering them in their work and in their search for professional status, they feel required to adopt a series of unpleasant adaptations.

1. The method of recognition and the method of presentation may become separate issues. The policeman may feel himself forced to "rationally reconstruct" what happened.[24]

A court officer noted that a particular police officer would behave in the following manner:

> He would state that he saw the defendant come down the street, knew him as a long time police game operator, stopped him, searched him, found policy tickets, and brought him in. The prosecutor would avise he had no case as the search was not legal, and unless the search was made pursuant to a lawful arrest, the evidence was inadmissible. The officer would then say "put me on the stand." When on the witness stand, he would testify he was standing under a street light when the defendant came by, a man known to him to have been previously convicted of policy violation, and that he saw his policy ticket sticking out of the defendant's coat pocket. Thereupon he arrested him, searched him, and found a number of such tickets and brought this prosecution.

> The court officer noted, in this case, that in one year two individuals each obtained $5,000 damages against this officer for false arrest. He was encouraged to resign from the force with his pension rights intact.

2. Once information has been gathered about criminal activities, the police may engage in staging observable crimes. For example, if the police know that someone is selling dope, they may—because they cannot say that the fellow was seen selling dope, only that an exchange of something was seen—arrange through the use of hired addicts for a purchase to take place which is sufficiently observable for recounting in court.

The staging of crimes is especially messy. First , the police may have to employ persons who would otherwise be institutionalized. In doing so they as-

---

[24]*Ibid.*, p. 160.

sure these persons at least a temporary freedom, sometimes indeed to pursue their illegal endeavors.[25] Second, where they are unable to get hired hands, they may themselves have to spend time in such activities as smiling in public toilets, making time with the lonely women who frequent bars, etc.

A SECOND SIMPLIFIED STATEMENT OF THE POLICEMAN'S PROBLEM

5. A policeman takes it that the persons he sees engaged in passing through the streets are oriented to a social order in terms of whose features they select the "proper or improper" courses of action which bring them to use the streets. His aim is to find a way of making activities observable in the particular sense of allowing him to see the passing of persons in terms of the courses they have selected.

Typically, he is in a position merely to observe persons passing in the street and does not engage in fully tracking their paths from entry to the streets to exit therefrom. In locating persons who are to be candidates in a test of their possible criminality he does not begin with information about the courses in which they are engaged. That they are possibly engaged in illegal activities must first be decided by way of the incongruity procedure, i.e. by way of a device for locating candidates from the set of observed persons.

Once located, his concern is to produce information about the paths candidates select and then to transform the information about the paths they select into evidence of the courses they have selected. He seeks, that is, to tranform information about the paths candidates select into a description of a set of acts which may be seen as the assembly of a crime.

His problem then seems to be:
Given that

1. he encounters persons in and by way of the streets, persons engaged in undetermined activities;

2. the activities are taken to be parts of selected courses of action constructed with an orientation to their propriety;

3. candidates for investigation are located prior to tracking their paths or knowing the course of action in which they are engaged;

Then:

How, by way of their street activities can one look at persons so as to be able to use their appearances to isolate candidates for investigation, and

---

[25]For example:
    After an unsuccessful effort to contact a source of supply for narcotics, the following occurred: The agents took Myra to A Street, somewhere near B Street where she was to begin hustling. Myra mentioned that she had not been picked up by the police for the past two weeks for some reason she could not explain, but facetiously guessed that the Detroit police "must know I've been copping for the Feds." Ibid., p. 90.

How can one then use what candidates do both as materials for discovering the courses of action in which they are engaged, and for determining in terms of those courses, that sense of their observable acts on the basis of which a strategy may be generated for demonstrating the observable character of their activities as the assembly of a crime?

5.a While the police might treat the streets as merely incidental locales of the persons they encounter, in fact they treat the streets with great seriousness. The police take it that what takes place in the streets stands in a determinable relation to that organization of concerted courses of action which involves persons in using the streets. If they discover who to investigate, then by tracking him they can at least determine the strategic problem that exposing the course to which he is oriented poses. Exposing the course itself will not be a problem patrolmen will be concerned with. But it is their job to determine who is to be tracked.

5.b As the police take it that those engaged in illegal activities do not randomly use the streets, so too persons routinely engaged in illegal activities are concerned to regulate the activities of those of their agents who use the streets in the course of work so that the use does appear random. Persons who organize illegal activities are concerned to minimize the clues that use provides to those who might, by analyzing street activities, expose the organization regulating those activities.

However, the strategic problem they face in doing so involves them in a bind similar to that the police were shown to face (4.c). Organizers of a numbers operation will, for example, regularly move the stations to which route-men go in delivering their slips. They may also attempt to have route-men vary the way they proceed through a territory. But the attempt to randomize has its drawbacks. Persons making purchases are kept in a far more viable mood if those they deal with keep a regular schedule. Then, too, those who keep a regular schedule will, if they are not held in suspicion, be less likely to arouse suspicion.

For the police, the problem of locating the persons using the streets as parts of coordinated illegal activities has a different purport than that of locating persons engaged in sole crimes. In the former case it is the organizers they seek to make observable, and the persons using the streets constitute not the sought-for criminals but possible resources by which organizers may be located. The police are oriented to the organizers, and are by and large willing to let the street operatives alone, because they are aware that those who use the streets are readily replaceable, and because, insofar as the organizers are not located, arrest of street operatives means only that the work of exposing the organization must begin again from the beginning, i.e. with an attempt to locate and track their replacements. Organizers, on the other hand, cannot rest content with the fact that their street operatives are not being bothered. For, even if this is so, it may be the case that the police are accumulating information that may soon be sufficient to crack the organization itself.

5.c Encountering by way of the streets what is taken to be a managed social order has a wide range of other imports.

1. Police seem often to treat an area as an "expressive unit." Suppose they see a group of persons standing on a street corner. The meaning they attach may be neither behavioral (e.g. how crowded they are) nor be conceived in terms of the conduct of those persons (e.g. what *they* are up to). A group of persons on a street corner may be seen as "the neighborhood is restless tonight," i.e. as a gesture of the territory. Conversely, in producing their own responses to neighborhood gestures they see their own actions as an answer to the neighborhood. Thus a policeman, having felt that the young toughs are getting over-rowdy, may pick one out and rough him up, taking it that this will be seen as instantial, as a remark that such persons had better get back in line. While such remarks often seem to be understood, i.e. the one that was beaten up takes it that he is incidental, and the others take it that police intend them to calm down, it seems also to be the case that when communication failures occur, the recipients of a gesture may experience both puzzlement ("why me, I was just standing on the corner?") and may have a hostility towards the police reinforced ("they have to maintain a quota of arrests, and don't care who they take in" or "they just pick on us, so what is the use of playing straight?").[26]

2. They also take it that the appearance of a neighborhood is attended to by those who pass within it as the shape in which it is maintained by the police. Thus, they may feel called on to make arrests because they feel that persons passing can see that the police see unshapely activities going on.[27]

> The wretched man positively insisted on being arrested. I'd been watching for a long time. And I didn't see how I could let him carry on much longer like that. He might get killed. Or someone might make a complaint at the police station. Then where would I be? There were a lot of people watching him and I thought most of them knew I had seen him. They would be thinking it was time I did something about it. They couldn't be expected to realize that I was a policeman who had never made an arrest. I could almost feel them looking at me, wondering how long it would be before I went into action.
>
> If only he would actually get on to a bus it would be all right. He would be whirled away, out of my uncomfortable little world, in no time at all. But he never did get on to a bus. He tried often enough, but usually the conductor waved him off, or he waited too long, grabbed wildly at the handrail as the vehicle drew away and, losing his balance, went reeling into the gutter. What a skinful he must have had! He was as tight as an owl.

3. For the police, the range of sights, sounds and the like which they observe while going through the streets is conceived in terms of the access these might give to private places. If the private places of a territory are the dominant setting for its activities, then the police attend to the streets with a highly refined sensitivity. Persons living in suburban areas report that "the only

---

[26]See Len O'Connor, *They Talked to a Stranger,* 1957. NY: Doubleday passim.

[27] A. Thorp, *Calling Scotland Yard*, p. 9, 1954. London: Roulledge Kegan-Paul

way" they can walk in the streets at night without being stopped by the police is if they can get a dog to accompany them. And the police chief of Beverly Hills notes that even this may not be sufficient, since his police are familiar with the persons and dogs who make a habit of walking at night.[28]

4. For the police, objects and places having routine uses are conceived in terms of favorite misuses. Garbage cans are places in which dead babies are thrown, schoolyards are places where molesters hang out, stores are places where shoplifters go, etc.

5.d For the police, each patrol of a beat is conceived as potentially adding items to a cumulative set of values; they want a patrol to count. What any patrol may, however, add to (or subtract from) an assembled body of knowledge, reputation, security, opportunity, etc. may vary considerably.

Given that some sort of mathematics seems attended to in the patrol as an occasion within a continuing set of occasions, we can appreciate the police concern with the matters that are seen as unordered, for example, the fact that "breaks," i.e. unexpected large accumulations (or losses) of units occur at undetermined points within a career. A policeman may, whether rookie or oldster, happen upon a crime in its course which, because of the public attention it gets, assures him then and there of fame and promotion. Or an old policeman, having assembled a large collection of units of value, may suddenly be caught in a compromising situation, and see himself stripped at a point when reassembly cannot be looked forward to. Or a policeman who knows the habits of the crooks he usually deals with may encounter a young hood who, being unaware of the business relations regular crooks and regular cops arduously establish, on being caught, fires and kills the cop.

The import of these unordered contingencies are, quite simply, that talk of the "course of a policeman's career" must recognize that the policeman is never able to say at what point he currently is in his career. Where he is now is radically a matter of where he will have turned out to be. This corner he approaches may be the corner at which he will have been killed.

5.e That the police seek to be professionals is well known.[29] While this might be accounted for in terms of a general search for status, one basis for the status seems to be their concern, and the concern of those they deal with, i.e. criminals, to develop means for establishing their relation as business-like, i.e. as impersonal, code-governed, etc.

The police claim that crime is a business is not merely a cry on their part for more adequate means to attack crime. It is as well an attempt to suggest, given quite limited means, that if criminals behave reasonably the police, too, will try to do so. The persons feared most by either side are the green groups of

---

[28] C. H. Anderson, *Beverly Hills Is My Beat*, 1960, pp. 33–4. NY: Archer

[29] One training manual states the matter neatly:

"Once a man has chosen police work as a career, he should do his part to make it a profession." J. Towler, *Practical Police Knowledge*, Springfield, Ill.; Charles C. Thomas, 1959.

the other. The new criminal is felt to be most dangerous; the old pro, trustable, almost a partner. And the criminal, too, is much more afraid of the rookie cop than of the veteran.

Throughout this century, each generation of olders seems to see the young members of the other as over-ready to engage in unwarranted violence, and to remark to their co-generationists about the businesslike relation they might have were it not for the young hot-heads.[30] A businesslike relation need imply no bribery, of course; merely that minimizable risks be minimized.

The Police
and Crime

James Q. Wilson

The average citizen thinks of the police as an organization primarily concerned with preventing crime and catching criminals. When crime increases or criminals go uncaught, the conventional public response is to demand more or better policemen. When the crime rate goes down or a particularly heinous crime is solved, the police often get—at least try to take—the credit.

For some time, persons who run or study police departments have recog-

---

[30]Once or twice he had gotten close to Sutton, but the wily bank robber seemed to have a second sense that told him Phillips was closing in. Phillips had picked up a former partner of Sutton's, and hoping for a lighter term than he faced, he had told Frank a lot about the fugitive. 'I seen Bill Sutton six weeks ago,' the prisoner said earnestly. 'He knows you're after him and he don't like it. Sutton never used a gun in his life, but he swears he'll kill you if he ever catches up with you. He's never forgotten what you did to Eddie Wilson.'

"He didn't tell her about this, but one of his partners did. When she mentioned it to him he laughed, 'Sutton is a professional like I am. He knows I have nothing personal against him. He's a crook; I'm a cop. He knows the rules of the game as well as I do. To Sutton I'm a business rival—nothing more. That punk I collared who sang about Sutton was just trying to make things easy for himself.'

"And so it proved. When Sutton was finally caught he told Phillips about the rumors he had heard about his reported personal vendetta against the detective. 'That bothered me,' Sutton said. 'Sure I was afraid you'd make me some day and grab me, but I knew there was nothing personal about you trying to collar me. Shooting a cop is for these trigger-happy young punks who are loaded with junk. I'm a bank robber, not a killer, Frank. Believe that. Of course,' he added with a grin, 'there were some days when I didn't like you so much. . . .'"

Reynolds, Q., *Headquarters*, pp. 15–16, 1955. Boston: Little Brown

REPRINTED FROM: James Q. Wilson, *Thinking About Crime*. New York: Basic Books, 1975 (81—97; 214).

nized that this public conception is misleading. The majority of calls received by most police are for services that have little to do with crime but a great deal to do with medical emergencies, family quarrels, auto accidents, barking dogs, minor traffic violations, and so on. And those calls that do involve serious crimes, such as burglaries, robberies, and auto thefts, typically occur after the event has taken place and the trail is cold; the officer who responds can often do little more than fill out a report that will contain few if any leads for further investigation.[1] The police themselves wish it were otherwise—most patrolmen would prefer to stop a crime in progress or catch a major felon—but only infrequently do they have the chance.

The growing realization among scholars and administrators of the importance of the service provision, order maintenance function of patrolmen has led some experts to dismiss or downplay the crime control function. A police department is often thought "advanced" or "progressive" to the extent it emphasizes community service rather than crime prevention. To a degree, this is well and good: For too long, police officers were given little training and no supervision in the performance of their most frquent duties, with the result that many citizens felt poorly treated and many officers felt frustrated and unsure of their mission.

But progress along these lines does not constitute an answer to the citizen's concern with crime. He believes, with reason, that if there were no police at all there would be more crime, and therefore he supposes that if there were more police there would be less crime. When he sees a policeman on a street corner, the citizen often feels more secure and assumes that the burglar or mugger seeing the same officer will feel less secure. If a crime is committed, the citizen believes that the police should diligently look for the criminal, even if it means neglecting their community service functions. The citizen is impatient with theories that argue that crime can only be prevented by reforming prisons or ending poverty. He thinks that crime—or at least crime that affects him—will be prevented if sufficient policemen walk by his home or business often enough.

There have been some attempts to test that belief, but until recently these efforts had serious shortcomings. One of the first was carried out in 1954 by the New York City Police Department (NYPD) under the direction of Commissioner Francis W. H. Adams.[2] Beginning on September 1 of that year, the police strength assigned to the twenty-fifth precinct in Manhattan (comprising much of East Harlem) was more than doubled. Most of the additional men were inexperienced patrolmen taken straight from the Police Academy who were assigned to foot posts, although experienced detectives and traffic, juvenile, and narcotics officers were also added to the precinct. Before the experiment, called "operation 25," began, as many as two-thirds of the foot posts (or beats) in the area were unmanned. During the experiment, no post was left vacant,

---

[1] See, for example, Albert J. Reiss, Jr., *The Police and the Public* (New Haven: Yale University Press, 1971), p. 71.

[2] The report on Operation 25 is from a brochure published by the New York City Police Department.

the number was increased from fifty-five to eighty-nine, and their average length was shortened.

Operation 25 lasted four months. During that time serious crimes declined and the reduction was greatest for "street crimes"—those that either occurred in public places or involved entry from the street into private places. Muggings fell from sixty-nine during the same period in 1953 to seven in the experimental part of 1954, and auto thefts dropped from seventy-eight to twenty-four. Burglaries declined as well, especially those for which the entry was made from the front of the residence or store. Murder, essentially a "private" crime, did not decline at all; indeed, it increased from six to eight cases. Felonious assault, which, like murder, frequently occurs in private places among "friends," did decline, but not nearly as much as street robberies or auto thefts.

Operation 25 was used to justify to the mayor and city council police demands for increases in manpower. The increases were forthcoming. Between 1954 and 1974, the size of NYPD increased by 54 per cent, while the total population remained about constant. However, crime increased even more rapidly than the police.

The subsequent increase in crime despite the growth in the size of the police force does not necessarily repudiate the findings of Operation 25. After all, the composition of the population has changed substantially during the years since 1954. Furthermore, not all officers added to a police department are added to the effective street force of that department. Thus, for every hundred officers added to the force, only a few may represent net increments to street patrol.

But if later history did not disprove Operation 25, problems in its design raised questions about its significance. There was no direct measure of true crime rates, only counts of reported crimes. More important, the comparison in crime rates was made with crime the preceding year. It is possible that crime might have declined during 1954 for reasons other than the increased police presence. But most important, no effort was made to discover whether crime in surrounding precincts increased as a result of the increased police activity of Operation 25. Perhaps crime was not reduced, only displaced. Finally, police administrators, if not citizens, would want to know whether increases of police manpower short of doubling the previous number will have any effect, and whether patrolmen in cars are more or less effective than those on foot.

In the 1960s, there were some fresh efforts to answer these questions. In Great Britain, J. A. Bright of the Home Office reported on the "Beat Patrol Experiments" carried out in 1965 to discover whether the number of crimes in an urban area would be affected by the number of foot patrolmen in that area.[3] In four British cities a number of foot beats were designated as experimental areas, and over successive four-week periods the number of officers walking those beats was varied systematically between zero and four. At the end of one year, Bright and his colleagues concluded that the number of reported crimes on a beat decreased when the officers patrolling it on foot increased from zero

---

[3]J. A. Bright, *Beat Patrol Experiment*. Report No. 8769 of the Police Research and Development Branch, Home Office, London England (July 1969).

to one, but that there were no further decreases resulting from raising the number of patrolmen to two per beat. There was some tentative evidence that a really sharp increase—say, from one to three or even four officers on a single beat—would produce still further reductions in crime, but the evidence supporting this was weak, and in any event it is not generally feasible to triple or quadruple a city's police force. In sum, Bright rejected the view that having more foot patrolmen in a neighborhood will produce a reduction in crime. Unfortunately, the beats in which the experiment was conducted were so small and the periods during which the changes were made so brief that the Home Office results can at best be regarded as tentative.

At about the same time, another project was underway in New York that sought to measure the results of having more cops on the beat. One of the objectives of this study, carried out by S. J. Press for the New York City Rand Institute, was to look closely at the possibility, overlooked in Operation 25, that reported crime rates might change for reasons having nothing to do with the additional officers on patrol.[4] To this end, Press studied two nearby precincts similar to the one (the twentieth precinct) in which, beginning in October 1966, police manpower was increased by 40 per cent, while the manpower assigned in the rest of the city remained about what it had always been.

The results, though not quite as dramatic as those claimed for Operation 25, were on the whole quite consistent with it. In the twentieth precinct, street robberies per week fell by 33 per cent, auto theft by 49 per cent, and grand larcencies "visible from the street" by 49 per cent. There were no appreciable decreases in serious crimes that occurred in private places, such as burglary and assault. Most important, these were *net* reductions in crime, over and above such changes as may have occurred in the similar precincts in which no additional policemen were deployed. Furthermore, these reductions seemed to be genuine—that is, little evidence was found that crime had simply been displaced to adjoining precincts.

Though the data from the twentieth precinct were better analyzed than had been those from the twenty-fifth precinct, the results were still inconclusive. Only changes in reported crimes, not in actual crimes, could be observed, and the reporting system itself changed early in the project, perhaps affecting the results in unknown ways. The time period was short—four months in the case of Operation 25, eight months in the twentieth precinct. Perhaps a sudden increase in police manpower will make criminals lie low or go elsewhere for a while, but then, as they become accustomed to the new situation, they resume their activities. This is often exactly what happens when better street lights are installed; crime decreases for a while but then returns to its previous level. Only rudimentary efforts were made to match socioeconomically the areas in which the police were strengthened with those in which they were not. In short, neither project was a true experiment.

Nonetheless, even discounting the results substantially to allow for these imperfections, the results in the two New York projects were sufficiently strik-

---

[4]S. J. Press, *Some Effects of an Increase in Police Manpower in the 20th Precinct of New York City*, Report No. R–704–NYC (New York: Rand Institute, 1971).

ing and consistent to warrant entertaining the belief that very large increases in police patrols may reduce "outside" or "street" crime significantly, at least for a short period of time.

Some of the limitations of the early studies were overcome in a careful analysis of subway robberies in New York City and the effect of increased assignment of police to the subway system. The proportion of crimes committed that are actually reported is probably much higher in the subway than in the city as a whole, because many victims are transit employees who must report crimes if they are to account for missing cash and tokens. And citizen victims are delivered by the subway to stops where police, dispatchers, and change-booth clerks are readily available, thus facilitating the reporting of a loss.

The two most common major crimes in subways are the robbing of passengers, an offense typically committed by young black boys of school age who, though unarmed, often use violence, and the robbing of change-booth clerks, a crime typically committed by somewhat older males, frequently narcotics users, who, though armed with guns, rarely use violence.

In the two years preceding 1965, subway felonies were increasing at an annual rate of about 50 per cent. In April of that year, Mayor Robert Wagner ordered a substantial increase in police patrols in the subways, from twelve hundred persons to over thirty-one hundred, with the objective, which was by and large met, of having a police officer on every subway train and at every station between the hours of 8 P.M. and 4 A.M..

The results of this manning schedule over an eight-year period were later analyzed by Jan M. Chaiken, Michael W. Lawless, and Keith A. Stevenson at the New York City Rand Institute.[5] This evaluation covers the longest period of patrol work ever studied in a comparable fashion. Following the introduction of heavy police coverage in 1965, there was a short-term decline in total subway crime. Within a year or so, however, the number of subway robberies began to rise again at a rapid rate, so that by 1970 there were six times as many robberies occurring as had occurred in 1965, when the extra police were first hired.

This discouraging result in total subway robberies concealed, however, a remarkable success story. The extra police were primarily deployed during the evening. The number of subway felonies occurring per hour during the night fell in 1965 *and remained low,* while the number of felonies occurring during the day, after a brief decrease in 1965 when the publicity about more transit police was at its peak, rose more or less steadily from 1966 on.

The Rand authors concluded that, though subway crime has tended to rise year after year, the addition of uniformed officers to the trains and platforms during the evening hours has caused a substantial decline in crime at those times, and that this deterrent effect of the police has persisted for several years. The cost was high, however—about $35,000 per deterred felony. And the circumstances were quite special: the subway is an enclosed place with few

---

[5]Jan M. Chaiken, Michael W. Lawless, and Keith A. Stevenson, *The Impact of Police Activity on Crime Robberies in the New York City Subway System.* Report No. R–1424– NYC (New York: Rand Institute, 1974).

exits. A would-be robber, seeing a police officer on a train or platform, will find it difficult to select a victim sufficiently removed from the officer as to eliminate the chance of being caught in the act, and to discover an escape route sufficiently convenient as to give him a good chance of getting away once a hue and cry is set up. In short, the subway patrol plan, while apparently of considerable value when it is in effect, offers few guidelines for patrolling the city streets.

In the late 1960s there was being developed a major new research technique of great potential value in studying police effectiveness. This was the "victimization survey," pioneered by the Task Force on the Assessment of Crime of President Johnson's Commission on Law Enforcement and Administration of Justice. A national survey of ten thousand households was carried out in 1966 by Philip H. Ennis and the National Opinion Research Center of the University of Chicago. Simultaneously, a survey of over five hundred persons in three precincts of Washington, D.C., was undertaken by Albert D. Biderman and the Bureau of Social Science Research, Inc.[6]

These surveys provided for the first time convincing evidence of the extent of unreported crime, a fact now widely accepted. There were, we learned, about twice as many major crimes being committed in the United States every year than appeared in official police statistics. In 1972–1973, the United States Bureau of the Census conducted even larger victimization surveys and in general confirmed the earlier finding.

The 1966 surveys, being one-shot enterprises, could not tell us anything about *changes* in true crime rates. But they offered a technique which, though quite expensive, could be applied to experiments in police patrol. By measuring victimization rates of individuals and business firms in experimental areas before and after changes in police deployment, and also in carefully matched control areas where no changes in deployment occurred, more reliable conclusions could be drawn about the extent to which various police strategies could affect crime.

In the early 1970s a few big-city police departments devised and began such experiments with funds, technical assistance, and evaluation studies provided by the Police Foundation, a private, independent foundation in Washington, D.C., created in the summer of 1970 by the Ford Foundation.

The first to be completed was done in Kansas City, Missouri, to test the effect of different levels of "preventive patrol." Preventive patrol, for long the fundamental assumption of police deployment, means having officers walk or drive through their beats whenever they are not answering a specific call for service or assistance. By their continuous, moving prescence, so the theory goes, crime will be prevented because would-be criminals will be aware of and deterred by the police presence. Furthermore, this patrolling may enable the

---

[6]The Ennis and Buderman studies were both reports to the President's Commission on Law Enforcement and Administration of Justice. Philip H. Ennis, *Criminal Victimization in the United States: A Report of a National Survey*, and Albert D. Buderman *et al., Report on a Pilot Study in the District of Columbia on Victimization and Attitudes Toward Law Enforcement* (Washington, D.C.: U.S. Government Printing Office, 1967).

officer to witness a crime in progress or to discover and stop fugitives, suspicious persons, and stolen cars.

Officers in Kansas City designed an experiment to test these assumptions. In the southern part of the city, fifteen police beats were sorted into five groups of three matched beats each. Each group was made up of beats that were as similar as possible in population characteristics (income, ethnicity, transiency, and so on), reported crime levels, and calls for police services. Within each group, three different patrol strategies were used for a one-year period. One beat (chosen at random) was patrolled in the customary fashion by a single patrol car that cruised the streets whenever it was not answering calls. These were the "control" beats. A second beat in each group had a greatly increased level of preventive patrol—cars were visible cruising these streets two to three times more frequently than in the control areas. This strategy was called "proactive patrol." In the third beat in each group, preventive patrol was eliminated altogether—a police car would enter the area only in answer to a specific request for service. When that run was completed, the car would either return to the periphery of the beat or cruise streets outside it. This was called "reactive patrol." Before and after the experiment, individuals and businessmen were interviewed to learn whether they had been the victims of crime, what they thought of the quality of police service, and to what extent they were fearful of crime.

The results analyzed by George L. Kelling and others were startling. After a year, no substantial differences among the three areas were observed in criminal activity, amount of reported crime, rate of victimization as revealed in the follow-up survey, level of citizen fear, or degree of citizen satisfaction with the police. For all practical purposes, the changes in the level of preventive patrol made no difference at all.

For reasons that are still hard to understand, citizen respect for the police increased somewhat in the control beats, where nothing was changed, and did not increase at all (indeed, declined slightly) on the proactive beats, where more police became available. And strangest of all, perhaps, the citizen living on the proactive beats felt more apprehensive than those living on others about the likelihood of being robbed or raped.

It is easy to misinterpret these results, and so it is important to state what was *not* found. The experiment does *not* show that the police make no difference and it does *not* show that adding more police is useless in controlling crime. All it shows is that changes in the amount of random preventive patrol in marked cars does not, by itself, seem to affect, over one year's time in Kansas City, how much crime occurs or how safe citizens feel. Very different results may have been obtained if important changes were made in *how* the police were used—for example, by having them patrol in unmarked cars, by having them walk beats out of uniform, by directing them to place under continuing surveillance frequently victimized homes or stores, or by assigning them to do more thorough follow-up investigations of crimes. Studies are underway that may shed some light on a few of these alternatives.

Even so, the Kansas City results offer an important opportunity for police administrators and public officials. If true generally and not just in one city, then these findings mean that there is no compelling reason to tie up large numbers of uniformed officers in the monotonous and apparently unproductive task of driving through the streets waiting for something to happen. By cutting back on preventive patrol, a substantial amount of manpower—in Kansas City, perhaps as much as one-third of all patrol man-hours—could be made available for other tasks, such as investigation, surveillance, or community service.

The key question, therefore, is whether other ways of using patrolmen will be more effective in terms of crime control or citizen satisfaction. Two kinds of patrol strategies have been designed to replace preventive patrol. One is the "community service" approach. It is based on the assumption that if officers are encouraged to become familiar with the neighborhoods in which they work and to take larger responsibilities for following through on citizen requests for assistance as well as on complaints of crime, they will win the confidence of those whom they are to protect and thereby elicit more cooperative assistance from the public and better intelligence about criminal activities. The other is the "crime attack" model which, while not logically incompatible with the former, is based on the assumption that the best use of patrolmen is to place them as close as possible, not to the citizens, but to the scene of a potential crime in ways that will enable them to apprehend the criminal in the act, or at least to cut short his crime almost as soon as it begins.

The community service model is variously called "team policing," the "beat commander project," the "basic car plan," or the "neighborhood police team." Variants of it have been tried in Syracuse, Los Angeles, New York, Cincinnati, Detroit, and elsewhere.[7] The essential idea is to assign a team of patrolmen and supervisors to a small area—say, one precinct or a few beats—and to leave them there with broad latitude to learn about the neighborhood, alter their own working hours to meet the demands of the area, conduct much of their own follow-up investigation on crimes, and serve as active intermediaries between citizens and various social service agencies. Instead of moving patrolmen about through many neighborhoods in response to radio calls for service, each team of patrolmen is expected to handle all the calls in their own neighborhood. Instead of turning all crime complaints, once the initial report is taken, over to detectives or other specialists from "downtown," the team is expected to do much of the initial investigation. The immediate objective is to develop among the officers a strong sense of territoriality—their beats are "their turf"—out of which will arise, it is hoped, a stronger sense of identification with the community and the fostering of reciprocity in information and service.

The crime attack model takes a much wider variety of forms, ranging from "Operation Identification" (designed to mark valuable items so as to simplify their recovery and thus discourage their theft) to stakeout squads stationed in the back rooms of liquor stores waiting for an armed robber to enter. In each case, the strategy is to make an object harder to steal or a thief easier to catch.

---

[7]An overview of efforts at team policing is Lawrence W. Sherman *et al, Team Policing* (Washington, D.C.: The Police Foundation, 1973).

Little effort goes into developing information from the community, because the police recognize that since the vast majority of citizens commit no serious crimes and know no serious criminals, they have little information to offer. A common crime attack tactic is the use of decoys—that is, officers disguised as derelicts, cab drivers, hippies, and other frequent targets of criminal activity. Some cities, such as New York, have used community service or team policing methods in some areas and decoys and stakeout squads in others.

Although there is no logical conflict, there sometimes appears to be tension between the two approaches. Stakeout squads and decoys may produce dead criminals rather than arrests. Decoys sometimes have difficulty convincing either criminals or innocent bystanders that they are police officers; indeed, there have even been stances in which a decoy has been unable to convince a fellow officer that he was a cop. As a result, police decoys have sometimes been attacked by citizens and shot at by skeptical officers. In racially tense areas, aggressive law enforcement, unless well managed, can give rise to community criticism.

At the same time, team policing may improve the morale of the officers or the image of the department without producing any increase in arrests or any decrease in crime. If crime rates are insensitive to the number of officers driving around on preventive patrol, they may also be unaffected by efforts to get to know the community.

So far, there has been virtually no independent evaluation of any crime-attack strategy, but statistics gathered by the police themselves seem encouraging. In 1971 the NYPD formed an "anticrime patrol" of about one thousand officers dressed in civilian clothes or in disguises who worked the streets of high-crime areas. The theory was that criminals recognize and avoid uniformed patrolmen (hence the ineffectiveness of random preventive patrol) and commit crimes that are infrequently solved by detectives. The objective of the NYPD effort was to catch criminals in the act. Although the plainclothes officers represented only about 5 per cent of the men and women assigned to each precinct, they made in 1973 over 18 per cent of the felony arrests, including over half the arrests for robbery and about 40 per cent of those for burglary and auto theft. Furthermore, three-fourths of these arrests resulted in convictions, far higher than the city-wide rate.[8] There is no way as yet, however, of determining with confidence the impact of these high arrest levels on crime rates.

Progress in evaluating the community service model has been somewhat greater. The most ambitious experiment of this kind ever done is underway in Cincinnati, where the police have implemented in District One (the downtown, inner-city area) a "Community Sector Team Policing Program," or COMSEC. Under COMSEC there was a slight increase (about 16 per cent) in police manpower assigned to District One, but a profound change in the way the police were organized and directed.

Formerly, motorized patrolmen in District One handled calls from throughout the area, even from a place outside their normal "sector" (i.e.,

---

[8] Data supplied by the New York Police Department.

beat). When particular problems arose, specialized units from headquarters were called in—to handle juveniles, burglary reports, narcotics, and so on. The patrolmen who took the initial call for service often performed no function beyond that of making a routine report. At the start of a tour of duty, the officers assigned to the district would muster together and listen to such information as a supervisor may have; much of it might not apply to their beat. There was little opportunity to exchange information in any systematic way with officers covering the same sector. Nor was there always a close correspondence between the number of officers on patrol in a sector and the workload at a given time in that sector. Finally, "community relations" was the responsibility of a community relations unit that worked out of headquarters. In all these respects, the Cincinnati police were organized in much the same way as other big-city police.

COMSEC changed much of that. Each sector in District One was now covered by a team that remained in that sector and handled almost all (91 per cent) of the calls for service from it. The team rarely called on specialized units for help on any matter except homicide. Not even the central traffic unit operates within District One except for some patrolling of the expressways. Detectives rarely appear. The Tactical Patrol Unit has been disbanded. Community relations became part of the ongoing responsibilities of each patrolman, to be discharged by involving local citizens in crime prevention and service activities. Officers on the beat appear at meetings in that neighborhood to answer questions and to gather information by, for example, showing pictures of known burglars operating in the area. Information developed by each officer is to be shared among his colleagues under the guidance of an information "collator." Working hours are changed frequently to adjust to actual workloads and neighborhood needs.

The eighteen-month experiment began in March 1973; six months later the preliminary results were analyzed by Alfred I. Schwartz of the Urban Institute. The total number of reported crimes decreased in Division One while it increased in the rest of the city. The greatest decrease in the experimental area was in the number of burglaries, which dropped by 7 per cent; in the rest of the city, burglaries increased by more than 2 per cent.

Curiously, citizens' fears of crime were not greatly allayed by the COMSEC program. The proportion of those living in District One who felt unsafe when out alone at night did not change substantially; the proportion who thought their neighborhood more dangerous than others actually went up; the proportion—about half—who believed their chances of being robbed had gone up in the past few years did not change. And this lack of any greater sense of security was not the result of the invisibility of the police—there was a significant increase in the percentage of citizens in District One who reported having seen police officers walking the area. Nor was it the result of any lack of public confidence in the police—about 90 per cent of the citizens interviewed thought the police handling of various incidents was "good" or "very good." In fact, even among those *arrested* by the police, 80 per cent thought the officers were basically honest, and more than half thought they were properly respectful to persons such as themselves.

Another experiment, this one in Rochester, New York, suggests, on the basis of preliminary results, that one aspect of the team policing model may have another advantage—namely, improving police effectiveness in investigating crimes that have been reported. In Rochester, two or three teams were allowed to combine the patrol and investigative (or detective) functions, instead of having separate units do each, as in most departments. The theory was that immediate follow-up on crime reports by officers assigned to a neighborhood permanently would lead to more crimes being solved (or as the police put it, "cleared") than if the follow-up was done by detectives sent in some time later to work independently of the patrolmen.

After one year, outside evaluators, led by Peter Bloch of the Urban Institute, concluded that there had been an impressive increase in the number of crimes cleared by the experimental teams as compared to the number cleared in other parts of the city by conventional detective units. For example, Team A more than doubled the number of robberies and burglaries they were able to solve (from about 18 per cent before they started to about 35 per cent after) and more than quintupled the number of larcenies being cleared. By comparison, conventional police in a similar part of the city showed no improvement over the same period.

It is too early to tell whether these striking results will continue and can be confirmed by further study and experimentation. Above all, there is as yet no way of knowing whether improved police ability to solve crimes will affect the crime rate.

Some will find the last statement inexplicable. If more crimes are solved because more criminals are arrested, the crime rate *must* go down—or so one would suppose. In fact, police ability to solve crimes may have very little affect on how many crimes are committed. The burglaries most easily solved may be random, impulsive crimes committed occasionally by amateurs; most burglaries may instead be committed by skilled professionals who are frequent violators and only rarely caught. Even more important, a criminal is not immobilized by an arrest, or at least not for long. Most are out on bail promptly—sometimes before the arresting officer can finish his paperwork. Trials are frequently delayed for months, convictions are not assured, and penalties may be light (e.g., probation). Finally, important social environmental changes, such as rapid population growth, the increase in the proportion of young persons, sharp movments in the business cycle, and abnormally hot or cold weather may have so much influence on the propensity to crime that gains resulting from police methods may be completely obscured.

At this stage of our understanding of police work it is hard to draw any comprehensive conclusions about the ability of the police to prevent crime that is not so guarded and cautious as to be useless. Since 1954, we have gathered more questions than answers. In general, however, these observations seem warranted:

First, a massive increase in police presence on foot in densely settled areas will probably lead to a reduction in those crimes, such as muggings and auto theft, that require the perpetrators to use the city streets. This seems to be supported by Operation 25, the manpower increase in the twentieth precinct, and the New York subway experience. No one can yet say with any confidence, however, how long this reduction will persist (except in the special case of the subway project, where it endured for many years), and how much crime is merely displaced to another location. The suggestion from the twentieth precinct that there is little displacement remains just that—only a suggestion, inadequately supported by data. And the cost of any massive increase is—well, massive.

Second, substantial increases in random preventive patrol by police in marked cars do not appear to have any affect on the crime rates, nor do they tend to reassure the citizenry about their safety. Police time spent driving the streets waiting for something to happen is not time well spent.

Third, the community service model of neighborhood team policing appears, on the basis of preliminary results from Cincinnati, to be of some value in reducing burglaries even without massive increases in police manpower. Ironically, the effort by the police to get closer to the community has not as yet reassured the community about its safety or made much difference in what the community thinks about the police, or vice versa.

Fourth, a crime-attack strategy aimed at specific offenses may hold great promise, but so far it has been the least well-evaluated of all police methods. More careful work is needed in this area than in almost any other aspect of police behavior.

Finally, whatever may be the value of the police presence as a deterrent to crime, the value of the police as apprehenders of criminals is not something that the police alone are capable of improving. The value of an arrest for incapacitating a criminal or for deterring would-be criminals from following his example depends crucially on what the courts elect to do with the arrestee, and here there has been virtually no careful experimentation at all. A few police departments in this country have shown themselves to be remarkably innovative, experimental, and open to evaluative research. There are not as yet many prosecutors or courts about which one can say the same thing.

PART IV
PRACTICE OF POLICING

The street-level interactions between the agents of a public service bureaucracy and members of the public is important, not only because of the citizen perceptions, feelings, and attitudes that are formed as a result of these face-to-face encounters, but also because the shape of these interactions represent, in effect, the operating policy of the bureaucracy. Nevertheless, the study of interaction episodes is a recent development in police research.* Specifically much of this research is directed toward gathering data that will independently measure aspects of policing that have previously been studied only by means of official and, often, quite unreliable data supplied to researchers by the police such as arrest statistics, traffic tickets issued, warnings given out, field investigation reports filed, calls answered, reported response times, and so forth.

More generally however, research on the practice of policing as it unfolds in citizen-officer interaction can potentially assess a variety of possible outcomes — verbal threats, tact, ignoring citizen requests, use of force, corruption, noble service, lying, errors, and so on. Such research can also examine the degree to which police officers act civilly toward members of the public, in line with departmental policies, and legally with respect to certain procedural guarantees. Yet, for a number of reasons, the focus of much of the research to date has been upon arrests. Such study reflects a most practical and significant interest in the police specifically and the legal system generally. Certainly, on one hand, arrests make possible the initiation of legal cases, feed the prosecutors' offices and the courts, reside at the heart of questions about police discretion, and represent the symbolic focus of police work. But, on the other hand, arrests occur rather infrequently, even in situations where suspects are present. Indeed, episodes that result in an arrest make up only a small fraction of the time the police spend on the street. In a sense, arrests and the use of force that often accompany them are "last resorts" to be used by a policeman only after other remedies have proved ineffectual. More common are citizen-officer interactions based upon matters of social discord, civil dispute, or requests for assistance of some kind. Consequently, since arrest is only one of a number of possible outcomes, and an unusual one at that, a study of arrest, as Black (1971:1092) elegantly suggests, "flatters the legal significance of the citizen-police encounter."

---

*Studies of police-citizen encounters are of several types: modified case studies (Chevigny, 1968; Wiley and Hudik, 1974); statistical analyses of formally coded and randomly sampled episodes that have been reported by trained observers (Black and Reiss, 1970; Lundman, 1974; Sykes and Clark, 1974); and ethnographic studies based on qualitative field-work data such as those produced by Rubenstein and Van Maanen (all represented in the readings of this section).

If other outcomes of police-citizen meetings are to be measured and examined, it is necessary to know something about the commonsense knowledge and street skills acquired and utilized by the police. Furthermore, we must also be able to characterize, in analytic and exhaustive detail, the features of interactions between the public and the police. Following Goffman (1961:11), interactions of the type we are interested in can be viewed as encounters — a coming together of strangers which is unrehearsed, requiring indications by the participants of their involvement in the "official" focus of the interaction, and evaporating when the participants disperse. Yet, the citizen-police encounter is of a unique character insofar as the police enter the occasion as authority figures with a special property of embracement or role involvement. In other words, the police see themselves in the encounter fully in terms of the imagery of their official role, meaning, in essense, that they can and will use coercion and violence if they believe it is necessary to do so. On the other hand, the citizen involved in the interchange may have little inclination to embrace the submissive-citizen role demanded of him by an involved authority figure. Since the citizen is likely to be under some sort of stress, and, is, at best, an irregular performer in such interactions, he may even be a bit reluctant to participate at all in the encounter. Following Goffman (1956:489) again, ". . . every civilian participant displays some of those very properties which are important *not* to display in focused interaction—embarrassment, lack of poise, distraction, failure to take proper turns at speaking and disregard of spacing rules." This situation is obviously troublesome because the police, fully in role, expect to be treated a certain way, yet the citizen may have difficulties providing such treatment. The police-citizen encounter, then, is a potentially deferential exchange between representatives of the legal order and persons acting in the citizen status. A slight of the officer, overt or covert, indicates disrespect not only for the person but also for the role of a representative of the state.

On the basis of a review of the expanding literature concerned with the police and their publics, we suggest that officer-citizen encounters contain the following key elements: (1) questions of authority; (2) the context of the encounter; (3) the components of the interaction; (4) the expected outcomes of the interactants; and (5) the interpersonal demeanor of both parties. We now discuss each of these five elements separately and, occasionally, in combination, taking care to note the correspondence between each element and the readings that are presented in this section.

1. Authority is always problematic when citizens and the police come together. Such encounters normally represent very brief interactions between strangers of different experiential familiarity with one another, and there is always the possiblity of coercion being exercised. Further, as Reiss (1971:17) points out, the modal encounter involves more citizens than police officers, placing the officers in a position of numerical disadvantage. As all the selections that follow make clear, establishing some degree of authority in the situation is the police officer's principal concern. It is also his principal difficulty, for without such authority he believes he cannot control the exchange. Thus, the major content of police-citizen interaction can be described as attempts to gain *interpersonal control*. To punctuate this point, Cruse and Rubin (1973:3) found that the vast majority of police actions in over 1,000 police-citizen en-

counters were described by observers as "controlling" in some specific fashion.

The explosive potential of this interactional feature is addressed directly by John Van Maanen in the first reading of this section, which is entitled "The Asshole." As Van Maanen argues, from the police point of view, "assholes" are social types created by the police because, in Goffman's (1956:489) refined phrase, "they fail to be properly demeaned." That is, they are persons who, from the police perspective, do not accept the officer's definition of who is to be in charge of the encounter and therefore act in ways that are seen as inappropriate in light of the situation. Such persons undergo what can be seen as a sort of character demotion whereby they become, in police argot, "assholes."

The issue of control is also examined in the next paper of this part- Peter K. Manning's essay on "Lying, Secrecy, and Social Control." Given that the basic orientation of a police officer in an encounter is one of authority and control, Manning argues that the basic distrust which characterizes a conflicted society provides the conditions under which lying occurs. Certainly, citizens lie to the police, and in fact, many officers expect that suspects and nonsuspects alike will do just that. But, the significance of police lying is that as representatives of the moral order, when the police lie, they raise basic questions about the legitimacy of societal authority. If the police lie and are thus impostors, what are the implications for social order and authority? Clearly, as Manning denotes, there are social contexts which make lying more likely, but nonetheless, police lies arise out of, and are shaped by, the officer's attempt to exert interpersonal control over the encounter.

2. Time and place are the crucial elements surrounding the *context* of any police-citizen encounter. Yet the orientation of police officers in time and space is constrained. Time, for instance, is tied closely to the expected use of certain locales. Thus, the citizen lounging in a public park at midday is viewed by the police as behaving in an entirely appropriate fashion, while the same behavior exhibited at midnight is sure to be seen by the police as entirely *de trop*, or "out of place." Consider, too, the following remarks concerning space made by Rubenstein (1973:129):

> He ([the patrolman]) usually carries with him on patrol a sector map of his district . . . . He has no need to know about places beyond the district's limits. The first thing he learns about his district, after the location of the station house, is its boundaries. His knowledge of what lies beyond them is limited and his curiosity restricted.

Other observers have also gone into some depth on the police officer's particularistic knowledge, in particular his knowledge of persons, places, and settings within his assigned territory (Van Maanen, 1974; Manning, 1977; Muir, 1977). Indeed, when places are known to an officer, this knowledge can be put to work and help structure an officer's orientation to subsequent encounters he may have with citizens in and around these places. Such specialized knowledge is therefore crucial and provides an immensely detailed backdrop of rich, nonshared, and particularistic knowledge that assists an officer when he is trying to make sense of an encounter with a citizen.

3. Some of the *components* of an encounter have been discussed previously. In particular, Manning's essay in Part II on "Rules, Colleagues, and Situationally Justified Actions" addressed various components of the police-citizen en-

counter. While discussing certain aspects of "good police work," Manning noted that officers believe they should maintain: proper emotional tone ("cool") and attitude ("neutral"); control of the information to be processed in the interaction; and display efficacious tactics and skills in the manipulation of objects. Here is where Jonathan Rubenstein's analysis of how the police attempt to control people — the third reading in this part — comes into play. No longer are we dealing with the subtleties of interpersonal dynamics, for, as Rubenstein notes, the police do not feel comfortable in any encounter until they are assured that their physical safety is not in immediate danger. Indeed, to a large extent, the instrumental nature of an encounter does not even begin until an officer's expressive concerns over his well-being have been, at least temporarily, laid to rest. These matters, as Rubenstein shows, are perhaps the most elemental, yet perhaps also the most invisible, aspects of any police-citizen exchange.

4. The degree to which any officer possesses a set of *expected outcomes* for a given situation is, in general, not well researched, although it seems that such expectations may be quite critical to the outcome of an encounter. Perhaps the more experienced officers, such as those discussed by Rubenstein, tend to have more systematic predictions of the kinds of outcomes they can expect from particular sorts of citizens in particular places and times and are thus better able to control their interactions on the street. It is likely that our notions about "good police work" (as well as the police notions) come primarily from articles, essays, and media depictions of experienced police officers who know their home territories, the types of persons they encounter there, and the sorts of crimes to look for. On the other hand, the young officer does not possess this detailed knowledge and in-depth understanding of his district. Clearly, knowledge is a variable, not a constant, among policemen. If firm expected outcomes, such as those carried perhaps by veteran patrolmen, make for greater police control over people and situations, other things being equal, then, younger officers with fewer experiences on the street are probably less able to control their interactions with citizens. As a result, an encounter for a relatively inexperienced patrolman is more problematic, more unstable, and more likely to deteriorate into a blatant exercise of coercive force through the officer's more frequent reliance upon his power of arrest or use of violence than is the case for experienced patrolmen.

5. As we have suggested, the failure of some citizen to exhibit *demeanor* that the police view as appropriate to their age, sex, and situational identity (e.g., offender, victim, witness, complainant) is a basis for differences in the quality of the interaction and in the *outcome* of the encounter. The most prominent example of the research accomplished in this area is the work Sykes and Clark (1974), who, in a study covering a fifteen-month period, observed almost 1,500 officer-citizen encounters unfolding in a heterogeneous urban area. Each transaction was recorded and content analyzed for patterns of verbal and nonverbal deference. Their findings show that as citizen status declined (based on role, seriousness of offense, class, and ethnicity), the level of deference the police displayed toward citizens declined. Also, the police, regardless of the status of the citizen, always displayed less deference than did the citizen.

Police minority interactions tend to be characterized by less mutual deference and more disrespect on both sides than other encounters. These data are rather convincing evidence of the importance of deference in shaping the exchange. That is, whether or not the expected deference to the officer is forthcoming patterns the response of both officer and citizen throughout the interaction. It is likely, then, that the presence or absence of deference toward the police would effect the probability of arrest. However, the evidence on the outcomes of citizen-police encounters, in terms of identifying the variables related to arrest or nonarrest, is somewhat more complicated. LaFave (1965) posited that in low-visibility situations where it was unlikely that the encounter would come to the attention of persons other than the officer, the absence of deference by a suspect or offender would increase the probability of arrest. Skolnick (1966) claims this is the case in traffic and vice enforcement, suggesting that rudeness, hostility, and resistance on the part of a citizen leads typically to police "overreaction" such as the applying of heavier penalties to the citizen offender. Lundman (1974) found in nondeferential situations police officers tend to reciprocate hostility, and, in the extreme, as Chevigny (1968) argues on the basis of his defense work for the ACLU in New York City, officers use brutality on citizens and cover their actions by bringing "resisting-arrest" charges against the citizen. A similar pattern is reported by Reiss (1971:55–62). Finally, police-juvenile encounters are probably the most subject to volatile disequilibrium or contests over status. This is perhaps due to the perception of the officer that a youth should defer to him not only as a citizen being confronted by an authority symbol but also as a youth being confronted by an elder. Considerable data support the notion that nondeferential youths are more likely to be handled officially than deferential youths (Piliavin and Briar, 1964; Ferdinand and Lucterhand, 1970). However, we should note, the work of Black and Reiss (1967) did not confirm these results.

Overall, the research reports on police-citizen encounters are somewhat equivocal in many areas. Furthermore, the studies are difficult to interpret and compare because they employ quite different methodologies and samples, and they focus on different categories of offense. Yet it is clear that the deference of the potential offender, particularly in the case of minor offenses (by far the majority of crimes), affects the outcome of an encounter when arrest or nonarrest is to be considered.

The rational model of police administration that is found in the conventional textbooks on police administrations or "criminal justice" does not take into account the obvious variability in police-officer behavior that these encounter-based matters introduce. From the standpoint of the work introduced here and in the readings that follow, the interpersonal tactics utilized by an officer to control his interactions with citizens on the street can always obviate whatever strategy the police organization is attempting to enact. In essence, patrolmen control the conditions of their work to a far greater degree than administrators seem willing to grant. Thus, once the effects of a given strategy are taken into account (see Part III), there is still an effect upon the arrest rate and crime rate caused by the dynamics and form of the typical police-citizen encounter.

In conclusion, social control encounters, where an officer's response to perceived deviance is central, involve degrees of mutual dependency between participants. Therefore, from this standpoint, all law enforcement is a matter of negotiation. But, as Edelman (1964:51) pointedly suggests, "when one of the groups is organized, the rules, as enforced, are likely to be rigged so as to favor it disproportionately." In characterizing law enforcement as a matter of negotiation, we conveniently return to the main theme of this part: namely, the face-to-face encounters between the police and the public are of critical importance, for it is these rule-negotiating situations that, in effect, shape and define public policy, help form many of the citizen's attitudes toward the police, and largely determine the patrolmen conceptions of their role. We will take up these issues again in Part V when we explore how policemen develop notions about what they are to do on the street as a part of their socialization for policing.

The Asshole

John Van Maanen

"I guess what our job really boils down to is not letting the assholes take over the city. Now I'm not talking about your regular crooks . . . they're bound to wind up in the joint anyway. What I'm talking about are those shitheads out to prove they can push everybody around. Those are the assholes we gotta deal with and take care of on patrol. . . . They're the ones that make it tough on the decent people out there. You take the majority of what we do and its nothing more than asshole control."

A veteran Patrolman[1]

I. POLICE TYPIFICATIONS

The asshole—creep, bigmouth, bastard, animal, mope, rough, jerkoff, clown, scumbag, wiseguy, phony, idiot, shithead, bum, fool, or any of a number of anatomical, oral, or incestuous terms—is a part of every policeman's world.[2] Yet the grounds upon which such a figure stands have never been examined systematically. The purpose of this essay is to display the interactional origins and consequences of the label asshole as it is used by policemen, in particular, patrolmen, going about their everyday tasks. I will argue that assholes represent a distinct but familiar type of person to the police and represent, therefore, a part of their commonsense wisdom as to the kinds of people that populate their working environment. From this standpoint, assholes are analytic types with whom the police regularly deal. More importantly, however, I will also argue that the label arises from a set of situated conditions largely unrelated to the institutional mandate of the police (i.e., to protect life and prop-

---

[1] All police quotes are taken from field notes I compiled of conversations and observations taking place during a year of participant observation in what I have referred to anonymously in my writings as the Union City Police Department (a large, metropolitan force employing over 1,500 uniformed officers). The quotes are as accurate as my ear, memory, and notes allow (see Epilogue—eds.) I should note, also, that in this essay I use the terms "police," "police officer," "patrolman," and "policemen" somewhat interchangeably. However, unless I indicate otherwise, my comments are directed solely toward the street-level officer—the cop on the beat—and not toward his superiors, administrators, or colleagues in the more prestigeful detective bureaus.

[2] I chose the term "asshole" for the title of this essay simply because it is a favorite of working policemen (at least in Union City). The interested reader might check my assumption by a casual glance at what several others have to say about this linguistic matter. Most useful in this regard are the firsthand accounts police have themselves provided and can be found, for example, in Terkel (1968, 1974); Drodge, (1973); Mass (1972); Olsen (1974); Whittemore (1973); Walker (1969). I should note as well that such labeling proceeds not only because of its functional use to the police but also because it helps officers to capture perceptual distinctions (i.e., labels are "good to think"). Thus assholes are conceptually part of the ordered world of police—the statuses, the rules, the norms, and the contrasts that constitute their social system.

erty, arrest law violators, preserve the peace, etc.) but arises in response to some occupational and personal concerns shared by virtually all policemen.

According to most knowledgeable observers, nothing characterizes policing in America more than the widespread belief on the part of the police themselves that they are primarily law enforcers—perpetually engaged in a struggle with those who would disobey, disrupt, do harm, agitate, or otherwise upset the just order of the regime. And, that as policemen, they and they alone are the most capable of sensing right from wrong; determining who is and who is not respectable; and, most critically, deciding what is to be done about it (if anything). Such heroic self-perceptions reflecting moral superiority have been noted by numerous social scientists concerned with the study of the police. Indeed, several detailed, insightful, and thoroughly accurate mappings of the police perspective exist.[3] For instance, learned discussions denote the various "outgroups" perceived by the police (e.g., Harris, 1973; Bayley and Mendelsohn, 1969); or the "symbolic assailants" which threaten the personal security of the police (e.g., Skolnick, 1966; Neiderhoffer, 1967; Rubenstein, 1973); or the "suspicious characters" recognized by the police via incongruous (nonordinary) appearances (e.g., Sacks, 1972; Black, 1968). These reports provide the background against which the pervasive police tropism to order the world into the "for us" and "against us" camps can most clearly be seen.

Yet these studies have glossed over certain unique but together commonsensical properties of the police situation with the attendant consequence of reifying the police position that the world is in fact divided into two camps. Other than noting the great disdain and disgust held by many police officers toward certain predefined segments of the population they presumably are to serve, these studies fail to fully describe and explain the range and meaning attached to the various labels used by the police themselves to affix individual reponsibility for particular actions occurring within their normal workaday world. Furthermore, previous studies do not provide much analytic aid when determining how the various typifications carried by the police are recognized as relevant and hence utilized as guides for action by a police officer in a particular situation. In short, if police typifications are seen to have origins as well as consequences, the popular distinction between "suspicious" or "threatening" and the almost mythologized "normal" or "respectable" is much too simple. It ignores not only the immediate context in which street interactions take place, but it also disregards the critical signs read by the police within the interaction itself which signify to them both the moral integrity of the person with whom they are dealing and the appropriate recipe they should

---

[3]See, for example: Rubenstein's (1973) report on the Philadelphia police; Westley's (1970) study of a midwestern police department in the late 1940s; Wilson's (1968) global accounting of the police perspective; Reiss's (1971) research into police-community interactions; LaFave's (1965) treatment of the police decision to arrest; Cain's (1973) and Banton's (1964) observations on the British police; and Berkeley's (1969) cross-cultural view of policing in democratic societies. What comes out of these excellent works is tantamount to a reaffirmation of Trotsky's famous dictum, "There is but one international and that is the police."

follow as the interaction proceeds.[4] Therefore, any distinction of the "types" of people with whom the police deal must include an explicit consideration of the ways in which the various "types" are both immediately and conditionally identified by the police. Only in this fashion is it possible to accurately depict the labels the police construct to define, explain, and take action when going about their routine and nonroutine tasks.

To begin this analysis, consider the following typology which suggests that the police tend to view their occupational world as comprised exhaustively of three types of citizens (Van Maanen, 1974). These ideal types are: (1) "suspicious persons"—those whom the police have reason to believe may have committed a serious offense; (2) "assholes"—those who do not accept the police definition of the situation; and (3) "know nothings"—those who are not either of the first two categories but are not police and therefore, according to the police, cannot know what the police are about.

This everyday typification scheme provides a clue to the expectations, thoughts, feelings, and behaviors of the police. For example, "suspicious persons" are recognized on the basis of their appearance in public surroundings. Such an appearance is seen as a furtive, nonroutine, de trop, or, to use Sacks's (1972) nicely turned phrase, "dramatically torturous." Crucially, such persons, when they provide the police reason to stop and interrogate them, are treated normally in a brisk, though thoroughly professional, manner. It is not their moral worth or identity which is at issue, but rather it is a possible illegal action in their immediate or not-so-immediate past which is in question. From the patrolman's point of view, he is most interested in insuring that formal procedural issues are observed. Hence the personal production of a professional police performance is called for and is presented—at least initially.[5] On the

---

[4]For example, Skolnick's (1966) idea that policemen are "afraid" of certain categories of persons distorts the nature of the occupational perspective. More to the point, policemen are disgusted by certain people, envious of others, and ambivalent toward most. At times they may even vaguely admire certain criminals—those that the British police call "good villians" (Cain, 1971). Fear must of course be given its due, but the occasion of fear hangs more upon unforeseen situational contingencies (the proverbial dark alley, desolate city park, or underlife tavern) than upon certain individuals.

[5]Certainly this may not always be the case. For example, some "suspected persons," due to the nature of their alleged crime (e.g., child molestation, drug dealing, indecent exposure, political sabotage, assault [or worse] upon a police officer, etc.) are likely to provide a strong sense of moral indignation on the part of the arresting (or stopping) officers. In such cases, once identity has been established to the satisfaction of the police (and it should be noted that errors are not unknown—particularly in these volatile cases), the person suspected is transformed immediately into an asshole and is subject to a predictably harsh treatment. Thus, in effect the label arises from an offense which occurred outside the immediate presence of the officers. However, since the spoiled identity must be reestablished anew in the immediate surroundings, the properties of the "affront" correspond analytically to the more familiar case outlines in the text. And while the distinction has theoretical value regarding the norms of the police culture (i.e., that it is not the denounced per se that is important, but rather it is the denouncer that matters—"say's who?"), its practical implications are questionable because patrolmen rarely encounter such situations.

other end of the continuum reside the "know nothings," the "average" citizens, who most generally come under police scrutiny only via their request for service. The "know nothing" may be the injured or wronged party or the seeker of banal information and as such is treated with a certain amount of deference and due respect by the patrolman.

"Assholes," by way of contrast, are stigmatized by the police and treated harshly on the basis of their failure to meet police expectations arising from the *interaction situation itself*. Of course, street interaction may quickly transform suspicious persons into know nothings and know nothings into assholes, or any combination thereof. But it is the asshole category which is most imbued with moral meaning for the patrolman—establishing for him a stained or flawed identity to attribute to the citizen upon which he can justify his sometimes malevolent acts. Consequently, the asshole may well be the recipient of what the police call "street justice"—a physical attack designed to rectify what police take as personal insult. Assholes are most vulnerable to street justice, since they, as their title implies, are not granted status as worthy human beings. Their actions are viewed by the police as stupid or senseless and their feelings as incomprehensible (if they can even be said to have feelings). Indeed, as I will show, the police consistently deny an asshole a rationale or ideology to support their actions, insisting that the behavior of an asshole is understandable only as a sudden or lifelong character aberration. On the other hand, suspicious persons are less likely candidates for street justice because, in the majority of cases, their guilt may still be in question, or, if their guilt has been in fact established, their actions are likely to seem at least comprehensible and purposeful to the police (i.e., a man steals because he needs money; a man shoots his wife because she "two-timed" him; etc.). Also, there are incentives for the suspicious person to cooperate (at least nominally) when subject to police attention. The suspicious person may well be the most cooperative of all the people with whom the police deal on a face-to-face basis. This is, in part, because he is most desirous of presenting a normal appearance (unafraid, unruffled, and with nothing to hide), and, in part, because if he is in fact caught he does not want to add further difficulty to his already difficult position. Finally, know nothings are the least likely candidates for street justice since they represent the so-called client system and are therefore those persons whom the police are most interested in impressing through a polished, efficient, and courteous performance.

At this point, I should note that the above ideal types are anything but precise and absolute. One purpose of this paper is to make at least one of these categories more explicit. But since I am dealing primarily with interior, subjective meanings negotiated in public with those whom the police interact, such typifications will always be subject to severe situational, temporal, and individually idiosyncratic restriction. Hence, an asshole in one context may be a know nothing in another, and vice versa. In other words, I am not arguing in this essay that a general moral order is shared by all policemen as their personalized but homomorphic view of the world. Indeed, the moral order subscribed to by police is complex, multiple, and continually shifts back and forth between that which is individual and that which is collective. What I will ar-

gue, however, is that particular situational conditions (i.e., provocations) pre-
dispose most policemen toward certain perceptions of people which lead to the
application of what can be shown to be rule-governed police actions. My objective, then, is simply to begin teasing out the underlying structure of police
thought and to denote the features of what might be called the secondary real
ity of police work.

The remainder of this essay is divided into four sections. The next section,
"Patrol Work," describes very briefly certain understandings shared by street-
level patrolmen as to what is involved in their work. In a sense, these understandings are akin to behavioral rules that can be seen to mobilize police action; hence they represent the grounds upon which the figure of the asshole is
recognized. The following section, "Street Justice," deals with the characteristic processes involved in discovering, distinguishing, and treating the asshole.
Some conclusions revolving around the relationship between the police and the
asshole are suggested in the next section. And, finally, a few of the broad implications that flow from this analysis are outlined in the last section.

II. PATROL WORK

Policing city streets entails what Hughes (1958) refers to as a "bundle of tasks."
Some of these tasks are mundane; many of them are routine; and a few of them
are dangerous. Indeed, patrol work defies a general job description since it includes an almost infinite set of activities—dogcatching, first-aid, assisting
elderly citizens, breaking up family fights, finding lost children, pursuing a
fleeing felon, directing traffic, and so forth. Yet, as in other lines of endeavor,
patrolmen develop certain insider notions about their work that may or may
not reflect what outsiders believe their work to be. Such notions are of course
attached firmly to the various experientially based meanings the police learn
to regularly ascribe to persons, places, and things—the validity of which is established, sustained, and continually reaffirmed through everyday activity.
Because these meanings are, to some degree, shared by patrolmen going about
similar tasks, their collective representation can be detailed and linked to certain typical practices engaged in on the street by the police. Thus, to understand the police perspective on, and treatment of, the asshole, it is necessary
also to understand the manner in which the policeman conceives of his work.
Below is a very short summary of certain interrelated assumptions and beliefs
that patrolmen tend to develop regarding the nature of their job.

Real Police Work

Many observers have noted the pervasive police tendency to narrowly constrict
their perceived task to be primarily—and to the exclusion of other alternatives—law enforcement. As Skolnick and Woodworth (1967:129) suggest
evocatively, "when a policeman can engage in real police work—act out the
symbolic rites of search, chase and capture—his self-image is affirmed and
morale enhanced." Yet, ironically, opportunities to enact this sequence are few
and far between. In fact, estimates of the time police spend actually in real

police work while on patrol vary from 0 percent (as in the case of the quiet country policeman for whom a street encounter with a bona fide "criminal" would be a spectacular exception to his daily tour of duty) to about 10 or 15 percent (as in the case of the busy urban patrolman who works a seamy cityside district in which the presence of pimps, dealers, cons, and burglars, among others, are the everyday rule). Nonetheless, most of the policeman's time is spent performing rather dry, monotonous, and relatively mundane activities of a service nature—the proverbial clerk in a patrol car routinely cruising his district and awaiting dispatched calls (see Cain, 1971; Reiss, 1971; Webster, 1970; and Cummings, Cummings and Edell, 1965, for further discussion on how the police, spend their time).

Within these boundaries, notions of real police work develop to provide at least a modicum of satisfaction to the police. To a patrolman, *real police work* involves the use of certain skills and special abilities he believes he possesses by virtue of his unique experience and training. Furthermore, such a perspective results in minimizing the importance of other activities he is often asked regularly to perform. In fact, an ethos of "stay-low-and-avoid-trouble-unless-real-police-work-is-called-for" permeates police organizations (Van Maanen, 1973, 1974, 1975). Only tasks involving criminal apprehension are attributed symbolic importance. For the most part, other tasks, if they cannot be avoided, are performed (barring interruption) with ceremonial dispatch and disinterest.

Territoriality

A central feature of policing at the street level is the striking autonomy maintained (and guarded jealously) by patrolmen working the beat. All patrol work is conducted by solo officers or partnerships (within a squad to whom they are linked) responsible for a given plot of territory. Over time, they come to know, in the most familar and penetrating manner, virtually every passageway— whether alley, street, or seldom-used path—located in their sector. From such knowledge of this social stage comes the corresponding evaluations of what particular conditions are to be considered good or bad, safe or unsafe, troubled or calm, usual or unusual, and so on. Of course, these evaluations are also linked to temporal properties associated with the public use of a patrolman's area of responsibility. As Rubenstein (1973) suggests, the territorial perspective carried by patrolmen establishes the basic normative standard for the proper use of place. And those perceived by patrolmen to be beyond the pale regarding their activities in space and time are very likely to warrant police attention.

Maintaining the Edge

Charged with enforcing ambiguous generalized statutes and operating from an autonomous, largely isolated position within the city, it is not surprising that police have internalized a standard of conduct which dictates that they must control and regulate all situations in which they find themselves. At one level, police feel they have the right to initiate, terminate, or otherwise direct all encounters with members of the public. Yet such perceptions penetrate more broadly into the social scheme of things, for police feel furthermore that the public order is a product of their ability to exercise control. The absence of trouble on their beat becomes, therefore, a personalized objective providing intimate feedback as to one's worth as a patrolman. Activity which may threaten the perceived order becomes intolerable, for it signifies to the patrolman that his advantage over the conduct of others (his "edge") is in question. It is a source of embarrassment in front of a public audience, and sometimes it is considered a disgrace to the police uniform if it is viewed by one's peers or departmental superiors. Clearly, such activity cannot be allowed to persist, for it may indicate both to a patrolman's colleagues and to his superiors that the officer no longer cares for his job and has, consequently, lost the all-important respect of those he polices (endangering, it is thought, other policemen who might work the same district). Hence, to "maintain one's edge" is a key concept vis-à-vis the "how to" of police work. And, as all policemen know, to let down the facade (for they do recognize the contrived nature of the front) is to invite disrespect, chaos, and crime.

The Moral Mandate

In light of the above three features of the police frame, it should be clear that police are both representatives of the moral order and a part of it. They are thus committed ("because it is right") to maintain their collective face as protectorates of the right and respectable against the wrong and the not-so-respectable. Situations in which this face is challenged—regardless of origin—are likely to be responded to in unequivocal terms. For example, Cain (1971) writes that when the authority of an officer is questioned by a member of the nonpolice public, the officer has three broad responses available to him. He may (1) physically attack the offender; (2) swallow his pride and ignore the offender; or (3) manufacture a false excuse for the arrest of the offender. What this suggests is a highly personalized view on the part of the police as to their moral position and responsibility, one in which an attempt on the part of the citizen to disregard the wishes of a policeman may be viewed by the police as a profaning of the social and legal system itself. Such an act can also be seen to provoke moral and private indignation on the part of the officer as an individual, thus providing him with another *de rigueur* excuse to locate an appropriate remedy. Since the police personally believe that they are capable of making correct decisions regarding the culpability of an involved party, justice is likely, in the case of an offense to the moral sensibilities of a police officer, to be enacted quickly, parsimoniously, and self-righteously—whether it be the relatively trivial swift kick in the pants or the penultimate tragedy involved in the taking of a life. Thus, the moral mandate felt by the police to be their just right at the societal level is translated and transformed into occupational and personal terms and provides both the justification and legitimation for specific acts of street justice.

This truncated picture of the occupational frame involved in the doing of police work provides the rubric upon which we now can examine the making of an asshole. As one would expect, assholes are not afforded the protection of the more structured relationships police maintain with other of their categories of persons—the suspicious and the know nothings. Rather, they fall outside this fragile shelter, for their actions are seen as "senseless," so "aimless" and "irrational" that recognizable and acceptable human motives are difficult for the police to discover (i.e., from the patrolmen's perspective, there are not legitimate reasons to distrust, disagree with, make trouble for, or certainly hate the police). In this sense, it is precisely the "pointlessness" of an individual's behavior that makes him an asshole and subjects him to the police version of street justice.

III. STREET JUSTICE

Policeman to motorist stopped for speeding:
"May I see your driver's license, please?"
Motorist:
"Why the hell are you picking on me and not somewhere else looking for some real criminals?"
Policeman:
"Cause you're an asshole, that's why . . . but I didn't know that until you opened your mouth."

The above sea story represents the peculiar reality with which patrolmen believe they must contend. The world is in part (and, to policemen, a large part) populated by individuals to whom an explanation for police behavior cannot be made, for, as the police say, "assholes don't listen to reason." The purpose of this section is to explore the commonplace and commonsense manner in which the tag asshole arises, sticks, and guides police action during a street encounter. This stigmatization process is divided into three stages which, while analytically distinct, are highly interactive and apt to occur in the real world of policing almost simultaneously. For convenience only, then, these phases are labeled *affront, clarification,* and *remedy.*

Throughout this discussion it should be remembered that the asshole is not necessarily a suspected law violator—although the two often overlap, thus providing double trouble, so to speak, for the labeled. Importantly, the police view of the asshole as deviant is a product of the immediate transaction between the two and not a product of an act preceding the transaction. This is not to say, however, that certain classes in society—for example, the young, the black, the militant, the homosexual—are not "fixed" by the police as a sort of permanent asshole grouping. Indeed, they are. Yet such bounded *a priori* categories can do policemen little good—except perhaps when dealing with the racial or bohemian obvious—for such stereotypes are frequently misleading and dysfunctional (e.g., the "hippie" who is a detective's prized informant; the black dressed in a purple jumpsuit who happens to be a mayor's top aide; the sign carrying protestor who is an undercover FBI agent). And, even in cases in which *a priori character* judgments are a part of the decision to stop an individual, the asshole label, if it is to play a determining role in the encounter, must arise anew. That is to say, if the asshole distinction is to have a *concrete* as opposed to *abstract* meaning, it must in some manner be tied fundamentally and irresolutely to observable social action occurring in the presence of the labeling officer.

Certainly, a policeman's past experience with an individual or with a recognizable group will influence his street behavior. For example, a rookie soon discovers (as a direct consequence of his initiation into a department) that blacks, students, Mexicans, reporters, lawyers, welfare workers, researchers, prostitutes, and gang members are not to be trusted, are unpredictable, and are usually "out-to-get-the-police." He may even sort these "outsiders" into various categories indicative of the risk he believes they present to him or the implied contrast they have with his own life-style and beliefs. Yet, without question, these categories will never be exhaustive—although the absolute size of what patrolmen call their "shit lists" may grow over the years. Consequently, to understand the police interpretation and meaning of the term "asshole" we must look directly into the field situations in which it originates.

Affront: Challenge

When a police officer approaches a civilian to issue a traffic citation or to inquire as to the whys and wherefores of one's presence or simply to pass the time of day, he directly brings the power of the state to bear on the situation and hence makes vulnerable to disgrace, embarrassment, and insult that power. Since the officer at the street level symbolizes the presence of the Leviathan in the everyday lives of the citizenry, such interactions take on dramatic properties far different from ordinary citizen-to-citizen transactions (Manning, 1974a; Silver, 1967). In a very real sense, the patrolman-to-citizen exchanges are moral contests in which the authority of the state is either confirmed, denied, or left in doubt. To the patrolman, such contests are not to be taken lightly, for the authority of the state is also his personal authority, and is, of necessity, a matter of some concern to him. To deny or raise doubt about his legitimacy is to shake the very ground upon which his self-image and corresponding views are built.

An affront, as it is used here, is a challenge to the policeman's authority, control, and definition of the immediate situation. As seen by the police, an affront is simply a response on the part of the other which indicates to them that their position and authority in the interaction are not being taken seriously. It may occur with or without intent. Whether it is the vocal student who claims to "know his rights," the stumbling drunk who says he has had "only two beers," or the lady of the evening who believes she is being questioned only because she is wearing "sexy clothes," the police will respond in particular ways to those who challenge or question their motive or right to intervene in situations that they believe demand police intervention. Clearly, overt and covert challenges to police authority will not go unnoticed. In fact, they can be seen to push the encounter to a new level wherein any further slight to an officer, however subtle, provides sufficient evidence to a patrolman that he may indeed be dealing with a certifiable asshole and that the situation is in need of rapid clarification. From this standpoint, an affront can be seen, therefore, as disrupting the smooth flow of the police performance. The argumentative motorist, the pugnacious drunk, the sometimes ludicrous behavior of combatants in a "family beef" all interfere, and hence make more difficult, the police task. Of course, some officers relish such encounters. In this sense, ironically, the asshole gives status to the police rather than takes it away. However, since the label is itself a moral charge (and it need not be made salient or verbally expressed), it is open theoretically for rebuttal and evidence may or may not be forthcoming which will substantiate or contradict the charge. Such evidence is gathered in the next analytic stage.

Clarification: Confrontation

Based upon a perceived affront, the patrolman must then attempt to determine precisely the kind of person with whom he is engaged. It is no longer an idle matter to him in which his private conceptions of people can be kept private as he goes about his business. But the patrolman is now in a position wherein he may discover that his taken-for-granted authority on the street is not exactly taken for granted by another. Two commonsensical issues are critical at this point in an encounter. *First*, the officer must determine whether or not the individual under question could have, under the present circumstances, acted in an alternative fashion. To wit, did the perceived affront occur by coercion or accident through no fault of the person? Did the person even know he was dealing with a police officer? Was he acting with a gun at his head? And so on. *Second*, and equally important, given that the person could have acted differently, the officer must determine whether or not the individual was aware of the consequences that might follow his action. In other words, was the action frivolous, naive, unserious, and not meant to offend? Did the person know that his actions were likely to be interpreted offensively by the police? The answers to these two questions, provide patrolmen with material (or lack of it) to construct and sustain an asshole definition. Let us examine in some depth these questions, for they raise the very issue of personal responsibility which is at the nexus of the asshole definition.[6]

McHugh (1969) argues persuasively that the social construction of deviant categories is a matter of elimination which proceeds logically through a series of negotiated offers and responses designed to fix responsibility for a perceived deviant act (i.e., a deviant act requires a charge before it can be said to have happened). Police follow a similar paradigm when filling, emptying, or otherwise attending to their person categories. Again, the first item to be determined in this process is the issue of whether or not the person had alternative means available to him of which he could reasonably be expected to be aware. For example, the speeding motorist who, when pulled to the side of the road, could be excused for his abusive language if it were discovered by the officer that the motorist's wife was at the same time in the back seat giving birth to a child. Similarly, juveniles "hanging out" on a public street corner at certain times of the day may be sometimes overlooked if the police feel that "those kids don't have anyplace to go." On the other hand, if it can be determined that

---

[6]In most regards, the asshole is a classic case of the deviant—although not transituationally so. See Matza (1969), Becker (1963), and Cohen (1965) for a systematic elaboration of the ideas which underpin this analysis.

there is no unavoidable reason behind the affronting action, the individual risks being labeled an asshole. The drunken and remorseless driver, the wife who harangues the police officer for mistreating her husband after she herself requested police service to break up a family fight, or the often-warned teenager who makes a nuisance of himself by flagrantly parading in public after curfew are all persons whom the police believe could have and should have acted differently. Their acts were not inevitable, and it could be expected that they had available to them conventional alternatives.

Given that there are no compelling deterministic accounts readily available to the patrolman to excuse a particular affront, the officer must still make a judgment about the offender's motive. In other words, as the second issue listed above suggests, the policeman must decide whether or not the person knows what he is doing. Could the person be expected to know of the consequences which follow an affront to an officer of the law? Indeed, does the person even realize that what he is doing is likely to provoke police action? Could this particular person be expected to know better? All are questions related to the establishment of a motive for action. For example, the stylized and ceremonial upright third finger when attached to the hand of a thirty-year-old man is taken by the police very differently from the same gesture attached to the hand of a four-year-old child. Loud and raucous behavior in some parts of a city may be ignored if the police feel "the people there don't know any better." Or the claim that one is Jesus Christ resurrected and is out to do battle with the wages of sin may indicate to the police that they are either in the presence of a "dope-crazed radical hippie freak" or a "soft-brained harmless mental case," depending, perhaps, on the offender's age. If the person is young, for instance, responsibility is likely to be individualized—"it is his fault"; however, if the person is old, responsibility is likely to be institutionalized—"he can't help it, he's a nut."

Summarily, the police have available to them two principles of clarification. One concerns the means available to a person guilty of an affront, and the other concerns the purposes behind the affront itself. If the affront is viewed as unavoidable or unintended, the person is unlikely to be subjected to shabby or harsh treatment at the hands of the police. The asshole, however, is one who is viewed as culpable and blameworthy for his affronting action, and, as the next section details, he will be dealt with by the police in ways they feel appropriate.

Remedy: Solution

The above portrait of the clarification principles utilized by police in labeling assholes suggests that certain typical police responses can be displayed by a simple fourfold typology. Figure 1 depicts the relationship between the police officer's assessment of responsibility for the affront and denotes, within each cell, the typical police response given the various possible assessments.

Cell A represents the subject case of this essay since it involves a flagrant (inexcusable) disregard for the sentiments of the police. To the police, those falling into this category are unmistakably assholes and are therefore prominent candidates to be the recipients of street justice—the aim of which is to punish or castigate the individual for a moral transgression. Persons placed in

FIGURE 1

DOES THE PERSON KNOW WHAT HE IS DOING

	YES	NO
COULD THE PERSON ACT DIFFERENTLY UNDER THE CIRCUMSTANCES?	YES A Castigate	B Teach
	NO C Ignore	D Isolate

this category are also the most likely to be placed under questionable arrest. This is not so because of the original intent of the encounter (which often, by itself, is trivial) but rather because of the serious extralegal means utilized by the police to enforce their particular view of the situation upon the recalcitrant asshole—"hamming-up" or "thumping" (beating).[7] And, as Reiss (1971) suggests, the use of force is not a philosophical question to the police but rather one of who, where, when, and how much.

The use of such means require of course that the officer manufacture post facto a legally defensible account of his action in order to, in the vernacular of the day, "cover his ass."[8] Such accounts in legalese most often take the form of "disorderly conduct," "assaulting a police officer," "the use of loud and abusive language in the presence of women and children," "disturbing the peace," or the almost legendary—due to its frequent use—"resisting arrest." The asshole from this position is subject to a police enactment of double jeopardy—justice without trial in the streets and justice, perhaps with trial, in the courts. And regardless of the outcome in the latter case, there is usually only one loser. I should emphasize, however, that I am not saying the behavior of the asshole may not be brutish, nasty, and itself thoroughly vicious. I am simply suggesting that behavior violating extralegal moral codes used by police to order their interactions—whether it be inconsiderate, barbarous, or otherwise—will be responded to in what police believe to be appropriate ways.

Cell B of Figure 1 also represents serious affront to police integrity, and it too may be an affront which calls for an extra-legal response. An illustration provided by the remarks of a patrolman is useful in this context:

> Those goddamn kids got to learn sooner or later that we won't take a lot of shit around Cardoza (a local college campus). Next time I see one of those punks waving a Viet Cong flag I'm gonna negotiate the little bastard back into an alley and kick his rosy red ass so hard he ain't gonna carry nothing for awhile. Those kids gotta be made to see that they can't get away with this type of thing.

---

[7]By the term "extralegal" I am merely implying that the formal police mandate excludes such moral considerations from actions inducing decisions made by officers on the street. The notion of professional policing makes this explicit when it is suggested that patrolmen must act impersonally without regard to individual prejudice.

[8]The "cover-your-ass" phenomena associated with urban policing is described in more depth in Van Maanen (1974). See also Manning (1974b) for a theoretical view of the more general construct, the police lie; and Chevigny (1968) for a presentation of numerous disturbing case studies.

Whether or not such a predicition was actually carried out does not matter, for the quotation itself indicates that "teaching" occupies a particularly prominent position in the police repertoire of possible responses. Thus, the uncooperative and surly motorist finds his sobriety rudely questioned, or the smug and haughty college student discovers himself stretched over the hood of a patrol car and the target of a mortifying and brusque body search. The object of such degradation ceremonies is simply to reassert police control and demonstrate to the citizen that his behavior is considered inappropriate. Teaching techniques are numerous, with threat, ridicule, and harassment among the more widely practiced. Other examples are readily available, such as the morally-toned lectures meted out to those who would attempt to bribe, lie, or otherwise worm their way out of what a policeman sees to be a legitimate traffic citation, the traditional—but vanishing—"kick in the ass" administered to a youngster caught stealing an apple or cutting school. The intent in all these cases is clear. The person must be taught a lesson. And whether the teaching occurs in public or in the back of an alley, the person must be shown the error of his ways. He has acted perhaps out of ignorance, but nevertheless the police feel they must demonstrate that they will not casually overlook the action. However, I should note that the person in this category will remain an asshole in the eyes of the police until he has apparently learned his lesson to the satisfaction of the officers on the scene. Here a display of remorse is no doubt crucial to the police.[9]

Cell C represents the case in which the police are likely to excuse the affront due to the extenuating circumstances surrounding the affront. When it is clear to the police that there are indeed mitigating conditions, their response is to ignore the error—to pretend, as it were, that such an affront never happened. For example, it is understandable to the police that the victim of a mugging may be somewhat abusive toward them when they interrogate him just after the crime (although there is a fine line to be drawn here). Similarly, if a teenage male vigorously defends the chaste and virtuous intentions of he and his girl friend while questioned by the police in a concealed and cozy corner of a public park, it is understood by the police that the boy has few other acceptable alternative lines available. The police response is typically to adopt a somewhat bemused tolerance policy toward actions which under different circumstances may have produced the orb and scepter.

Finally, cell D in Figure 1 concerns the case of an affront which police take to lie beyond the responsibility of the actor. While such action cannot normally be allowed to continue, the moral indignation felt by police is tempered by the understanding that the person is not aware nor could be easily made aware of the rule-breaking nature of his actions. The police response is to isolate the offender, not to punish him. Thus, the "mental case" is shipped to the county

---

[9]Arrests are, of course, sometimes used to teach someone a lesson. However, police believe that in many cases the asshole will arrange his release before the patrolman will have completed the paperwork necessitated by the arrest. And since the affront was moral, the legal justification to "make the case" in court may be lacking. Thus, the classroom more often than not is in the street. Given the opportunity to teach the asshole either by "turning him in" or "doing him in," most police would choose the latter.

hospital for observation and treatment; the "foul-mouthed child" is returned to those responsible for his behavior; the out-of-state tourist prowling an area close to his hotel but frequented by prostitutes is informed of his "oversight" and told in unmistakable terms to vacate the territory. It is important to note that police feel justified in using only enough force or coercive power to seal off the offender from public (and, by implication; their own) view. To use more force would be considered unreasonable.

It has been my purpose here to suggest that much of what the general public might see as capricous, random, or unnecessary behavior on the part of the police is, in fact, governed by certain rather pervasive interpretive rules which lie close enough to the surface such that they can be made visible. Certain police actions, following the model presented above, can be seen, then, to be at least logical if not legal. Furthermore, much of the power of these rules stems from their tacit or taken-for-granted basis. Indeed, were the rules to be questioned, the game could not continue. However, while these rules are applied in a like fashion by all police in a given interactional episode, the specific situated behavior of a citizen that is taken as a sign which leads to isolating, ignoring, teaching, or castigating a given individual is no doubt quite different across patrolmen. Here, the police game continues as it does because, in part, the asshole label swallows up and hides whatever individual differences exist across patrolmen. Thus, language neatly solves the problem of misunderstanding that would arise among the police were the rules to be articulated and standards sought as to how they should be applied.

IV. SOME CONCLUSIONS

It is possible, of course, to see the preceding ritualized sequence as an isolated and rarely indulged propensity of the police. However, in this section, I will argue that indeed such a sequence and the corresponding identification and treatment of the asshole is intimately related to the police production and represents an aspect of policing that is near the core of the patrolman's definition of his task. In essence, the existence of an asshole demonstrates and confirms the police view of the importance and worth of themselves both as individuals and as members of a necessary occupation. However, several other, somewhat more practical and everyday features of police work insure the ominous presence of the asshole in the police world.

First, the labeling of individuals as assholes can be seen as a technique (although invisible to most) useful to patrolmen in providing distance between themselves and their segmented audiences—to be liked by the people in the street is, in the defensive rhetoric of patrolmen, a sign of a bad cop. By profaning and degrading the actions of another, social distance can be established and maintained—a guarantee, so to speak, that the other will not come uncomfortably close. Thus, the asshole simplifies and orders the policeman's world and continually verifies his classification scheme regarding those who are "like him" and those who are "unlike him." Relatedly the labeling serves also as an immediate call to action, denoting a consensually approved, (by the police culture) means for remedying "out-of-kilter" situations.

Second, the label not only describes and prescribes but it also explains and makes meaningful the statements and actions of others. In fact, an entire set of action expectations (i.e., "they are out to make the police look bad") can be ascribed as motives to the asshole. In this sense, the police function in street interaction is not unlike that of a psychiatrist diagnosing a patient. Both explain perceived deviancy in terms of a characterological genesis. Hence, the label implies that a different, inappropriate, and strange motivational scheme is used by the "type of person" known as an asshole. In this manner, an act is made understandable by stripping away whatever meaning might be attributed to it by the actor. Thus, to make sense of the act is to assume that it does not make sense—that it is stupid, irrational, wrong, deranged, or dangerous. Any other assumption would be too threatening.

Third, the labeling process must be viewed as serving an occupational purpose. I suggested previously that the urban policeman is primarily a keeper of the peace yet he defines his job in terms of law enforcement. Furthermore, as others have noted, many patrolmen try to convert peacekeeping situations to those of law enforcement (e.g., Bittner, 1967, 1970; Wilson, 1969; Piliavin and Briar, 1964). Since real police work is seldom available, marginally legitimate arrests of assholes provide a patrolman excitement and the opportunity to engage one's valued skills. Perhaps the police cliché, "a good beat is full of deadbeats," reflects structural support for the asshole-labeling phenomena.

Fourth, the discovery and subsequent action taken when the police encounter the asshole provides an expressive outlet—almost ceremonial in its predictability—for much of the frustration policing engenders. To the patrolman, one particular asshole symbolizes all those that remain "out there" untouched, untaught, and unpunished. Such emotional outbursts provide, therefore, a reaffirmation of the moral repugnance of the asshole. Whether the officer responds by placing the handcuffs on the person's wrists such that they cut off circulation (and not incidentally cause intense, almost excruciating pain) or pushes a destitute soul through a shop window, these actions release some of the pent-up energies stored up over a period in which small but cumulative indignities are suffered by the police at the hands of the community elites, the courts, the politicians, the uncaught crooks, the press, and numerous others. The asshole stands, then, as a ready ersatz for those whom the police will never—short of a miracle—be in a position to directly encounter and confront.

Finally, the asshole can be seen as a sort of reified other, representing all those persons who would question, limit, or otherwise attempt to control the police. From this standpoint, knowing that there are assholes at large serves perhaps to rally and solidify police organizations around at least one common function. Thus, the police are, to a limited degree, unified by their disdain of those who would question their activities. Perhaps one could say that the police represent what Simmel (1950) referred to as an "invisible church" in which the faithful are fused together through their common relation to an outside phenomenon.

Consequently, assholes are not simply obscure and fanciful figments of the bedeviled imagination of the police. On the contrary, they define to a surprising degree what the police are about. And while the internal satisfactions and rewards involved in "slamming around" an asshole may seem esoteric if not loathsome to the outsider, to the patrolman who makes his living on the city streets it is not.

V. POSTSCRIPT

The foregoing description and explanation of an overlooked aspect of urban policing highlights the fact that the police officer is anything but a Weberian bureaucrat whose discretion and authority are checked rigidly. The collective myth surrounding the rulebound "policeman-as-public-servant" has no doubt never been very accurate. By virtue of their independence from superiors, their carefully guarded autonomy in the field, their deeply felt notions about real police work and those who would interfere with it, and their increasing isolation from the public they serve (as a result of mobile patrol, rotating shifts, greater specialization of the police, and the growing segmentation of the society at large with its own specialized and emerging subcultures), police-community "problems" will not disappear. And, since the police view their critics as threatening and as persons who generally should be taught or castigated, one could argue that the explosive potential of citizen-police encounters will grow.

Additionally, if the police become more sensitive to public chastisement, it could be expected that something of a self-fulfilling prophecy may well become a more important factor in the street than it is presently. That is to say, if the police increasingly view their public audience as foes—whose views are incomprehensible if not degenerate or subversive—it is likely that they will also magnify clues which will sustain the stereotype of citizen-as-enemy escalating therefore the percentage of street interactions which result in improper arrest and verbal or physical attack. Thus, the fantasy may well become the reality as stereotypes are transformed into actualities. In fact, the future may make prophetic Brendan Behan's half-jesting remark that he had never seen a situation so bad that a policeman couldn't make it worse.

To conclude, this essay has implied that there is a virtual—if unintended—license in this society granted to police. In particular, when it comes to the asshole, police actions are not governed at all, given the present policies of allowing the watchers to watch themselves. It would seem that something is amiss, and, if the practical morality in urban areas is not exactly inverted, it is at least tilted. If the asshole is indeed a critical aspect of policing, then there is serious risk involved in the movement to "professionalize" the police. As other observers have remarked, successful occupational professionalization inevitably leads to increased autonomy and ultimately increased power for members of the occupation (Becker, 1962; Hughes, 1965). Professionalism may well widen the police mandate in society and therefore amplify the potential of the police to act as moral entrepreneurs. From this perspective, what is required at present is not professional police but accountable police.

REFERENCES

Banton, Michael, (1964) *The Policeman in the Community*. New York: Basic Books.

Bayley, P. H. and H. Mendelsohn, (1969) *Minorities and the Police: Confrontation in America*. New York: Free Press.

Becker, Howard S., (1962) "The Nature of a Profession," in *Education for the Professions*, 61st Yearbook of the Society for the Study of Education, Part 2. Chicago: University of Chicago Press. (1963) *Outsiders*. New York: Free Press.

Berkeley, George E., (1969) *The Democratic Policeman*, Boston: Beacon Press.

Bittner, Egon, (1970) *The Functions of the Police in Modern Society*. Washington, D.C.: United States Government Printing Office. (1967) "The Police on Skid Row," 32, *American Sociological Review*, 699–715.

Black, Donald, (1968) "Police Encounters and Social Organization: An Observational Study." Unpublished Ph.D. Dissertation, University of Michigan.

Cain, Maureen, (1973) *Society and the Policeman's Role*. London: Kegan Paul. (1971) "On the Beat: Interactions and Relations in Rural and Urban Police Forces," in S. Cohen (ed.) *Images of Deviance*. Middlesex, England: Penguin Books.

Chevigny, Paul, (1968) *Police Power: Police Abuses in New York*. New York: Pantheon.

Cohen, Albert K., (1965) "The Sociology of the Deviant Act," 30, *American Sociological Review*, 5–14.

Cumming, E., I. Cumming and L. Edell, (1965) "The Policeman as Philosopher, Guide and Friend," 12, *Social Problems*, 276–286.

Drodge, Edward F., (1973) *The Patrolman: A Cop's Story*. New York: New American Library.

Harris, Richard N., (1973) *The Police Academy: An Inside View*. New York: John Wiley and Sons.

Hughes, Everett C., (1965) "Professions," in K. S. Lynn (ed.) *Professions in America*. Boston: Beacon Press.(1958) *Men and Their Work*. Glencoe, Ill. Free Press.

LaFave, W. R., (1965) *Arrest: The Decision to Take a Suspect into Custody*. Boston: Little, Brown and Company.

Manning, Peter K., (1971) "The Police: Mandate, Strategies and Appearances," in J. Douglas (ed.) *Crime and Justice in America*. Indianapolis: Bobbs-Merrill. (1974a) "Dramatic Aspects of Policing: Selected Propositions." *Sociology and Social Research*. 59 (October). (1974b) "Police Lying." *Urban Life* 3 (October).

Maas, Peter, (1973) *Serpico*. New York: The Viking Press.

Matza, David, (1969) *Becoming Deviant*. Englewood Cliffs, N.J.: Prentice-Hall.

McHugh, Peter, (1969) "A Common-Sense Preception of Deviancy," in J. Douglas (ed.) *Deviance and Respectability*. New York: Basic Books.

Neiderhoffer, Arthur, (1969) *Behind the Shield*. Garden City, N.Y.: Doubleday, 1967.

Olsen, Jack, (1974) *Sweet Street*. New York: Simon and Schuster.

Piliavin, I. and S. Briar, (1964) "Police Encounters with Juveniles." 70, *American Journal of Sociology*, 206–214.

Reiss, Albert J., (1971) *The Police and the Public*. New Haven, Conn.: Yale University Press.

Rubenstein, Jonathan, (1973) *City Police*. New York: Farrar, Straus and Giroux.

Sacks, Harvey, (1972) "Notes on Police Assessment of Moral Character," in D. Sudnow (ed.) *Studies in Social Interaction*. New York: The Free Press.

Silver, Allen, (1967) "The Demand for Order in Civil Society," in D. Bordua (ed.) *The Police: Six Sociological Essays*. New York: John Wiley and Sons.

Simmel, Georg, (1950) *The Sociology of Georg Simmel*. Translated, edited, and with an introduction by Kurt H. Wolff. New York: The Free Press.

Skolnick, Jerome, (1966) *Justice Without Trial*. New York: John Wiley and Sons.

Skolnick, Jerome and J. R. Woodworth, (1967) "Bureaucracy, Information and Social Control," in D. Bordua (ed.) *The Police: Six Sociological Essays*. New York: John Wiley and Sons.

Terkel, Studs, (1968) *Division Street: America*. New York: Random House. (1974) *Working*. New York: Pantheon.

Van Maanen, John, (1972) "Pledging the Police: A Study of Selected Aspects of Recruit Socialization in a Large Police Department." Unpublished Ph.D. Dissertation, University of California, Irvine.(1973) "Observations on the Making of Policemen," 32, *Human Organizations*, 407–418. (1974) "Working the Streets: A Developmental View of Police Behavior," in H. Jacobs (ed.) *Reality and Reform: The Criminal Justice System*, Beverly Hills, California: Sage Publications.(1975) Police Socialization. *Administrative Science Quarterly*, 20, 207–228.

Walker, T. Mike, (1969) *Voices from the Bottom of the World: A Policeman's Journal.* New York: Grove Press.

Webster, J. A., (1970) "Police Task and Time Study," 61 *Journal of Criminal Law, Criminology and Police Science*, 94–100.

Westley, William, (1970) *Violence and the Police.* Cambridge, Mass.: MIT Press (originally a Ph.D. Dissertation, University of Chicago, 1951).

Whittemore, L. H., (1973) *The Super Cops.* New York: Stein and Day.

Wilson, James, Q., (1967) "Police Morale, Reform and Citizen Respect: The Chicago Case," in D. Bordua (ed.) *The Police: Six Sociological Essays.* New York: John Wiley and Sons. (1968) *Varieties of Police Behavior.* Cambridge, Mass.: Harvard University Press.

Lying, Secrecy and Social Control

Peter K. Manning*

Communication is possible because the symbol (the thing by which a message is conveyed) is not intrinsic to its referent (that which the message describes). As Rappaport writes, "Lies are the natural offspring of symbols. They are transmitted by symbolic communication and symbolic communication only . . ." (1971:67–68). If one cannot assemble complete information on the source of a communication, or on the message itself, or the thing which the message describes, then one must, to some degree, rely on trust. The sort of trust involved, of course, is not unitary, for although "Modern life is based to a larger extent than is usually realized upon the faith in honesty of the other (Simmel,

*Author's Note: This paper is based in part on my research on the London Metropolitan Police during my tenure as Visiting Research Scholar at University of London, Goldsmiths' College, London, 1972–1973. I gratefully acknowledge the assistance provided by Chief Superintendent Stephen O'Brien, Chief Superintendent Benjamin Plunkett, Superintendent Angus Pattison, and the many men who so willingly gave of their time and energy to facilitate my inquiries. Mike Chatterton and Maureen Cain were very helpful in the early stages of my investigation. I am grateful to John Van Maanen for his critical readings of earlier drafts. I appreciate the opportunity to utilize observations made by Van Maanen and William Sanders. This research was supported in part by an All-University Research Grant from Michigan State University and a grant from the General Research Fund of the College of Human Medicine, Michigan State University.

Revised from Peter K. Manning, Police Lying. *Urban Life.* 3, *1974* (283–306).

1964:313)," the sort of "faith" required is itself highly *situational*. The standards which persons apply to communication vary; their tolerance for ambiguity is wide; the degree of intimacy is quite variable and changing; and the risk involved in the outcomes is certainly not unchanging across situations. The amount of knowledge itself is quite different for individuals in different situations (compare the amount of information you have about the operation of a bicycle with that of a nuclear reactor or even a large automobile engine). Where one has little information, where the situation contains little risk, and where there is little trust involved in the relationship, then lying either will be irrelevant to the outcome or will be little penalized even if it is revealed. Think, for example, of the difference between being told a lie by a cab driver when you are casually seeking a ride and being told a lie about the whereabouts of a lover who does not spend the night at "home." Although on a general level of cross-cultural comparisons, complex industrialized societies are based on, or require a higher degree of, trust than those which are based on face-to-face relations and frequent intimate communication, the degree of trust varies from situation to situation. Lying is both more destructive in intimate relations and more common there precisely because such verbal misrepresentation of facts is necessary to retain control, to retain trust, to manipulate others to fulfill one's desires, and so forth. Global trust is not at all necessary in a highly segmented, specialized world of work.[1] Let us look at some of the general features of lying before examining police lying.

That false information is often transmitted, intentionally or unintentionally, and that it is perceived by others as false is incontrovertible. Moreover, it is clear that lying is a feature of modern life as common as, or more common than, honesty and authenticity.[2] The labels "lie" and "lying" are socially derived, socially utilized and constructed, and are thus always tied to some delineated relationship between an audience and a speaker. A lie can be labeled

---

[1]". . . The importance of trust greatly raises the risk of lying—he who is caught is really screwed. If that argument is true. But I don't think it is. I think trust is vastly more important in close, intimate relations. Trust is important in itself in intimate relations—it is a vital part of intimacy and a condition of it. For example, I know from experience that I cannot trust some of my closest colleagues concerning political matters (in the case of X), sexual matters (in the case of Y and Z), and other matters. Academics don't lie about money very often. They lie about politics and sex—the really important things to them. And political power is the most important. But this does not mean that I cannot work with and like X, Y, and Z. I do. The point is that as a practical actor in a conflictful world I have complex understandings (grasps, because they are largely presymbolic) of what leads people to lie—the situations in which they lie. I try to make sure I do not take their word about such matters—I watch them, silently categorize their comments as "shit," avoid discussing the matters so they won't have to lie, etc. A vital part of the whole thing is avoiding situations where they will have to lie, for that is disruptive of relations, especially because they will suspect I know they are lying, because they know I know too much about them to take these lies at face value. They would probably even suspect I was trying precisely to pin a lie on them . . ." (personal communication, anonymous academic).

[2]The most systematic discussion of lying in contemporary social life, the conditions under which it occurs, and the implications of lies for social research is found in Jack D. Douglas's *Investigative Social Research* (1976) 67–73.

as such either by a hearer or by the speaker, each independent of the other's knowledge or awareness. A lie clearly can refer to such independent judgments (which might, for example, be independently solicited by a third party). However, sociologically, one must investigate the knowledge each actor possesses (or infer it from actions or deeds) and seek comprehensive knowledge of the relationship in which what can be considered a lie emerges or has consequence.[3] Any communication can be considered to be a lie if an observer is able to ascertain intention and attribution. These tentative analytic distinctions permit us to distinguish at least two types of lies: the *recognition case* where an observer who makes an assessment of intention and attribution and decides that a lie has been perpetrated, and the hearer recognizes that such is the case,[4] and the *nonrecognition* case where the observer makes the same decisions concerning intention and attribution but where the hearer does not recognize the communication as a lie or potentially a lie.

Lies are thus features of situations to be analyzed. The implicit premise of this paper is that if subsequent behavior or talk is available, the observer can infer that the relationship between speaker and audience is modified by non-recognized lies. This article, based on field work in London,[5] considers cases of intentional lying unrecognized at the time of their utterance by the audience(s) to which they were directed by officers. Since the audience to which the lie is directed plays an important role in determining the type of consequentiality associated with the act, I distinguish between *internal lies* (told to fellow officers in the department) and *external lies* (told to the public).[6]

---

[3]One of the most difficult decisions to make in discussing cases of lying is to separate lying (conscious deception) from such things as self-deception (where a person conceals to himself what he feels or thinks, although other behavior reveals that he recognizes his own distortions); ignorance (where one simply does not know that the facts told another are in whole or part incorrect); and evasions (half-truths, avoiding situations where lies might have to be told, partial answers which are partial truths); etc. That these often occur together is clear to anyone who has observed any complex interactional sequence, and it is only by radical simplification (such as is done here) that lying can be discussed in "clear cases." Douglas's *Investigative Social Research* (1976) brilliantly explicates the nuances and interconnected nature of evasions, lies, and self-deceptions in chapts. 4 and 5.

[4]The recognition case requires a dynamic analysis of the consequences of the recognition of one actor that another has lied to him. Such an analysis, beyond the scope of this paper, would require a rather elaborate framework, perhaps as suggested in Goffman's *Strategic Interaction* (1970).

[5]Observational and focused interview techniques were employed. I took field notes while walking home beats, riding in police cars, sitting in the reserve room (the main information room of the station) or canteen or in the office of the chief superintendent. I also gathered statistics and assisted officers by collating phone and teleprinter messages received at the station. Eighty-four hours were spent in observation (additional details are found in Manning, 1977).

[6]My focus is uniformed patrolmen and sergeants, not detectives (CID in England). Lying in detective work is more subtle and difficult to establish. William Sanders, who has done an extensive study of detective work on the West Coast of the United States, comments on lying (personal communication, Feb. 14, 1974): "Lying was not characteristic of the detectives in our study. Events formulated as 'bullshitting,' 'conning,' and 'twisting' took place in the context of interrogations, but they lacked the texture of lying."

POLICE LYING

The police-public relationship is not characterized by intimacy but by public trust derived from the centrality of the police as representatives of the moral and political order (Buckner, 1967:413; Manning, 1977a: Chapter 9). It often contains risks for participants and cannot be easily avoided as can collegial contacts; it is consequential for participants in the sense that police-citizen encounters are suffused with obligations of citizenship and of authority (cf. Sykes and Clark, 1974; see Goffman (1961), on the consequentiality of encounters). Three principal conditions of policing as an occupation in large, urban areas can be seen to underly and to be conducive to police lying. These are endemic features of policing; they lead to conflict over or ambiguity about the locus of judgment for the criteria establishing truth or falsehood. The police can be seen as performing two types of functions at least: *order-maintaining* functions (enforcing order in disturbances, domestic squabbles, traffic, and in morals offenses), and *law enforcement* functions (using the criminal or civil law to coerce compliance with their directives; see Banton, 1964; Wilson, 1968). The place of lying is quite different in the two situations, not the least of which is that law enforcement situations hold potential perjury charges should the lie be revealed in court.

In the maintenance of public order, the police confront many conditions which do not involve lawbreaking. The law in these situations is a weak resource (Bittner, 1967). The law does not always provide a means for controlling "irritating" behavior—for example, a car being routinely parked next to one's driveway so that it is difficult to manipulate one's own car safely and easily from the garage into the street. Yet this is often the type of situation where, having received the complaint, the police feel constrained to act. (They may not take action to alleviate the phenomenon but to mitigate the pressure on themselves.) The police often rely on nonlegal and sometimes illegal means of controlling the public, including lying, duplicity, and secrecy.

When dealing with situations covered by the criminal law (as the patrolman perceives and understands it—one should appreciate that his working knowledge of the law is in fact limited to those laws he routinely enforces [cf. Buckner, 1967; Rubenstein, 1973; Harris, 1973], the police believe that because of their unique experiences in dealing with criminals and the public they "know" the guilt or innocence of the parties they arrest. (They are legally required to possess this certainty as a precondition to making an arrest.) However, the "final" decision on guilt or innocence is a complex matter negotiated by defense and prosecuting lawyers, judges, juries, and the persons charged (Blumberg, 1967; Newman, 1956). The police provide evidence, and are required, usually with the assistance of legal advice, to construct the strongest case for conviction. Often conflict results between the police, legal advisors, and court representatives. Once their discretionary tasks are performed in founding a crime, investigating an allegation, and arresting and charging a person, the police cannot control final outcomes (Reiss, 1971:125–134; 1974; Skolnick, 1966). It would appear that this tentative ascription of guilt combined with the fact that the courts possess final control leads the police to utilize a contrived and legalistic language in describing their activities to "outsiders" (sociological investigators, journalists, lawyers, and the courts). Although they may see the construction of a legal case as a bit of a sham (a partial or "legally admissible" presentation of the facts they actually possess), they describe their own activities in a quasi-legal rhetoric. As one consequence of their "dependent" position in the legal system they use such tentative and legalistic phrases as "proceeded on information received" (for example, when making an investigation to search for and confiscate drugs in a private setting based upon an informer's word that drugs are present) and fill their reports with terms indicating uncertainty—"alleged," "the suspect," or "it can be assumed that . . ." Because there is a constant awareness of the tentativeness of their facts, given the court's capacity to exclude evidence, to redefine the facts of the case, and the prosector's discretion in the use of materials, the police withdraw commitment to "paper reality." They tend to see what happens "on the ground" in face-to-face encounters as "real police work";—that which they can control; and to see paperwork and legal decisions as both beyond their control and subject to redefinition of relevance. Hence, the risk of perjury often hangs in a courtroom when police testify, especially in vice cases where the case often devolves to a matter of the credibility of two versions of an incident, the police version and the alleged offender's version.

Second, one consistent theme is the centrality of *controlling and concealing* information which police possess on the activities of criminals (e.g., their movements, addresses, past criminal records, associates, present occupations, automobiles driven/owned), and the activities of other categories of people who might cause police trouble (e.g., political activists, families frequently involved in marital/family disputes, "dishonest" businessmen, potential or actual drug users, youthful "troublemakers"). It is assumed that if criminals in particular (although the general public is also to be suspect to some degree) are aware of police priorities (policy emphases, patrol patterns, allocation of resources, personnel concentration on particular types of activities), they might modify their behavior to avoid or minimize surveillance and/or arrest. Enforcing the law requires preserving a degree of ignorance on the part of the public (and especially what is seen as the criminal element in society). Posing as a prostitute, a "john," or an eager buyer of narcotics is feasible only where appearances are taken to be just that. Further, the protection of informants, so critical in vice work, often conflicts with variable public expectations regarding arrest and conviction of known offenders. It is assumed that if the "respectable" public were aware of, for example, the monetary rewards or drugs paid to informants (Knapp Report, 1972: Chapter 5; Whittemore, 1973:323; Manning and Redlinger, 1977), police protection of their informants from prosecution or the highly variable and sometimes personalistic interpretations of the law or departmental policy which occur in all departments, the public might hamper police work and thus "inadvertently" endanger their own safety. The alternative theme, present in traffic enforcement and to some degree in drug enforcement, is the *deterrent* strategy. In this case, it is assumed that information communicated to the relevant target populations concerning the risk inherent in criminal acts will deter. Social groups made aware of such *required* and intrinsic matters of police operations as discretion, differential attention to certain activities, and variable administrative policy directed to given problems in a community, might conceivably, in police eyes, withdraw support from the department. Legalist theorists (Davis, 1969, 1975) have argued that these pressures are the root source of the "full enforcement doctrine" which police employ. These observers have pointed out that the police claim when it is to their advantage that they possess no discretion in enforcement—that the legislature, the law, and the courts do not provide for active discretion—while privately simultaneously exercising wide choice in the enforcement of nearly all laws. It is quite clear that the desire to conceal information and to protect their own interests in controlling the public, and not the law, is the basis for the facade of full enforcement and associated public lies.

Third, the police in a large urban setting are in adversary relationships with large segments of the community. Their services are often unwanted and, from their point of view, seldom properly appreciated.

The social psychology or *sentiments* of the policeman reflect these structural conditions. The police view many of their "clients" as ingrates, and in the context of a semisecret society this is conducive to police cynicism (Wilson, 1968; Skolnick, 1966; Westly, 1970; Cain, 1973). The role institutionalizes and rewards a degree of systematic *suspiciousness* and *distrust* (Banton, 1964). A police officer learns to be suspicious of appearances and of what people say. He often perceives risk to himself or others as implicit in police-citizen encounters. He identifies with the legal and moral order. Rule violations and challenges to authority are seen as violations of self-esteem (see Manning [1977a: Chapter 8] for a summary of studies of this process). Because he looks for evidence of criminality in everyday situations; doubts appearances and verbal statements; views people cynically; uses incongruity (e.g., of facts, of persons/settings, of "normal" versus "odd" behavior) in a sharpened way; employs his senses in a strategic and explicitly self-aware fashion; and organizes and maintains these facts, feelings, and perceptions in a notebook, the police officer quite consciously suspends at least one principal feature of everyday life—the principle of trust (Buckner, 1967; Sacks, 1972). Once others are seen as untrustworthy and different (since they do not share the secrets of the police world), they become, like all clients to some degree, objects to be controlled, manipulated, coerced, and perhaps lied to.

These external and social psychological conditions are intrinsic and inseparable aspects of police *internal* operations and of the pattern of police transactions, and are the principal conditions supportive and nurturant of police lying. The internal operations of police organizations, as Schutz noted, "[are] understandable only by those who have participated in the common past experiences in which it took rise in the tradition connecting them" (1944:505). The police conception of people in general as fallible and stupid, as translucent Machiavellis, is to an important degree also the policeman's view of his colleagues. As the senior sleuth in Colin MacInnes's brilliant story, *Mr. Love and Mr. Justice*, tells the young copper, Mr. Justice, in reply to the query whether he trusted his colleagues in the force: "Colleagues! I trust them for one thing, and one thing only. There are exceptions—but in a fight they're brave and they're reliable. Alone in a dark lane with a bunch of Teds, they won't stab you in the back—no, they'll help you come what may. But otherwise . . ." (1970:31). This perceived hostility, a part of the police relationship to the public, and to some degree each other, is manifested in their tendency to conceal information from the public and thereby to become a secret organization.

The secrecy often associated with lying (a secret being something about which nothing can be told to those outside the secret-sharing group) serves to pattern the structure and functioning of organizations.

> "As soon as a whole group uses secrecy as its form of existence, the significance becomes internal: the secret determines the reciprocal relations among those who share it in common . . . [therefore] the sociology of the secret society is confronted with the complicated problem of ascertaining how intra-group life is determined by the group's secretive behavior toward the outside." (Simmel, 1964:345)

The police as an organization do not possess a "common culture" when viewed from the *inside*. Instead, there is an elaborate hierarchical rank structure which replicates the social distribution of secret knowledge. Police organizations are segmented, specialized, and covert to a striking degree. Social relationships among policemen are based to an unknown extent upon *differential information* and ignorance, a structural fact that maintains organizational stratification (Moore and Tumin, 1949; Manning, 1977).

Police work is diverse and involves great discretion on the part of the patrol officer, a member of the least visible and least easily controlled segment of the organization (Wilson, 1968:8–9). Since 1829, when one of the first commissioners of police was an ex-military man, policing has been *publicly* represented as a paramilitary organization (Jacobs, 1969), characterized by very strict internal disciplinary codes, investigatory units (including trials and hearings), and high rates of punishment and disciplinary violations (Reiss, 1971:169 ff.). Nevertheless, the proliferation of rules and overt presentation of the organization as efficient and tightly controlled (Manning, 1971) does *not* eliminate and is perhaps conducive to internal lies.

Organizational rules, general orders, and public statements of policy are in fact constantly transformed in interaction into social and behavioral realities. What is claimed to be the case in the organizational plan, latest policy statement or supplement to the *General Orders,* is subject to *doubt.* The rules and records are viewed tactically and strategically, while idealized explanations are employed to cover pragmatic decisions. Police officers see rules as resources, and the actions of supervisors (sergeants and inspectors) as expedient means of protecting themselves against higher echelons—superintendents and above. There are a great many internal rules; it is probably impossible to pass a day on the job without violating one or more of them. Rule enforcement by supervisors seems to resemble a mock bureaucracy where ritualistic and punitive enforcement is applied after the fact. Since rules are surrounded with uncertainty, when disciplinary action is taken it tends to be viewed as arbitrary and the supervisors as self-serving (McNamara, 1967; Manning, 1977a: Chapter 6). "Supervisors do not enforce what they want to enforce, but what they are told to enforce." This view of senior officers makes communication upward problematic and fraught with lies, duplicity and avoidance of situations."[7]

Given this mode of harsh discipline, arbitrary enforcement practices, and the high discretion and invisibility of the patrolman, it is not surprising that the patrolman, in particular, is inclined to be secretive and to protect himself variously from internal surveillance and from public control. The police possess enormous amounts of recorded detailed information, but it is seldom shared or made public. "Police departments accommodate a colossally complicated network of secret sharing, combined with systematic information denial," (Bittner, 1970:64). The police rarely share unrecorded information, partly because they trust neither each other nor the public. Virtually all policemen know occupationally relevant facts unknown to other policemen; this information is useful in maintaining informants, in keeping public order, and in maximizing effectiveness in increasing arrests. They do not share knowledge, since others might use it to their own advantage. Bittner observed that the overriding rule within departments is: "no one ever tells anybody else more than he absolutely has to" (Bittner, 1970:64).

Let us now turn to external lies and internal lies, the two patterns of lying identified above.

EXTERNAL LIES

Our intent here is to illustrate the variety of situations—some involving possible criminal charges, others dealing with public order maintenance—which virtually require policemen to lie.[8] Skolnick (1966:79) notes that police officers may use deceit to uncover information about a person wanted for a traffic warrant:

> If the warrant is for John Smith, the policeman might ring the bell of the residence listed in the warrant and ask for Richard Roe.
>
> 'Richard Roe doesn't live here,' will be the reply.
>
> 'Well, who does?' asks the policeman.
>
> 'I do,' says the resident.
>
> 'Who are you?' asks the policeman.

---

[7]The star sleuth tells Mr. Justice, the fledgling copper, "We have also, of course, certain rules and regulations . . . I don't know by whom and don't much care because there they are, they exist, and they've got to be observed . . . *Observed*, I said, mark you. But not necessarily, in every case to be *obeyed*. (MacInnes, 1970:109). "Observing" means for the most part honoring the breach, or when one is discovered or cannot avoid disclosure.

[8]Some of the examples below are adopted from Buckner (1967).

'John Smith.'

'Well, I happen to have a warrant for your arrest.'

Initial misrepresentation of a situation may occur in order to justify a field interrogation where an official stop is not used. Innocuous conversation is used to draw information from the person stopped. Lies may be utilized to detain a suspect without making him aware that he is under surveillance; for example, asking someone to describe tenants in a building under the guise of seeking a fictitious party and thus obtaining the sought person's description. Duplicity may be used to control such distressing but legal behavior as "loud parties" by suggesting that the host can and will be arrested (possible, but extremely unlikely) if officers return to the scene. Officers may gain entrance to an apartment, house, or car by asking permission to enter and then engaging in a search. An individual can be deceived into accepting an arrest when officers actually have no definite charges in mind or when the suspect might flee if he were aware of a threat to himself. Usually, this is accomplished by implying to the person that the officer's intent is innocent. A person may be asked to "chat" while sitting in the back of a police car and subsequently be taken in and charged. Further, once in custody, persons may be subject to interrogation, which involves their being manipulated in order to gain a confession or admission of guilt (Cummins, 1967). Misleading information or suggestions are used to obtain signatures on confessions and to convince persons to plead guilty.

Undercover police work and vice work, whether it involves vice or patrol officers, hinges upon and requires deception. For example, vice officers will dress as patrol officers in order to observe drug dealing (drug dealers assume that patrol officers are ignorant and harmless and will leave most drug offenses, unless they are insults or flagrant, to vice officers); patrol officers will "pose" as police officers investigating a phony traffic offense at a house and invite the owner out so that narcs can hit the open door and rush inside before the occupant understands what is happening. Sometimes a lie is executed by patrol division at the behest of another police unit: they will stop drug users or dealers repeatedly to "hassle them," to keep them under surveillance, to search their cars, or to run computer checks on outstanding warrants for traffic or other offenses. The beauty of such a strategy of deception is that by having the patrol officer lie by saying it is a "routine check" the drug dealers do not perceive that it is actually the narcotics officers who have them under suspicion! In addition, this action may be based on an internal lie, since narcotics officers may tell patrol officers a misleading story (that they just want to see if the person has a driver's license) or lie in order not to have uniform officers inadvertently reveal their interest to the suspect. Of course, these more circuitous lies are complemented by the more straightforward lies told by officers in order to search a house without a search warrant (a raid in which I participated fully ignorant of the necessity of having a warrant for a search).

> One night, we (a sergeant, a PC, a temporary detective constable and myself) were in a plainclothes car. We planned to search a flat occupied by a suspected (convicted) drug dealer. We did not have a search warrant. We "talked our way in" by asking if we could come in and simultaneously

showing badges (I was told to flash anything that "looked official" and I used my American Express Card). The woman who rented the flat and answered the door had been in bed with another woman. A young man was watching t.v. in the living room. The flat-renter asked presently to see our search warrant. The sergeant said, "Under paragraph 721 of the Police General Orders-Criminal Code, officers are not required to show a warrant during a preliminary investigation." He told me later that "People never listen to you, and believe what a copper says about the law.' He explained that he always refers to some fictitious passage in the code and quotes it if asked.

Other types of lies are not as easily analyzed and result from *pressures* which the police perceive from the public, or from their fears that a complaint or investigation may result if they do not convince the public that some action, however ineffectual, is being taken. They are not criminal matters and require interpersonal skill without the "back-up" force of the law. Van Maanen (personal communication) lists several cases in point:

> The stolen vehicle victim who is told that the department will "get right on it"; the missing person report taken solely as a public relations gesture to give a distraught parent something to do—or a feeling of doing; cooling out an angry spouse whose husband has been arrested with the statement, "don't worry lady, he'll be home for dinner."

These might be considered "white lies" in the sense that they are perceived by the police as doing little harm and representing "what the public really wants" from the police. Many responses to "cranks" who regularly call the station are handled in this way, both to reassure the caller and to avoid a nuisance. I observed inspectors (the ranking officer in the station at the time) on several occasions talking from ten to fifteen minutes with callers complaining about legally but inconveniently parked cars, about backyard trash which was annoying the rear neighbors, and about "suspicious characters." Callers were told that the matter would be "checked out," but in none of these cases, to my knowledge, was anything further done.

Lying serves to relieve situations not easily solved by recourse to the law or where following stipulated procedures ("policing by the book") might make organizational action impossible. Three examples may serve to illustrate this point:

> 1. We were on patrol in the wireless car, parked in the downtown area to watch the girls on a Saturday afternoon. A citizen approached the car and told the officers that he had purchased a ticket for the city lot (adjacent to the ferry), had forgotten to stick it on the car, and had been given a parking ticket. (London policemen do not handle routine ticketing; it is done by specialized Traffic Wardens.) The citizen was very worried and kept repeating his story, emphasizing his innocence, and asking advice. The driver asked him when he had purchased the ticket, when he had returned, and established that the story was reasonably accurate. He then advised the man to tell the desk officer at the station that he had placed the ticket on his window as per instructions, and that when he returned he found that the wind had blown off the parking voucher, and

that he had a ticket. The citizen said, "thanks, . . . I just forgot, and don't think I should have a ticket." The officer called him back as he started, in relief, to walk away, "Don't tell them you forgot, be certain to say you placed it on the windscreen and that the wind blew it off."

2. I interviewed a PC who emphasized the centrality of truth and honesty in police work: "To be a good policeman, you must have honesty with yourself and with others; you must, basically, create the respect necessary to carry out your duties." Subsequently, we talked with a tailor in his shop on the beat. The tailor was telling how a known juvenile offender had been employed in his shop for a short time, but then did not show up after a very few days. It was concluded by the PC and the tailor that "you can't trust the young much anymore"; that they are untrustworthy and don't really want to work. We left the shop and strolled ("proceeded") past what the PC called the "poor man's bank"—the social security office. He recalled that he knew the man working at the tailor's was on social security and had called them to inform on the man. He had been forced to quit the work at the tailor's or lose his social security payments. The PC recalled, "I didn't tell the tailor. I couldn't. That's one of the things that bothers you in this job, you have to be sort of two-faced. You have to tell people a few lies, to use them. You can't tell them you're doing it, because you have to keep up contacts so you can do the job. . . ."

3. A citizen came into the station who was a known "nutter" (mental case). He had been complaining for months that a neighbor had been transmitting television pictures into his head. He wanted the police to arrest his neighbor. The police had previously refused, but the citizen kept returning. The Sergeant on the desk was talking with him and listening again to the complaint and explaining that it was not a police problem. The citizen kept demanding police action. Finally in desperation the sergeant hit on an idea. "You say that your neighbor is transmitting television pictures into your head? Does he have a license to broadcast? That matter is covered by the GPO (the General Post Office and Communications Department). You had better take your complaint to the GPO." The man left, temporarily satisfied.

That lying serves a number of important functions, latent and manifest, should be apparent in these three cases. The first case illustrates the tentative legalistic frame of mind. The facts are not the issue. The task is that of creating a legalistic construction such that omission and inclusion of legally relevant facts result in the most expeditious solution. In the second case, the policeman is consciously aware that he must employ at least three different types of truth: one to "criminals, villains and slag"; one to "respectable citizens"; and another to the courts when he is required to testify in legal format and style. This experience of seeing simultaneous multiple truths loosens the tie between morality and the law and between duty to the citizenry and duty to oneself or other policemen. The third case is a rather innocent but frequently used ploy. A "white lie" or misleading advice is given to a person when the police cannot legally intervene but where they perceive that they must act in response to a matter brought to their attention. In sum, each case begins with a situation where legal constraints or public attitudes provide little freedom for proper action, where the police are required and internally rewarded for "successful intervention," or where patrolmen wish to avoid internal disciplinary action; and each is "solved" by manipulation of the public through lying.

INTERNAL LIES

The structure of police organizations is such that "mistakes" are viewed as intentional by senior officers, thus introducing a constant ambiguity in interorganizational relationships, especially between officers and their supervisors. Lower participants fear sanctioning, feel it is not predictable, difficult to defend against, ambiguous as to meaning and prospective significance for their reputations, and based on personal relationships rather than on the behavior labeled as rule-breaking (Manning, 1977). Thus, internal lies are frequent, as my field notes and the writings of others suggest (where other observers' examples are superior to my own, I have used them as illustrations). There are at least four types of internal lies. The first is the arrest-and-charge situation, where typically a sergeant and a patrol officer negotiate the charge that will be lodged against an arrested person.

They mutually decide what to conceal and what to reveal, and where the final details are to be written up in the charge book. Subsequently, the charge book will be examined and signed by the Chief Superintendent or Superintendent. Van Maanen, who observed an urban U.S. police department, provides a detailed example of this process of formulating a lie, and its corollary "covering your ass."

> The sergeant plays a critical role for he screens all reports written by his men. If an arrest report contains an ambiguous phrase which could possibly be interpreted negatively by the court or [if it] fails to mention a detail (factual or otherwise) which might keep an officer (and, by implication the squad and the sergeant) out of trouble, [or includes one which will get them in trouble—PKM], he will have the man rewrite the report until it is flawless in his eyes:

> When Blazier was placed under guard in the hospital (after a rather brutal encounter in which Blazier, a black homosexual, was severely beaten in the back of a patrol wagon), we returned to the precinct station to handle the paperwork. Officer Barns filled out the many reports involved in the incident and passed them to his sergeant for approval. The sergeant carefully read each report and then returned the "paper" to Barns saying that he better claim he was kicked in the face *before* he entered the patrol wagon or Barns would get a heavy brutality complaint for sure. He also told Barns to change the charge on Blazier to felonious assault from refusal-to-obey and add drunk-in-public to the disturbing-the-peace charge Barns had originally thought appropriate. According to the sergeant, the heavier charges were necessary to protect Barns from IID (Internal Investigation Division). Finally, after some discussion and two re-writes, Barns finished a report which the sergeant said "covered their asses."

This "cover your ass" perspective pervades all of patrol work. In a sense, it represents a sort of bureaucratic paranoia which is all but rampant in police circles (Van Maanen, 1974:110).

The second type of situation involves a "threat of discipline." Whittemore, in his monograph on two New York policemen, gives an example of lying and obfuscation used to *avoid* being put on report by a supervising Captain (A "Shoofly") for wearing a "summer hat" in winter.

"What'd you say?" Captain Weiner asked.

"Summer or winter," Bob said, "it's the thing about my grandmother, who's very, very sick at the moment, and of course the hat is used for my brother, whose hair is falling out, sir, and I know that this is my normal hat, some cop was wearing lipstick the other day and, uh, too much hair on his chest for that role, so we wear these hats now as before in the future—"

"*Wait a minute!* Captain Weiner was saying. "Wait, hold on! Tell me again, now. *Why* are you wearing a summer hat?"

"It's part of the uniform," Bob said. "I can't go into the street without a hat, Captain. You should know that."

"Look, *something's* happening now. But I just can't figure it. Once more—why a summer hat?"

Dave started to laugh.

"What's so funny?" Captain Weiner asked.

"Well," Dave said, "here you're the shoofly, and you're supposed to go around enforcing department regulations, and you don't even *know* the regulations."

"*What do you mean, I don't know the regulations?*"

"Well, the T.O.P. came down last week, saying that there's no longer any difference between summer and winter hats. Summer hats became optional all year long."

"What?"

"Yeah," Dave bluffed [lied-PKM] "And that's what I'm laughing about."

"Oh, yeah," Bob said. "That's right. I remember reading that. Captain, you should know about the new orders."

The discussion went on for another half an hour. Captain Weiner asked everybody in the precinct house if they had seen the new Temporary Operating Procedures. They all said no, but then few cops ever read them, anyway (Whittemore, 1973: 293–294).

A third type of situation is lying by silence in order to omit relevant information to supervising officers, for example, about a constable's location or present activities. To understand the relevance of such concealment, it is necessary to outline the ambiguity inherent in the pattern of controlling constables by two-radio communication systems. Cars are allocated to scenes by radio. Walking constables and drivers of the small neighborhood ("panda") cars are supplied with a personal radio (PR). The range of the PR is limited to about a mile radius of the station because of the weakness of the batteries and physical obstructions such as hills and buildings. All levels of the subdivision are aware of the difficulties experienced in communicating with officers by PR. Further, there are legitimate reasons for turning off the radio (interrogating a suspect, taking a statement, observation). PRs were often turned off in my presence without "legitimate" reason—what constables called "skivving." Skivving, or avoiding work, may be accomplished by turning the radio off while having a pint, a cup of tea, or running a personal errand. If the officer cannot be raised, it is normally assumed that either he has legitimately turned off the radio or he cannot be reached because of transmission difficulties. The "area" or "wireless" car is assigned to cover an entire subdivision, and is second in priority (or third if there are two cars operating, that is, when a "reserve" area car can be staffed) in accepting radio calls from the force radio. The force radio in the Metropolitan Police Headquarters receives citizen calls (999 in London) and relays them to the appropriate Divisional area cars. The "radio man," or a third man if riding in the car, carries a PR by which to receive messages transmitted from the subdivisional headquarters.

As a consequence of the fact that the PR is weak and fallible in its operation, and may legitimately be turned off, and that area car crew members often must leave the car for investigation, there is persistent ambiguity in the location of the cars and men on the subdivision.

> Two PCs were sitting in a private club having a few pints and filling out reports of earlier incidents they had handled. They left the area car parked outside, but were reached by PR concerning the disposition of a juvenile they had previously taken to a hospital for treatment. It was assumed when they reported that arrangements had been made for the boy's return to his foster home that they were in the car on patrol, not drinking in a club.

Silence conceals: "Among [the] noblest professions is the secure feeling of knowing where one must speak, and where one must be silent" (Simmel, 1964:349).

A fourth type of situation is that of lying to a fellow officer in order to protect an informant. Police work often requires, as was suggested above, the protection of informants (rather than the control or manipulation of the public). Van Maanen provides the following useful example (personal communication):

> A small time pimp who had been feeding narcotics information to patrolman II told an entirely different story to another patrolman about his whereabouts early in an evening than the story originally told patrolman II by patrolman I.

Again, the rules of keeping one's knowledge to one's self (patrolman II had told patrolman I that the informant was lying because he wanted to protect him from arrest by patrolman I), and of particularistic knowledge of crime as fundamental to policemen (as they see it), encourage deception of one's colleagues.

COMMENT

The examples of police lying presented here are significant if they are a feature of a large number of police organizations. Insofar as the structural and social psychological features of police organizations in Anglo-American society are generic, lying is also potentially very common. Since the police are representatives of the moral order in everyday life, their credibility reflects upon the legitimacy of the politico-moral order. If lying is endemic in police operations, it is not only a commentary on the moral status of police officers and police organizations; it is a commentary on the society in which the activity is rooted. There are three implications of the centrality of lying to the operation of social-control agencies. The first is that it is assumed by many in our society that one must lie at some times to protect oneself, some higher goal or purpose, or an agency. All of these motives are well illustrated in the scenario of Watergate. This accepted-as-normal misrepresentation can be seen in the ways in which police conceal their practices under the full-enforcement doctrine; prosecutors fail to publicly state and develop policies on what will be plea bargained; judges use complete discretion without control by any agency but superior court appeal and the CIA lies concerning their activities in Cuba, Chile, Iran, and Latin America. A semisecret organization depends on the fact that people believe two things at once: that it lies, and that the lies are "true" in the sense that one "should" believe them. This type of organization can work effectively only when it retains credibility.

The police, as many have noted (Cain, 1973; Manning, 1971; Wilson, 1968), are mobilizing to gain more and more control over law enforcement, and acceding less and less power to the unorganized citizenry. If the police continue their present policies, we are likely to gain further public evidence that the police, although posing as representatives of morality and truth, are "impostors":

> Paradoxically, the more closely the impostor's performance approximates the real thing, the more intensely we may be threatened, for a competent performance by someone who proves to be an impostor may weaken in our minds the moral connection between legitimate authority to play a part and the capacity to play it (Goffman, 1959:59).

Such a situation of doubt and distrust of public police performance will certainly be exacerbated by further decline in police credibility coming as a result of public investigation and knowledge of police scandal. If the police succeed in their present drives for professional autonomy, it is unlikely that the public will see any significant modification in the police practices outlined here. Continued professionalization of the police without internal changes (horizontal recruitment into administrative positions, decentralization, greater clarification of public policies, and additional formal legal advice) and external changes (citizen review of complaints against the police; legal changes, especially in the case of crimes without victims; and greater clarification of the lines of accountability of police to the political structure) will only perpetuate many of the present means (e.g. lying) employed by officers to deal with structurally induced conflicts.

A second implication of this analysis is that if lying is a pervasive matter resulting from the conflict between rules, meanings, and power groups, then other corollaries implied by Goffman to be essential to the maintenance of the self are also essential to agencies of control in this sort of mass society. I refer here to frontwork (the manipulation of appearances, especially by means of physical props); evasion and half-truths passing a public policy; leaving unsaid or implied unpleasant truths; or responding to only some aspects of questions, which we can see in policing: for example, the police use the frontwork of rapid arrival with flashing lights and sirens to crime scenes even though they know that rapid response time bears little relationship to the probability of an arrest being made (Beick, 1976); they claim to be enforcing all drug violations when in fact they plea bargain away many petty crimes in order to get informants, or overlook crimes committed by their informants; they argue for an association between crime and drug use, although this empirical link has never been proven (Manning and Redlinger, forthcoming). These are of course ways of inducing public favor, maintaining public ignorance of their "real" activities, and avoiding using the third basis for control (after manipulation and ignorance)—violence. Thus, dramaturgical activities appear when violence is low but is a feature of all social control (Manning, 1974, 1977a).

A third implication bears on the significance of this analysis for other analyses of deviance. Lying, misrepresentation, and entrapment, more than the violation itself, must be considered a fundamental cause of the rates reported by the police (see Marx 1974, 1976; DeFleur, 1975; Manning and Redlinger, 1975, 1977b). If this proposition is true, then the strategies which lie behind or produce different arrests must be considered; for example, the use of undercover as opposed to patrol enforcement of drug laws. Finally, all control agencies must involve agents in dissembling and lying at some point to handle problematic situations with clients and publics. How is this dissembling and lying learned and sanctioned? Perhaps the detailed ethnographies of Rubenstein (1973), and more specifically, the work of Van Maanen (1973, 1974, 1975) and Harris (1973) will produce leads to the understanding of organizational socialization (Manning, 1970; Blankenship, 1973). These implications should be understood as signposts to students of deviance and control, for much of what has been studied in this field has been based on official records, statements, and ideologies (Polsky, 1967); as a result, we have been producing an official criminology, and the results have been often intellectually impoverished.

REFERENCES

Banton, M. (1964) The Policeman in the Community. New York: Basic Books.
Beick, W. (1976) Police Response Time Study. Washington, D.C.: Police Foundation.
Bittner, E. (1970) The Functions of the Police in Modern Society. Washington, D.C.: Government Printing Office.

————(1967) "The police on skid row" Amer. Soc. Rev. (October):699–715.

Blankenship, R. (1973) "Organizational Careers," Sociological Quarterly 14 (Winter):88–98.

Blumberg, A. (1967) Criminal Justice. Chicago: Quadrangle.

Buckner, H. T. (1967) "The Police: the culture of a social control agency," Ph.D. dissertation. University of California, Berkeley.

Cain, M. (1973) Society and the Policeman's Role. London: Routledge & Kegan Paul.

Cummins, M. (1967) "The frame-up," Ph.D. dissertation. University of Colorado.

Davis, K. (1975) Police Discretion. St. Paul: West Publishing Co.

————(1969) Discretionary Justice. Urbana: University of Illinois Press.

DeFleur, L. (1975) "Biasing influences on drug arrest records: implications for deviance research," American Sociological Review 40 (February):88–103.

Douglas, J. D., Investigative Social Research. Santa Monica, Calif.: Sage, 1976.

Goffman, E. (1970) Strategic Interaction. Philadelphia: University of Pennsylvania Press.

————(1961) Encounters. Indianapolis: Bobbs-Merrill.

Harris, R. (1973) The Police Academy: An Inside View. New York: John Wiley.

Jacobs, J. (1969) "Symbolic bureaucracy: a case study of a social welfare agency," Social Forces 47 (June):413–422.

Knapp, W. (1972) The Knapp Report on Police Corruption [in New York City]. New York: George Braziller.

MacInnes, C. (1970) Mr. Love and Mr. Justice. New York: Ballantine.

Manning, P. (1977) "Rules, colleagues and situationally justified action," in R. Blankenship (ed.) Colleagues in Organizations: The Social Construction of Professional Work. New York: John Wiley and Sons.

————(1977a) Police Work. Cambridge, Mass.: MIT Press.

————(1974) "Dramatic aspects of policing," Sociology and Social Research. 59 (October):121–129.

————(1971) "The police: mandate, strategies and appearances," in J. D. Douglas (ed.) Crime and Justice in American Society. Pp. 149–193. Indianapolis: Bobbs-Merrill.

————(1970) "Talking and becoming," in J. D. Douglas (ed.) Understanding Everyday Life. Chicago: Aldine.

Manning, P. K. and L. J. Redlinger (1977) "Invitational edges of corruption: some consequences of narcotic law enforcement," in P. Rock (ed.) Drugs. Rutgers: Society Books.

————(1975) "The working bases of corruption: some consequences of narcotic law enforcement," presented to the American Society of Criminology, Toronto.

————(forthcoming) "Observations on the impact of police strategies upon the trade in opiates," IROS: The International Review of Opium Studies. Philadelphia: Institute for the Study of Human Issues.

Marx, G. (1976) "The new undercover police work," unpublished paper, MIT, Cambridge, Mass.

————(1974 "Thoughts on a neglected category of social movement participant: the agent provocateur and the informant," American Journal of Sociology 80 (September):402–442.

————(1973) "Alternative measures of police performance," American Psych. Association (unpublished).

McNamara, J. (1967) "Uncertainties in police work: the relevance of recruits' background and training," pp. 163–252 in D. J. Bordua (ed.) The Police. New York: John Wiley.

Moore, W. and M. Tumin (1949) "Some social functions of ignorance," American Sociological Review 14 (December):787–795.

Newman, D. (1956) "Pleading guilty for considerations: a study of bargain justice," Journal of Criminal Law, Criminology and Police Science 46 (March/April):780–790.

Polsky, N. (1967) Hustlers, Beats and Others. Chicago: Aldine Publishing Co.

Rappaport, R. (1971) "Ritual, sanctity and cybernetics," American Anthropologist 73 (February):59–76.

Reiss, A. J., Jr. (1974) "Discretionary justice," in D. Glaser (ed.) Handbook of Criminology. Chicago: Rand McNally:679–699.

———(1971) The Police and the Public. New Haven, Conn.: Yale University Press.

Rubenstein, J. (1973) City Police. N.Y.: Farrar, Straus and Giroux.

Sacks, H. (1972) "Notes on police assessment of moral character," from D. Sudnow (ed.) Studies in Social Interaction. New York: Free Press:280–293.

Schutz, A. (1944) "The stranger," American Journal of Sociology 49 (May):499–507.

Simmel, G. (1964) The Sociology of Georg Simmel. New York: Free Press.

Skolnick, J. (1966) Justice Without Trial. New York: John Wiley.

Sykes, R. and J. Clark (1974) "A theory of deference exchange in police-citizen encounters," ASA paper.

Van Maanen, J. (1975) "Police socialization: a longitudinal examination of job attitudes in an urban police department," Administrative Science Quarterly 20 (June):207–228.

———(1974) "Working the street . . . ," in H. Jacobs (ed.) The Potential for Reform of Criminal Justice. Beverly Hills, Calif.: Sage.

———(1973) "Observations on the making of policemen," Human Organization 32 (Winter):407–418.

Westley, W. (1970) Violence and the Police. Cambridge, Mass.: MIT Press. (Originally a Ph.D. Dissertation, University of Chicago, 1951.)

Whittemore, L. H. (1973) Super Cops. New York: Bantam.

Wilson, J. Q. (1968) Varieties of Police Behavior. Cambridge, Mass.: Harvard University Press.

Controlling People

Jonathan Rubenstein

A policeman's principal concern is to physically control the people he is policing. While he sometimes wants to hurt or humiliate them, that is not nearly so often his purpose as it is the consequence of his efforts to control them. When he intervenes in a person's life, his attitude is basically instrumental. He mainly wants to place himself as quickly as possible in a position that will allow him to control the person, if that is required, or hopefully to discourage any inclinations to resist him or his orders. That is why he ignores the risks he takes in driving and violates departmental regulations by refusing to use the safety belt provided for him. The idea of being confined and prevented from moving quickly out of his car terrifies him.

Policemen act as though all people are right-handed. If he has any choice in the matter, the patrolman tries to move in a leftward direction toward a person in order to control his fighting arm. This allows him to stand at the person's right, at a slight angle, when he is facing him, which keeps his gun away from the man he is seeking to dominate. He consistently violates the normal distances which people seek to maintain when they are engaged in friendly conversation, often causing discomfort and nervousness when he does not mean to. He is not formally trained to do this, nor does he do it consciously, but an understanding of his actions would not deter him, since his objective is the

---

REPRINTED FROM: Jonathan Rubenstein, *City Police*. New York: Farrar, Straus and Giroux, *1972* (302–317).

maintenance of his personal security and not the discomfort of others. By constantly crowding people, he reduces their opportunities for kicking and punching him effectively. When he can, the patrolman stands slightly at an angle to the person he is confronting to avoid a crippling blow to the groin. Naturally he can be grabbed and wrestled with; this is the main reason why most policemen wear clip-on ties and hate any gear that offers someone a handhold on them.

The first and sometimes the only thing a policeman looks at when approaching someone is his hands. Recruits are warned repeatedly to train themselves to check people's hands first ("If the guy's got a brick, he better be building a house"). But he must do more than just look—he must learn to expect to see things. A policeman is frequently called into the presence of people who are distressed, depressed, angry, or fearful. It is not surprising that many of them are holding some kind of weapon, which they do not necessarily intend for use against him. He must be prepared to disarm them swiftly without resorting to force. Often he sees boys walking down the street carrying sticks or boards; he usually disarms them and sends them on their way, unless there has been a specific call or an order to bring them in. Anyone who comes into his presence is unceremoniously disarmed. A boy carrying a bow and arrow has the toy taken from him, and given to his mother after the policeman finishes talking with them. A woman opens her door for an officer taking a meet complainant, and he quickly grabs a butcher knife and pistol. He enters the house, unloads the gun, places the knife in a drawer, sits down for a cup of coffee and a little conversation, and leaves after the woman has had a good cry and he is reasonably sure she will not commit suicide. People often tell him of weapons in their houses and offer to get them, but the experienced patrolman will not let anyone handle a gun in his presence. People holding paper bags are looked at carefully, because every policeman knows that it is not an elegant manner of transporting a gun but it is one that is used often enough. He is not concerned about hurting the feelings of the people whom he handles unceremoniously in these moments. He only cares about disarming them, for there are occasions when the door opens and he is looking directly into the barrel of a shotgun, and then is stripped of everything he is but his blue suit.[1]

Anyone whose hands are concealed, wittingly or not, risks serious injury or worse when he attracts the attention of a policeman. Hidden hands imply danger to a policeman, and he must decide in a few seconds what course of action to take. Whatever he decides to do, he must continue until he has succeeded or failed, because there is no possibility of mediation with a policeman intent on assuring his security, and he will be satisfied only by seeing empty hands.

---

[1]"A 26-year-old man armed with a Luger pistol and a rifle disarmed three policemen early today and held them at bay for nearly two hours . . . . The man finally gave up his weapons and surrendered after having a cup of coffee with two of the policemen. The drama started when police received a report of a 'disturbance.' . . . The first officer to respond was Policeman Robert Patrick . . . who said he saw Hansen standing at the front door, his back toward the street. 'Did you call, sir?' Patrick asked. Hansen turned around and according to Patrick, 'The next thing I knew I had a rifle to my head.' " *Philadelphia Daily News*, July 27, 1971 (footnotes renumbered—eds.).

A young white officer noticed a man standing near a street corner turn away as the patrol car approached. He stopped his car and rolled down the window to look at the elderly Negro man. Instead of getting out of the car, he yelled across the deserted street to him, "Take your hand out of your coat." The man had turned back toward the car when it stopped, and he had his right hand jammed inside. He did not react to the command. They were frozen for several seconds; then the patrolman repeated his demand. When the man remained silent, the officer drew his pistol, continuing to remain seated in his car. He placed his gun in plain view and again ordered the man to show his hand. The man was very agitated but he remained silent. Slowly he began to extract his hand, but he gave the appearance of concealing some intention which threatened the patrolman, who cocked his gun and pointed it directly at the man. Suddenly the old man drew out his hand and threw a pistol to the ground. He stood trembling. The patrolman uncocked his gun with a shaking hand and approached. He was on the verge of tears, and in a moment of confusion, fear, and anxiety, he struck the man with the butt of his pistol. "Why didn't you take your hand out when I told you? I almost shot you, you dumb bastard." The man protested the treatment he had received, complaining that there was no reason to hit him. He said he had had no intention of using the gun but was carrying it for self-protection. The patrolman recovered from his fright, but despite his regret for striking the man in anger, he refused to acknowledge any responsibility. "Are you wearing a sign? How the fuck am I supposed to know what you're gonna do?"

From a purely technical point of view, the patrolman had initially made an error by failing to close the distance between himself and the suspect, allowing himself no alternative but to leave or use his gun. If he had charged the man immediately upon suspecting him of some misdeed, any passer-by might have "seen" an elderly black man being "assaulted" by a policeman, but the patrolman would have avoided the chance of a much more serious incident. The presumption here is that the policeman was behaving correctly in having suspicions about the man and stopping to make any kind of investigation. Nobody obliged him to stop the man, and if he had continued on his patrol, his superiors and colleagues would not have known. But the patrolman makes these stops because they are his job. He knows colleagues who do not make them, or seldom do so, to avoid moments like the ones he had passed through, but if his morale is high and if he treats his job in a serious way, he has little choice but to exercise the skills he has developed. Whether these stops should be allowed is a political issue. They have tactical value to the police, but the use of suspicion stops as a police tactic cannot be decided from a simple, technical viewpoint but must be made in terms of the political values of the people who pay the police.

The positioning and distance of a patrolman in relation to the person he is seeking to control are absolutely critical. When they are separated by many feet, the chances of the policeman drawing his gun are considerable. But even if he is in close proximity to the suspect, the policeman can still fail unless he positions his body to do what he wants to. He uses his gun infrequently when he is close to a suspect, relying instead on his hand weapons and his physical assets. When he commits himself to this kind of action and fails, he is in serious trouble.

Consider the predicament of the patrolman turning off his fifteenth hydrant on a hot, steamy day. He approached the gushing hydrant, wrench in hand, watching the children splashing and a young man washing his Irish setter. He asked them to stand back, but the man continued to wash his dog, splashing water freely about and entirely ignoring the presence of the officer. He was told again to move, this time forcefully but without insult. The fellow looked up and said, "Fuck you, pig!" In that split second the patrolman committed himself. He lunged in anger, but trying to avoid the water, he arched his body and limited his reach. The fellow leaped back into the middle of the street and taunted the policeman with obscene gestures and remarks. If the policeman gave chase, he might capture him, but the chances were not good. Every time he took a step forward, the fellow sprang back, yelling louder and attracting larger and larger numbers of onlookers. The policeman grew angrier by the moment and was very reluctant to withdraw, although he realized his situation was untenable. He concluded the incident by vowing to "get" the fellow.

The policeman had every intention of settling the "score" with the young man and mentioned him to his sergeant and several colleagues, who urged that he remain away. The policemen did not find the young man, although one night he found them. When they were answering a call at another house, the fellow allegedly dropped a jug of water out of a second-floor window, narrowly missing a patrolman. The officer called an assist, broke into the man's house, and arrested him after an altercation. A number of law suits erupted out of this event, and the fellow moved out of the district.

The policeman's intense concern with position, his ability to see a suspect's hands and to make some judgment about his physical capacity and inclinations combine to make all car stops potentially explosive moments. A policeman usually stops a car because he thinks that it is stolen, that the occupants are trying to avoid him, or that there has been some kind of traffic violation. He has used his power to stop the car. He can see the driver and the other occupants, but he cannot make any judgments about what they are doing. He cannot see their hands or how big they are, or determine what they might do. All the unknowns he fears are present as he proceeds to investigate.

The patrolman is under orders—often disregarded—not to make suspicion car stops when he is working alone. Each time he makes a car stop, he is supposed to inform his dispatcher and, before getting out of his car, give his location and the color, make, and license number of the car. If he is alone and his stop is on suspicion, he is supposed to await the arrival of a back-up before proceeding. If his suspicion is strong and the stop is made at night, the patrolman tries to blind the driver by shining his spotlight directly onto the car's rearview mirror. He does not take his eyes off the car once he has signaled the stop. He counts the number of occupants he sees and makes sure that they all remain visible. If he is alone and waiting for another officer, he will stay in his car and order anyone trying to get out to remain seated.

If two men are making a suspicion stop, they use speed and position to overcome the deficiencies in their situation. Both patrolmen emerge quickly, stepping out with one leg so that their bodies do not turn away from the car they are going to approach. The recorder stations himself at the right rear of the car, looking through the back windows to make sure nobody is hiding on the floor or concealing something under the seat. The driver approaches the front of the car and positions himself to maximize his advantage over the occupants. He stands to the rear of the front door and well away from it, to avoid the possibility of someone opening the door and knocking him down. By standing back, he obliges the person to turn around to him, an awkward and uncomfortable position. Policemen are urged to adopt this posture whenever they stop a car, but when a patrolman is issuing a traffic ticket, he finds it difficult to maintain a hostile posture without seeming aggressive. Few policemen walk directly to a car window without first making some judgment about the driver.

There is no way for the policeman completely to settle his anxieties when making a car stop. The people he is seeking to control are right before him; he is close to them, but he cannot get near enough to place them under his physical control. His personal estimate of his own vulnerability greatly increases his tension. Many patrolmen not only unlatch the strap on their holsters before approaching a car but actually pull their guns. At night it is not uncommon to see policemen unholster their guns and conceal them behind a thigh as they approach a suspicious car. There is relatively little the occupants of a car can do to ease the situation. Occasionally people who have considerable experience with the police place their hands on top of the steering wheel to indicate their peaceful intentions. But this does not calm him; rather it tells the officer that he is approaching someone who is cop-wise and his wariness increases.

The policeman's unease does not result from the attitudes of the people but from the constraint of the situation. Even when he sees people who give every appearance of peace, he is unlikely to relax his wariness. Two patrolmen approached a parked car with a running motor. It was very early on a frosty Sunday morning. The white policeman walked directly toward the driver, but his black partner restrained him. "Sleeping like a baby, right? Made a load and can't get home, so he pulls over and parks. Well, you want to check 'em out, see he ain't dead. But before you open the door or knock on the window, look inside first. You gotta make sure the car is in park and the guy don't have a knife in his hand. A lot of these dudes have been rolled so many times they keep an open knife on their lap before they doze off, for protection, you know. That's O.K., you know, but you don't want no surprises when you wake him up. Some of 'em been rolled by guys in blue suits, too, and you can't forget that neither."

A car stop combines the anxieties of entry into an enclosed space where concealment is possible with the frustrations of being unable to control people who are visible and in some sense publicly available. The policeman must try to balance his need to give a stern and forceful appearance, his "I mean business" manner, with a recognition that most stops turn into nothing, that they are false alarms that can get out of hand if he acts too aggressively or, in his desire to control the people, is insulting. In moments of extreme tension, when the police are mobilized in search of "cop killers" or feel that the department is being beseiged and threatened, some men cast caution to the wind and openly use their guns to control car stops. A faultlessly polite patrolman pointed his revolver directly at a person's head, saying, "Sir, would you please stand out of your car?" But even having a gun ready is not always a guarantee of success.

Two patrolmen stopped a car they knew to be stolen. The plate was listed on the hot sheet and they had checked it with the dispatcher before moving. They were on special patrol in search of some men who the day before had murdered a policeman. Both policemen had their revolvers out as they approached the car, which held two men. The driver had his hands on the steering wheel and was looking back over his shoulder at the advancing officer. According to the patrolman, the fellow smiled and said to him, "Shit, man, you don't need that." He suckered the officer, who hesitated and then holstered his gun. He later claimed that he knew he had made an error the moment he did it. The man dropped his hand and came up with a .45, shooting the policeman twice, while the other man wounded the second officer. The two men were captured a short while later. There is no point in a policeman having his gun out unless he is prepared to shoot someone, and the police cannot be allowed to think of shooting except in defense. Their assailant must be allowed the first move, however slight, but the police have to be able to protect themselves. If they are not allowed to approach people closely, carefully controlling their movements and even violating their bodies, the only way they can make suspicion stops is with their guns unhooked and their sticks ready to hit.

A patrolman with twenty years' experience had recently arrested two robbery suspects on a car stop. He recalled that although he had drawn his gun several times, he had never shot anyone. "I don't know, they were just bad, the way they were acting. The detectives found a gun under the seat. I was real close to them, working alone. I had my gun pointed right at the driver's head. If one of them had bent down, I would have shot him. It would have been too bad for me if it had been a handkerchief under there, but I would have shot him."

The policeman knows that he does not have an unrestricted right to interfere with people's privacy, but his decision to violate their bodies is not made with regard either to their feelings or to their rights. At the police academy the distinctions between a frisk and a search are carefully explained to him, and the limitations of his authority are defined as clearly as the law allows, but his instructors stress that he should not hesitate to frisk anyone if he feels it is necessary.[2] Any judgment you make is gonna have to be backed up in court,

---

[2]A policeman may examine the outer clothing of any person he stops on suspicion if he feels the person means him harm or may be concealing a weapon. If he feels anything that might be a weapon, he may go into the person's clothing and extract the object for examination. If in the course of the frisk he discovers any contraband or evidence implicating the person in some crime, it is not considered to be legally seized since the policeman has conducted what amounts to a search without reasonable grounds. The distinctions between stop and frisk are discussed in Lawrence P. Tiffany, Donald M. McIntyre, Jr., and Daniel L. Rotenberg, *Detection of Crime* (Boston: Little, Brown, 1967), pp. 44–57. The general issue is still under intense legal review, and the recent Supreme

but if you think you should, do it." Body control is treated as a technical issue; considerable time is spent teaching recruits how to efficiently violate the privacy of fellow citizens.

Several recruits at the academy were arbitrarily selected to enact a stop and frisk in class. They were given a situation; first one and then the other played the officer and the suspect. Almost everyone failed. They spoke in muffled tones, asked politely for some identification, and muttered questions about why he was loitering in the alley at so late an hour. "You just gonna stand there and ask him to put his hand in his coat pocket? Hey, boy, you're up an alley, it's dark, and we ain't here," the instructor piped in. Everyone, including a few ex-policemen back for a refresher, failed badly and knew it. How do you frisk someone? How do you not violate him? He's your friend and buddy.

The instructor concealed several guns and knives on a student collaborator and arranged to demonstrate frisking. "O.K., it ain't so easy. Half you guys would be on your ass by now, and this guy's gonna play football with your head, remember that. So now, we learn how to frisk." The collaborator and another student were called to the front of the room. Two others were called up to frisk them. "O.K. Put 'em on the wall and frisk 'em down," the black instructor ordered. The recruits mumbled their orders, and without using their hands or stepping in close to the men, they positioned the "suspects" on the wall. Both men used their feet to kick at the subjects' legs, spreading them to keep the man off balance. "Hey, wait a minute. Why all this kickin'? Everybody starts kickin' the guy's legs. Why all the rough stuff?" The men finished their frisk and were followed by two other recruits. Throughout the hour nobody found any of the weapons, and each man commenced his frisking by kicking or roughing up his classmate.

The instructor exhibited his mock displeasure (his students rarely find any weapons the first time) and demonstrated a proper frisk on his collaborator. "When you frisk someone, it is for your own protection. You don't have to kick him. You have to put him under your control and frisk him systematically." The instructor used his entire body, placing the man in the position he wanted him, feet back and spread wide, every muscle tensed to keep his head, which was far forward, from slipping down and causing him to fall. "You want to stand right in there. Don't be afraid of him. You gonna be afraid when he ain't in this position. Now you got him. Put your leg inside his, and if he moves you can trip him up. If he takes a few bumps, that's resisting. Frisk him

---

Court and federal court decisions will be amended and refined in upcoming cases. The most recent decisions are *Terry vs. Ohio.* 88 S.Ct. 1868 (1968); *Sibron vs. New York,* 88 S.Ct. 1889 (1968); *United States vs. McMann,* 370 F.2d 757 (2d Cir. 1967). The stop-and-frisk authority of the police in a number of other countries is discussed in Sowle, *Police Power and Individual Freedom.* In no country do the police appear to have less formal power than they do in America, although the actual practices may differ. A cursory discussion of police frisking in London and the negative responses of people is in Peter Laurie, *Scotland Yard* (London: Bodley Head, 1970), pp. 62–65.

systematically. Don't use your fingertips. Use your palms. Start with the palms on his head and work one side of his body and then the other. Look at his hair, and don't be afraid to put your hands in his crotch, it won't bite. And if the guy gives you any shit, why you can give him a little shot to remember you while you're there."

The instructor showed them the concealed knives and guns and told them, "They were hardly hidden. But you are gonna learn. And listen, the rough stuff is for nothing. It doesn't help you find anything. If you're nervous, the guy out there is gonna know it. He may have more experience at this than you. You give him a chance, he'll take it. Don't talk to him or let him distract you, just frisk him. Then if he don't stand still, you make him, but don't get tough just because you're nervous and don't like the guy's color or looks or whatever."

After several weeks of practicing and discovering the many places a weapon can be concealed (one student sliced open his finger on a razor blade stuck behind a belt), the students' admiration for their instructor was unbounded and their efficiency at frisking vastly improved. Most of the kicking had disappeared, and the recruits were beginning to use their bodies to place people on the wall and to control them while they were there. But even using loaded guns (with blanks) and switchblades did not create the necessary ingredients to make it all real—fear and anger.

Most frisking is actually done casually and in an offhand manner. When a policeman is working alone, he is reluctant to bend down, which he must do in a full frisk from the rear, and he will forgo it unless he has strong reasons to believe the person is armed. A decision to frisk is also affected by the relative size of the people involved. Few policemen frisk youngsters (unless they are quite large), because an officer assumes that if gets any trouble from a kid, he can put him down. He contents himself with casually feeling the outer pockets of his jacket and his waist area. But the experienced man does not waste these few motions. He is not delicate in poking his hands about while he is making conversation.

A frisk usually occurs after a stop is made and the patrolman has made some determination about his initial suspicions, but there are numerous occasions when the frisk and stop occur almost simultaneously.

Two patrolmen were searching an area for suspects in the shooting of a police officer. There was little information about the killers except that they were young. Driving slowly down an almost deserted street, they passed a young man walking in the opposite direction. "Did he turn away? Yeah, let's get him. Shit, I hate backin' up on these dudes," he muttered to his recorder, throwing the car into reverse. He jumped out, ran between two parked cars, grabbed the man, and turned him about. He was frisking his midriff when the man said, "Hey, Hank, what's the matter, man?" The patrolman, surprised at hearing his name, looked up and noticed that he had stopped the brother of a close friend. He stopped the frisk and apologized. They smoked a cigarette, chatted, and parted. He had been so intent on quickly approaching the suspect without losing sight of the man's hands that he did not even look at his face. He was not embarrassed but considered the action an excellent example of how to do his job properly. "He might have been a killer. When you go up on someone like that, you got no business lookin' at his face," he said.

If the policeman has not stopped a person on suspicion or encountered him under circumstances that suggest involvement in disorder or crime, he will not frisk him unless in the course of conversation something is said suggesting violence or resistance. He does not search everyone he meets or everyone he stands next to on a dark street. He is never relaxed in the presence of strangers, and he assumes that his alertness and readiness are sufficient to handle surprises, but if there is a hint of a weapon present, his entire manner changes abruptly.

The patrolmen were interviewing a man who claimed that two acquaintances had robbed him of a thousand dollars. "Wow, that's like a million bucks in this neighborhood. You must be a number writer, pal," one officer said, with a grin. The alleged victim did not think it funny, and the more he talked of his loss, the angrier he became. He was quite vague in giving a description of the robbers, and the patrolmen began to think the man was just another drunk. "I'm gonna kill them motherfuckers!" he mumbled, and in a second one officer had grabbed him by the arm, twisted him about, and started frisking him. From inside the man's overcoat he extracted an ice pick. "I didn't like the way he said 'kill.' You hear that kinda shit all the time, but he really meant it. An ice pick is the worst, too, because there's no hole when you pull it out. All the bleeding is on the inside," he said to his inexperienced partner.

Whenever he is making a suspicion stop, the patrolman conducts some kind of frisk. How he proceeds depends on whether he is working alone or with a partner. If he is alone, he will not bother to back-frisk anyone he thinks has no chance of overpowering him. But if the person appears to be strongly built and willing to "give it a go," he will turn him about, often accompanying his commands with a few threats, but he will not bend down to do a thorough search. Instead he uses his stick to feel the man's legs or, if he has no stick, does not bother to do a complete job. If he bends down, the policeman is vulnerable, and while the man may not hurt him, he has a chance to "make it"; no policeman wants to give anyone the opportunity of involving him in a chase.

When patrolmen work in pairs, their approach alters completely. Two men who work together regularly come to understand each other's attitudes and routines. They divide responsibilities, and each knows what he is going to do when they make a stop or go into a place where there is some kind of trouble. Whether they are stopping one man or five, one officer conducts the interrogation and the frisk, and the other stands back and controls the scene. If they have stopped a group of men, the patrolman does not hesitate to unholster his gun in order to make them more responsive to his commands. Working in pairs, one man can focus his attention on the frisk and does not have to worry about the chances of assault or flight.

Working alone, the patrolman's control of the situation is slight and tenuous. If he is working one to one, only fear prevents the person he has stopped from proceeding. The degree of force the policeman must use to make him obey depends as much on his willingness to appear forceful as it does on the actual use of force. There are many policemen who rarely use force for the simple reason that they appear willing (and possibly are) to do almost anything to subdue resistance. Other patrolmen, who misjudge their power (or like to abuse it), often find themselves in situations where they are risking serious danger for little reward.

A young, aggressive patrolman told of a problem he had encountered when he stopped six men outside a bar. "I had all six on the wall, you know, and I was gonna search the one on the end when one guy said they should rush me. I cocked my gun and nobody moved, and I told him if they came, I'd burn him. What else could I do? I started to frisk the one guy when the guys at the other end started drifting around the corner. I lost two, but I finished the other four." If he had expected solace and comfort from his colleagues, he was disappointed. "Carl, you are a dumb motherfucker. You keep up that crazy shit, you are gonna be in the hospital or dead."

Even if the policeman is careful not to exceed the limits of his capacity to safely control suspects, he cannot focus his attention closely on what he is doing when he frisks someone. Most frisks are done quickly and informally to assure the officer that the suspect does not have anything on him which might be used against the policeman. Patrolmen who fancy themselves specialists in gun pinches frisk people very thoroughly, but they are exceptional. Every time a person is arrested he is usually frisked twice, first by the arresting officer and then by the wagon crew, before he is transported to the station, but weapons are still overlooked, concealed behind belt buckles, in armpits, and even in a folded wallet.

A patrolman recalled a time when he was working plainclothes and was arrested during a raid on a speakeasy. The police missed the small revolver he had stuck behind his belt buckle. "I was sittin' on the bench in the station, waitin', you know, to tell 'em who I was when we was in private, but I was worried if they noticed the gun they'd kick the shit outta me. So I called a cop over and real quiet I told him I was still carryin'. He almost shit." On another occasion, a young man was sitting in a station, handcuffed, waiting for some detectives to come for him. He acted quite nervous, kept looking about and fidgeting. Finally a patrolman approached and told him to keep quiet. He apologized and said he was very nervous because he had a gun in his pocket that the policeman had not taken from him. The patrolman seized him by the lapels, twisted him about as he raised him from the bench, and grabbed the gun.

Frisking is much more common in some parts of the city than in others, and it is not an activity engaged in exclusively by the police. There are bars and restaurants where regular patrons "bump" into strangers, checking whether or not they are armed. Prostitutes who work out of bars frequently seek to protect themselves from entrapments by plainclothesmen by holding hands and pretending affection for a potential client while actually checking to see if the man's hands match what he claims to do for a living and if he is carrying a small gun or a jack somewhere about his middle. These people frisk for protection, as a policeman does. An officer is forbidden by regulation to frisk a woman except in an extreme emergency; he must turn her over to a matron or a policewoman. Undoubtedly the number of complaints against the police would increase if this restriction were lifted, but so, too, would the number of stops and arrests. There are many reasons why a policeman does not look with suspicion on women in public places (except in areas where prostitutes work), but one of them certainly is his inability to protect himself. Not only can he not frisk a woman, a policeman is reluctant to hit a woman, and even when he has justification (from his point of view), he recalls doing so with regret and chagrin.

Although a policeman views frisking as a defensive act devoid of personal comment, those he stops cannot help but feel angered by their powerlessness, if for no other reason. Regardless of how the policeman behaves or what he says, he is compelling the person to submit to him and to turn his body over for examination. Younger men in some parts of the city are so familiar with the routine that when they are hailed by the police, they stop and spread their arms to the side before the officer has asked a question or even approached. They understand that this signal of submission will gain them more gentle and circumspect treatment. Sometimes a patrolman runs his hands absentmindedly over a man's pockets while engaging in conversation, not really meaning to frisk him but just letting him know that he is in control, that for the moment the man belongs to the patrolman. It is not a consciously hostile or aggressive act. It is an expression of the policeman's belief that regardless of the momentary tone of the interaction, his place in that relationship is supported ultimately by his personal will and readiness to exercise all of the authority invested in him. There is no way he can make this point without causing discontent, because the authority given to him can be exercised only by restraining the liberty of some persons and violating their autonomy. A policeman does not enjoy frisking people. During a busy tour he may wash up several times because many of the people he stops are filthy. He constantly grumbles about the dirt and the odors, but they do not cause him to keep his distance or to avoid intimate contact. He knows that when he is on the street, it is only his readiness to demonstrate his power that maintains the edge necessary for him to do his work and come home safely each day.

PART V

SOCIALIZATION FOR POLICING

Police work offers a person far more than merely a job. Indeed, from the time a recruit first dons his uniform he enters into a distinct way of life that largely defines what he is to think, feel, and do. Up to this point, we have focused primarily upon responses of the police to the various institutional and situational attributes of their work. As a consequence, we have given relatively short shrift to the indigenous manner in which such responses arise. In particular, we have neglected the question of how it is that the patterns of police thought and action are passed from one generation of policemen to the next. Since this process necessarily involves the transmission of information and knowledge, it is fundamentally a cultural matter.

The occupational culture constructed by the police consists of long-standing rules of thumb, a somewhat special language and ideology that help edit a member's everyday experiences, shared standards of relevance as to the critical aspects of the work, matter-of-fact prejudices, models for street-level etiquette and demeanor, certain customs and rituals suggestive of how members are to relate not only to each other but to outsiders, and a sort of residual category consisting of the assorted miscellany of some rather plain police horse sense. All of these cultural modes of thinking, knowing, and doing are, of course, so rooted in the recurrent problems and common experiences of the police that they are regarded by insiders as perfectly natural responses to the world they inhabit. Indeed, cultures arise as a way of coping with, and making sense of, a given environment. That this occupational culture has displayed such remarkable stability through time is itself testimony to the persistence of the problematic habitat within which police work takes place.

In the operational environment of the patrol division, the street level of policing, many old habits and traditions have survived largely intact despite the persistent efforts of officialdom to introduce new ideas, tighter organizational controls, and sophisticated technologies into the daily affairs of patrolmen. Even the introduction of better educated and more highly trained recruits has provided precious little encouragement for those seeking to alter the police culture from the inside. This latter point is particularly crucial, for it suggests that there are powerful means available within the occupation that act to systematically discourage innovation while they encourage the status quo.

This is not to say, however, that the transfer of occupational perspectives from generation to generation of policemen occurs altogether smoothly and without difficulty. New members always bring with them at least the potential of trouble because they may, for example, question old assumption, be ignorant of rather sacred traditions, and fail to properly appreciate the ideology shared by the more experienced members. And, in police organizations, where the work setting is populated by members who have very firm notions regarding what they are about, this potential is likely to be evaluated quite closely. The novice carries with him into the occupational life different biographical experiences, faulty, or, at least romanticized conceptions and knowledge of the job, and perhaps values or purposes at odds with those of the working membership. To the veteran practitioners of the trade, ways must be found, therefore, to assure that the recruit does not disrupt or bring into question the various cultural solutions worked out previously by those on the scene to handle the robust practical problems they face. Put bluntly, new members must be taught to see the world as do their more experienced colleagues in the setting if the pragmatic traditions of the occupation are to survive. The manner in which this problematic intergenerational continuity has been maintained in police agencies rests precariously, but predictably, on what we call here the police socialization process.

At heart, occupational socialization is a jejune phrase used by social scientists to refer to the process by which a person learns the ropes of a particular job. Across jobs, the process may appear in many forms ranging from a relatively quick, on-the-job, trial-and-error process to a far more elaborate one which requires a lengthy preparation period of education and training, followed by an equally drawn out period of apprenticeship. Even on the job, socialization usually involves several sequences of diverse activities In fact, if one takes seriously the notion that learning itself is a continuous and lifelong process, the entire occupational career of an individual can be seen as a socialization process. At any rate, given a particular job, socialization refers simply to the way an individual comes to absorb the collective understandings necessary to perform that job. As such, it requires learning what is customary and desirable in the work setting as well as what is not.

The results or content of an occupational socialization process include, for example, a readiness to select certain events for attention over others, a stylized stance toward one's routine activities, some idea of the appropriateness of various behavioral responses to recurrent situations in the work world, and so forth. In short, socialization entails the learning of a cultural perspective that can be brought to bear on occupational matters. To illustrate this highly contextual process, consider the following hypothetical, but altogether plausible, exchange between an experienced patrolman and a colleague in a police department. When asked about what happened to him during a given shift, the veteran officer might well respond by saying "We didn't do much police work, just wrote a couple of movers and brought in a body, a stand-up, you know." The raw recruit could hardly know of such things, for the description given clearly presumes a specific kind of knowledge shared by experienced patrolmen as to the typical features of their work and how such knowledge is used when going about their daily tasks. The rookie must learn of these understandings and eventually come to utilize them in an entirely matter-of-fact way. This is the cultural material of which occupational socialization is concerned.

There are several rather important temporal features of the police socialization process that are quite influential in terms of the occupational understandings policemen develop toward their work. First, the process begins in a unequivocally formal fashion. To wit, selection procedures and academy training for policemen sharply distinguish the candidates and recruits from all others within the organization. In general, the greater the separation of a person from the day-to-day reality of the work, the less the person will be able to carry over any abilities or skills learned in the formal setting to the particular position for which he is being prepared. Formal processes concentrate, therefore, far more on attitudes than on acts, at least implicitly if not explicitly. To a degree, formal processes stress the "proper" or "correct" way of behaving in lieu of the "practical" or "smart" way, followed perhaps by the more experienced members of an occupation who have learned that a member who strictly adheres to the proper practices is seen as something of a cultural dope, one who has not been socialized fully. This is the case, not because the normative teachings of formal, role-segregated socialization programs are thought to be necessarily wrongheaded or false by the experienced members, but rather because, given the complicated and contingent realities of the work itself, most normative prescriptions do not translate well into specific recipes for action—they are viewed as far too abstract and general to be of much practical use. In short, the rules fail to provide for their application. Thus, "proper" procedures become part of the presentational background of the occupation and are seen, for the most part, to be somewhat irrelevant to the more gritty operational matters at hand.

The above discussion anticipates the second temporal feature of the police socialization process; namely, that because the formal initiation of recruits into the occupation is necessarily incomplete, the socialization process will always include a closely observed, informal, on-the-job period of introduction. In the former phase universal standards are applied rather uniformly to each recruit, but in the latter phase the process becomes very particularistic and shifting standards are applied to each recruit more or less at the whims of each recruit's official or unofficial overseers in the patrol squad to which he has been assigned. However, it is in this latter phase where the "proper" information is separated by the recruit from the "smart." And it is at this point in the process that a recruit's full recognition of the police role is likely to occur. Sociologically, this temporal phase of socialization is marked by a serial characteristic whereby experienced members groom the newcomers about to assume similar roles in the organization. Since such grooming takes place in an intense, affectively laden, and consequential situation, it is accomplished with relative ease. Within the police world, this serial feature is virtually taken for granted and accounts in large measure for the stability of patrolmen behavior patterns.

The third temporal feature is a more general one, and in a sense encompasses the above two. It refers to the degree to which the police socialization process is organized, whether advertently or inadvertently, first, to dismantle the incoming identity of the recruit, and second, to rebuild that identity along lines that are thought occupationally appropriate. Ordinarily, dismantling processes vary directly with the degree to which a people-processing system resembles an ordeal to those passing through it. Rebuilding processes often occurring simultaneously with dismantling procedures, are marked by the presence of visible and appropriate role models (often with much fate control over a target of socialization); a collective peer group of recruits who share identical problems and are allowed considerable interaction time; and, most critically, a set of externally defined problems and dangers to which the new identity, situationally based of course, can be shown to be applicable. The degree to which both dismantling and rebuilding processes are at work in police agencies is sometimes startling. Consider, for example, police selection processes which appear to be organized primarily to allow the department to discredit a man's biography rather than to honor it. Certainly, candidates undergoing this time-consuming, often embarrassing social and mental interrogation procedure are fully aware that their selectors are out to disconfirm, not to confirm, their presented self. The process continues at the Police Academy where whatever trace of individualism possessed by a recruit is to be minimized in favor of the collective front or shared symbolic representation of police work accepted and honored by the present membership. Appearances are to be uniform, and the cohort group is expected to display such characteristics as group solidarity and unity. And, upon joining the patrol division, the recruit quickly learns to appreciate the teamwork involved in policing as he discovers the local understandings carried by his new colleagues regarding how the work is to be carried out. Consequently, the stripping away of an individual's character upon entering the police world does not leave the recruit demoralized and alone. Rather, the occupation offers up a very seductive and appealing alternative identity to the recruit to replace the one he has left behind. Given that the process works to everyone's satisfaction, he is invited to be a fellow cop; for those who accept this identity, the gap separating themselves and the veterans narrows appreciably, whereas the gap separating members from nonmembers grows concomitantly.

With this short overview in mind, the readings that follow discuss some of the typical features of the police socialization process. First, Richard N. Harris gives a detailed examination of the "professional policeman" as seen by the recruits and described by the training staff of a police academy. Standing alone, the notion of professionalism is a topical and significant subject, for much has been made of late about the promise of a professional police service—or danger, depending on one's point of view. Since Harris attended the academy alongside the recruits of whom he writes, few observers can match his inside account of how the concept of a professional policeman is presented to, and received by, newcomers to the occupation. The value of this analysis goes further, because Harris delves deeply into the workings of the training academy itself and suggests that there is much going on in such settings that is "out of sight" and normally does not meet the eye. For example, he points to the inchoate beginnings of an esprit de corps, a personalized morality, and a masculine ethos, all of which seem to define the social contours of the police world. Here is an important point. Many students of policing, laymen and social scientists alike, have been apparently all too willing to accept the working cop's view of things and have summarily dismissed the academy as an irrelevant and inconsequential experience for a recruit. It may, in fact, forcefully and consequentially help to shape the patrolman's later working style.

The second reading presented here implies that there may well be a common language available to describe the socialization of American police recruits. John Van Maanen describes, in a fashion notably similar to the preceding selection, the manner, tempo, and results of a police academy in a larger, more urban community than that examined by Harris. However, by following the socialization process through the recruit's initiation into the patrol division, Van Maanen also emphasizes the critical importance of the small squad of officers and the partner to whom the novice is first assigned. Thus, during his early days on patrol, the rookie discovers that "knowledge about" and "knowledge of" city streets are too different things. To a recruit, this is a period of felt ineptness, insecurity, and discomfort, for he is something of an alien among natives. While the academy may prepare a recruit to accept the definition of police work transmitted by his squad, it cannot tell him precisely what such a definition might be. Indeed, everyday matters of policing must be explained verbally to the recruit and exemplified with reference to certain incidents he comes upon. He is highly dependent upon the goodwill of his colleagues. According to Van Maanen's observations, veteran officers close to the recruit are, in general, supportive, though they are slow in coming to trust the prudence, motives, and abilities of the newcomer in their midst. Furthermore, they try to insure the obedience of the recruit by warning him through both word and deed of the mean and dark spirits out to get him if he goes too far astray. That these mean and dark spirits are to be found in the department as well as on the street is perhaps the central point of Van Maanen's essay.

While Harris and Van Maanen stress the powerful role played by the recruit socialization process in the making of policemen, both would reject the notion that a single, unitary "cop personality" is somehow created as a result of this process. Such a view would be mistaken not only because of the numerous psychological responses potentially available to police recruits as idiosyncratic ways of coping with the police culture, but also because the police culture itself is hardly monolithic. The assignment of recruits, for instance, to different precincts, shifts, and beats will provide for different recruit experiences, as will the assignment of recruits to different supervisors, colleagues, and patrol partners. Indeed, as others have pointed out, the various task and structural arrangements within police organizations promote considerable segmentation in the perceptions of policemen toward such aspects of their work as task predictability, danger on the job, organizational production pressures, autonomy from supervision, and even encounters with citizens (e.g., Tift, 1974; Sterling, 1972; Bayley and Mendelson, 1969). Nor is the occupational socialization of policemen confined strictly to the early "breaking-in" period of a police career. To recall a point made earlier: the socialization of police is a continuous process that occurs at least to some degree, every time an individual crosses hierarchical, functional, or social boundaries within the organization. It is therefore the case that the analytic insights provided into the patrolman's occupational world in the selections by Harris and Van Maanen are but a first step, for we still know far too little about the personal and collective adjustments made when patrolmen move into other police worlds such as traffic enforcement, undercover narcotics work, or first-level supervision. Potentially, any police career can take many twists and turns, periodically requiring an individual to adapt to novel circumstances and surroundings. Perhaps future work will examine diverse types of police careers allowing for further specification and depth in our emerging understanding of the police life.

Before proceeding to the readings, we should make some mention of the Epilogue that follows. Fundamentally, the last selection in this book represents an attempt to provide the reader with a perspective on the sometimes opaque observational methods used by many of the authors represented in this book. To be sure, the Epilogue is a personalized, first hand account of a single police research project, but we suspect that many, if not most, of the difficulties highlighted by Van Maanen in the context of beginning his Union City work are common to all ethnographic attempts to uncover the illusive meanings contained within the police culture. The essay is not intended as either a subjective autobiography of the author's time in the field or an explicit "how-to" manual for conducting research in police organizations, though there are elements of each contained in the selection. Rather, the purpose of its inclusion here is to suggest as directly as possible the sweep of both substantive and methodological issues that are raised when an outsider seeks to develop and, to the degree possible, structure a research relationship with the police. Additionally (and perhaps more subtly), we believe that something of the existential flavor and texture of the police socialization process comes through in the Epilogue, thus complementing the materials presented in Part V. Too often sociologists seem to swallow up the stark yet personal reality of what they study by conveniently writing themselves out of what they observe. As others have noted, there is a curious envelope of silence surrounding the role of the participant-observer in police organizations. The Epilogue is, in small measure, an attempt to correct for the apparently obvious fact that although the researcher is rarely if ever the unobserved observer, discovering that this is so from the researcher's writings is a task to try the patience of the most interested and dedicated of readers. Even persistent efforts to read between the lines may not yield a person behind a carefully crafted research report.

Finally, appended to Van Maanen's Epilogue is a tabular presentation drawn from but representing an extension of Manning's (1976) summary of police research. The table lists and describes in some detail most of the major published and unpublished sociological field studies of Anglo-American policing. The majority of these studies have been conducted since 1965 — though all of the research of which we are aware is included. This Appendix, along with the bibliographic references accompanying all the selections presented in this book, provides a comprehensive guide to the available sociological material on, and understanding of, the police in American society.

The Police Academy
and the Professional
Self-Image

Richard N. Harris

Every occupation appears to have what Everett C. Hughes terms a "moral division of labor." That is, some members of an occupation are able to conform to norms of respectability because other members fulfill the requirements of the less respectable, or "dirty," facets.[1] For instance, Jerome Carlin notes that "respectable" lawyers do not usually handle divorces, which can become rather messy, since there are always less well-off lawyers who snatch up those kinds of cases. Because these lawyers are less well-off financially, they feel fewer compunctions in some of their unscrupulous practices.[2] In other words, the respectable lawyer has clean hands at the expense of someone else's dirty hands.

The phenomenon Hughes observes within occupations also operates on a more macrosocial level. Society is able to function with smoothness and a sense of moral cleanliness because there are *entire* occupations insulated from public observability, that wash the dirty linen or keep it out of sight. The respectable people of society recognize the need for distasteful work to be done. This work may involve objects (picking up garbage) or people (processing rejected or dead persons). While the respectables want the job done, they are less concerned with the particulars of how it is to be accomplished. Indeed, in the respectables' desire for cleanliness — physical, psychological, and social — they prefer to know as little as possible about the job. Discretion is the better part of valor: "Don't tell us your problems, just do what you're paid to do; we don't care how you do it, but do it!"

Police work seems to be an example of dirty work. The low prestige of police work stems partly from the "dirty" facet of policing: enforcing laws that support interest groups, but becoming scapegoats when things go wrong. That is, the respectables hire the police to do their dirty work for them. Although respectables ask the police to enforce the laws, they become indignant when they are asked to obey them. Vaguely aware that police officers have the tasks of touching diseased bodies, crawling under trains to tie up a bloody stump on the end of a leg, and subjecting themselves to continual time shifts in tours of duty which take their toll on the body later in life, respectables do not want to be reminded of such troubles. In dealing with police problems, respectables would dirty their own hands by being reminded of the sordid aspects of life that

---

[1] Everett Cherrington Hughes, *Men and Their Work* (Chicago: The Free Press 1958), pp. 44–45, 49–51, 71–73, 92–95, 121–122, 137, (footnotes renumbered — eds.).

[2] Jerome E. Carlin, *Lawyers' Ethics* (New York: The Russell Sage Foundation, 1966), p. 177.

REPRINTED FROM: Richard N. Harris, *The Police Academy: An Inside View*, New York: Wiley, *1973* (3–7; 17–20; 77–94).

the police officer must contend with each day. Although they are aware of the need for law and order, they refuse to take responsibility for their personal involvement: they do not train their children to respect the police; they keep information from the police; and they do not participate in police-community relations programs.

If this is the respectables' perspective of the police, one may well ask what the public really means when it demands law and order. The recent saliency of the law and order issue in political campaigning may reflect several areas of confusion for respectable middle-class America. It may reflect the increasing crime rates and disrespect for authority on all levels. It may be a reaction to middle-class youth's rejection of the value orientations of their parents. It may be a reaction to the national guilt rooted in the ambivalence toward the Vietnam War. It may also reflect the anger over the welfare subsidation of the very people who riot. And surely, it reflects consternation over some recent Supreme Court decisions that, many claim, seem more protective of the rights of the criminal than of the rights of the victim.

On a more latent and unrecognized level, the present demand for law and order appears to invoke repression and prejudice, as a substitute for effective programs of action, in order to deal with major social problems. At times, the police are used to support the interests of power groups. For example, at the turn of the century, police were used by management to break up union activities.[3] Presently, the law has been used to suppress those who do not subscribe to political orthodoxy, and it has become clear to lessees that the law favors landlords. The cry for law and order is used to cover up important social issues just as the expense for "national defense" provides some politicians with the excuse that funds are not available to solve urban, poverty, and medical problems. The question then becomes: To what extent is law enforcement "dirty"? That is, to what extent is law enforcement following the public's unspoken and secret wishes?

The dirty facet of police work does not only refer to actually *doing* the dirty work of the respectables. To ask a police officer to resolve the "student problem" is only part of the process of "dirtying" the officer's occupation. There is another side of the coin. Dirty work may also be physically disgusting, such as dragging a vomiting drunk to a call box, or morally disgusting, such as handling and being exposed to family squabbles. Police work may be dirty by other respectable standards, too, because it often requires physical and even violent means of control. What the police officer must face every day seems to be too demanding, too sordid, and too dangerous for the citizen to involve himself in law, order, and justice.

Given this state of affairs, how are policemen trained to work within this social context and what are their modes of adjustment? Researchers have not considered these questions sufficiently. A partial explanation for this neglect

---

[3] A Task Force Report Submitted to the National Commission on the Causes and Prevention of Violence. *The Politics of Protest,* under the direction of Jerome H. Skolnick (New York: Simon and Schuster, 1969), pp. 268–269.

is that policemen themselves regard academy training as discontinuous with everyday occupational demands. Apparently students of police work accept the notion that the police academy is isolated from the ordinary policeman's world of work. Speaking about a Midwestern police department of the late 1940's, William Westley reports:

> . . . everyone expects [the recruit] to take himself seriously *at first,* but he will not obtain the trust and confidence of the other men until he begins to see the formal rules as they are. . . .[4]

And, in 1967, Arthur Niederhoffer speaks of the highly rated New York City Police Department:

> The more experienced men tell [the recruit] that in order to become a real policeman, he will have to forget everything he is learning at the Academy . . . that attendance at the recruit school is "just a waste of time . . . .[5]

If academy training is an experiential stage of the police career, surely the time and energy spent in the academy has some subjective meaning to the recruit, for better or worse. The impact of academy training on the recruit cannot be so easily dismissed as inconsequential unless evidence exists to support this position. Thus far, no study has been available to offer evidence one way or the other.

Why, then, is academy training considered to be ineffective and discrepant with the everyday demands of police work? Kai Erikson suggests that social control agencies are oriented toward regulating social deviance rather than toward its elimination. He goes on to say that social deviants may be useful to society by their testing and retesting of the degree of flexibility of rules and laws, or even because they point to needed changes in some of those rules and laws. He asks whether society possibly organizes itself in such a way as to *promote* deviancy:

> Indeed, the institutions devised by society for discouraging deviant behavior are often so poorly equipped for the task that we might well ask why this is considered their "real" function at all.

If institutions of social control have the unintended or unrecognized function of merely regulating deviance, inadequate police training may be perceived as part of the "poor equipment" for one of the institutions of social control—law enforcement. Perhaps this is why police officials, politicians, and the citizenry seem to place little interest in police training; they do not want policemen to perform too well. Indeed, as I demonstrate in the following pages, even up-graded police training is likely to boomerang and maintain both the low prestige and the "dirty" qualities of police work.

---

[4]William A. Westley, *Violence and the Police* (Cambridge, Mass.: The MIT Press, 1970), p. 156.

[5]Arthur Niederhoffer, *Behind the Shield* (Garden City, N.Y.: Doubleday, 1967), pp. 44 and 47.

RECRUIT REQUIREMENTS

Before a person can join RCPD (Rurban County Police Department—ed.), he must take a competitive civil service examination. The higher his score, the more likely that he will be able to enter the recruit class before the quota is met. In addition to the examination, the applicant must successfully pass physical endurance tests, a medical examination, and an in-depth investigation into his background. Part of the investigation includes a preliminary interview with the applicant and his wife at their home; this is followed by another interview at the academy. Only then can he be accepted as a candidate. Following the successful completion of 12 weeks in the academy, he is on probation for nine more months, during which time he can easily be dismissed from the department.

To graduate from the academy, he must meet four basic requirements. He must have a good attendance record. He must score 200 out of 300 points on the pistol combat course and 70 out of 100 points on the bull's-eye range, both under time pressure. He must have a typed notebook that is transcribed from class notes. Finally, he must attain an overall average of 75 points on his three monthly written examinations based on class lectures.

The subjects to which the recruit class was exposed can be categorized as follows. Next to each category and its examples are the number of hours devoted to each grouping. The number of hours are not altogether accurate, but they do demonstrate the emphasis given to these various topics.

Topic	Hours
Patrol procedures (including 40 hours in the field)	89
Law and the courts (excluding laws related to traffic)	78½
Traffic (laws, accident forms, driving skills, procedures)	40½
Police subdepartments: structure and functions (homicide, narcotics, canine, juvenile aid, arson, inspection, communications, etc.)	32½
Self-defense (karate, koga, riot training)	26
Drill and inspections	21
Departmental forms and regulations	20
First aid (including maternity cases)	16
Orientation (community relations, police ethics, professionalism, race relations, county geography)	16

THE DAILY SCHEDULE

Although the recruits were required to be in formation by 8:45 A.M., about half of them arrived a good half hour early. They drank coffee and sat or stood around in small groups along the drill floor. Shortly before 8:45 the two platoon sergeants called their respective platoons to formation. Each platoon consisted of three rows of about nine men in each row. The first man of the row was its squad leader. His main responsibility was to check the attendance within his squad. Through a series of salutes and reports, each squad leader passed his information to the platoon sergeant. As Patrolman Arsenault came to take his position in front of the platoons at precisely 8:45, the sergeants called their platoons to attention. Patrolman Arsenault ordered each sergeant to report the state of the platoon's attendance. If anyone was reported absent, his name was taken and a patrol car was dispatched to his home to check on his safety. This precaution is a department regulation because of the inherent dangers of police work. Even if absentees live outside the police district, other police departments cooperate in this procedure.

Roll call was followed by inspection or drill, which lasted anywhere from 5 to 20 minutes. If inspection was brief, there might still be time for a few drill movements. If not, the platoons were called to attention and dismissed for a brief break before classes.

The first of the three morning classes began around 9:00. For every 50 minutes of class time, the recruits were given a ten-minute coffee break. It was not long before they tried to extend their breaks to 15 minutes or more. After the first week of classes, for instance, the instructors always had to call the recruits back to the class. Once in the room the recruits talked to one another from their seats until the instructor or staff member walked in. The recruit who sat closest to the door yelled "Atten-hut!" at which time the rest of the recruits jumped to attention. After they were reseated, the lecture began.

The lunch period was from 12:00 to 12:45. Some recruits brought their own lunches; others bought hero sandwiches provided at the academy. Some recruits who rebelled at the prices of the sandwiches drove to a nearby store and brought back food to eat. Every now and then a recruit who lived near enough to the academy went home for lunch.

At precisely 12:45 roll call was taken again. Following roll call, the recruits either practiced drill or riot formations, or they were dismissed for their 1:00 class. There were four hours of classes in the afternoon. The last hour or two was often spent in participatory activities such as koga, self-defense, and riot tactics. For physical training, karate, and self-defense, the recruits changed into sweat clothes in the men's room before classes. Although military drill sometimes took place outside the building during cold days, riot formations were practiced outside only when the weather warmed. At 4:50 or whenever the last class of the day was dismissed the recruits rushed out of the building. Inside of 10 minutes, there was hardly a car left in the parking area.

Until the first test was given at the end of the first month, the mood of the recruits seemed anxious. Although the tests were based on lecture material alone, instructors passed out large mimeographed sheets and constantly referred to portions of the penal code. Not only did the recruits have to worry about their lessons but they were expected to do physical exercises, practice koga and karate moves, keep their leather spit-shined, and practice dry-firing with their revolvers (to develop finger control)—all on their own time. If the first month of recruit training could be characterized by anything, it seemed to be a feeling of too little time to learn too many things. As one recruit told me, "I can tell you. . . . They're worried about what they are going to do if they flunk out, with their wife and kids."

The mood of the recruits seemed to shift significantly during the last month of the session. Throughout the training program the staff had tried to counter the prejudices against classroom training by having police officers from the field lecture on most of the subjects. But once the recruits spent their week in the field, complaints about the irrelevancy of the academy increased.

With the approach of graduation day, the recruits became more and more restless. Each day was characterized by boredom. The sense of boredom was aggravated by circumstances other than just the anticipation of graduation. For one reason or another, the staff was unable to keep to the schedule, usually because lecturers did not arrive on time. Breaks between classes lengthened into 30 minutes; and some of the classes were objectively more boring than they had been in previous weeks. Indeed, one entire morning, sponsored by Green Cross, on traffic safety seemed to be geared for elementary school children. In spite of the increasing restlessness and ennui, however, there was a visible sigh of relief after the final written examination as if nothing else could stand between them and graduation.

FIRST STEPS TOWARD PROFESSIONALISM

Education

The same day the recruit took the oath making him a bona fide member of the department, he was given a brief introductory speech while he stood at attention on the drill floor with the other in-coming members. He was at once instructed that he was a professional within a profession and must act accordingly. "You will look like professionals, read like professionals, and study like professionals who are joining other professionals in a profession within the community." It was not until later in the day that the recruit was finally given a hint of what was meant by "professional."

Education was presented as the *sine qua non*, the indispensable ingredient, or professionalism. That is, the recruit was told that a professional is "recognized by his education"; if RCPD wanted to be professional, its members had to be educated. But while education might have been the key to attaining professional status, high salary seemed to be the real criterion for success. Said one instructor:

> You may come up against someone who won't join law enforcement because of the pay. And you'll be able to say, "Whoo, we're professionals. We require a minimum of two years of college and we can start at $15,000." Education is the thing.

During a coffee break, a recruit offered his opinion. If the community wanted professional policemen, it would have to pay for it. ". . . I can tell you why all these guys are here: for the retirement and for the security. You've gotta have the money if you want professionals."

To become acquainted with their educational opportunities, the recruit class spent a day at State College where there was a police science program. The program consisted of a two-year college level degree and covered three required areas. The number following each subject equals its semester hours.

Area 1: Sociology 3, Psychology 3, Physical Science 6, English 6
Area 2: Police Science courses (law, traffic) 36
Area 3: Electives in Social Sciences and the Humanities 10

The state allowed the academy training session to be worth five semester hours, which would be applied to Area 3, in order to encourage the recruit to enter the program. In effect, the liberal arts courses were superseded by police technology courses. By not applying the five credits to Area 2 (which would seem to be the appropriate choice), the department and State College emphasized courses that were mainly technological. Instead of giving priority to courses that were more likely—but certainly no guarantee—to cultivate the use of reason, contemplation, and discourse as instruments for achieving order, "nuts and bolts" courses took precedence. RCPD and the state might have believed that education was necessary for the development of a well-rounded police officer, but unlike the professions that they try to emulate, the quality of their education was essentially vocational.

Esprit de Corps

Even with the vocational orientation in the police science curriculum, the recruit was taught that he was more professional than the members of the classical professions of medicine, law, theology, and education. The police profession became the superprofession, one that overlapped with each of the elite professions but performed its job with more dedication. A tinge of self-righteousness ran throughout a lecture presented by a popular instructor which seemed to set the tone regarding professions for the duration of the session.

> I submit, too, gentlemen, that the average attorney is not as dedicated as the average law enforcer. When you get your gun, you are given the power of life and death. Not even the Supreme Court has that power. I submit to you that the legal attorney is guilty of moral prostitution—by that I mean he says one thing and means another. The 1920's showed how an attorney who could circumvent the law was hailed as successful—one who could twist a perhaps inept police testimony.

> The leading attorney is not F. Lee Bailey, but Mr. Foreman, who defended Candy and her nephew, who were in an incestuous relationship (but after seeing her picture, you could forgive him that) and who conspired in killing her husband. Yet Foreman got an acquittal. And I quote from Foreman after the trial, "My clients want freedom, not justice." It's rare when a police officer bastardizes the law, while I feel attorneys do, and Foreman succinctly stated their position. The public is very willing to retain the stereotype of the fat, slouchy policeman. We're trying to change that stereotype.

Now let's talk about medicine. Here again we take a profession which used to be dedicated to the citizenry turning to the cash register. One night you may have a grisly accident on Franklin Turnpike that turns your stomach, don't pick up a phone to call a doctor because you won't get one. Your first aid is what saves lives. If you and your first aid weren't there, he'd be in the morgue. The average physician here is making $40,000 clear. A number of med schools have even dropped giving the Oath of Hippocrates. Someone must have had a conscience and realized that it didn't apply to the present medical profession.

... We are bound to get some bad apples who smear the badge; what they do smears the badge of everybody across the country. Every profession has its cancers. How many of the clergy betray the cloth by going into sex? How many educators hide behind academia—the homosexuals who warp our children's minds? At least when *we* get a bad apple, we get rid of him.

The disparagement of the elite professions by the lecturer apparently found willing ears among the recruits, some of whom had their own stories about lawyers and doctors. As in the lecture, the lawyer was never given the benefit of the doubt: he connives to distort the law for his own selfish ends. Tales abounded about the lawyer who got his client off through a legal technicality. As for the doctor, recruits complained how useless it was to try to get a doctor to make a house call. One recruit who had been an ambulance driver recounted an experience of his at a hospital. He had brought a badly injured car accident victim into the emergency room. Because the victim was a "mess," the attendants walked by pretending not to see him. Finally, the driver grabbed a doctor and ordered him to take care of the injured man. "That's the way you have to talk to them," he finished.

Not only was law enforcement projected as the most noble and sincere profession, but the instructors increased recruit enthusiasm and professional distinctiveness by setting up their own department as a paradigm for other police departments.

If you stay with us, we can be the best—including Megopolis Department; they aren't so good. And with all due respect to those from Megopolis Department, all they have is size and strength; but they can't compare to us because we're professional, and we want to be professional about our job.

Recruits who came from other police departments confirmed the excellence of RCPD. From the first day of the training session, these recruits compared their departments unfavorably with Rurban County's. Several recruits from Megopolis Department referred to it as "the factory." One of them told me that 55 percent of the force would "love to leave Megopolis Department, but they are either overage or cannot afford the move." Another recruit remarked about a city policeman who gave up a soft job in order to stay on the beat. "He was really dedicated, that's very rare; out here, everyone is dedicated." Still another recruit explained, "We were told not to make any arrests. They kept trying to stop me, but I wouldn't. . . . We were told right off not to make any arrests, not to get involved."

Suburban County Police Department, contiguous to Rurban County, fared no better. "They accept false rumors and get rid of you. They back you up all right—with a knife in your back." And, "Jeff even went through Suburban Academy before he came here, but he quit; he saw right away that it was political. You never know where you stand."

In summary, the first steps taken by the staff and visiting lecturers seemed to be the construction of a feeling of specialness—a "we are best" syndrome. The law enforcer was not just equal to the professional with the most status, he was better. Professions were in a hierarchical relationship to one another with law enforcement at the apex. And within the law enforcement profession itself, RCPD was the best. The lateral relationship in which a professional is recognized as an expert in his respective area seems to characterize the "classical" professions because they are secure in their status. On the other hand, the insecure occupations such as law enforcement are too insecure and too competitive to feel comfortable in a lateral relationship, especially when they have not been recognized by those who have "arrived." To be told that the recruit would learn in 12 weeks what the lawyer had to know for his bar examinations reinforced these feelings of inequity. In the following section, the content of the "professional image" as it seemed to be defined to the recruit will be examined.

THE PROFESSIONAL IMAGE

The Physical Image

Once having established an espirit de corps, it remained for the instructors to teach the recruit to be a professional police officer. One way was to look the part. Great stress was placed on the recruit's physical appearance. At first, the emphasis was not apparent.

> We aren't going to inspect you today, but we expect you to always have a neat appearance. Shoes are to be shined. . . . Haircuts are preferred to be crew cuts; we aren't strict, but we won't tolerate long sideburns or pompadours.

The recruit soon learned that shined shoes were not enough: they had to be spit-shined on the toe at the very least. Even the recruit's leather equipment (holster, belt, handcuff case, and bullet case) had to be as close to a spit-shine as possible. The result was a patent leather look that seemed to contradict the recruit's image of himself as an officer of the law and as a man of action. Regular haircuts were not enough either. While the staff had said crew cuts were not required, the recruit found that they might just as well have been required.

On the other hand, the staff claimed that the requirements they placed on the recruits' physical appearance were necessary because "with fifty-four recruits, we don't have time to worry about a picayune thing like appearance." Judging from the amount of time the staff spent on inspections during the training session, however, appearance had to be more than a picayune matter. Shoes not only had to be polished, they had to be spit-shined. Haircuts could not only be neat, they had to be cut almost weekly. Uniforms not only had to be tidy, they had to be ironed after each day's use.

Surely the staff had other criteria in mind by which to evaluate a recruit's appearance than what it at first described as a "neat appearance." The stress on the recruit's dress habits was more than an expression of discipline although that, too, was involved. Nor could it be explained away as part of a hazing process characteristic of fraternal or military organizations as an essential part of their rites of passage.[6] For example, a staff member wrote me about this. He thought I might have missed the point of inspections: "The minute harassment was only designed to make the new man, who would be wearing the uniform for the first time, more conscious of his appearance." On a recognized and intended level he is, of course, correct. But on an unrecognized and unintended level, the attitude that seemed to be translated to the recruit was that a neat physical appearance was professional.

Appearance was not only an end in itself, that is, professional, but it was also a means to convince the public that a new breed of policeman was at its service. Whereas the "old style" cop might have been sloppy, overweight, and cigar smoking—the image associated with police corruption—the image of the new breed would replace the stereotype. As one instructor put it baldly, "Look sharp and impress the public." In spite of the instructors' insistence on a new breed of police officer, a few interesting incidents suggested that at times something resembling the old breed was still desirable.

The tenth day of the session, the staff selected several men from each of our two platoons. The recruits were to shout commands to their respective platoons, and the two who performed to the staff's satisfaction would become platoon sergeants. What struck me was that the recruit who became my platoon sergeant seemed to earn his position by booming Neanderthal grunts, for I never understood a command he gave. It was as if he were chosen on volume alone. Nevertheless, the "sharp appearance" and the deep voice of authority expressed a realistic need in the field. Said one instructor, "In this job if you don't look the part, forget it. You must project confidence. You are going to be put into an emergency situation sometime in your career, and you have to step in and take charge when everybody else is emotional." Thus, a large and necessary part of the emphasis on appearance seemed to be for its effect on the public.

The second incident occurred right after the completion of the first week of the session. During the night a severe snowstorm put the community into an official state of emergency. Protocol was for a recruit to call the academy 15 minutes before roll call if he would be late or absent during the day. Most recruits, including myself, had called up to find out if classes would be held that

---

[6]Sanford Dornbusch, "The Military Academy as an Assimilating Institution" *Social Forces*, 33 (May 1955), 316–321; Arnold Van Gennup, *Rites of Passage* (Chicago: University of Chicago Press, 1960); Frank W. Young, *Initiation Ceremonies* (New York: Bobbs-Merrill, 1965).

day. We were informed by Headquarters that classes were canceled. However, a few recruits had not checked about classes and had staunchly made the trip. For salary adjustments because of the cancellation, the pay for the missed day was to be applied to the day that a recruit would spend at the Communications Center during a weekend. Those recruits who had come to the academy in the aftermath of the storm and found the doors closed were to be paid in full for the day that they would spend at Communications.

The other recruits balked at the rewards granted to those who came to the academy (or at the punishment received for not coming). Their feeling was either that it was impossible to reach the academy and the matter was out of their hands, or that they would have come to the academy if classes had met. Nevertheless, it was interesting that the department rewarded those recruits who did not have the foresight to call headquarters before leaving their homes, while those who did not bulldog their way to the academy were penalized. It became a question of which kind of recruit the department actually wanted: the one who would charge straight ahead impervious to the conditions surrounding him (as the brave but unthinking soldier assaulting a defended hill), or the one who would respond to a situation flexibly and with deliberation (supposedly a characteristic of the new breed). The department seemed to have opted for the "heroic" style.[7]

The Moral Image

The physical image seemed to be closely associated with the moral image, which connotes respectability, convention, piety, virtue, and honor. Physical appearance was used as an indicator of a person's place in the moral structure. A person who shaved each day, kept his hair short, shined his shoes regularly, and wore pressed clothes could be expected to be a respectable, law-abiding, and moral person. Conversely, those persons who grew beards, wore their hair long, and wore unkempt clothes—in short, those who deviated from convention—could be expected to connote something less than the moral.

> Kids want to be like adults in some ways. They want sex, but not the responsibilities that go with it . . . or I'll braid my hair for spite . . . So we want good appearances. Everything is going to look good.

Therefore, the recruit was told he was not allowed to grow sideburns, mustaches, or long hair because he had to "set an example" for the citizenry and because he would then offend fewer people. (I understand that the academy has since become more lax in this respect.)

Of course, there was a screening process that included an evaluation of how the investigators thought the candidate would project the new police image before he was admitted to RCPD. Only one recruit in the class had been given a decidedly unfavorable report during his precandidacy interview. His report read something like this: needed a shave, haircut, hair hanging over his ears and shirt collar [he had a "mod" haircut]; he lacked any kind of military bearing, slouching down in chair during interview; he lacked enthusiasm

---

[7]Morris Janowitz, *The Professional Soldier* (New York: The Free Press, 1960), p. 21.

shown by other candidates. Although his appearance obviously did not disqualify him, and he did have an opportunity to "prove" himself, it is interesting that his hair style and mannerisms during the interview were questionable in the eyes of the interviewers. In contrast, candidates from other law enforcing agencies had the following remark of approval: he has the background that indicates he can adjust to police work well. There was no further elaboration; the fact that the applicant had some previous police experience made him a suitable candidate. The former recruit, however, did not have the image that the department hoped to project to the public; he looked too unconventional for them. Ironically, I thought he was one of the few recruits who believed in and tried to conform to the "new image" beyond surface manifestations.

While this aspect of the moral image may be offensive to some readers, it nevertheless exists and has a bearing on police behavior. No instructor, no staff member, and no recruit ever explicitly stated that a person's physical appearance was a sign of his moral worth. But inferences can be and were made based on comments regarding the unconventionally attired. No instructor made a positive or accepting statement about the unconventionally dressed; only two recruits verbalized their tolerance for such persons. Furthermore, it seemed to be the general consensus that people with long hair or a beard, for example, deserved a different quality of law enforcement than their opposites. Here, then, is another example of a process and relationship that may not have been intended or recognized but did exist and should be recognized.

Integrity, the capacity to be honest with oneself and with others, was the second component of the moral image as it seemed to be presented to the recruit. "Without integrity you cannot be a professional." The recruit seemed to think he had this quality: that was one reason why he entered law enforcement. Consequently, he resented persons in the elite professions who did not always display moral characters, yet apparently had a monopoly of high salaries and prestige. The police officer was only trying to do his job, what the people hired him to do, but all he seemed to find were stumbling blocks in his path. The doctor, lawyer, clergyman, and educator did not seem to fulfill their jobs with as much personal sacrifice and moral discipline as the policeman did, yet the public refused to treat him as a professional. To the recruit, the disparity of rewards seemed unjust. The righteous indignation directed toward the elite professions increased his feeling of moral superiority. This feeling of superiority seemed to serve as a basis for an in-group identity that was continuously set off against the implied moral inferiority of various out-groups. In his envy of the elite professions, he deprecated them and thereby bolstered his own self-image.

The Courteous Image

Professionalism included what a patrolman *did* as well as how he looked.

> Every person who walks in the precinct is entitled at that moment to your undivided attention—whether he is green, a Buddhist, or an atheist. We are going to expose you to the worst kind of treatment, and how you handle it will determine whether you're a professional or just another policeman.

Various reasons were given to the recruit as to why he should behave courteously. One of these reasons was defensive. That is, one should be courteous because the public generalizes from the behavior of one policeman to every policeman in the nation. The department and recruit seemed to resent this necessity for being defensive, since they considered themselves professionals of good moral character. Apparently, anybody could be discourteous to a policeman, but he in turn could not be. "But how you respond to this is what makes the difference between a professional or unprofessional." Hearing this, the recruit responded, "What about our side, don't they care about us?"

Another reason offered to the recruit for acting courteously was that the way a patrolman presented himself could aid him in performing his duties with the least amount of trouble.[8]

> Treat lovers nice. There's no reason to bust their balls. Because they don't forget it. Today we have to use professionalization. Give them time to adjust themselves if you suspect any hanky-panky.

Thus, as one's physical appearance seemed to be identified with professionalism, courtesy was also.

The community itself seemed to support politeness, self-control, and deference as definitions of professionalism. During a sit-in at State University, the police department was commended by community newspapers for its "professional" behavior. Deans, professors, and police officials kept the situation cool and persuaded most of the demonstrators to leave the building. The few students who remained were arrested and escorted out without harshness or bodily harm. The police department was praised for "looking good," they "looked like professionals."

The professional image, then, had three components: appearance, morality, and demeanor. Although these components were defined as ends in themselves, for the most part, the rationale for them seemed to be expediency.

THE PROFESSIONAL IMAGE AND THE CLASSROOM

The Teaching-Learning Situation

Modes of teaching and learning in the classroom offered further insights into the image that the instructors hoped the recruit would inculcate. The classroom situation is particularly important to discuss, since it was there that the recruit spent most of his day. The typical classroom situation seemed to be based on the traditional setting in which a teacher talked and students quietly listened at their desks. Even the goals of the classes seemed to parallel those of the traditional style of training—the accumulation of subject matter and the memorization of facts. In addition, the assumption of discipline usually

---

[8]Erving Goffman, "The Nature of Deference and Demeanor," *Interaction Ritual* (Chicago: Aldine, 1967), pp. 57–95, and *The Presentation of Self in Everyday Life* (Garden City, N.Y.: Doubleday, 1959), pp. 104 and 217, discuss the role of courtesy as a basis for normal face-to-face interaction.

associated with the "old guard" classroom setting was in evidence. Explained one instructor to the class:

> We harass you because we know the requirements you need. . . . We are trying to develop objective people who can think situations through . . . we have to impose our authority on you to get you to know how to respond to situations and rationally deal with a situation.

Discipline was not only a necessary force for the cultivation of rationality and objectivity; it also seemed to be a necessary force for motivating the recruit to learn his lessons. "I'm sorry we have to bear down on you, but we have to watch over you like this in order for this training to have an impact on you."

The instructors might not have been too far off the mark when they assumed the recruit needed an external source of authority. Perhaps the recruit accepted his relatively passive role in the classroom because he placed little worth in "book learning."[9] If the recruit participated in lectures at all, it was usually to ask questions of clarification. When instructors extended their classes into the coffee break time, he became noticeably restless and squirmed noisily in his seat in order to politely indicate that they were going beyond their "allotted" time.

To the recruit it seemed that on-the-job training was more practical than classroom learning: one learns by doing, not by listening. He appeared wary of the scholar who might perform well in the classroom but who would be unable to be depended on in field situations. Lectures that offered practical tools for police work were valued (such as role plays, law, and how to effect a legal arrest), but lectures that seemed unrelated to the necessities of field work were ignored. Indeed, most of the recruits seemed to think that they learned more about police work in one week of field experience than in the previous six weeks of classes, as the following statements indicate.

> You find out that what you learn in the academy isn't so; it's a waste of time.

> I learned more on the precinct in one week than I did here.

> I'm glad I saw how things were really done. If we followed the book, we'd never make any arrests.

To what extent these statements reflected the recruit's true attitudes regarding academy training is debatable. To give an outward sign that the academy did not fit into the needs of the officer in the field seemed acceptable among the recruits; perhaps it was even expected by them. In contrast, when he was alone, a recruit told me, "I know I wouldn't like to go straight on the job without some background." And when I passed out a questionnaire asking the recruits to evaluate their training for field work, 31 of the 52 recruits who filled them out gave positive responses; thus, one should be cautious in forming any generalizations.

---

[9]Joseph Kadish, "Mental Health Training of the Police," *Mental Hygiene*, 50 (April 1966), 205–211.

If the recruit was biased against classroom training, some of the instructors, though by no means typical, seemed to be also. However, the recruit tended to accept their comments as being more realistic than those of the majority of instructors.

> . . . don't worry about that now. Wait till you get out of the academy. In here, we stick by the book.

> There are tricks of the trade we can't teach you in the academy, but you'll learn them.

These sparse comments seemed to have such an impact on the recruit that he believed that many of his classes were either irrelevant or misrepresentative, for example, Community Relations classes. It appeared that the recruit perceived the academy program as an initial phase of training that he would have to tolerate for a few months.

If he was expected to sit quietly for six or seven hours a day, the recruit seemed to feel that the instructors should, at least, make their lectures entertaining. The need for a gimmick was recognized by one recruit who said, pointing to an instructor:

> Doesn't he look like Jonathan Winters? Look at the way he walks. He's really funny. All he'd have to say was "Hello," "Good-bye" [he accompanied the words with the comedian's mannerisms], and he'd have the whole class listening to what he says. Here he comes; look at the way he walks.

Here, at least, the staff and most of the instructors seemed to agree with the recruit: a gimmick was needed for each class if the recruits were to pay attention to them. There were two general techniques that they used to capture the interest of the recruit. Sexual jokes during the lecture was one technique. Hardly a lecture went by without some off-color joke. A second method used by instructors who accompanied their lectures with slides was to intersperse the slide collection with pictures of nudes. As the nudes flicked across the screen, the recruit's attentiveness, shifting positions, and craning neck contrasted sharply with his earlier sedateness.

In addition to the more general techniques, a few lecturers tried to motivate the class to learn their material in more specific ways. Often it was said that the knowledge in question would protect the recruit from embarrassment, departmental discipline, or lawsuits once he left the academy. For example, in a lecture on arrests, the recruit was admonished with:

> Baby, you better learn this, or your ass will be in the sling! . . . If you don't know the elements of the law, you'll end up looking like a fool or even lose your case.

More notable were the department's formal incentives to encourage the recruit to perform well during academy training. The awards sponsored by police organizations such as the Detectives Association and the Police Brotherhood Association were established specifically to induce "professionalization" among the recruits. An off-duty gun worth $60, required of all departmental members, was presented at graduation to each of the two recruits with the highest overall average in the academy written examinations and to the recruit with the highest firearms average score. The recruit with the second highest firearms average received a $25 savings bond. A $500 scholarship toward tuition for a police science degree was awarded to the recruit selected by the staff for his all-around excellence.

Interestingly, three of the five prizes awarded, in the words of the staff, to "encourage professionalization" were revolvers—especially since the revolver appeared to be an important symbol of the police image for the recruit. During the first day of the session, the recruit was warned, "If you can't shoot a gun, you shouldn't be here." Of all the skills necessary in police work, it was the officer's marksmanship that was periodically evaluated throughout his career. If an officer lost his accuracy, he lost his right to be a policeman. "You must be checked out with firearms once a year, and occasionally we have to drop somebody for this."

Thus it seemed that the intellectual competence image of the policeman was superseded by an action image. While the recruit wore weaponry within two weeks of the session, the training was two-thirds over before he received his wallet-sized card with the Miranda warnings. One instructor remarked, "They give you a gun but not [the Miranda cards]. Well, people like to see a police officer with a gun." Unfortunately, then, the public also identifies the gun with the policeman. In any case, perhaps the department was expressing in another unrecognized way through its training methods the kind of image it really had in mind when it claimed to be developing professional police officers.

Ethic of Masculinity

As in many predominantly male occupations, there were ribald jokes, profanities, and boasts about sexual encounters throughout the academy session. However, it appeared that these displays of masculinity went beyond mere joking, swearing, and boasting. They seemed to show to the recruit that he was, indeed, among men and thereby testified to his own manhood. The phrase "ethic of masculinity" refers to the apparent need of the recruit to confirm his masculine image to others and to himself by exaggerating the characteristics associated with manhood. These characteristics include physical and sexual prowess, courage, profanity, and aggression toward authority.[10]

The man-of-action image, emanating from the ethic of masculinity, seemed to be an important but implicit component of the professional image. The recruit seemed to perceive the police officer as a man of action with the emphasis both on the *man* of action and the man of *action*. A police officer was physically strong, virile, and courageous. Less inclined to depend on persuasion through discourse, he would rely on physical force. Not afraid of dangerous work, his code of loyalty included putting his life "on the line" in order to

---

[10]Jackson Toby. "Violence and the Masculine Ideal: Some Qualitative Data," *Annals*, 364 (March 1966), 19–27.

help a fellow officer. The recruit who did not manifest the man-of-action image was not as highly esteemed by his fellow classmates, and he certainly was not accessible to the inner circles.

In one case in particular, the recruit class expressed disapproval when it thought some fellow recruits were rejecting the image of the policeman as a man of action. It occurred after an announcement that the class was to participate in a murder investigation. This was the first opportunity the class had had to leave the classroom situation for "real" police work. However, the academy staff needed six men to remain behind to help move some furniture. The reaction of the group as the volunteers left ranks was a friendly but critical hissing as if the six men were not making the proper response as police officers.

Sometimes the image of the officer in action had its humorous spots. One example occurred when an alert recruit became suspicious (over a weekend).

> I was parked in my car when I saw a man slink along the side of the drug store and then turn and go around the back. Thinking I was on to something, I got out and went around the other side. The guy was taking a leak!

The second incident occurred during Field Week. The sergeant asked if anybody had a family call during his tour of duty. About ten hands went up, and a voice spoke softly, "I responded to one call; I ran around the back [of the house] and the dog got me."

In contrast, the police academy image, in which a recruit passively sits at his desk while listening to a lecturer and whose spit-shined leatherwork turns him into a "patent leather soldier," ran against the grain of the recruit. To be a "good" recruit implied a docility and childlike conformity that contradicted the man-of-action image. Consequently, the recruit rejected, through subtle acts of rebellion, the image intentionally or unintentionally defined by the academy. During drill a recruit pushed the man in front of him, who almost collided with the recruit in front of him. One recruit pulled out the back of another recruit's shirt while still another recruit grabbed someone else's memo book and let it drop to the floor. During inspection, ties were pulled off and shirts were pulled out. Instead of running through riot exercises, some recruits danced or walked whenever the instructor's back was turned. Class breaks and lunch hour afforded more time for the men to pull off ties and pull out memo books or blackjacks from otherwise smartly dressed recruits. Once someone placed a blackjack in my empty holster (I was never allowed to carry police weaponry), which I interpreted as a show of disdain for the police academy image.[11] Manliness, then, may also have involved a defiance against leaders and authority; for total conformity meant that one surrendered his freedom to act as an individual.

Physical prowess was esteemed as part of the man-of-action image. On the other hand, mental action seemed not to be defined as action at all, since more

---

[11]These behaviors may be aptly applied to Erving Goffman's concept of role distance in *Encounters* (Indianapolis: Bobbs-Merrill, 1961), pp. 84–152.

prestige was attached to performing well on the pistol range and playing football during coffee breaks than to doing well on written examinations on class lectures. In fact, my willingness and capacity to play football contributed toward my acceptance as a "regular guy." As one recruit remarked to me as we played football during a lunch period, "When you first came, I thought you were a canary-ass brain—you know, those smart guys."

Off-color jokes, profanity, and stories heard or experienced in the military or in police work were typical of many group discussions. The jokes, the use of profanity, and the tales about sexual encounters seemed to confirm the manhood of the recruit. It appeared important for a recruit to confirm his masculinity by contributing some jokes of his own, but lacking these, he should laugh robustly with those recruits who did. In each case, ribald jokes were aggressive toward someone or something, usually an out-group. Many times a police officer was the protagonist, in which case the male made his conquest. Male protagonists who were not policemen turned out to be naive, stupid, or cuckolds.

> You ever hear about the guy who always wanted to be a cop? He could never pass a test, so he bought a uniform and whistle. He's having fun until a broad asks him for directions, but she asks him to get into the car. He gets in, and she strips—she's got a pair of 44's. . . . "Go ahead," she says, "touch 'em." "Uh, there's just one thing lady, I ain't a real cop."

Conversations, such as the following, never failed to draw a group of attentive recruits. "Experienced recruits," those who had served in other police departments, shared some of their encounters with females in the past—all in the line of duty. In this example, several recruits were discussing their experiences patrolling areas of parked lovers.

> R₁: He [his partner] was a fucking sadist. He'd wait until they were stripped, and then he'd rush up and pull them out of the car. He was really a sadist.
>
> R₂: We'd wait till dark, and then we would go around hoping to catch some couple.
>
> R₃: I know a guy who used to crawl into the ventilating units of the toilets. . . .

The "raw recruits" offered stories heard from their brothers or friends who were police officers or who were themselves abused with their dates. For instance, one recruit claimed that his brother found a parked couple heavily petting. After he comically illustrated how the couple must have tried to cover themselves, he said his brother began questioning them and then chatting with them. After a while, the boy fell asleep, so his brother and the half-naked girl went to the patrol car where he remained with her for most of the night. The listening recruits dreamily sighed to each other as they possibly envisioned themselves in similar circumstances. At the very least, they expressed the enviable position in which this recruit's brother had found himself.

The acting out of the ethic of masculinity may indicate why police officers tend to react personally to an affront on police authority. It would seem that an officer would be less likely to react to disrespect personally if he feels secure with himself. Concomitantly, it would be those officers least secure in their masculine image who are prone to react violently to perceived threats to their masculinity. Thus, while William Westley suggests that violence by police officers emerges when they perceive threats to their authority, he does not appear to go far enough.[12] What people may be doing when they challenge an officer's authority is to challenge his masculinity which he, in part, identifies with authority and respect.

Dirty workers probably place as much esteem on their occupations as do other members of the community. Although some dirty workers see their work as a calling, I suspect that most know that they are doing dirty work. Some may try to romanticize their work, but underneath their bravado may be resentment about their work and an envy of "clean" workers. Certainly this was true among the police recruits. Consequently, the dirty worker, in his low self-esteem, may embrace the ethic of masculinity, but *not* necessarily because he is insecure about his manhood. Rather he embraces it because, if he is nothing else, he is at least a man. Many men can rationalize away their limitations, their subservience, and their lack of prestige, but few can calmly ignore threats or ridicules about their masculinity.

In the case of the recruit, the public may have defined his total identity as "cop," as dirty worker. But the recruit seemed to be saying through his ethic of masculinity that while he was indeed a "cop," it was only a subidentity. First and foremost, he was a man. The recruit and dirty worker exaggeration of masculine characteristics may merely be an affirmation that although they do someone else's dirty work, they are still men.

---

[12]William A. Westley, "Violence and the Police," *American Journal of Sociology,* 49 (August 1953), 34–41. See also, Arthur E. Hippler, "The Game of Black and White at Hunters Point," *Trans-Action,* 7 (April 1970), 56–63.

Observations on the
Making of Policemen

*John Van Maanen**

In recent years the so-called "police problem" has become one of the more in-stitutionalized topics of routine conversation in this society. Whether one views the police as friend or foe, virtually everyone has a set of "cop stories" to relate to willing listeners. Although most stories dramatize personal encounters and are situation-specific, there is a common thread running through these fre-quently heard accounts. In such stories the police are almost always depicted as a homogeneous occupational grouping somehow quite different from most other men.

Occupational stereotyping is, of course, not unknown. Professors, taxicab drivers, used-car salesmen, corporate executives all have mythological coun-terparts in the popular culture. Yet, what is of interest here is the recognition by the police themselves of the implied differences.

Policemen generally view themselves as performing society's dirty work. As such, a gap is created between the police and the public. Today's patrolman feels cut off from the mainstream culture and unfairly stigmatized. In short, when the policeman dons his uniform, he enters a distinct subculture governed by norms and values designed to manage the strain created by an outsider role in the community.[1]

To classify the police as outsiders helps us to focus on several important things: the distinctive social definitions used by persons belonging to such marginal subcultures (e.g., "everybody hates a cop"); the outsider's methods for managing the tension created by his social position (e.g., "always protect brother officers"); and the explicit delineation of the everyday standards of

*I would like to gratefully acknowledge the generous cooperation and support of men like M.C., Dave, Doug, Leon, and Jim, who, like myself, learned what it means to live by the police culture. Their integrity, honesty, and defiance of popular stereotypes made this study a most enlightening and enjoyable experience. Also, I would like to thank my academic colleagues, in particular, Edgar H. Schein, Lyman W. Porter, Robert Dubin, and Mason Haire for their insightful suggestions and assistance during various phases of this research. Finally, I wish to express my appreciation to the Office of Naval Research, the Organizational Behavior Research Center at the University of California, Irvine, and the Organizational Studies Group at the Massachusetts Institute of Technol-ogy for partial support and total encouragement throughout this project.

[1]The use of the term "outsider" in the above context is not intended to invidiously portray the police. Rather, the term simply connotes the widespread conviction carried by the police themselves that they are, of necessity, somehow different, and set-off from the larger society. To most police observers, isolationism, secrecy, strong in-group loyalties sacred symbols, common language, and a sense of estrangement are almost axiomatic subcultural features underpinning a set of common understandings among police in general which govern their relations with one another as well as with civilians. (Bayley and Mendelsohn, 1969; President's Commission, 1967; Skolnick, 1966). Such a perspective emphasizes the necessity to view the world from the eyes of the outsider—a perspective which ideally is empathetic but neither sympathetic or judgmental.

REPRINTED FROM: *Human Organization.* 32 1973 (407–418).

conduct followed by the outsider (e.g., "lay low and avoid trouble"). Further-more, such a perspective forces a researcher to delve deeply into the subculture in order to see clearly through the eyes of the studied.

CONTEXT

While observation of the police in naturally occurring situations is difficult, lengthy, and often threatening, it is imperative. Unfortunately, most research to date relies almost exclusively upon interview-questionnaire data (e.g., Bayley and Mendelsohn 1969; Wilson 1968), official statistics (e.g., Webster 1970; President's Commission on Law Enforcement and the Administration of Justice 1967), or broad-ranging attitude surveys (e.g., Sterling 1972; McNa-mara 1967). The very few sustained observational studies have been concerned with specific aspects of police behavioral patterns (e.g., Skolnick 1966—vice ac-tivities; Reiss 1971—police-citizen contacts; Bittner 1967, Cicourel 1967 police encounters with "skid row alcoholics" and juveniles, respectively). This is not to say these diverse investigations are without merit. Indeed, without such studies we would not have even begun to see beneath the occupational shield. Yet, the paucity of in-depth police-related research—especially from the outsider perspective—represents a serious gap in our knowledge of a criti-cal social establishment.[2]

In particular the process of becoming a police officer has been neglected.[3] What little data we presently have related to the police socialization process come from either the work devoted to certain hypothesized dimensions of the police personality (e.g., dogmatism, authoritarianism, cynicism, alienation, etc.) or cross-sectional snapshots of police attitudes toward their public audi-ences. Using a dramaturgic metaphor, these studies have concentrated upon the description of the actors, stage setting, and "on stage" performance of the police production. Little attention has been paid to the orientation of the per-formers to their particular role viewed from "backstage" perspective. Clearly, for any performance to materialize there must be casting sessions, rehearsals, directors, stagehands, and some form(s) of compensation provided the actors to insure their continued performance. Recognizing that to some degree organi-zational socialization occurs at all career stages, this paradigm focuses exclu-sively upon the individual recruit's entry into the organization. It is during the breaking-in period that the organization may be thought to be most persua-sive, for the person has few guidelines to direct his behavior and has little, if

---

[2]If one takes seriously research findings regarding esoteric subcultures, social scientists interested in police behavior are limited in their choice of methodological strategy. If we are to gain insight into the so-called police problem, researchers must penetrate the official smoke screen sheltering virtually all departments and observe directly the social action in social situations which, in the last analysis, defines police work.

[3]One exception is Westley's (1951) insightful observational study of a midwestern police department. However, his research was devoted mainly to the description of the more salient sociological features of the police occupation and was concerned only peripherally with the learning process associated with the police role.

any, organizationally based support for his "vulnerable selves" which may be the object of influence. Support for this position comes from a wide range of studies indicating that early organizational learning is a major determinant of one's later organizationally relevant beliefs, attitudes, and behaviors (Van Maanen 1972; Lortie 1968; Berlew and Hall 1966; Evan 1963; Hughes 1958; Dornbush 1955). Schein (1971) suggested perceptively that this process results in a "psychological contract" linking the goals of the individual to the constraints and purposes of the organization. In a sense, this psychological contract is actually a modus vivendi between the person and the organization representing the outcomes of the socialization process.

METHOD

The somewhat truncated analysis that follows was based upon the observation of novice policemen in situ. The study was conducted in Union City over a nine-month period.[4] Approximately three months of this time were spent as a fully participating member of one Union City Police Academy recruit class. Following the formal training phase of the initiation process, my fully participating role was modified. As a civilian, I spent five months (roughly eight to ten hours a day, six days a week) riding in patrol units operated by a recruit and his FTO (i.e., Field Training Officer charged with imputing "street sense" into the neophyte) as a back-seat observer.

From the outset, my role as researcher-qua-researcher was made explicit. To masquerade as a regular police recruit would not only have been problematic, but would have raised a number of ethical questions as well (particularly during the field training portion of the socialization sequence).[5]

The conversational data presented below are drawn primarily from naturally occurring encounters with persons in the police domain (e.g., recruits, veterans, administrators, wives, friends, reporters, court officials, etc.). While formal interviews were conducted with some, the bulk of the data contained

---

[4]Union City is a pseudonym for a sprawling metropolitan area populated by more than a million people. The police department employs well over 1,500 uniformed officers, provides a salary above the national average, and is organized in the classic pyramidal arrangement (see Van Maanen, 1972). Based on interviews with police personnel from a number of different departments and, most importantly, critical readings of my work by policemen from several departments, the sequence of events involved in recruit socialization appears to be remarkably similar from department to department. This structural correspondence among recruit training programs has been noted by others (see Ahern, 1972; Berkeley, 1969; Neiderhoffer, 1967).

[5]While it cannot be stated categorically that my presence had little effect upon the behavior of the subjects, I felt I was accepted completely as a regular group member in my particular police academy class and little or no behavior was (or, for that matter, could be) altered explicitly. Furthermore, the lengthy, personal, and involving nature of my academy experiences produced an invaluable carry-over effect when I moved to the street work portion of the study. The importance of continuous observation and full participation as an aid for minimizing distortions and behavior change on the part of social actors has been strikingly demonstrated by a number of social scientists (e.g., see Whyte, 1943; Becker, 1963; Dalton, 1964; Greer, 1964; and, most recently, Schatzman and Strauss, 1973).

here arose from far less-structured situations. (See Epilogue for a further discussion of the methods employed in this study— eds.)

THE MAKING OF A POLICEMAN: A PARADIGM

For purposes here, the police recruit's initiation into the organizational setting shall be treated as if it occurred in four discrete stages. While these stages are only analytically distinct, they do serve as useful markers for describing the route traversed by the recruit. The sequence is related to the preentry, admittance, change, and continuance phases of the organizational socialization process and are labeled here as choice, introduction, encounter, and metamorphosis, respectively.

Preentry: Choice

What sort of young man is attracted to and selected for a police career? The literature notes that police work seems to attract local, family-oriented, working-class whites interested primarily in the security and salary aspects of the occupation. Importantly, the authoritarian syndrome which has popularly been ascribed to persons selecting police careers has not been supported by empirical study. The available research supports the contention that the police occupation is viewed by the recruits as simply one job of many and considered roughly along the same dimensions as any job choice.

While my research can add little to the above picture, several qualifications are in order which perhaps provide a greater understanding of the particular choice process. First, the security and salary aspects of the police job have probably been overrated. Through interviews and experience with Union City recruits, a rather pervasive meaningful work theme is apparent as a major factor in job choice. Virtually all recruits alluded to the opportunity afforded by a police career to perform in a role which was perceived as consequential or important to society. While such altruistic motives may be subject to social desirability considerations, or other biasing factors, it is my feeling that these high expectations of community service are an important element in the choice process.

Second, the out-of-doors and presumably adventurous qualities of police work (as reflected in the popular culture) were perceived by the recruits as among the more influential factors attracting them to the job. With few exceptions, the novice policemen had worked several jobs since completing high school and were particularly apt to stress the benefits of working a nonroutine job.

Third, the screening factor associated with police selection is a dominating aspect of the socialization process. From the filling out of the application blank at City Hall to the telephone call which informs a potential recruit of his acceptance into the department, the individual passes through a series of events which serve to impress an aspiring policeman with a sense of being accepted into an elite organization. Perhaps some men originally take the qualifying examination for patrolman lightly, but it is unlikely many men proceed through the entire screening process—often taking up to six months or more—without becoming committed seriously to a police career. As such, the various selection devices, if successfully surmounted, increase the person's self-esteem, as well as buttress his occupational choice. Thus, this anticipatory stage tends to strengthen the neophyte's evaluation of the police organization as an important place to work.

Finally, as in most organizations, the police department is depicted to individuals who have yet to take the oath of office in its most favorable light. A potential recruit is made to feel as if he were important and valued by the organization. Since virtually all recruitment occurs via generational or friendship networks involving police officers and prospective recruits, the individual receives personalized encouragement and support which helps sustain his interest during the arduous screening procedure. Such links begin to attach the would-be policeman to the organization long before he actually joins.

To summarize, most policemen have not chosen their career casually. They enter the department with a high degree of normative identification with what they perceive to be the goals and values of the organization. At least in Union City, the police department was able to attract and select men who entered the organization with a reservoir of positive attitudes toward hard work and a strong level of organizational support. What happens to the recruit when he is introduced to the occupation at the police academy is where attention is now directed.

Admittance: Introduction

The individual usually feels upon swearing allegiance to the department, city, state, and nation that "he's finally made it." However, the department instantaneously and somewhat rudely informs him that until he has served his probationary period he may be severed from the membership rolls at any time without warning, explanation, or appeal. It is perhaps ironic that in a period of a few minutes, a person's position vis-à-vis the organization can be altered so dramatically. Although some aspects of this phenomenon can be found in all organizations, in the paramilitary environment of the police world, the shift is particularly illuminating to the recruit.

For most urban police recruits, the first real contact with the police subculture occurs at the academy. Surrounded by forty to fifty contemporaries, the recruit is introduced to the harsh and often arbitrary discipline of the organization. Absolute obedience to departmental rules, rigorous physical training, dull lectures devoted to various technical aspects of the occupation, and a ritualistic concern for detail characterize the academy. Only the recruit's classmates aid his struggle to avoid punishments and provide him an outlet from the long days. A recruit soon learns that to be one minute late to a class, to utter a careless word in formation, or to be caught walking when he should be running may result in a "gig" or demerit costing a man an extra day of work or the time it may take to write a long essay on, say, "the importance of keeping a neat appearance."

Wearing a uniform which distinguishes the novices from "real" policemen, recruits are expected to demonstrate group cohesion in all aspects of academy life. The training staff actively promotes solidarity through the use of group rewards and punishments, identifying garments for each recruit class, inter-class competition, and cajoling the newcomers—at every conceivable opportunity—to show some unity. Predictably, such tactics work — partial evidence is suggested by the well-attended academy class reunions held year after year in the department. To most veteran officers, their police academy experiences resulted in a career-long source of identification. It is no exaggera-tion to state that the "in-the-same-boat" collective consciousness which arises when groups are processed serially through a harsh set of experiences was as refined in the Union City Police Department as in other institutions such as military academies, fraternities, or medical schools.[6]

The formal content of the training academy is almost exclusively weighted in favor of the more technical aspects of police work. A few outside speakers are invited to the academy (usually during the last few weeks of training), but the majority of class time is filled by departmental personnel describing the more mundane features of the occupation. To a large degree, the formal acad-emy may be viewed as a didactic sort of instrumentally oriented ritual passage rite. As such, feigning attention to lectures on, for example, "the organization of the Administrative Services Bureau" or "state and local traffic codes" is a major task for the recruits.

However, the academy also provides the recruit with an opportunity to begin learning or, more properly, absorbing the tradition which typifies the department. The novices' overwhelming eagerness to hear what police work is really like results in literally hours upon hours of war stories (alternately called "sea stories" by a few officers) told at the discretion of the many instruc-tors. One recruit, when asked about what he hoped to learn in the academy, responded as follows:

> I want them to tell me what police work is all about. I could care less about the outside speakers or the guys they bring out here from upstairs who haven't been on the street for the last twenty years. What I want is for somebody who's gonna level with us and really give the lowdown on how we're supposed to survive out there.

By observing and listening closely to police stories and style, the indi-vidual is exposed to a partial organizational history which details certain per-sonalities, past events, places, and implied relationships which the recruit is expected eventually to learn, and it is largely through war stories that the de-partment's history is conveyed. Throughout the academy, a recruit is exposed to particular instructors who relate caveats concerning the area's notorious criminals, sensational crimes, social-geographical peculiarities, and political structure. Certain charismatic departmental personalities are described in de-

---

[6]Significantly, a recruit is not even allowed to carry a loaded weapon during the classroom portion of his academy training. He must wait until graduation night before being permitted to load his weapon. To the recruit, such policies are demeaning. Yet, the policies "stigmatizing" the recruits-as-recruits (e.g., different uniforms, old and battered batons, allocation of special parking spaces, special scarfs, and name plates) were exceedingly effective methods of impressing upon the recruits that they were members of a particular class and were not yet Union City Police Officers.

tail. Past events—notably the shooting of police officers—are recreated and informal analyses passed on. The following excerpt from a criminal law lecture illustrates some of these concerns.

> I suppose you guys have heard of Lucky Baldwin? If not, you sure will when you hit the street. Baldwin happens to be the biggest burglar still operating in this town. Every guy in this department from patrolman to chief would love to get him and make it stick. We've busted him about ten times so far, but he's got an asshole lawyer and money so he always beats the rap.... If I ever get a chance to pinch the SOB, I'll do it my way with my thirty-eight and spare the city the cost of a trial.

The correlates of this history are mutually held perspectives toward certain classes of persons, places, and things which are the objective reality of police work. Critically, when war stories are presented, discipline within the recruit class is relaxed. The rookies are allowed to share laughter and tension-relieving quips with the veteran officers. A general atmosphere of comraderie is maintained. The near lascivious enjoyment accompanying these informal respites from academy routine serve to establish congeniality and solidarity with the experienced officers in what is normally a rather harsh and uncomfortable environment. Clearly, this is the material of which memories are made.

Outside the classroom, the recruits spend endless hours discussing nuances and implications of war stories, and collective understandings begin to develop. Via such experiences, the meaning and emotional reality of police work starts to take shape for the individual. In a sense, by vicariously sharing the exploits of his predecessors, the newcomer gradually builds a common language and shared set of interests which will attach him to the organization until he too has police experience to relate.

Despite these important breaks in formality, the recruits' early perceptions of policing are overshadowed by the submissive and often degrading role they are expected to play in the academy. Long, monotonous hours of class time are required, a seemingly eternal set of examinations are administered, meaningless assignments consume valuable off-duty time, various mortifying events are institutionalized rituals of academy life (e.g., each week, a class "asshole" was selected and received a trophy depicting a gorilla dressed as a policeman), and relatively sharp punishments enacted for breaches of academy regulations. The multitude of academy rules make it highly unlikely that any recruit can complete the training course unscathed. The following training division report illustrates the arbitrary nature of the dreaded gigs issued during the academy phase.

> You were observed displaying unofficerlike conduct in an academy class. You openly yawned (without making any effort to minimize or conceal the fact), (this happened twice), you were observed looking out the window constantly, and spent time with your arms lying across your desk. You will report to Sergeant Smith in the communications division for an extra three hours of duty on August 15 (parentheses theirs).

The main result of such stress training is that the recruit soon learns it is his peer group rather than the "brass" which will support him and which he, in turn, must support. For example, the newcomers adopt covering tactics to shield the tardy colleague, develop cribbing techniques to pass exams, and become proficient at constructing consensual ad hoc explanations of a fellow-recruit's mistake. Furthermore, the long hours, new friends, and ordeal aspects of the recruit school serve to detach the newcomer from his old attitudes and acquaintances. In short, the academy impresses upon the recruit that he must now identify with a new group—his fellow officers. That this process is not complete, however, is illustrated by the experience of one recruit during this last week of training before his introduction to the street. This particular recruit told his classmates the following:

> Last night as I was driving home from the academy, I stopped to get some gas. . . . As soon as I shut off the engine some dude comes running up flapping his arms and yelling like crazy about being robbed. Here I am sitting in my car with my gun on and the ole buzzer (badge) staring him right in the face. . . . Wow! . . . I had no idea what to do; so I told him to call the cops and got the hell away from there. What gets me is that it didn't begin to hit me that I WAS A COP until I was about a mile away (emphasis mine).

To this researcher, the academy training period serves to prepare the recruits to alter their initially high but unrealistic occupational expectations. Through the methods described above, the novices begin to absorb the subcultural ethos and to think like policemen. As a fellow recruit stated at the end of the academy portion of training:

> There's sure more to this job than I first thought. They expect us to be dog catchers, lawyers, marriage counselors, boxers, firemen, doctors, baby-sitters, race-car drivers, and still catch a crook occasionally. There's no way we can do all that crap. They're nuts!

Finally, as in other highly regulated social systems, the initiate learns that the formal rules and regulations are applied inconsistently. What is sanctioned in one case with a gig is ignored in another case. To the recruits, academy rules become behavioral prescriptions which are to be coped with formally, but informally dismissed. The newcomer learns that when The Department notices his behavior, it is usually to administer a punishment, not a reward. The solution to this collective predicament is to stay low and avoid trouble.

Change: Encounter

Following the classroom training period, a newcomer is introduced to the complexities of the "street" through his Field Training Officer (hereafter referred to as the FTO). It is during this period of apprenticeshiplike socialization that the reality shock encompassing full recognition of being a policeman is likely to occur. Through the eyes of his experienced FTO, the recruit learns the ins and outs of the police role. Here he learns what kinds of behavior are appropriate and expected of a patrolman within his social setting. His other instructors in this phase are almost exclusively his fellow patrolmen working the same precinct and shift. While his sergeant may occasionally offer tips on how to handle himself on the street, the supervisor is more notable for his absence than for his presence. When the sergeant does seek out the recruit, it is probably to inquire as to how many hazardous traffic violations the "green pea" had written that week or to remind the recruit to keep his hat on while out of the patrol car. As a matter of formal policy in Union City, the department expected the FTO to handle all recruit uncertainties. This traditional feature of police work—patrolmen training patrolmen—insures continuity from class to class of police officers regardless of the content of the academy instruction. In large measure, the flow of influence from one generation to another accounts for the remarkable stability of the pattern of police behavior.

It was my observation that the recruit's reception into the Patrol Division was one of consideration and warm welcome. As near as interviewing and personal experience can attest, there was no hazing or rejection of the recruit by veteran officers. In all cases, the recruits were fully accepted into the ongoing police system with good-natured tolerance and much advice. If anyone in the department was likely to react negatively to the recruits during their first few weeks on patrol, it was the supervisor and not the on-line patrolmen. The fraternal-like regard shown the rookie by the experienced officers stands in stark contrast to the stern greeting he received at the police academy. The newcomer quickly is bombarded with "street wise" patrolmen assuring him that the police academy was simply an experience all officers endure and has little, if anything, to do with real police work. Consequently, the academy experiences for the recruits stand symbolically as their rites de passage, permitting them access to the occupation. That the experienced officers confirm their negative evaluation of the academy heightens the assumed similarities among the rookies and veterans and serves to facilitate the recruit's absorption into the division. As an FTO noted during my first night on patrol:

> I hope the academy didn't get to you. It's something we all have to go through. A bunch of bullshit as far as I can tell. . . . Since you got through it all right, you get to find out what it's like out here. You'll find out mighty fast that it ain't nothing like they tell you at the academy.

During the protracted hours spent on patrol with his FTO, the recruit is instructed as to the real nature of police work. To the neophyte, the first few weeks on patrol is an extremely trying period. The recruit is slightly fearful and woefully ill-prepared for both the routine and eccentricities of real police work. While he may know the criminal code and the rudimentaries of arrest, the fledgling patrolman is perplexed and certainly not at ease in their application. For example, a two-day veteran told the following story to several of his academy associates.

> We were down under the bridge where the fags hang out and spot this car that looked like nobody was in it. . . . Frank puts the spot on it and two heads pop up. He tells me to watch what he does and keep my mouth

shut. So I follow him up to the car and just kind of stand around feeling pretty dumb. Frank gives 'em a blast of shit and tells the guy sitting behind the wheel he's under arrest. The punk gets out of the car snivelling and I go up to him and start putting the cuffs on. Frank says, "just take him back to the car and sit on him while I get the dope on his boyfriend here." So I kind of direct him back to the car and stick him in the backseat and I get in the front. . . . While Frank's filling out a FIR (Field Investigation Report) on the other guy, the little pansy in the backseat's carrying on about his wife and kids like you wouldn't believe. I'm starting to feel sorta sorry for arresting him. Anyway, Frank finishes filling out the FIR and tells the other guy to get going and if he ever sees him again he'll beat the holy shit out of him. Then he comes back to the car and does the same number on the other fag. After we drove away, I told Frank I thought we'd arrested somebody. He laughed his ass off and told me that that's the way we do things out here.

To a recruit, the whole world seems new, and from his novel point of view it is. Like a visitor from a foreign land, the daily events are perplexing and present a myriad of operational difficulties. At first, the squawk of the police radio transmits only meaningless static; the streets appear to be a maze through which only an expert could maneuver; the use of report forms seems inconsistent and confusing; encounters with a hostile public leave him cold and apprehensive; and so on. Yet, next to him in the patrol unit is his partner, a veteran. Hence, the FTO is the answer to most of the breaking-in dilemmas. It is commonplace for the rookie to never make a move without first checking with his FTO. By watching, listening, and mimicking, the neophyte policeman learns how to deal with the objects of his occupation—the traffic violator, the hippie, the drunk, the brass, and the criminal justice complex itself. One veteran reflected on his early patrol experiences as follows:

> On this job, your first partner is everything. He tells you how to survive on the job . . . how to walk, how to stand, and how to speak and how to think and what to say and see.

Clearly, it is during the FTO phase of the recruit's career that he is most susceptible to attitude change. The newcomer is self-conscious and truly in need of guidelines. A whole folklore of tales, myths, and legends surrounding the department is communicated to the recruit by his fellow officers—conspicuously by his FTO. Through these anecdotes—dealing largely with mistakes or "flubs" made by policemen—the recruit begins to adopt the perspectives of his more experienced colleagues. He becomes aware that nobody's perfect and, as if to reify his police academy experiences, he learns that to be protected from his own mistakes, he must protect others. One such yarn told to me by a two-year veteran illustrates this point.

> Grayson had this dolly he'd been balling for quite a while living over on the north side. Well, it seemed like a quiet night so we cruise out of our district and over to the girl's house. I baby-sit the radio while Grayson goes inside. Wouldn't you know it, we get an emergency call right away. . . . I start honking the horn trying to get the horny bastard out of there;

he pays me no mind, but the neighbors get kind of irritated at some cop
waking up the nine-to-fivers. Some asshole calls the station and pretty
soon Sparky and Jim show up to find out what's happening. They're cool
but their Sergeant ain't, so we fabricate this insane story 'bout Sparky's
girlfriend living there and how he always toots the horn when passing.
Me and Grayson beat it back to our district and show up about 45 minutes late on our call. Nobody ever found out what happened, but it sure
was close.

Critical to the practical learning process is the neophyte's own developing
repertoire of experiences. These events are normally interpreted to him by his
FTO and other veteran officers. Thus, the reality shock of being "in on the action" is absorbed and defined by the recruit's fellow officers. As a somewhat
typical example, one newcomer, at the prodding of his patrol partner, discovered that to explain police actions to a civilian invited disrespect. He
explained

Keith was always telling me to be forceful, to not back down and to never
try and explain the law or what we are doing to a civilian. I didn't really
know what he was talking about until I tried to tell some kid why we
have laws about speeding. Well, the more I tried to tell him about traffic
safety, the angrier he got. I was lucky to just get his John Hancock on the
citation. When I came back to the patrol car, Keith explains to me just
where I'd gone wrong. You really can't talk to those people out there,
they just won't listen to reason.

In general, the first month or so on the street is an exciting and rewarding
period for the recruit. For his FTO, however, it is a period of appraisal. While
the recruit is busy absorbing many novel experiences, his partner is evaluating the newcomer's reaction to certain situations. Aside from assisting the recruit with the routines of patrol work, the training officer's main concern is in
how the recruit will handle the "hot" or, in the contemporary language of the
recruits, the "heavy" call (i.e., the in-progress, or on-view, or help the officer
situation which the experienced officer knows may result in trouble). The
heavy call represents everything the policeman feels he is prepared for. In
short, it calls for police work. Such calls are anticipated by the patrolmen with
both pleasure and anxiety, and the recruit's performance on such calls is in a
very real sense the measure of the man. A Union City Sergeant described the
heavy call to me as follows:

It's our main reason for being in business. Like when somebody starts
busting up a place, or some asshole's got a gun, or some idiot tries to
knock off a cop. Basically, it's the situation where you figure you may
have to use the tools of your trade. Of course, some guys get a little
shaky when these incidents come along, in fact, most of us do if we're
honest. But, you know deep down that this is why you're a cop and not
pushing pencils somewhere. You've got to be tough on this job and situations like these separate the men from the boys. I know I'd never trust
my partner until I'd seen him in action on a hot one.

While such calls are relatively rare on a day-to-day basis, their occurrence
signals a behavioral test for the recruit. To pass, he must have "balls." By plac-

ing himself in a vulnerable position and pluckily backing-up his FTO and/or other patrolmen, a recruit demonstrates his inclination to share the risks of police work. Through such events, a newcomer quickly makes a departmental reputation which will follow him for the remainder of his career.

At another level, testing the recruit's propensity to partake in the risks which accompany police work goes on continuously within the department. For example, several FTO's in Union City were departmental celebrities for their training techniques. One officer made it a ritual to have his recruit write parking citations in front of the local Black Panther Party headquarters. Another was prominent for requiring his recruit to "shake out" certain trouble bars in the rougher sections of town (i.e., check identifications, make cursory body searches, and possibly roust out customers, a la *The French Connection*). Less dramatic, but nonetheless as important, recruits are appraised as to their speed in getting out of the patrol car, their lack of hesitation when approaching a suspicious person, or their willingness to lead the way up a darkened stairwell. The required behaviors vary from event to event; however, contingent upon the ex post facto evaluation (e.g., Was a weapon involved? Did the officers have to fight the suspect? How many other patrolmen were on the spot?), a novice makes his departmental reputation. While some FTO's promote these climactic events, most wait quietly for such situations to occur. Certainly varying definitions of appropriate behavior in these situations exist from patrolman to patrolman, but the critical and common element is the recruit's demonstrated willingness to place himself in a precarious position while assisting a brother officer. In the police world, such behavior is demanded.

Although data on such instances are inherently difficult to collect, it appears that the behaviorally demonstrated commitment to one's fellow officers involved in such events is a particularly important stage in the socialization process. To the recruit, he has experienced a test and it provides him with the first of many shared experiences which he can relate to other officers. To the FTO, he has watched his man in a police work situation and now knows a great deal more about his occupational companion.

Aside from the backup test applied to all recruits, the other most powerful experience in a recruit's early days on patrol is his first arrest. Virtually all policemen can recall the individual, location, and situation surrounding their first arrest. One five-year veteran patrolman stated:

> The first arrest is really something. I guess that's because it's what we're supposedly out here for. . . . In my case, I'd been out for a couple of weeks but we hadn't done much. . . . I think we'd made some chippies, like stand-ups, or DWI's, but my partner never let me handle the arrest part. Then one night he tells me that if anything happens, I've got to handle it. Believe me, I'll never forget that first arrest, even if it was only a scumbag horn (wino) who had just fallen through a window. . . . I suppose I can remember my first three or four arrests, but after that they just start to blur together.[7]

---

[7]By "chippies," the officer was referring to normal arrests encountered frequently by patrolmen. Usually, a chippie is a misdemeanor arrest for something like drunkenness. The chippie crimes the officer noted in the quotation, "stand-up" and "DWI's," refer to drunk-in-public and driving-while-intoxicated, respectively.

It is such occurrences that determine the recruit's success in the department. To some extent, both the back up test and the first arrest are beyond the direct control of the newcomer. The fact that they both take place at the discretion of the FTO underscores the orderliness of the socialization process. In effect, these climactic situations graphically demonstrate to the recruit his new status and role within the department. And after passing through this regulated sequence of events, he can say, "I am a cop!"

Continuance: Metamorphosis

This section is concerned broadly with what Becker et al. (1961) labeled the final perspective. As such, the interest is upon the characteristic response recruits eventually demonstrate regarding their occupational and organizational setting. Again, the focus is upon the perspectives the initiates come to hold for the backstage aspect of their career.

As noted earlier, one of the major motivating factors behind the recruit's decision to become a policeman was the adventure or romance he felt would characterize the occupation. Yet, the young officer soon learns the work consists primarily of performing routine service and administrative tasks—the proverbial clerk in a patrol car. This finding seems well-established in the pertinent literature and my observations confirm these reports (e.g., Wilson 1968; Webster 1970; Reiss 1971). Indeed, a patrolman is predominantly an order taker—a reactive member of a service organization. For example, most officers remarked that they never realized the extent to which they would be "married to the radio" until they had worked the street for several months.

On the other hand, there is an unpredictable side of the occupation and this aspect cannot be overlooked. In fact, it is the unexpected elements of working patrol that provides self-esteem and stimulation for the officers. This unpredictable feature of patrol work has too often been understated or disregarded by students of police behavior. To classify the police task as bureaucratically routine and monotonous ignores the psychological omnipresence of the potential "good pinch." It is precisely the opportunity to exercise his perceived police role that gives meaning to the occupational identity of patrolmen. Operationally, this does not imply patrolmen are always alert and working hard to make the "good pinch." Rather, it simply suggests that the unexpected is one of the few aspects of the job that helps maintain the patrolman's self-image of performing a worthwhile, exciting, and dangerous task. To some degree, the anticipation of the "hot call" allows for the crystallization of his personal identity as a policeman. One Union City patrolman with ten years' experience commented succinctly on this feature. He noted:

> Most of the time being a cop is the dullest job in the world . . . what we do is pretty far away from the stuff you see on Dragnet or Adam 12. But, what I like about this job and I guess it's what keeps me going, is that you never know what's gonna happen out there. For instance, me and my partner will be working a Sunday first watch way out in the north end and expecting everything to be real peaceful and quiet like; then all of a sudden, hell breaks loose . . . Even on the quietest nights, something interesting usually happens.

Reiss noted perceptually the atypical routine enjoyed by patrolmen. After examining the police "straight eight"—the tour of duty—he stated:

> No tour of duty is typical except in the sense that the modal tour of duty does not involve the arrest of a person (Reiss 1971:19).

Still, one of the ironies of police work is that recruits were attracted to the organization by and large via the unrealistic expectation that the work would be adventurous and exciting. In the real world such activities are few and far between. Once a recruit has mastered the various technical and social skills of routine policing (e.g., "learning the district," developing a set of mutual understandings with his partner, knowing how and when to fill out the myriad of various report forms) there is little left to learn about his occupation which can be transferred by formal or informal instruction. As Westley (1951) pointed out, the recruit must then sit back and wait, absorb the subjective side of police work and let his experiences accumulate. The wife of one recruit noted this frustrating characteristic of police work. She said:

> It seems to me that being a policeman must be very discouraging. They spend all that time teaching the men to use the gun and the club and then they make them go out and do very uninteresting work.

It has been suggested that for a newcomer to any occupation, "coping with the emotional reality of the job" is the most difficult problem to resolve (Schein 1963). In police work, the coping behavior appears to consist of the "learning of complacency." Since the vast majority of time is spent in tasks other than real police work, there is little incentive for performance. In other words, the young patrolman discovers that the most satisfying solution to the labyrinth of hierarchy, the red tape and paperwork, the plethora of rules and regulations, and the "dirty work" which characterize the occupation is to adopt the group norm stressing staying out of trouble. And the best way in which he can stay out of trouble is to minimize the set of activities he pursues. One Union City veteran patrolman explained:

> We are under constant pressure from the public to account for why we did or did not do this or that. It's almost as if the public feels it owns us. You become supersensitive to criticisms from the public, almost afraid to do anything. At the same time, the brass around here never gives a straightforward answer about procedures to anyone and that creates a lot of discontent. All communication comes down. But, try and ask a question and it gets stopped at the next level up. It gets to the point where you know that if you don't do anything at all, you won't get in trouble.

In a similar vein, another veteran officer put it somewhat more bluntly. He suggested caustically:

> The only way to survive on this job is to keep from breaking your ass . . . if you try too hard you're sure to get in trouble. Either some civic-minded creep is going to get outraged and you'll wind up with a complaint in your file; or the high and mighty in the department will come down on you for breaking some rule or something and you'll get your pay docked.

These quotations suggest that patrolman disenchantment has two edges. One, the police with the general public—which has been well-substantiated in the literature—and two, the disenchantment with the police system itself. In short, a recruit begins to realize (through proverb, example, and his own experience) it is his relationship with his fellow officers (particularly those working the same sector and shift—his squad) that protects his interests and allows him to continue on the job—without their support he would be lost.[8]

To summarize, the adjustment of a newcomer in police departments is one which follows the line of least resistance. By becoming similar in sentiment and behavior to his peers, the recruit avoids censure by the department, his supervisor and, most important, his brother officers. Furthermore, since the occupational rewards are to be found primarily in the unusual situation which calls for "real" police work, the logical situational solution is for the officers to organize their activities in such a way as to minimize the likelihood of being sanctioned by *any* of their audiences. The low visibility of the patrolman's role vis-à-vis the department allows for such a response. Thus, the pervasive adjustment is epitomized in the "lie low, hang loose, and don't expect too much" advice frequently heard within the Union City Police Department. This overall picture would indicate that the following tip given to me by a Union City veteran represents a very astute analysis of how to insure continuance in the police world. He suggested:

> There's only two things you gotta know around here. First, forget everything you've learned in the academy 'cause the street's where you'll learn to be a cop; and second, being first don't mean shit around here. Take it easy, that's our motto.

The above characterization of the recruit socialization process, while necessarily a drastic condensation of a much more complex and interdependent process, does delineate the more important aspects of becoming a policeman. Furthermore, this descriptive narrative hints that many of the recent attempts to alter or reform police behavior are likely to meet with frustration and failure.

---

[8]In most ways, the patrolmen represent what Goffman (1959) calls a team. In Goffmanesque, a team is "a set of individuals whose intimate co-operation is required if a given projected definition of the situation is to be maintained" (1959:104). The situational definition to be sustained in the patrol setting is that "all-is-going-well-there-are-no-problems." The covert rule for patrolmen is to never draw attention to one's activities. An analysis I conducted on written weekly FTO progress reports illustrates this point convincingly. Of over 300 report forms, only one contained an even slightly negative evaluation. Uniformly, all forms were characterized by high praise for the recruit. The topics the FTO's chose to elaborate upon were typified by such concerns as the recruit's driving skill, the recruit's pleasing personality, the recruit's stable home life, and so on. The vast majority of reports contained no reference whatsoever to the types of activities engaged in by the recruits. The point is simply that in no case was an FTO report filed which might result in departmental attention. It should be clear that such behavior does not pass unnoticed by the recruit. Indeed, he learns rapidly the importance and value of his team as well as the corresponding definition of the police situation.

A CODA FOR REFORMERS

Most police reformers view the behavior of individual patrolmen as a problem for the department or society, not vice versa. I have, in a small way, tried to correct this bias by describing the point of view of the entering recruit. This emphasizes the intelligibility of the newcomer's actions as he works out solutions to his unique problems. In short, we "looked up" at the nature of the network above the recruit rather than using the usual approach which, in the past, has "looked down" on the "outsider." Perhaps this approach indicates the dilemma in which our police are indeed trapped.

In a very real sense, this article suggests a limit upon the extent to which the police can be expected to solve their own problems. Regardless of how well-educated, well-equipped, or professional the patrolman may become, his normative position and task within society will remain unchanged. From this perspective, the characteristic response of police officers to their present situation is indeed both rational and functional. Clearly, the police subculture—like subcultures surrounding bricklayers, lawyers, or social workers—will probably exist in even the most reformed of departments. To change the police without changing the police role in society is as futile as the labors of Sisyphus.

The long-range goal should be a structural redefinition of the police task and a determination of ways in which the external control principle—so central to the rule of law—may be strengthened. Of course, ways must be found to make the policeman's lot somewhat more tolerable, both to him and to the general citizenry. Organizational change can aid this process by designing training programs which place less stress on the apprenticeship relationship. However, it is doubtful that without profound alterations in the definition and structural arrangement of the police task (and in the implied values such arrangements support), significant change is possible.

Thus, plans to increase the therapeutic and operational effectiveness of police institutions by "in-house" techniques must be judged in terms of what is being done now and what might be done—and, given the features of the police institution as described here, the difference is painfully small. The particular pattern of police practices is a response to the demands of the larger complex and, as such, reflects the values and norms prevalent throughout society. The extent to which the police system undermines the rule of law; the extent to which the public is willing to alter the crime fighter image of police; the extent to which the police bureaucracy will allow change; and ultimately, the extent to which the police system as presently constructed can operate under strict public accounting—these are the major issues confronting the police, not the degree to which the individual policeman can be professionalized.[9]

---

[9]I have attempted to suggest in this article that the intelligibility of social events requires they be viewed in a context which extends both spatially and in time. Relatedly, social actors must be granted rationality for their behavior. Given the situational imperatives faced by patrolmen, is it any wonder our police recoil behind a blue curtain? Perhaps we have reached what R.D. Laing (1964) calls the "theoretical limit of institutions." According to Laing, this paradoxical position is characterized by a system which, when viewed as a collective, behaves irrationally, yet is populated by members whose everyday behavior is eminently rational.

REFERENCES CITED

Ahern, J. F., (1972) Police in Trouble. New York: Hawthorn Books.
Bayley, P. H., and H. Mendelsohn, (1969) Minorities and the Police. New York: The Free Press.
Becker, H. S. (1963) Outsiders: Studies in the Sociology of Deviance. New York: The Free Press.
Becker, H. S., B. Greer, E. C. Hughes, and A. Strauss (1961) Boys in White: Student Culture in Medical School. Chicago: University of Chicago Press.
Berkeley, G. E., (1969) The Democratic Policeman. Boston: Beacon Press.
Berlew, D. E., and D. T. Hall, (1966) The socialization of managers; effects of expectations on performance. Administrative Science Quarterly 11:207-23.
Bittner, E., (1967) The police on skid row. American Sociological Review 32:699-715.
Cicourel, A. V., (1967) The Social Organization of Juvenile Justice. New York: John Wiley and Sons.
Dalton, M., (1964) Preconceptions and methods in men who manage. In Sociologists at Work, P. Hammond, ed. New York: Doubleday.
Dornbush, S. M., (1955) The military academy as an assimilating institution. Social Forces 33:316-21.
Evan, W. M., (1963) Peer group interaction and organizational socialization: a study of employee turnover. American Sociological Review 28:436-40.
Goffman, E., (1959) The Presentation of Self in Everyday Life. New York: Doubleday.
Greer, B., (1964) First days in the field. In Sociologists at Work, P. Hammond, ed. New York: Doubleday.
Hughes, E. C., (1958) Men and their Work. Glencoe, Illinois: The Free Press.
Laing, R. D., (1964) The obvious. In Dialectics of Liberation, D. Cooper, ed. London: Institute of Phenomenological Studies.
Lortie, D. C., (1968) Shared ordeal and induction to work. In Institutions and the Person, H. S. Becker, B. Greer, D. Riesman, and R. T. Weiss, eds. Chicago: Aldine.
McNamara, J., (1967) Uncertainties in police work: the relevance of police recruits' background and training. In The Police: Six Sociological Essays, D. J. Bordura, ed. New York: John Wiley and Sons.
Neiderhoffer, A., (1967) Behind the Shield. New York: Doubleday.
President's Commission on Law Enforcement, (1967) Task Force Report: The Police. Washington, D.C.: Government Printing Office.
Reiss, A. J., (1971) The Police and the Public. New Haven: Yale University Press.
Schatzman, L., and A. Strauss, (1973) Field Research: Strategies for a Natural Sociology. Englewood Cliffs, New Jersey: Prentice-Hall.
Schein, E. H., (1963) Organizational socialization in the early career of industrial managers. Paper presented at the New England Psychological Association, Boston, Massachusetts. (1971) Organizational socialization and the profession of management. Industrial Management Review 2:37-45.
Skolnick, J., (1966) Justice Without Trial: Law Enforcement in a Democratic Society. New York: John Wiley and Sons.
Sterling, J. W., (1972) Changes in Role Concepts of Police Officers. Washington, D.C.: International Association of Chiefs of Police.
Van Maanen, J., (1972) Pledging the police: a study of selected aspects of recruit socialization in a large, urban police department. Ph.D. Dissertation, University of California, Irvine. (1976) Breaking-in: socialization to work. In Handbook of Work, Organization, and Society, R. Dubin, ed. Chicago: Rand-McNally.
Webster, J. A., (1970) Police task and time study. Journal of Criminal Law, Criminology and Police Science 61:94-100.
Westley, W. A., (1951) The police: a sociological study of law, custom and mortality. Ph.D. Dissertation, University of Chicago, Chicago, Illinois.
Whyte, W. F., (1943) Street Corner Society. Chicago: University of Chicago Press.
Wilson, J. Q., (1968) Varieties of Police Behavior. Cambridge, Massachusetts. Harvard University Press.

Epilogue
On Watching the Watchers*

John Van Maanen[1]

I. INTRODUCTION

In this essay, I discuss and detail various methodological issues and nuances endemic to the ethnographic study of the police. The ethnographic approach is that of anthropology, and, to a more limited extent, sociology, under the stiff but precise tag, participant observation.[2] As practiced, both methodologies utilize the culture manufactured by the subjects of study (the

*Support for my study has come from whomever and wherever I could find it. At various times, I have received financial assistance from: the Office of Naval Research, the Organizational Behavior Research Center at the University of California, Irvine (now defunct); the Ford Foundation; the Industrial Liaison Office at MIT; the Graduate Division at the University of California, Irvine; the Sloan School of Management at MIT; the Department of Labor; and the quiet sacrifice of my working wife, Colleen McCallion. This monograph represents an attempt to detail some of the actions that fall between these perfunctory lines. A number of people have read and commented upon one or more of the several versions of this paper that I have circulated about for criticism. Among them, Professors Chris Argyris, Lotte Bailyn, Peter Harris, Edgar H. Schein, and Donald Schon have provided some very careful and helpful remarks. In particular, I wish to thank my colleague and partner Peter K. Manning for his assistance in clarifying what, in retrospect, turned out to be some very muddy analytic and descriptive work on my part. While those mentioned may not recognize their contributions here, I have written this paper with many of their comments in mind.

[1]In September 1969, I began contacting police officials across the country seeking permission to conduct a one-man field study inside a metropolitan law enforcement agency. I wished to study, by firsthand observation and participation, the processes by which young men go about learning the ropes of city policing. My proposed study was accepted by a large, urban police department (herein called Union City) in April 1970, and I began my work in residence later that month. After attending the thirteen-week recruit training academy, I spent approximately five months as an armed backseat and frontseat observer of patrolmen. I returned to Union City for two months in early 1973 and again spent considerable time watching the police from patrol units. Since that time, I have been back to Union City on three brief occasions to renew acquaintances and check out particular findings, although I did not engage in any announced research activities.

[2]There is a substantial body of work devoted to the *in situ* observation of social life which identifies various generic areas of problematic concern. For some representative writings on the sociological side, see: Junker (1960); Adams and Priess, eds. (1960); Bruyn (1966); McCall and Simmons, eds. (1969); Habenstein, ed. (1970); Lofland (1971, 1976); Filstead, ed. (1970); Schatzman and Strauss (1973); Johnson (1975); Suttles (1976); and Douglas (1976). Of course, the sociological primer for all students of social organization is Goffman (1959). On the anthropological side, see: Radcliff-Brown (1958); Berreman (1962); Malinowski (1961), (1967); Powdermaker (1967); Conklin (1968); Frake (1969); Freilich (1970); Wax (1971); Gulick (1973); and Pelto and Pelto (1973). Certainly these field guides are helpful when planning, organizing, and attempting to focus a study before entering the field. But these guidelines are of somewhat less assistance when one enters a *specific* social world except to remind the field worker that the difficulties and anxieties raised by involvement in unfamiliar surroundings are common to all strangers, sojourners, tourists, immigrants, recruits, novices, missionaries, and social scientists.

socially acquired and shared knowledge available to the participants in the examined setting) to account for the observed patterns of human activity.[3] The practice of the method itself is described elegantly by Conklin (1968:172) as involving: "a long period of intimate study and residence in a small, well-defined community, knowledge of the spoken language, and the employment of a wide range of observational techniques including prolonged face-to-face contacts with members of the local group, direct participation in some of that group's activities, and a greater emphasis on intensive work with informants than on the use of documentary or survey data."

Significantly, a large body of knowledge relevant to various aspects of policing has been gathered through ethnographic field studies (as the readings presented in this book indicate). Yet, the actual process by which such information has been generated remains something of a mystery. What we have at present are terse descriptions of the time spent observing by a particular researcher or team of researchers; curious illustrations of the formal capacities by which the observers observed; and, in a relatively few cases, suggestive examples of the social and psychological problems posed by observation *au naturel*.[4] In fact, there appears to be something of a discrete illusion and growing mystique associated with the conduct of police field work. It is as if the field worker, as he is presented in the published works, simply vanished for a period of time into an obscure and often-unnamed police world; became involved in the activities that took place there; attained something akin to a state of grace with the observed; and, then, presto, emerged with the data in hand. Clearly, important contacts were initiated, roles were carved out, and certain kinds of events were (and were not), observed while the researcher was out of view, but we know not how such things were accomplished.

---

[3]The ethnographic or cultural approach as discussed in the text should be distinguished from the more popular behavioral approach which presently seems to dominate the social sciences. Mather (1976:5), in a very insightful look at the ethnographic study of trial courts, notes: "the behavioral model ignores what is going on inside of people's heads (because it is said to be inaccessible to the researcher) and accounts for behavior by observing behavioral input and output, or stimulus and response." Behavioral models seek then to predict human responses according to a predefined set of prior stimuli whereas ethnographic models seek to discover, not prescribe, the important stimuli in a particular social world. This difference is captured nicely by Frake (1969:124), who writes, "the model of an ethnographic statement is not: 'if a person is confronted with stimulus X, he will do Y,' but: 'if a person is in situation X, performance Y will be judged appropriate by native actors.'"

[4]Ironically, Polsky's (1967:117–149) comments on observing criminals are most appropriate for a police researcher (e.g., "In studying a criminal it is important to realize that he will also be studying you" [p. 118]). But perhaps the best discussion of the problems raised when the observer is deep within a police organization is found in the appendix of Buckner's (1967) unpublished doctoral dissertation. Other relevant examples of field methods, although brief, can be located in Reiss (1968, 1971: Preface); Westley (1970:11–14; 196–201); Skolnick (1966:23–41); Cain (1971:1–12; Appendices); Rubenstein (1973: Preface); Harris (1973:20–26; Appendix); and Banton (1964: Preface). Several reviews of the field methods employed in studying the police across agencies are now also available, see Manning (1972, 1976b); McCall (1975: Chapter 3); Fox and Lundman (1974) and Lundman and Fox (1974).

What follows is an attempt to fill in some of the essential incompleteness surrounding the conduct of field research in police organizations. Of necessity, I lean heavily on my own experiences. However, my primary purpose is to deal as directly and candidly with certain general issues that are unavoidably raised when any outsider seeks to construct a research relationship with the police. To accomplish this task, I *first* consider why and how I chose to undertake a police study. *Second,* I discuss several rather omnipresent and salient obstacles present whenever outsiders seek to conduct field work inside a police agency. *Third,* I take a retrospective look at my own process of obtaining access in the Union City Police Department, and *fourth,* I examine some of the issues that arose during the doing of the research itself. The implicit argument running throughout these four sections is simply that access is continually problematic for the field researcher. Entry into the police system is no guarantee that one will be allowed to remain, or, perhaps more to the point, it is no guarantee that one will be able to produce useful or enlightening data while there. *Finally,* I conclude with a brief but more abstract consideration of the kinds of roles available to, and apparently used by, field researchers in police settings. When all is said and done, it will be perhaps easier to understand Manning's (1972:235) rather sharp assertion that the police have been ". . . the source of several superior sociological studies and the demise of probably three times that number."

II. FOCUSING ON THE POLICE

In 1969, I wrote in my thesis proposal submitted to, and accepted by, the faculty of my graduate department: "The police are quite possibly the most vital of our human service agencies. Certainly they are the most visible and active institution of social control, representing the technological and organizational answer to the Hobbsian question of social order, the *deus ex machina*. Through their exclusive mandate to intervene directly into the lives of the citizenry, the police are crucial actors in both our everyday and ceremonial affairs, and, as such, deserve intensive and continual study for their role and function in society is far too important to be taken-for-granted, or, worse, to be ignored."

Such high-sounding sentiments, similar to those above, provide, I am sure, the sort of doctrinal or ideological canopy covering virtually all police studies. Yet, speaking sociologically, such statements are inadequate explanations of a given study for at least two reasons. First, questions about the *place* of police studies within the social sciences are glossed over neatly when a researcher points only to the "peculiar and significant" aspects of a specific research location. Second, research, especially research conducted in the field work tradition, is both a social and a personal act, and as such is subject to the same sorts of biographically and situationally specific understandings through which any individual act is rendered sensible. Thus, to fully account for the reasons standing behind a given research project, both of the issues must be explored.

Social scientists generally express something of a hierarchy of professional interests on which personal motives rank low and scientific motives rank high. At the apex of such a hierarchy are usually the formal theoretical concerns—

what is it that is to be explained by the research? In my case, I was interested in questions surrounding adult socialization and the formation of occupational identities. As such, I searched about for a work world that might involve a good deal of personal change on the part of newcomers in the process of becoming fully accepted members of an occupation and an organization. From this analytic (and remote) standpoint, the police seemed to be a logical, if not downright dramatic, choice. Yet, alternative possibilities were most certainly available—doctors, lawyers, professors, crooks, priests, accountants, architects, railroad workers, and so on. At this point, then, more gritty matters (though matters rarely addressed in print) concerning why a specific researcher chooses to study a certain social world must necessarily be raised. Of course, to establish a motive, even one's own, is a tricky business. Nevertheless, it is an important task, because there are some rather popular but misleading accounts available in the culture at large to explain why *particular* people study *particular* institutions.

On one hand, people who have sought close ties with the practitioners of police work are sometimes thought to be expressing deep-seated desires to be what they study—"they really want to be cops." The police themselves will sometimes subscribe to this flattering diagnosis of the field worker's hidden but "true" motives when, for example, they speak of the researcher as a "cop buff" (the thrill seeker who has come to experience the dangerous life). During my study, some of my police (and even nonpolice) acquaintances occasionally accused me of "growing a badge." Apparently, it is assumed by people that those who study a particular line of endeavor must have more than a professional or detached interest in it.[5] On the other hand, people sometimes see much darker and insidious motives behind an individual's choice to study the police. Researchers are frequently taken to be crusading and treacherous journalists in disguise who undertake their studies solely to expose wrongdoings and embarrass law enforcement agencies.

Both accounts sometimes fit the person and the situation. Some people do in fact study the police for many of the same reasons that other people join the police. Research in police organizations can be a challenging, adventurous undertaking in a sociologically rich environment. This no doubt contrasts sharply with research carried out in many other organizational settings which are marked, at least on the surface, by what appears to be a more humdrum and commonplace work routine. Manning (1977: Preface) speaks, for example, of

---

[5]This seems particularly the case for those who carry out research in deviant subcultures. The popular logic goes something like this: anyone who would bother to study, say, homosexuals, must be one, or why in the world would he go to the trouble to study them? To some people, the police are the deviants of a given moral order and, by implication, so are the people that study them. Among a few of my university cohorts in 1969, this logic seemed to prevail. This appeared to be particularly the case after I had begun to negotiate for access in a police department and my physical image underwent a rather dramatic transformation (eliminating my cultivated but altogether shaggy studentlike appearance and effecting a more crisp, militarylike appearance). Other researchers have remarked on a similar sort of altercasting by which friends, students, family members, and occupational colleagues apparently "make sense" out of the researcher's decision to study the police. See Manning (1972:242–255).

the "childlike quality" that accompanied much of his field-work experiences with the police. I have heard other social scientists cast the advantages of studying the police in terms of the vast and ceaseless variety of problematic concerns encountered in police settings (e.g., "it keeps one well fed with new ideas"). This hardly differs from the policeman who justifies his occupational choice on the grounds of seeking task variety and social significance (Muir, 1977:13–36). And it is also true that a muckraking tradition is built into any analytic perspective based upon an operating premise which states that things are rarely what they seem. Since most social scientists subscribe to the notion that reality does not present itself with a label, much of the research into the workings of organizations and institutions debunks official lines and takes issue with managerial pronouncements that things are operating as they should be. To the social scientist, this is merely demystification, but to administrators, this can be an unscrupulous form of vile muckraking.

Granted that there are some partial truths in the above popular attributions of motive, neither account is very informative—at least when it comes to framing my interest in the police. Aside from a theoretical concern with occupational socialization, three rather personal and perhaps pivotal factors seem to best explain my particular choice to study the police. First, when I began thinking seriously of the police as a topic for research in the late 1960s, the police were prominently fixed in the imagery of the day. Whether damned or praised, they were both participants and subjects in the dramatic and searing issues of public debate. Indeed, the police were visible reminders that the American society was a bitterly divided one, and one did not require a Ph.D. to grasp their social significance in the scheme of things. Second, not much seemed to be known about the police. While everyone I knew had cop stories to tell, there remained in all these tales something of a mystery as to why the police acted as they did. I discovered rather quickly that the police-related literature was at that time relatively thin, particularly when it came to describing the actual activities of policemen. Third, the available literature did not seem to square with my own random observations and run-ins with the police. Certainly, with few exceptions, the arid portraits which represent a good portion of the social science literature of the day (circa 1968) did not match my own visceral beliefs.[6] As a young man growing up in a Los Angeles suburb, I had many times been subject to police attention. To wit, as a teenager driving a series of unusually shabby but stylized automobiles, it seemed as if I could never undertake a journey of any length without being stopped by the police for some reason or another. I had even been arrested several times for minor misdeeds such as underage drinking, curfew violations, petty theft, and fight-

---

[6]There were of course some significant exceptions. In particular, I was very much impressed by what I took then and now to be the intellectual honesty of the works of Westley (1951, reprinted in 1970) and Banton (1964). However, it was Skolnick's (1966) study of "Westville" detectives that was most influential on my as yet uncrystallized ideas. Perhaps because Skolnick chose not to write himself out of many of his observations, I read and reread his book several times. In the process, I slowly came to frame and justify a substantive interest in the police and a methodological means to such substantive ends.

ing.[7] And, of more immediate experience, the cordons of grim, often antagonistic, policemen that demarked the boundaries of every political demonstration I attended could not easily be forgotten. In many ways, I both feared and loathed the police.

During the preparation phase of observational studies, I think it reasonably important for the investigator to sort through and try to classify not only the scholarly justifications but the personal reasons which lie behind the study. What is being accomplished at this stage is not so much a definition for the study as it is a fixing of interest such that the potential researcher can begin to judge whether or not the proposed study is sufficiently attractive to him personally—attractive enough to carry him through a long and perhaps frustrating period of field work. Out of these various cognitive forays into the field comes a more elaborate rationale for the study itself, a rationale the researcher will have to live with long after the study has begun.

In terms of the formal preparation required for field work in police settings, I am ambivalent. There is now a substantial and rapidly growing research base that can be staggering if not paralyzing for the novice. Often an elaborate soaking up of the literature leads to a very narrow research interest. Far too many studies merely document the "believing-is-seeing" paradigm, for a full set of preconceptions can easily lead to a loss of sensitivity for the discrepant observation which may occur in the field. This is not to say that plowing through others' perspectives on the police is of no benefit, but it is crucial that the would-be researcher not become so steeped in the prevailing logic that his vision is impaired. Such a conclusion is somewhat in opposition to the sentiment ruling among many social scientists, who believe that empirical data are best used to test, not discover, current theory. Since alternative theories for any given social activity are usually available, it is all too convenient for the investigator simply to pick one and go about testing it in the field. Such an arcane model for police research is unlikely to discover much of anything new nor to provide much insight into the business of policing.[8]

At any rate, while the researcher is engaged in the task of looking over various empirical and analytic perspectives on the police prior to going to the field, a methodological self-consciousness also begins to emerge. However,

---

[7]Such "minor misdeeds" were a cause for some concern on my part, since a requirement for police service is, at least according to most civil service recruiting brochures, a personal history that reflects "exemplary" conduct. If, in fact, any checking on my past police record was accomplished, no direct mention of such checking was ever made to me by police officials in Union City. Furthermore, to my partial surprise, my record was by no means unusual among recruits of my academy class or their veteran police peers (note: my evidence here comes from both the informal storytelling and banter among my recruit acquaintances and a surreptitious look at individual personnel records).

[8]To avoid any misunderstanding, I should note here that I have nothing against one's being *au courant* with the literature in the social sciences before entering the field. Good training in methods and theory is not necessarily the same as being tied down to preconceived ideas. But, as Malinowski (1961:9) remarked, "If a man sets out on an expedition determined to prove certain hypotheses, if he is incapable of changing his views constantly and casting them off ungrudgingly under the pressure of evidence, needless to say his work will be meaningless." The notions of Glaser and Strauss (1967) concerning the discovery of "grounded theory" are perhaps most pertinent in this regard.

when discovering what so-and-so learned about this-or-that, one is very unlikely to also discover how such learning actually took place. Some insight can
be gained by carefully combing the prefaces and methodological supplements
contained in a few of the books and articles dealing with the police. For example, I learned that observing the police might well be a risky business morally,
that problems of impression management were likely to be vast, that police
values and my values were likely to be far apart, and so forth. Still, one cannot
know on the basis of what can be gleaned from the literature how to create and
manage a research relationship with the police. Of course, a number of clues,
usually in the form of research findings and personal anecdotes, can be collected enabling one to form a fantasy around the ideal role he wishes to build
from which to observe the typical scenes of police work. But in reality such an
ideal is, at best, a background expectancy which contains only the potential for
use after the study has begun.

Of most use to me during the preliminary probleming phase, was simply
talking with policemen from various departments. In most cases, a blind phone
call or haphazard visit to various departments put me in touch with a public
relations officer, an Officer Friendly type, who arranged for me to spend some
time riding with selected patrol units. Most cities of even moderate size offer
citizen "ride-along" programs of one sort or another. Although one is given
what Union City officers referred to as a "whitewash tour" on such ride-alongs,
one also has the opportunity to begin to develop a perspective on the ambiance
surrounding the police function from the basic unit of the police
organization—the patrol car. More often than not, the units used in citizen
ride-along programs are unofficially but effectively "out of service" (as they
were in Union City), although perhaps on occasion some routine service assignments will be dispatched. At the time, I found this exercise useful, and I
later discovered that such experience served as a useful conversational gambit
when police talk turned to a discussion of interdepartmental comparisons.
What one learns on these tours is, of course, only what the hand-picked officers
who guide the tours choose to reveal. This usually means one is told about recent technological innovations the department has instituted, various hints for
personal protection a la Dick Tracy "crime stoppers," or carefully sanitized
versions of the latest gimmick in the police repertoire of public service gestures. Less obvious, however, but of far greater importance, one learns some
helpful lessons in how to talk with the police. While one is quite unlikely to
view much police activity, there are ample opportunities to engage in some
conversational give-and-take, thus allowing the researcher to develop some
understanding of the current police argot and sensibility.[9] Yet, as Rubenstein
(1973) suggests, police talk in such circumstances will be moderated by the

---

[9]In particular, through this exercise, I first became dimly aware of the pervasive
anecdotal style of communication used by policemen in general. Indeed, as my notes on
these experiences attest, the patrolmen with whom I rode were terrible in making the sort
of careful generalizations I had been taught to appreciate in graduate school. To wit, many
patrolmen would think nothing of saying, "all hippies are scum," and then go on to give
one or two pointed illustrations of some altogether exemplary hippies they knew. Yet,
despite my keen sociological ear (or perhaps because of it), it took me some time to see the

careful etiquette that governs the kind of information that can be exchanged
between the police and those strangers who might report on their doings.

The final phase of my prestudy activity involved the interviewing of six-
teen patrolmen from a medium-sized city near the university I was then attending. These interviews took place with the approval of the chief of police
and were conducted inside the departmental headquarters, although on pleasant days we often drifted across the street to a city park. The interviews were
quite unorganized, ranged in length from a half hour to three hours, and were
aimed at what Westley (1970) called getting a kind of "acquaintance with" the
police life. While I did not succeed in getting more than a rather facile view of
the police life, the interviewing process did perhaps help to reduce my naiveté
and to establish something of a comparative perspective on police work such
that when I finally began my intensive field work in Union City I was better
able to separate some of the local attributes of the occupation from the generic
ones.

III. SOME OBSTACLES TO RESEARCH

Before moving on to discuss the process of securing access, a brief review of
what I take to be the more serious obstacles to police research—particularly
observational studies—is presented below. This discussion is organized for
convenience under seven separate headings, although clearly each topic is related in complex and multiple ways to the others. While some of the following
points are general to organizational studies of all types, this discussion is
premised upon the specific peculiarities of attempting to do research in police
systems.

1. Stereotypes, Predecessors, and the Fear of Exposure: Antipathy and distrust
of the academic researcher is endemic to most police departments. A good part
of this hostility is based on the cultural stereotype of the social scientist as social critic, who, if not outright subversive, does seek to cast a disparaging light
on the institutions of the day. The outside researcher in police organization is
therefore rarely asked in by police administrators and even more rarely wel-
comed by the rank and file if he should somehow succeed initially in getting
through the door.[10]

Some of this police hostility toward the social scientist can be located in
recent events. During the last decade or so, the police have been penetrated

---

value of anecdotes for my studies. Though I do not wish to minimize the problems I had and
still have in understanding everyday police talk, anecdotes, at least to the field worker,
are both convenient and attractive bits of data. As Klockers (1974) points out, first, they do
not require great prior understandings to grasp their meanings. Second, they represent
complete units in themselves with neat beginnings, middles, and ends. And third,
remembering them is relatively easy, thus promoting a close correspondence between
one's field notes and what people actually said.

[10]There are apparently some notable exceptions to this rule. Rubenstein (1973) in
particular mentions in his preface the "generous treatment" he received from his sponsors
in the Philadelphia Police Department. "I was granted unrestricted freedom of inquiry,"
says Rubenstien, "by an agency which some people judge to be committed to stifling

and, at times, permeated by various industrial consultants, efficiency experts, systems analysts, training specialists, program evaluators, clinical psychologists, and so on. The majority of these so-called applied behavioral scientists have come onto the scene with a battery of fixed, though sometimes sophisticated, techniques thought applicable to different aspects of a predecided police "problem." Yet for a number of reasons, most of them structural, when the behavioral scientists have departed the police are left still with their basic problems intact. Social scientists are often seen as mischievous "ivory-tower types who talk and write a good game but can't deliver the goods" (personal interview with a chief of police).

The field worker who seeks to locate a representative urban department in which to practice his craft will no doubt have difficulty these days finding one uncontaminated by predecessors who have not left some sort of legacy of disillusionment or irrelevancy. Previous experiences have left even the most professionally oriented police administrators with the not-unfounded impression that social science research is often useless and unintelligible. Such impressions live long lives. The presence of a scholarly visitor is always something of an inconvenience, interruption, and imposition. From the police perspective, care must be taken to protect his safety, to try to insure his goodwill, and to properly locate him somewhere within the department. Thus, many police administrators will have little tolerance to do so unless a researcher can directly answer the question, "What good will this study do?" Needless to say, this is a question to which most ethnographers cannot easily, nor specifically, respond. However, it is not true that *all* administrators feel this way. As the studies represented in this book imply, there are no doubt a number of high-ranking police officials who are interested in, as they might put it, "research for research sake." Indeed, I have known several police administrators who were intrigued with the idea of simply getting a scholarly and outsider perspective on what their respective organizations or divisions were actually doing, irrespective of whatever use they might eventually find for such information (if any). While antipathy to academic research within police organizations may be the rule, there are many exceptions.

Nevertheless, individuals aside for the moment, the most important explanation for the police reluctance to open their doors to a curious social scientist adheres in the nature of any relatively closed system. Outsiders to such systems are troublesome and even dangerous. Police fears on this score are not

---

dissent and diversity of opinion" (p. xiv). Wilson (1968) and Banton (1964) also go out of their way to note the cooperative spirit of their police contacts. Yet such statements presumably reflect primarily the attitudes of high-ranking officials and not those of the middle- and lower-level operatives in the police system. Nor should it be altogether surprising that high-placed administrators may welcome the opportunity to have a social scientist around, to act perhaps as a spy and warn them of unrest or misconduct at other levels in the organization. Other equally critical problems of access are apparent only when the researcher attempts to break into the ground levels where, to a large degree, the police culture is manufactured and maintained. Manning (1972) refers to this problem as "securing secondary access" and considers it to be perhaps as difficult as securing primary, or administrative, access.

groundless, since there are many illegal and potentially embarrassing activities that go on within their boundaries. Moreover, these fears differ in content and consequence at each level of the organization (Williams, Manning, and Redlinger, 1977:11). For example, upper-level officials in police systems may be less worried about themselves and more worried about the image of their organization. Lower-level members may be less concerned about the organization qua organization, and more worried about the image of their own unit (or even themselves). However, at any level, one of the only ways for the police to be sure the dangers of exposure do not inhere in a researcher (despite whatever claims for confidentiality may be made) is to subject that investigator to effective organizational control (editorial or otherwise) so that if a trust is betrayed the transgressor can be brought to account. This is usually thought to be inimical to the requirements of "good" social research. Thus, the scholarly stranger to the police is often beyond organizational control and, therefore beyond trust, and is perhaps best sent on his way before a study begins.[11] True, the researcher can always be asked to leave after he has initiated a study, but from the perspective of the gatekeepers in the organization this tactic is problematic since delicate information may already have been gathered by the investigator and to throw him out belatedly is not only an awkward occasion for all concerned, it may even further provoke the researcher into exposing and making public what the organization wishes to keep private.

2. Public Image of the Police: Anyone considering doing a study on the police runs the risk of being blinded by the abundant imagery of the police prevalent in the society as a whole. The public view of police departments features such attributes as elaborate ritual, dangerous duty, militarylike ceremony, esoteric rank distinctions, exaggerated bureaucratic pageantry, and so on. Added to this partially fictive picture is the police encouraged stereotype of the cop-as-crime-fighter. Indeed, the popular literature and mass media have contributed to the mystique rather than illuminating it. Such imagery casts long shadows, thus making it considerably more difficult to identify common human features associated with policing that are readily comparable with other organized social settings in society. The police are seen as anomalies, somehow quite different from the rest of us. Apparently, the drama of police business makes it quite difficult to discern the complex, though normal, web of social phenomena that forms the background of policing from the manifest appearance of police agencies characterized by what Manning (1977) calls the threat-danger-hero symbolism of policing.

3. Police Fraternity: As virtually all policemen will witness, the initiation into police circles is a costly process both socially and psychologically. Those who achieve membership are reluctant to accept others who have not undergone a similar set of experiences. Access to police departments seems at times to be

---

[11]To know whether or not another can be trusted means essentially that one can locate the other within a known social structure. The outside observer in police settings has no known location within the structure initially and is thus caught in the classic anthropological "marginal-man" position. The observer must in effect create and maintain a role on his own. A good discussion of this problem can be found in Berreman (1962).

directly proportional to the researcher's fraternal credentials. That is, if one cannot claim status as a former police officer or is otherwise experienced in police matters, doors will be difficult to open. The police view, along with John Dewey's and Mao Tse-tung's, is that experience is the only teacher. If one has not "been there" one cannot possibly understand what it is like to be a policeman. In short, many policemen feel that a person has no business studying them unless he too belongs to the club. While such sentiments nicely rationalize a closed-door policy and are no doubt to be found in other occupations such as medicine, professional athletics, and industrial management, in the police world fraternity has its own special, and sometimes quite personal, meanings. One patrolman in my study put this well when he said, "How the fuck can I tell anyone who ain't a cop that I lie a little in court or that sometimes I won't do shit on the street 'cause I'm tired or that I made some asshole 'cause he was just all out wrong . . . the only people that can understand are people who've had to pull the same shit" (Van Maanen, 1974:103).

4. *Occupational Secrecy:* A very serious obstacle to research is the secrecy that attends too many police matters. Secrecy is important to the police not only in terms of content as outlined above but also as an organizational form. Like the military, the police regard the disclosure of information about their affairs as potentially a threat to their success, and even their survival. Related to this guarded, mission-oriented perspective are the commonsensical implications attached by the police to the terms "research," "study," or "investigation." These terms are usually interpreted as a means for establishing responsibility in general (organizational) and sometimes in particular (individual) for a culpable action. If research to the police means finding a culprit, why, from their standpoint, should it be different for anyone else? So strong is this occupationally induced belief that a principal problem for an outsider in police organizations is to avoid being taken as a spy. While this may be a familiar organizational phenomenon, the legal nature of police work probably intensifies this fear of the investigator—of any variety. I am reminded here of the only half-humorous police saying that "Anytime you get more than five cops together, you can be sure one of them is a fink" (i.e., an informer).

Briefly, secrecy as an obstacle to research in a police organization has at least three distinct, although broad, meanings. First, secrecy about certain operational policies is often deemed a strategic necessity by the police insofar as the success of such policies are concerned. That is, research directed at, say, narcotics enforcement may be seen by the police as potentially damaging to the very tactics of enforcement presently in use. If drug dealers are, for example, to discover how narcotics agents make their cases, they might be able to alter their modus operandi such that their chances of getting caught are lessened. Second, secrecy is important to the police because of the potential embarrassment a disclosure about mistakes, misguided policies, cover-ups, and so on might bring the institution, organization, division, or other collective units in a department. This is the image question, and it is of consequential value to the police to keep a good one—both internally and externally. Third, secrecy is obviously an issue at the individual level, since all policemen are potentially subject to a vast number of rather strict controls. Thus, exposure of certain activity may bring organizational, colleagual, and legal sanctions to bear upon a person. All of these features make difficult the task of pursuing research inside police agencies.

5. *Value Conflicts:* Hughes (1974:330), in a most telling remark, noted that ethnographic investigations always entail the study of one kind of people by those of another kind. The police are marked by political and social conservatism; a preference for action and decisiveness; a distrust of, if not prejudice against, racial minorities; and an ambivalent, instrumental attitude toward the law, an attitude that can come only from the frustration of trying to interpret and enforce the law on a day-to-day basis. The social scientist, on the other hand, tends toward the politically liberal, is intellectually inclined, strives to appear tolerant of racial minorities, and usually regards the law in expressive, abstract, almost utopian terms. Clearly, the values (and often the class backgrounds which contribute to such values) of the social scientist and those of the police are widely discrepant. This discrepancy, of course, makes for an uncomfortable research situation. Yet there is a necessity on the researcher's part to accept, as Buckner (1967) suggested, value relativism at a gut level and forgo the single-minded (perhaps simpleminded) moralism that requires one to openly denounce sentiments and acts that are at variance with one's own standards. To many a social scientist, this is an impossible and untenable position, especially when one considers the fact that the researcher may be called upon to assist police officers in certain activities which may be personally distasteful and sometimes illegal.

6. *Uniqueness, Partitions, and Street-level Isolation:* Rubenstein (1973: Preface) noted that while policing is universally practiced, it is always localistic in character. In the United States, each police department seeks to enforce and publicize its uniqueness vis-à-vis other departments. To an observer, the implied differences can be bewildering. There seems to be such an acknowledged diversity of approaches to policing that to find a "representive" department is an impossibility. Even within a given department the variety of tasks performed by various divisions is sometimes astonishing. The police world is partitioned into so many subworlds that it is quite difficult to see any unity of purpose or overall strategy behind police actions. Furthermore, if the researcher wishes to observe problematic police situations at the street level—where trouble arises, decisions are made, and the direct control of the citizen is exerted—he faces an elaborately scattered, spatially independent, subject population who will tell him if he asks that each district is quite unique. Moreover, since so much police work (at least at the patrol level) is patently unpredictable, there is no guarantee that one's time in the field will be even roughly commensurate with the naturalistic observation of what the researcher might consider critical events. As many others have pointed out, the first hand observation of the police in action can often be a boring and frustrating affair, since there is no assurance that one will see what one came to see (Reiss, 1971; Cain, 1973; Manning, 1976b). For example, I recently spent an evening riding with a Watch Commander during a special-event tour who

spent inordinate amounts of time simply trying to locate his assigned lieutenants, who, when they were located, remarked that they were having difficulty
finding their sergeants, who, had we found them, undoubtedly would have said
something to the effect that they too could not locate the patrolmen under their
not-so-watchful eye. This is what Rubenstein (1973) called the game of
"finding-your-men," and to a researcher who wishes to generalize from his
findings, the knowledge that such a game exists may be disturbing.

7. *Environmental Turbulence and Danger:* There are various kinds of environmental turbulence that act as barriers to research in police organizations. One
sort of turbulence is the all-too-familiar police scandal. Police departments in
New York, Boston, Detroit, Seattle, and Cincinnati are all examples of organizations that have recently undergone public scrutiny and exposure of manifold
types of corruption—bribery, extortion, brutality, drug dealing, burglary, and
so on. City police seem to undergo almost regular cycles of public concern with,
and investigation into, their internal affairs. Given the rather precarious political position of the directors of any department under investigation, it is no
mystery that their doors are usually tightly shut to outsiders during and for
some time following these periods. Indeed, since the threat of scandal is omnipresent in virtually all large departments, it is something of a small wonder
that we have the number of police studies we do.

In my own case, I entered the Union City Police Department to begin my
work only six weeks before a major scandal erupted. As the series of screaming
headlines in the local and national press documented, the public disclosure of
police misconduct left a trail of criminal indictments throughout the police
hierarchy. Had I begun my negotiations for access as little as a month later, I
have no doubt (and was told so by several high-ranking police officials) that my
proposed study would have been turned down. Following the indictments—
one of which involved a departmental sponsor of mine—the organization was
headed by a sequence of interim chiefs of police. A permanent chief was not
selected and seated until the fourth month of my initial nine-month study
period. Although I was insulated from having to contend with much of the
police anger and fear that followed in the wake of the investigation and the
change of command by virtue of my location at that time in the police training
academy, I most certainly could sense a residue of resentment among veteran
officers against the curious outsider when I finally began to work the streets.
While I cannot say the extent to which the scandal influenced or in various
ways interfered with my study, I am sure that such effects were not insignificant. There were, for example, several older officers who flatly refused to
speak with me during my stay in Union City on the grounds that they no
longer trusted anyone who had connections with the "new" brass in the department (i.e., the "reform" brass).

This last anecdote bears further examination because it sheds light on
matters of more general importance. Despite popular conjecture, the internal
order in which the police work is anything but a consensual one, even in the
most placid of times. As Bittner (1970) and Rubenstein (1973) note, police officers rarely tell each other any more than they absolutely have to. Horizontal
and vertical cliques abound, and most members have a refined sense for the

politics of the organization.[12] A novice researcher in the department cannot know directly of such matters and may, for example, find himself outside looking in as a result of inadvertently forming an alliance with a particular administrator who, for various reasons, is pushed well outside the central power structure of the department. Again, in my case, the indicted police official who was instrumental in my gaining initial access to the department was, whatever his legal status, a relatively popular leader among the men under his command. Had this not been true, I probably would have been ushered as unceremoniously out of the department as my sponsor was ushered ceremoniously into court. Luckily, then, I was allowed to remain, although at every administrative change in command I suffered through some anxious moments, not knowing if I would be allowed to continue my work. Such shifts in the political wind are common to many police departments whether or not the organization is embroiled in the throes of a scandal.

Another problem related to the internal affairs of policing is the exaggerated degree to which the appearance of a supervisor is regulated by the performance of his subordinates. It is said in police circles that "First, the chief makes his decision, then the locker room boys make theirs." And if a police administrator has reason to suspect that an uncomplimentary picture of his area of responsibility will be forthcoming from certain ecological or functional niches in the department, a researcher without an explicit mandate to examine these niches that comes from the top of the organization is almost sure to be denied access into these regions. More common, however, is the reverse effect where an administrator grants access to a particular region of the department, yet the researcher finds upon his arrival little openness or desire among the men to discuss their work and a great suspicion of the researcher's motives. Discipline in police departments is at times lax and at times harsh, but it is virtually always of the personal sort and therefore seen by most members at the lower levels as particularly capricious (Reiss and Bordura, 1967; Rubenstein, 1973; Manning, 1976a). A researcher who aligns himself with an administrator whom the men do not trust finds, understandably, that the men will not trust him either. Reputations cannot be created or learned in a day, and the inexperienced police student is well advised to follow the police example in

---

[12]In many respects, police organizations represent a hodgepodge of cliques, cabals, and conspiracies. Since members often do not trust each other (let alone an outsider), deceit, evasiveness, duplicity, lying, innuendo, secrecy, double-talk, and triple-talk mark many of the interactions in police agencies. In part, the police are organized around cleavages in the interpretation of their mission, the meaning and application of disciplinary rules, and the importance and value of various tasks performed by members of the department. From this standpoint, conflict is obvious between the staff and the line, the upper and lower ranks, the professionally oriented and traditionally oriented members of the department, and the union and the nonunion participants within the organization. Social cleavages too are not unknown, as the sometimes bitter conflicts between blacks and whites, men and women, and younger and older officers suggest. Manning (1976a; 1977), Wilson (1968) and Cain (1973) are good on the organizational and situational cleavages, whereas Alex (1969), Neiderhoffer (1967), and Muir (1977) are good on the social and individual cleavages.

such matters and keep quiet about his sponsors in the department until he knows the system quite well indeed.

Finally, certain obstacles to research derive from the day-to-day troubles that are associated with police work. Stabbings, shootings, civil unrest, violent police-citizen encounters, volatile demonstrations, and bizarre homicides all occurring within a delicate political situation are, to a degree, "normal" features associated with police work. A researcher in such a context is often a liability to the police, slowing their actions and forcing them to contend with yet another meddling civilian. They will not like it. Moreover, there are risks for the researcher who wishes to see for himself what the police life is like. I wanted to be, for example, in a position like Rubenstein (1973) where the various contingencies of the work itself would compel the police to ignore my presence, or, on the other hand, to be in a position where the police would have to rely on my being there.[13] It is my impression that those observers who wish to stand quietly in the background, removed from the action, cannot do so for long in the police world. Indeed, the researcher must be willing to share the risks, and, to a degree, share the "dirty work" associated with the everyday job. I will return to this crucial issue in another section, but for now, suffice it to say that the environment in which policing takes place is hardly conducive to the traditional but remote research role played most comfortably by the so-called detached academic scholar.

IV. NEGOTIATING ENTRY

There is, as I have suggested, a shroud of silence surrounding the circumstances under which social scientists have been granted permission to conduct research in police settings. Very few published studies have discussed the negotiation process by which a specific research site was chosen and secured. Those that have invariably imply that the process was an aleatory one (Manning, 1976b). The would-be police researcher is left therefore with the sense that his success in gaining inside privileges depends primarily on external, perhaps serendipitous, occurrences and contacts.

There is a partial truth to this assumption. I established contact with fourteen departments and actively negotiated with five of them before being granted access to one department to carry out my study. While there may be researchers in the field who are sufficiently attractive, slippery, independently powerful, or well connected to gain access on their own without such a wide search for cooperation, most of us are not. Presumably, what typically occurs is that the investigator selects several departments which are roughly equivalent

---

[13]From this perspective, it should be clear that one of my operating goals was to maneuver myself into a position where I would be close at hand whenever anything dramatic or important occurred. At such moments, the police could not help but talk about what was going on, for they were far too excited to be reticent and far too interested in the matters at hand to be reluctant to supply the contextual details. Needless to say, however, such a tactic required me to first become sufficiently part of the everyday scene such that my police acquaintances were not alarmed by my presence.

on certain descriptive dimensions and is willing to settle for any one of them.[14]

My quest for access was directed toward "large" departments (i.e., over 1,000 men in uniform) and operating in an "urban" environment (i.e., cities over 500,000 people). Such a strategy left considerable and obvious variation among the departments I contacted—size, structure, policy, and so on. For convenience sake, my search began with those departments located reasonably close to the university I was attending but quickly expanded territorially on the basis of various personal contacts I developed whom I thought might help me secure access.[15] After several discouraging months of getting nowhere, I would have been just as content with access in, say, Portland, Oregon, as in Baltimore, Maryland.

It has been suggested by some that the introduction of a "professional orientation" among the police is a prerequisite for the growth of police-related research (Banton, 1970; Manning, 1972; Reiss, quoted in Manning, 1973; and McCall, 1975). This may be the case in general, although in my case it did not seem to operate in particular. In fact, it appeared to me as I pursued my efforts at breaking into a police system that the more professional a department was thought to be, the less chance I had to gain access to it. To wit, the Los Angeles City Police Department, considered by many to be the foremost example of a professional force, flatly turned down my study on the grounds that "it would unnecessarily interfere with the primary functions of the department" (personal communication from the commander of the LAPD Training Division). It is naive to believe that the so-called professionalization of the police will solve access problems for the outside researcher. My own feeling on this matter is that professionalism has exasperated, not eased, the situation. While professional departments are perhaps more likely to undertake certain sorts of research projects (i.e., those that are initiated internally and oriented toward managerial problems), they are at least as likely as traditional departments to

---

[14]This is hardly unique to those interested in studying the police. All organizations are rather careful about allowing the curious outsider inside their boundaries. In fact, Chris Argyris (personal communication) suggests that police organizations, because of their explicit public mandate, may even be somewhat easier to study than those private organizations in which management is held accountable to only a small and usually reclusive board of dirertors. To illustrate his point, Professor Argyris remarked that when he was about to conduct his first field study, he was turned down flatly by eleven banks before finding one willing to allow his presence in the organization. Dalton (1964) presents a similar picture of the private firm. While police departments are difficult to enter as a researcher, too much can be made of their isolation and reluctance to be examined as a unique and peculiar organizational characteristic. See Lofland (1976) and Douglas (1976) for some further variations on this theme.

[15]Manning (1976b) suggests and illustrates four types of police contacts that have apparently been instrumental in securing access for those researchers who have acted more or less on their own. The four are: informal social contacts; friends or friends of friends; family contacts; and work-related contacts. The would-be police researcher without acquaintances in any of these categories would be well advised to get some before trying to break into a police agency. Academic credentials alone, unless they are backed up by institutional support of some kind, are unlikely to allow one to penetrate very far into most police organizations.

refuse access to the field worker who is necessarily vague at the outset about his specific research aims.[16]

Consequently, the inescapable conclusion here is that a researcher who is seriously desirous of conducting field work inside a large, urban police department, and has no obvious inside connection (or prestigious police research organization such as the Police Foundation, the Urban Institute, or an LEAA-related sponsor), must knock on many doors and be willing to settle for what he can get. And the responses to the researcher's initial inquiries are often slow in coming. I spent six months of fairly intensive letter writing, telephone calling, interviewing, and site visiting before finally arranging access to a police agency. Some departments did not answer my letters of inquiry at all, and, of those that did reply, all were noncommittal and oblique. In person, a line I encountered several times from aids to a chief of police went as follows: "The Chief has not yet had time to consider your request—he is a busy man, you know—but we'll contact you as soon as your request has been looked at." The process is akin to a modified version of Goffman's (1952) "cooling out of the mark." Sooner or later, these officials must have reasoned, my interest would sag and I would abandon my efforts. Such a tactic of course allows the department to maintain an appearance of openness without revealing that it is, in fact, closed. It is significant, perhaps, that my efforts in fourteen departments resulted in only three written refusals. Directness and decisiveness may characterize the actions of men at the lower echelons in police agencies, but these characteristics did not typify the behavior of the men of the upper ranks whom I had tentative dealings with. The researcher in such cases may become knowledgeable on the metaphysics of waitingness, but not on the police.

Some might suppose, as I did, that the direct or blind approach to gaining access is foolish. That is, as everybody knows, the "wise" researcher seeks out intermediaries who can proffer advice, set up inside contacts, and run interference for the researcher attempting to break into the system. Obviously, where intermediaries are available, such cultural wisdom should be heeded. I had indirect contacts for twelve departments. My contacts ran the gamut from people who claimed they knew the chief of police, the mayor, or the city manager of the town, to those who had relatives in "high places," to those proverbial contacts "who knew somebody that knew somebody (. . . who knew somebody . . .)"

---

[16]There are several other reasons here as well. First, professional departments usually have more to lose from research—particularly the open-ended, ethnographic variety of research which could quite possibly puncture part of the carefully constructed public image of the organization—than do departments without strong professional pretensions. Second, the more professionalized a department, the more likely it is to have its own internal research division in which to conduct the studies administrators deem appropriate (and, not insignificantly, to bring in outside dollars for various purposes under the guise of research). An outside researcher may compete with this division, thus causing some degree of tension and strain inside the department. In short, I believe that unless the researcher: (1) brings with him money, and a lot of it, to support his research activities to the profit and perhaps growth of the department; (2) has impeccable credentials via governmental or foundation support; (3) has the study couched in a programmatic and experimental framework; and/or (4) has very high sponsors within the organization, he will find the doors to most professionalized departments tightly shut.

inside a particular police department. Most of these leads led nowhere. One lead in particular took me to a member of the Human Relations Commission in a West Coast city who directed me to a local chief of police. When I arrived at my appointed time to meet with the chief, I mentioned the name of the commissioner who had directed me to him. At that point, whatever opportunity for access I might have had in this department quickly disappeared and I was treated to a verbal lambasting of the commissioner's moral character and abhorrent attitudes toward the police. I was soon escorted to the door with the remark, "No friend of David Belknap is a friend of the police." (Note: all names used here are fictitious.)

Needless to say, I became more and more discouraged in my attempts to secure access. Even my academic supporters were beginning to suggest that I look elsewhere for a research topic. I once visited a rather famous sociologist who had conducted one of the major police studies published up to that time. I was told by him to either select a small, suburban, or rural police department in which to conduct my study, or forget the matter entirely.

It is important also to note that in some of my efforts I had attempted to frame my proposed research in terms of managerial questions, not sociological ones. I emphasized to some departments my affiliation with a school of administration, hoping that, as a result, I would be viewed as less of a threat than if my social science background and interest were brought to the fore. This approach is, of course, double-edged, because such a "pitch" to members of the organization at the lower levels is likely to work to the disadvantage of the researcher. But this, I felt, was an issue I could deal with when I came to it. First, I had to get access. It is the case, too, that at the upper levels of a "mismanaged" organization, such a pitch is unlikely to be received with great favor. At any rate, regardless of my emphasis, I grew increasingly disenchanted with the possibility of ever carrying out my proposed study.

Finally, after a little over five months of trying, I got a break. A clinical psychologist who had recently joined the University of California, Irvine faculty overheard a conversation I was having with a fellow graduate student in which I was loudly bemoaning my fate and cursing the police for their closed-mindedness. He intervened in the conversation to tell me that he had some police contacts that might be of interest to me. It turned out that he had once run a two-week sensitivity training program for the middle and upper level managers in the Union City Police Department (a department I had not yet contacted) and claimed to have established considerable rapport with a few of the participants, a rapport that perhaps only a sensitivity-group trainer can achieve. He then offered to see if he could help place me in that department. A few days later, after I had briefed him on my purposes and research plans, he called an acquaintance in the department, an assistant chief of police, who, my psychologist friend assured me, was on the "good side" of the chief. During the short conversation which I was invited to overhear, but not to participate in, my go-between attested personally to my character, my scholarly aims, and my willingness to listen to police problems. Over the phone, to my great surprise, the assistant chief said he would "back" the research idea but that final authority would depend on the chief's approval. Since only the briefest of mention had been made as to what, in fact, I was interested in, I was instructed to write a captain in the Training Division and explain my research purposes. I did so and a week later I was invited to Union City to meet the captain, the assistant chief, and the chief himself. I flew to Union City, and after an hour's meeting with the captain and considerably shorter meetings with the assistant chief and the chief I was granted access to the agency on what could only be called open terms. Less than a month later I entered the department to begin my work.

I have gone into these procedural matters, not because I think good fortune and happenstance are subject to analytical dissection, but because I think my no-doubt-unique case study conveys some rather pragmatic lessons about the process of gaining access to police departments. First, the process can be immensely time consuming, uncertain, and very unlikely to conform to academic calendars. Second, without a sponsor in a high place within a department (or a contact with a personal link to one), it may well be impossible to obtain access. Third, even in densely populated urban areas where there are many police agencies, it is necessary that a would-be researcher assume much flexibility vis-à-vis his choice of a department and therefore be willing to be geographically mobile.

V. STRIKING THE RESEARCH BARGAIN(S)

The above sketchy details of the access problem do not deal with what was gained (other than access itself) and what was sacrificed from the researcher's perspective (other than time and energy). Nor does it deal with features of the internal politics of a police organization, which are, no doubt, critical of the outcomes of the access process. Furthermore, I have not touched upon the impression management tactics available to both parties in the access negotiation interactions. In this section, I will cover these and other issues from a perspective which suggests that the negotiation process, when successful, results in what Becker (1970) calls the "Research Bargain."

At the outset, I must emphasize that the research bargain is not one bargain nor an explicit contract; rather, it represents many bargains involving a set of loose promises and expectations held by both researcher and hosts as to what will occur before, during, and after the study. Thus, an initial bargain may be and usually is renegotiated many times throughout the organization. The research bargain does not represent one master agreement but rather represents many agreements with a number of people in the research setting. Indeed, the bargain that is struck between researcher and hosts becomes over time to represent a multileveled political and moral agreement that is episodically in flux—although there are usually stable agreements contained within it. As Manning (1976) suggests, the researcher "buys" stability in the field only by continuous exchange with a number of actors. In the subsections that follow I discuss four analytically distinct features of research bargains. This is, however, only a convenient gloss, for these four features are hopelessly interconnected.

A. *Contacts:* Perhaps the most important structural feature of police organizations (particularly large ones) for a field worker to be aware of is the degree to which these organizations display a magnified version of nonconsensual solidarity. That is, police departments represent various social groupings not linked together by any basic agreement but rather organized around cleavages in interests and values. They are knit together at certain places, both vertically and horizontally, by patterns of collusion, accommodation, compromise, and nescience, but nevertheless, police departments are marked by enduring, sometimes bitter internal conflict. Most of these conflicts are, of course, acted out in what Goffman (1959) would call "backstage regions" and are therefore often outside a researcher's initial awareness. But a researcher should be cognizant that his study will quickly raise questions concerning, for example, the patterned evasion of certain organizational rules or raise questions about the particularistic implementation of ostensibly universalistic regulations and laws (Manning, 1976a). In short, there are many definitions and meanings available and utilized inside any department concerning what a police agency is about.[17] The acceptance of the researcher in one part of a police organization does not therefore guarantee his acceptance in another part; it may, in fact, prohibit his acceptance in other parts of the organization. Realization of these features of police life suggests that a researcher must very carefully pick and choose the members of the organization he will align himself with, recognizing in the process that his choices are problematic in many ways.

More specifically, it is usually the chief of police whom the researcher must initially convince of the worth of his study if he expects to gain access. The chief is thought to be the crucial contact, the final authority. Reiss and Bordura (1976) characterize police organizations as patrimonial bureaucracies, meaning, in part, that the chief takes formal responsibility for virtually all decisions taking place in the organization and often takes a very personal interest in even the most petty of matters bearing on his command.

In Union City, my one and only meeting with the chief of police who authorized my entrance into the department lasted maybe fifteen minutes. We exchanged pleasantries; he asked a few almost *pro forma* questions (primarily about who was to finance my study and provide personal support while I was in Union City); he extracted a promise that I would not identify people, places, or

---

[17]This suggests that whatever bargains may be struck between the researcher and various groups and individuals within the organization, such bargains may also be in conflict. Indeed, there is no requirement for the investigator to create research agreements that are internally consistent. For example, a researcher could not inform a high-ranking police administrator that he will maintain absolute silence if he happens to observe illegal activities on the part of subordinates, even though it is clear that this is the bargain the researcher must make at another level in the organization. As Dalton (1964) argued, organizational studies require a researcher to negotiate recursively throughout the organization with the hidden recognition that each social agreement reached at any given level may violate the implicit or explicit agreements reached at other levels. Needless to say, the field worker walks a thin line here and can only trust that his deceptions will not be discovered before he completes his work.

the department in any of my writings,[18] and he mentioned that I would be expected to provide the department with periodic written reports whenever requested (none was ever requested). Hierarchically, I was to be under the supervision of the assistant chief, who, although assuring me later that he would be available should I get lost in the labyrinth of the organization, informed me that whatever my request, I was to work through the Captain of Training. Over the next few weeks the captain and I worked out some details of my study by telephone. And, before the study proper had begun, the police had agreed to provide me with: a reserve commission in the department; a slot in the next recruit-training class; approval should I choose to administer the questionnaire I had prepared prior to my first meeting in Union City; tentative approval for my work in the patrol division (subject to my graduation from the Police Academy); and, most important, something of an administrative commitment to see my work completed. It was not at all apparent from these negotiations what the police were to receive in exchange for their efforts. From my perspective, I could hardly have asked for better terms.

B. Legitimacy: A researcher obviously must be concerned with how his work is viewed by those whom he contacts in the setting, both before and after access has been negotiated. Prior to gaining entry, a large part of the legitimacy question is answered for the hosts on the basis of how contact was initiated—through whom? Because of my relationship with a particular academic acquaintance, I had inherited a certain amount of a priori respectability by virtue of his reputation within certain well-placed circles in the department. Through this fortuitous contact I had been able to carve out a most favorable research bargain with the highest officials in the department. Similarly, I justified my presence in the department throughout the study to other police officials on the lower managerial rungs by virtue of my personal contract with the ranking officials. This was apparently respected by most members of the department at face value, although I am sure that on occasion some people did check out my story with the higher authorities.

After the department was rocked by the scandal (and both the chief and assistant chiefs were relieved of their command), my position in the department became less clear. However, since I had by then begun to develop relationships of a personal sort with policemen I encountered every day, no noticeable change in my informal research contacts occurred despite my apprehensiveness. I was, in fact, assured by the Captain of Training that my role would continue as before. I was never contacted by the interim chiefs, nor did I

---

[18]I must rank among my faux pas in Union City this agreement to keep confidential the name of the department. I was not asked directly about this matter but volunteered such an agreement in my initial meeting with police officials. I did so out of perhaps a sense of nervous anxiety, and correspondingly, an overwhelming desire to please my potential departmental sponsors. However, once my promise was out there was no backing away from it, for I was reminded of the agreement many times before I departed. Whether or not departmental anonymity would have eventually surfaced as a condition for continuing the research I cannot say, but nonetheless the fact remains that I did blunder into what I consider now to be an unfortunate artifact of too many police studies.

contact them. When a permanent chief of police was appointed, I was in the final month of my training program and was concerned naturally as to whether my opportunity to observe in the Patrol Division would still be forthcoming. Working through the captain, I scheduled an appointment with the new chief to discuss this matter. Again, my meeting lasted only a few minutes and was marked by an exchange of pleasantries having to do with how I was getting along and whether or not I was enjoying my stay in Union City. The new chief told me that there were "no problems" associated with my observing in the Patrol Division, and I was given the name of a patrol captain who would presumably assist me in my initiation into that division. He would also be available should any problems arise. I was told, however, that I could remain in the division only until the first of the year (about four and a half months).[19] And, as far as the chief was concerned, I could work with whomever I could convince to have me along. Thus, the new chief had adopted, as had his predecessors, something of a hands-off policy, leaving it to me to handle the day-to-day problems of the study. Barring any incident (as yet undefined), the chief would not interfere with matters of the research. The only substantive issue that arose during this brief meeting was the chief's apparent concern for what he called a "sick-leave abuse problem." He asked that I keep "my ears open" for information that might be pertinent to this problem. I said I would, and the topic was never discussed again.

What accounts for such a research bargain? Certainly I had been somewhat open about the more general aims of my research, but I was not required to be very specific. Once the study began, however, I avoided full disclosure and chose not to be candid with anyone in the department either about my initial sentiments regarding the police or about certain findings I felt I was making after the research was under way. Of course, I attempted to appear sincere, to be a hardworking, if naive, student of the police, genuinely interested in the welfare of the department and my field contacts. But whether or not such definitions took hold, I cannot say.

My own description of my thoughts and actions are perhaps best captured by the felicitous phrase, "cautious sophistry." That is, whenever possible I opted to explain my doings to people in only the most general of ways, and then only when asked directly to do so. Following a standard methodological ploy, I continually defined my purposes in most nebulous of terms, such as, "discovering what it was like to be a policeman," or "finding out how one learns to be a

---

[19]Interestingly, my original bargain struck with the former chief of police did not specifically deal with the time I was to be allowed in the Patrol Division. Although I had made clear my desire to observe for an extended time in the division following the academy, both the chief and I agreed to consider the matter later. Perhaps the conditional terms of this tentative agreement to permit me to observe in the Patrol Division only after I had attended the Police Academy was based on the latent premise, well stated by McCall (1975:70), at the researcher will become discouraged and drop his planned study or at least that i. . will come to acquire the police view of policing." At any rate, these matters are unknowable, but I must admit that I was both pleased and surprised by the new chief's willingness to extend my stay in the department because, at the time, I had been told by the Captain of the Training Division that three months was about all I could expect.

policeman." I emphasized that whatever preconceptions I might have had upon entering the department had been shattered by my experiences to date. Furthermore, I pictured myself as working for very stern and relentless taskmasters located back at the university who were sure to pick apart my study if I failed to return with good information. Perhaps they would even flunk me if I was not to get accurate data and I would be unable to follow my chosen profession. This evoked considerable sympathy from a few officers, who several times chided others for what they took to be incomplete or evasive answers to my questions. On many occasions, I attempted to define myself as a compassionate medium by which they could tell their story to the hostile outside world. Of course, not everyone wished to tell their story, although some did. While I am sure not everyone I encountered in the department fully accepted such accounts as the "true" reasons behind my questioning, most of my lasting acquaintances in the department appeared, after a time, to accept some, if not all, of them as legitimate ones from their perspective—although for the most part these reasons stood in the background and were rarely discussed.

Without doubt, my "credentials" also played an important part in helping to establish my legitimacy in the organization.[20] I presented myself as a student of organizations, a Ph.D. candidate from a graduate school of administration. Although I was not sponsored by a research organization associated closely with the police, I was supported partially by the Office of Naval Research. This ONR source was probably seen by the police as complimenting their sense of propriety in a way that maybe an NIMH (National Institute of Mental Health) grant might not. Yet this is mere speculation, for the only matter explicitly part of the research bargain was the requirement that full financial support come from sources outside the department. After my initial statement as to where my funds originated, the question was never again raised at the administrative level, although I was time and time again asked to explain my situation to acquaintances at the lower levels in the department. This is an important matter, for certainly the fact that I was not on the departmental payroll was a most critical part of my presentation of self within the department. Indeed, my legitimacy as a researcher, not a spy, was at stake in such presentations.

Of relevance to this legitimacy issue is the researcher's ability to clearly differentiate himself from other intellectual types with whom the police are familiar. In particular, the field worker must take pains to impress upon his police contacts that he is not closely akin to the journalist or reporter who might potentially cause the police harm. Usually the fact that the researcher has a known university affiliation, is willing to spend a lengthy amount of time in residence, and comes equipped with certain tools of his trade that offer physical evidence that he is, in fact, who he says he is will suffice. I tried to

---

[20]There are perhaps many examples of researchers who have been granted access into police organizations without the elaborate preparation, procedural runarounds, and credential worries discussed here. But, if so, it is not apparent from the literature, where in even the most cursory of acknowledgments prominent mention is made of the researcher's close association with a prestigious university and the support of various funding agencies. See Manning (1972:235–236).

assume the appearance of a conventional academic researcher with a variety of scientific instruments (and theories). To wit, I had a prepared questionnaire and a tentative interview schedule ready to submit to police officials for examination and approval at my first meeting. Such a tactic helped, I think, to make my purposes seem more or less benign, hence easing my entry into the department.

This is an interesting road to hoe, for, as I mentioned earlier, the field worker must also defuse the sometimes dangerous and explosive social-scientist-as-critic role the police may wish to assign to him. Here, time in the field as well as personal friendships are crucial factors, particularly after access has been achieved. To a certain extent, this is the "nice-guy" ploy so idealized by writers on field methods.[21] But clearly, while the researcher may succeed in being seen as a "nice guy," he is still a researcher and sometimes must take pains to enforce that definition lest people with whom he has marginal contact think he is up to no good. At the outset of my studies, for example, I discovered a few formal routines such as collecting career histories from the recruits in my academy class (a process not unlike the anthropologist collecting kinship genealogies during his early days in the field) that helped perhaps to establish a "nice-guy" image as well as to defuse whatever dangers others may have seen in my work. In a sense, such formalities helped normalize my work. Indeed, people may be quite suspicious of the field worker, since he appears to be doing little more than "hanging around" much of the time. By collecting career histories, I was in essence saying to my police associates: "Look, I really am doing some research. See, I am working on my trade right now by asking questions and writing down what people tell me."[22]

Finally, my legitimacy—especially among the patrolmen—depended, to some degree, on how I chose to explain my particular choice of Union City as the site for the study. I initially began with appeals to their pride (e.g., "it is a good, professional, interesting department"). This seemed to satisfy only a few rookies. Many continued to wonder (as I did myself) why I had traveled so far to enter the Union City Department, since there were obviously other depart-

---

[21]The "nice guy" is, of course, one who is rarely angry, never hostile, concerned for everyone's welfare, does little favors for others, and generally expresses humility and the milk of human kindness in his everyday encounters. This was an emotionally trying role for me to play. In particular, there were some people on the scene that I frankly did not care for no matter how hard I tried. Indeed, there were a few people who I truly loathed, and I avoided them wherever and whenever I could. Yet, when we came face to face, I tried to avoid communicating my disgust for them, though I am quite sure that on some occasions I was less than successful. While the "nice-guy" front is proclaimed usually as the appropriate field-work approach, it is surprising that so few authors have bothered to comment upon just how difficult and wearisome it is to maintain on a day-to-day basis. It seems as if ethnographers are almost expected to come to love their studied tribes, informants, subcultures, or whatever, so that being the "nice guy" is a natural and easy stance. Perhaps this myth will eventually be shattered, for I suspect more than a little posturing is involved when a literature is so silent about such human emotions as indignation, disdain, fear, and even hate. Malinowski's (1967) candid diaries go some distance in this direction.

[22]Irrespective of the researcher's credentials, honorable objectives, and friendly behavior, some people in the setting will have great difficulty accepting the field worker

ments, equally good, which were closer to home. I tried explaining this in terms of Union City's relative accessibility; the aesthetic surroundings of Union City; the content of the department's training program; and, my own favorite, which stressed the department's similarity to other police agencies. But clearly the most satisfactory explanation was simply that my presence was a result of chance. Everyone agreed, with the possible exception of the various chiefs of police, that fate was the real reason I was there.

C. *Offerings:* To the field worker entering a police system, a principal difficulty is to cast his research interests so that they correspond to the police sense of what is important. This suggests, as Roy (1970) advised in another context, that the researcher waive questions of substantive merit to those studied. In the police world, this means that the primary offering made is to study problems the police themselves consider relevant. This does not mean one must agree with former Police Chief Tootham from Oakland, California, who once remarked, "There are no police problems in this community, only people problems" (quoted in Murray, 1970:67). Rather, it means that if the researcher is to create and maintain a role for himself within a department, he must listen carefully to police perspectives (and there are many) and try to transform his scholarly interests into a language that is at least understandable to the police. That is, the researcher must make himself sensible to the police by addressing and articulating problems that the police can recognize. Furthermore, he must allow ample opportunity for the police to contribute to his research definitions. Indeed, I suspect the police tire rather quickly of the oversocialized academic bore whose didactic conversational mannerisms leave him comfortable in human interaction only when he is lecturing another. Such a style is especially handicapping in police circles, if not in all circles.

But this offering a flexibility is not merely a matter of stylistic or pragmatic concern. It reflects deeper theoretical questions about the utility of the formal and deductive research models. The praxis model suggested here requires a certain suspension of beliefs on the part of the researcher when entering a setting with which he is unfamiliar. Problems are to be discovered, not to

---

because his day-to-day work is of a kind that few will have witnessed before. To some extent, as Freilich (1970) suggests, the field worker is a collector of esoteric trivia, personal confessions, and sometimes scandalous gossip (evil talk). From an informant's point of view, if the ethnographer is in fact what he pretends to be and is not gathering information for some purpose harmful to those studied, his work is likely to seem all that more bizarre. The spy, however dastardly, is at least understandable. In Union City, I learned that there were a few officers who thought me to be some kind of scholarly bum since I was constantly seen as "hanging around" without displaying any interest in finding a job that paid better than my small research stipend (350 dollars per month). On my return to the field after an absence of some two and one half years, these attitudes changed dramatically since I was by then a fully accredited professor at, of all places, the Massachusetts Institute of Technology. Although my work style probably seemed no less bizarre and puzzling to these men, I was no doubt more respectable to those who continued to be skeptical of the work involved in field work. This form of incredulity (and perhaps mild suspicion) was captured elegantly by one officer who remarked quite sincerely, "You mean they pay you to just ride around and talk to cops?" The more common attitude, however, was of the "nice-work-if-you-can-get-it" variety.

be assumed. It would be illusionary for the field worker to believe he knows what is important to members of a particular social group before he begins his work. I have found much sympathy among police on these grounds. Indeed, many policemen feel that they have been exploited by social scientists who have used their departments and people as if they were guinea pigs in some grand but obscure and ultimately meaningless experiment. In Union City, my presentation from the outset included a statement that I needed considerable help in discovering the areas the police felt were particularly problematic and troublesome. Furthermore, I continued by noting that since I was an outsider there was no way I could know beforehand what these areas might be. This sort of open-textured research stance is usually interpreted as existential concern. When it is made a part of the research bargain, it means that the researcher is committed to listening closely to the dramatic and mundane complaints of the police. In brief, it is a commitment to empathize, not to judge.

From this standpoint, lengthy written statements about what one wants to research in the department are likely to be liabilities rather than assets. I chose not to disclose in Union City a long statement of purpose and method I had prepared, choosing instead to provide a short, two-page summary highlighting only a few questions I had in mind and attesting to the fact that I was a student, not an expert, on matters of concern to the police. Since a researcher cannot predict in advance how his aims will be interpreted, the more flexibility he can build into the research plan the better.

This brings up the matter of what to disclose. Although I think it sound for the ethnographer to make known to the people he studies that his purpose is to learn about their way of life (i.e., in my case, I told others that I wished to learn what happens to people after they join a police organization), I do not believe it is ethically necessary, nor methodologically sound, to make known specific hypotheses, background assumptions, or particular areas of interest. To this point, Berreman (1962:18) writes, "participant observations, as a form of social interaction, always involves impression management. Therefore, as a research technique, it inevitably entails some secrecy and some dissimulation. . . ."

To take my police acquaintances into full confidence may well have precluded the possibility of acquiring information essential to the study. For example, I had an interest in how officers on the street learned techniques to cover their mistakes; or, as they would say, "to cover their asses." An admission of this interest, to most people in the department, would have been harmful to the research effort itself, for they most certainly would have quickly become suspicious of my motives for wanting to collect such information. Similarly, had I felt morally constrained to avoid all dissimulation, I would have had to forgo whatever insights I gained into such topics as graft, perjury, and police violence by not announcing that these were matters in which I was very much interested. Perhaps in other types of organizations a researcher can reveal his "true interests," but even here I doubt that few field workers can aspire to access and acceptance initially through full and complete disclosure.

This is not to imply that one's general purposes are to be concealed. Certainly, every time a new face is encountered in the setting, the research-bargaining process begins anew and the field worker must reveal his reasons for also being on the scene if he expects to remain in place and learn anything at all about what is going on. Some people may wish to know why he is asking what they consider awkward or dumb questions. Some may wish to know about the opinions the researcher has formed of them. And some may wish also to know what the researcher plans to do with the results of his work. The field worker's response to these matters of everyday discourse represent the flesh on whatever skeleton the research bargains are being negotiated. Indeed, the information the researcher provides others in the setting represents, to a large degree, the quid pro quo for the information they provide him. In the early stages of my own research work, I was able, for instance, to trade certain biographical elements of my background for those of another's background.[23] Such reciprocity occurred when dealing with purposes or intentions as well. It is expected in human affairs.

To those knowledgeable of social science matters, the issue of research pure and research applied is bound to arise. And research for research sake is unlikely to carry much weight in police departments. Applied research, directed at police demarked areas, is viewed with considerably more favor, though the investigator must be careful to avoid the implication that his findings will be of the cut-and-dried variety. In talking recently with various police administrators from several departments, it appears as if social scientists typically oversell their research programs—perhaps just as social scientists typically overpredict individual behavior. Most police administrators believe that social research rarely, if ever, contributed much in terms of a solution to police problems. Therefore, the researcher must avoid making claims that will not stand up to practical test. Perhaps the best way to avoid this is to make as few claims as possible.

In my own case, I tried to avoid justifying my study solely on the grounds that it would "be good" for the department. However, I did imply that I felt my study could contribute some fresh ideas in certain problem areas; for example, recruit training, management practices, personnel assignments, and so forth. I also noted continually to whomever appeared interested that I would be happy at the conclusion of my studies to discuss the findings in terms of what might be done differently from what was currently being done in the department. Interestingly, I was never asked to do so (and did not so volunteer).

There are certain other more specific elements related to the research bargain that fit under the general heading of offerings. Perhaps of critical importance is the researcher's demonstrated willingness to spend large amounts of time in the field listening to police stories, learning the language, and displaying the appropriate demeanor and respect that policemen as human be-

---

[23]It is true of course that the researcher is not "anyman." As Douglas (1976) notes, the personal relationships a field worker builds with his informants are not "biographically transparent." Certainly few, if any, relationships are independent of either party's race, sex, age, socioeconomic background, speech patterns, or religion. In the police world, there is, for example, a rather realistic and impenetrable boundary surrounding what a fifty-six-year-old veteran patrolman will tell a twenty-eight-year-old "greenpea," regardless whether or not that greenpea is a rookie cop or a social scientist.

ings feel is their due. This means, in part, that the researcher follow roughly the same bureaucratic norms of address, composure, and attire; the same procedural routines; and the same work schedules followed by the men he is studying. Furthermore, a researcher in a police organization should not expect (nor should he request) immunity or protection from the consequences of whatever actions he may engage in while conducting the research. In other words, not only must the researcher adhere to the same rules as those whom he studies, but the researcher should also expect to be judged by others in the department by roughly the same standards on which they judge each other. One of the standards in police organizations, for example, is discretion. That is, if one is to be granted the status of an insider in any particular police subgroup, the price for that status is the researcher's silence when it comes to exposing matters that might harm members of that subgroup. It is important, therefore, that the researcher understand this dilemma at the outset. If he is to gather valid data, he must not inform on the activities of any individual or group in the organization. However, he is not beyond the law (or the administrator) on this matter. His participation in certain activities or a refusal to answer inquiries about certain activities will subject him to the same sorts of disciplinary measures other members of the department face. This is the only ethical bargain the field worker can hope to make—to be treated as others are treated. Any other agreement could lead to a crippling interpretation of the researcher's role as spy—or worse, as agent provocateur.[24]

As I implied earlier in this section, it is somewhat puzzling to me what it was that my police sponsors hoped to gain, if anything, by allowing me into their department. Perhaps they hoped to gain some associative respectability among the academic community—an unlikely sort of objective. Perhaps they wished to gain some insight into their recruitment, selection, and training programs. Or perhaps they hoped to convey the appearance of openness to the public at large through the presence of a civilian researcher in the department. Internal political purposes are possible, too, of course. Indeed, some of my sponsors inside the department may have viewed me as a potential ally on an issue of their concern. Public relations or image-building purposes are perhaps also relevant. For instance, the department most likely garnered some favorable publicity as a result of my presence in the organization when a local television news crew filmed a portion of the Police Academy graduation exercises. During the ceremony, my classmates presented me with an unexpected gift, a Smith & Wesson .357 magnum revolver, after which it was only proper that I ceremoniously respond. My impromptu speech of gratitude was filmed and featured on the six- and eleven-o'clock news that evening, during which I was erroneously referred to as a California college professor who went through the training academy because "the Union City program was among the best in the

---

[24]I do not wish to wave my hands over the serious moral questions raised by a researcher's observation and participation in police systems. These are important and weighty matters, but there is hardly space to adequately discuss them here. For a treatment of the ethical dilemmas involved when a researcher maintains close ties with a police organization, see Van Maanen (forthcoming), wherein these matters are described from the researcher's point of view as a "moral fix."

country." No doubt a member of the department had supplied the station with their information. And, to a viewer, I suspect my "I-wish-to-thank-all-the-people-who-made-this-possible" remarks did not in any way tarnish the image of the department.

But, public relations aside, whatever political or other latent purposes any ranking members of the department may have had remain unknown. Perhaps they would have surfaced had my sponsors remained with the department throughout the study. Yet it is nonetheless impossible to know, though if my experiences are at all typical, it is a little surprising we have as many police studies as we do, for police administrators have much to lose by allowing a researcher access to the inner regions of their departments and apparently little or nothing to gain, at least in the short run.[25]

D. Testing: A research project that entails lengthy firsthand observation and participation places the field worker in a socialization setting similar to the situation any newcomer would face in the group under study. While the researcher may be especially attuned to the consequences of the socialization processes taking place in the setting, he is not immune from such processes, and may, in fact, be the object of intensified attention on the part of the members of the group he is examining. A newcomer to any group engaged in ongoing, defined, and established activity is sure to be tested by others in the setting as to his ability and intention to keep the performance moving as smoothly as possible (Van Maanen, 1976). And, under most conditions, membership will not be extended to the would-be member until others are reasonably sure that the newcomer will behave himself in such a fashion that they will not be shamed, hurt, or otherwise embarrassed by his presence. From this standpoint, participant observation in a police agency, as Reiss (1968:325) remarked, "can be socialization with a sociological vengeance."

Social science literature is replete with examples in which strangers to various groups are inspected, questioned, and called upon to demonstrate a commitment to an aspired-to group before the strangers are taken in, and hence enlightened on both the symbolic and the practical affairs of the group (e.g., Dornbush, 1955; Schein, 1956; Sykes, 1958; Lofland, 1966; Van Maanen, 1976, 1977). A similar passage, though considerably less ritualized and without the chorus of exhortation in the background, awaits the researcher in police departments. Some of the tests applied to the researcher are common to all new members; others are not.

The first test shared by all members is the police selection process itself. It is a time-consuming, arduous, uncertain, and at times humiliating process

---

[25]I do not wish to overemphasize either the promise or the influence of social science in the world at large. Certainly many, if not most, police administrators believe that, in general, social science research is likely to have little influence beyond the self-contained world of social science. From this standpoint, some police officials really don't care about a researcher in their midst—provided he does not create internal disturbance—since they believe, with some justification, that the results of his study will merely produce more esoterica to be consumed in a rather closed academic community. Only the future will demonstrate how accurate such predictions prove to be.

which weeds out many of the less committed aspirants to the occupation (Van Maanen, 1973). A like function is served by the selection process associated with research projects submitted by outsiders, to which I have directed most of my comments up to this point.

The academy training program stands as the second hurdle awaiting a recruit to the organization. Lortie's (1962) phrase, "the shared ordeal," elegantly describes some of the training program's main properties. To a researcher seeking to understand the police milieu, attendance at and matriculation from a police academy serves several purposes. On one hand, however idealized they may be, the technical lessons that are taught in the academy, promote an instrumental appreciation on the researcher's part for the organizational, legal, and procedural difficulties of a variety of police tasks. On the other hand, attendance at the academy serves the expressive function of providing the field worker with at least one common and, for most policemen, significant experience to share with other members of the organization. It links the researcher with all others who have been through the academy and dramatically displays and documents the researcher's willingness to associate closely, cooperatively, and on roughly equal terms with the men who are his subjects. As one veteran policeman told me, "Anyone who's willing to put up with that academy bullshit can't be all that bad." For a researcher wishing to get as close to the lives of policemen as possible, attendance at the academy represents a very fruitful first step.

Naturally enough, my Union City experiences bear this out. From the outset, I made no effort to conceal my identity and general purposes from my academy classmates. To be sure, I was an anomaly, but the day-to-day exigencies of academy life made treatment of me as an anomaly problematic, if not impossible. For example, when the field worker is on the ground doing calisthenics with forty other men, or taking a competitive exam on traffic codes together, or simply swapping stories and sharing a few beers with other recruits in a tavern after classes are over for the day, it makes relatively little difference whether one is a researcher or not. The person is, for all intensive purposes, a passenger on the same boat and will be judged primarily on the same grounds as are all other passengers.[26] Given that virtually all recruits were strangers to one another on the first day of the academy, I had precisely the same opportunity as everyone else to prove worthy of group respect. Certainly

---

[26]Some of the grounds upon which friendship and colleagual respect developed in the all-male Police Academy are hardly unique to police departments—although they may be somewhat more visible, since the imagery of the police, like that of the military, conjures up an excessive concern for physical toughness and strength. Both Harris (1973) and Cain (1973) do skillful jobs exploring some of these gender-related matters. Certainly, the Police Academy (as similar to other fraternal programs where much of the everyday talk turns on cars, sports, and sex) stresses an ethos of masculinity; and the glib recruit who can, for instance, boast of his sexual adventures, speak of his victorious street fights, and demonstrate his knowledge of the "practical world" wins considerable respect from his peers. Indeed, the raconteur with a gift for gab—who apparently lives outside the puritanical morality—is something of an internal folk hero to policemen. Wambaugh's (1975) most recent novel, *The Choirboys*, capitalizes quite nicely on such legendary figures (and themes) inside police agencies.

my credentials entitled me to a certain amount of status in the group, but the status that counted to the cohort group undergoing the academy experience was status on recruit concerns. From this standpoint, I had, as did everyone else, thirteen weeks to prove myself dumb, clever, foolish, or smart on the trials that were of our collective concern.[27]

The third test common to recruit experiences occurs during the early post-academy days on the street, under the watchful eye of veteran officers. I have referred to this sort of test elsewhere as a "balls test"—an evaluation made by colleagues of a recruit in the Patrol Division as to the recruit's willingness to share the risks of policing (Van Maanen, 1973, 1974). The essence of this test is captured nicely by Rubenstein (1973:318) when he writes, "Every policeman learns to accept in silence much that he dislikes about some colleagues—their indifference, viciousness, dishonesty—but he does not have to keep quiet about someone he considers unreliable or dangerous."

For an armed researcher with a reserve commission riding with the police in either the front seat with a "solo" officer or in the back seat of a patrol car with a two-man partnership, this test is in all likelihood less extreme than it is for the fully sworn, novice officer. However, there were more than a few occasions where I felt compelled to assist, or, in police parlance, to "back-up" the policemen I was ostensibly observing. I must also hasten to add that during such moments I was hardly making a rational, conscious, or instrumental decision "for the good of my study." Rather, I was reacting as police react to what I took to be unavoidable contingencies of the situation at hand. In one case, for example, I wrestled on a living room rug with an irate husband, trying to keep him from bursting into a bedroom where two officers were attempting to determine whether a woman was comatose because of drugs, drink, or illness. On another occasion, I stood alongside a veteran officer blocking a driveway while a man suspected of felonious assault (on a police officer) made up his mind whether he was going to try to run us down with his automobile or submit to questioning. This was a particularly terrifying incident, for my hand was wrapped around my gun and all I wanted at the moment was to be out of the situation intact.[28] Whether or not I "passed" such tests with colors flying or

---

[27]I finished the academy ranked in about the middle of my training class. These rankings were based solely on academic performance and included a recruit's score on such things as weekly spelling tests, pop quizzes and short tests on lecture or reading materials, and three most comprehensive and lengthy examinations. Though it was difficult indeed to flunk out of the program for academic failures, no one knew this to be a certainty and therefore we all studied reasonably hard, though few of us would admit to so doing publicly.

[28]Only one other time did I fear having to make use of the ever present bulge under my sport coat while on patrol. I was involved in a "shakeout" of a three-level parking garage in which it was thought that at least two armed men were hiding. In the darkness, eight patrolmen and I searched the building from bottom to top, aiming flashlights into every nook and cranny of the structure. All of the men had their holsters unsnapped, and several had their service revolvers out and pointed ahead of them with their safety catches off and their finger on the trigger. The patrolman I was teamed with told me to get my gun out also, since it would have been somewhat awkward for me to draw quickly from inside my coat if the need arose. I did so, hoping, perhaps as did the others, that the objects of our

dragging I cannot say. I can say, however, that most men seemed to accept my presence in the department and appeared pleased when I would spend a shift with them. Some confirmation of this appeared after I had spent about six weeks in the Patrol Division when I began to be smothered with invitations to ride along and with stories which began, "Boy, you shoulda been with us last night." I am certain as well, though, that there were some occasions (particularly during my early experiences in the Patrol Division) in which I was an added burden to the men and represented perhaps the sort of bother that they would have preferred to do without. This brings us to the last test common to recruits and researcher, one I will call here the "prudence test."

Danger comes to a policeman from many sources. To his body, it comes in the form of physical violence, a fact of life in city streets. To his soul, it may come from the dirty work he performs, or the vulgarities he must endure, or the toll that is taken by attempting to enforce the unenforceable. But to his career, danger comes from a careless word or a lie that he cannot cover up. Virtually all policemen (of course, some more frequently than others) have engaged in activities that, if known, could get them fired—or worse, land them in jail. A researcher who spends more than a trivial amount of time with the police quickly discovers this. More quickly, the researcher's police subjects will make some character judgments as to the prudence to be expected from the particular researcher. A statement attesting to the researcher's confidential intent will not be taken at face value. Nor will his professed professional ethics be believed until it has been subjected to some sort of practical test. Circumspection on the researcher's part can only be demonstrated over time.[29] If time passes, for example, without a rumor drifting back to the sender or if time passes after an illegal or questionable event has occurred in the presence of an observer without incident, the field worker's prudence can be tentatively documented. More often are those occasions when a researcher inadvertently overhears or actually witnesses a potentially harmful event or series of events. And, if and when the field worker stumbles into a flagrante delicto, those involved will of necessity be particularly alert for clues regarding the prudence of the stumbler. Of course, the embarrassment may work in the researcher's favor, since those embarrassed are under some obligation to oblige the researcher for his discretion in the matter. They may not like it, but they have little choice.

One tactic available to others on the scene to more or less neutralize this power of observation (whether it rests in the rookie policeman or in a researcher) is to involve the faultless in potentially embarrassing acts them-

---

hunt had long since vanished. As we suspected, they were not to be found. But, in retrospect, I think I was more frightened at the time of drawing the fire of my nervous colleagues by tripping over a trash can or by throwing a threatening shadow on the wall than I was at the prospect of encountering our imagined adversaries.

[29]Polite acceptance and even friendship are not sufficient to get one into the backstage regions of police departments. Indeed, liking a person is no guarantee that one can also trust him. The police too know this and are consequently very guarded in their talk and actions around all nonpolice acquaintances, including, many times, close family members.

selves. Thus, the faultless are made vulnerable to the same sanctions as others, and discretion on their part can be expected. Debts and obligations are therefore equalized.

I was party to much discrediting information regarding the legality and propriety of police actions in Union City. On several occasions I was present when illegal acts took place and, although not directing the line of action, I was as culpable legally as any witness to such actions would be. During and after such incidents, it was clear that I had moral choices to make regarding my conduct. I made these choices as would most policemen. I kept my mouth shut. And, after a short time, I too was vulnerable to legal sanction, for I had not reported what I heard or saw. As Manning (1972:255) cautioned, "observing the law involves, at times, not observing it."

These four tests are, as I have noted, not unique to a researcher engaged in observational study, but are common to all new members of the organization. To the degree that the researcher can live with, and measure up to, these tests, he will be rewarded with data inaccessible through any other means. Some of these data may in fact be beyond verification, but if his goal is to discover and understand the possible shams, pretenses, and contradictions of police work, there is no other way. The best advice I could offer to a researcher just entering a police system would be precisely the same he would hear were he a recruit: simply keep quiet and to himself virtually everything he hears and sees during his early days in the field.

Less crucial perhaps but nonetheless important were certain other forms of testing which appeared to be specially tailored to discover something about the character and commitment of the researcher qua researcher. For example, early in my academy experience I was given a series of "gigs" (punitive assignments) for what I thought to be imagined offenses—a "dirty weapon"; "jogging, not running, while in the parking lot" (note: recruits were required to run to and from their automobiles, classrooms, and locker room); "not paying attention in class"; and so on. In a short period of time, I had amassed enough gigs to convince myself that the academy staff was pushing to discover whether or not, as several staff members later told me, "I could take it." Grudgingly, I accepted my extra assignment and did not utter verbal protest. Ironically, the effect of such special treatment brought my classmates and I closer together.[30]

---

[30]It is perhaps more generally the case that the displayed hostility of management often works to a researcher's advantage in that it opens certain doors to a population of subjects who are also potential targets of punitive managerial attention. Indeed, when lower-ranking members of an organization see that the researcher is also having his troubles with the bosses, they may grant him more legitimacy and credibility than might otherwise be the case. This phenomenon was helpful to me, not only in the academy, but also in the Patrol Division, where the curt, sometimes caustic, treatment I was accorded by several captains and lieutenants in the division provided me with increased respectability among patrolmen. I was also able to gain access to certain personnel statistics from the Policeman's Benevolent Association, apparently on the grounds that the department itself had been unwilling to provide them. Union officials therefore had documented evidence that I was not in league with management. From their perspective, I was probably thought to be "open-minded" on matters of their concern, and even perhaps capable of being influenced by their cooperation.

They too felt that I was being singled out, and, although there may have been some secret relief that it was me and not them who was being punished, they were supportive in words and sometimes, deeds of my plight. This unique form of testing was shortlived, however. By the end of the first month, the training staff eased off, apparently satisfied that I could "take it" and was around to stay.

Another sort of test occurred during one of my brief visits back to Union City several years after the bulk of my field work had been completed. I was observing informally one evening with an officer I knew quite well, and after "lunch" (about 10:00 P.M.) he suggested we have a drink. I agreed. While not a frequent event, I had in the past several times shared a drink with on-duty officers. We drove to an almost empty parking lot adjoining a city park, a lot frequented by other cars working this particular district. My friend parked the squad car and opened his ever present attaché case and produced a bottle of brandy from which we both took several sips. Suddenly, there was a loud banging on my side of the car, and there in apparent moral outrage was the squad sergeant, a sergeant I knew only in passing. I sat with a three-quarter-full and open bottle of brandy in my hand and had, no doubt, a look of utter chagrin on my face when the sergeant opened the door and ordered me to explain my doings. I looked first to my colleague to no avail; he was tight-lipped and staring straight ahead. I then turned to the sergeant and, with great difficulty, stammered out a weak excuse that went something like, "Goddamn it, Sarge, I'm sorry, it's my bottle. Jimmy told me not to bring it along." At this point, both my partner for the night and the sergeant broke out in almost hysterical laughter, and I realized that I had just been made the proverbial sucker of a well-executed practical joke. After a period of mock outrage I joined the laughter, and then all three of us shared another warming nip of brandy. But there was a lesson for all of us in that surface moment of unseriousness. Had I said that the bottle was not mine, the ruse would have still been revealed, although my character might very well have undergone considerable and perhaps irreparable damage. It is true, of course, that the significance of such a light and playful test was not apparent to the conspirators. On the other hand, perhaps it was.

In summary, the testing aspect of the research bargain is more subtle and less visible than the other three features, for it surfaces indisputably only when there are failures. Furthermore, testing is continual and provides, in the final analysis, the basis upon which the field worker creates and re-creates a viable research role in the organization. It would be foolish to assume that once trust has been established it is maintained without effort or that it never waxes or wanes over time. Indeed, a field worker may be trusted for awhile and then, without warning, tossed out on the grounds of some real, or fancied, failure in a particular situation that the police view as a critical test of some sort. In essence, as Becker (1966) suggests, the researcher is being asked during such tests, "Whose side is he really on?" Will he side with the brass or bigwigs in the department? Will he side with the men of one sector against the men of another? Will he side with the patrolmen against their sergeant? Long (1958) once described the urban milieu as an "ecology of games." Such a description fits police departments as well. Some of the games pit vertically partitioned players against each other such as the ongoing conflict between the patrolman and the brass over the applicability of certain departmental rules and regulations. Other games pit horizontally partitioned players against each other such as the continual monopolization for personal use of information gathered at the street level. There are no doubt as many teams, in Goffman's (1959:77–105) sense of the term, at work in police departments as there are special interests. A field worker, by becoming closely attached to any one team and hence appearing to accept that team's definition for what the police are about, may in the process alienate potential informants from other teams and hence cut off some promising research directions. Thus, the researcher must try to walk a nerve-wracking tightrope, appearing to accept as many definitions as he can get away with. From this perspective, the research bargain that is appropriate to the ethnographic task merely provides a license for the field worker to engage in these games. And, as with any other kind of license, it can always be revoked.

VI. SOME CLOSING COMMENTS ON THE PARTICIPANT-OBSERVER IN POLICE ORGANIZATIONS

Levi-Strauss (1972) uses the apt French term *bricoleur* to describe the participant-observer. The *bricoleur* is the proverbial jack-of-all-trades who draws on whatever material is at hand, raw or polished, to fashion a needed product. I know of no better way to describe what the participant-observer or ethnographer does. The field worker develops a style and a method that presumably best fits the situation he is in. The methodology then unfolds on the basis of contextual contingencies. The tools of the researcher working from this mode are primarily his eyes and ears, although at times they may include other information-generating and information-gathering techniques such as surveys, formal interviews, archival or official documents, and so on.

Participant-observers do not appear of course on organization charts. Nor is there likely, as I have suggested, to be much lay knowledge as to what researchers committed to this method actually do, as is less true, perhaps, with researchers using questionnaires or formal interviews to gather data. In effect, the participant-observer must construct a role and definition for himself and his activities as best he can, given what other people on the scene deem appropriate. And every time one definition wears thin, another must be created. In my case, I was to various people at various times, a cop buff, a writer of books, an intruder, a student, a survey researcher, a management specialist, a friend, an ally, an asshole, a historian, a recruit, and so on. Some of these definitions I could control, and can, therefore, properly speak of manufacturing my appearance to fit the occasion. Other definitions I could not control, nor could I avoid or disclaim them with much success. In either case, however, there is much to learn, for the labels available and utilized by any group tell us a great deal about the social patterns, behavioral requirements, and associated problems of that group.

The methods literature surrounding field work often discusses what is thought to be the proper etiquette, demeanor, and distance to be assumed by a researcher as well as some of the scientific consequences associated with the use of the human instrument to gather data. In particular, this literature invariably discusses the relative trade-offs among the various roles thought to be available to the participant-observer.[31] As the label implies, there are two crucial dimensions on which role choice is assumed to turn. First, the researcher has a decision to reach concerning the degree to which he wants to participate in the day-to-day life of the group under examination. In theory, he can be active, simulating or achieving membership, thus assuming all the duties, rights, and responsibilities that go with membership. Or he can be passive, standing off to the side, as it were, quietly watching the ongoing performances. Second, in either of the participation realms, the researcher is thought to have a choice as to whether or not he will reveal his identity as a researcher. On this dimension, he can be overt, providing a full explanation to those on the scene as to his role and objectives, or he can be covert, masking his purpose and identity. There are then four logical or pure types of role available to the ethnographer or the participant-observer. These roles are presented and labeled in Figure 1.

FIGURE 1

PURE TYPES OF PARTICIPANT-OBSERVER ROLES

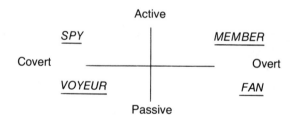

The vast majority of police studies have been conducted by researchers working out of a fan's role. Westley (1970), Skolnick (1966), Reiss (1971), Cain (1973), Banton (1964), Wilson (1968), Manning (1977), Muir (1977), and others all made their purposes known at the outset; were not full-time or part-time sworn officers; and, if they took a role in police actions, one gathers they did so on a most limited and perhaps reluctant basis. Other work falls somewhere between the member role and the fan role. Rubenstein (1973), while not formally a police officer, spent over nine months riding patrol in civilian garb on a regu-

---

[31]On observational research roles see, for example, Gold (1958); Merton (1972); Lofland (1971:93–116); and Schatzman and Strauss (1973:58–63). There is a good deal of controversy over the "proper" research role, and most of it centers either on the degree to which the observer should participate within the studied scene or on the ethical soundness of a researcher's decision to adopt a covert role for collecting data. A good selection of position papers representing both sides of these controversies can be located in Filstead, ed. (1970), and McCall and Simmons, eds. (1969).

lar work schedule and engaged in police activities whenever possible.[32] My role in Union City as I have described it here was similar. Harris (1973) too falls between these roles. He was a member of a police academy training class, though not recruited or selected on the same grounds as his cohorts. A few studies have been accomplished by a researcher in a full-member role. For example, Neiderhoffer (1969) draws on twenty years of work experience in the New York City Police Department for background pertaining to his study of police cynicism.[33] Since there is also something of an exposé literature regarding the police, some work has been accomplished from the spy perspective. These writings, by and large, come from ex-policemen who draw on their departmental experiences and deal largely with graft, corruption, brutality, and other damaging aspects of police conduct (e.g., Drodge, 1973; Walker, 1969). Finally, there is a smattering of journalistic writings accomplished by non-policemen who either surreptitiously investigated police activities (e.g., Hersey, 1968; Chevigny, 1968, 1972) or vicariously experienced the police life through documents, records, or personal information provided by police-officer confidants (Maas, 1973; Whittemore, 1973; Knapp, 1972).

It is possible, therefore, to describe what can be called a dominant research style in terms of these four pure types. However, to do so distorts what I think is actually the case as I have tried to show in this paper. Despite the formal rhetoric of justification attached to post facto descriptions of an applied methodology, I suspect most participant-observers in the police world shift back and forth continually among the four available roles. The ethnographer, then, must be seen to play all of these four crude roles to varying degrees. The notion that with one swift, succinct statement of purpose and identity the researcher neatly boxes himself into an ethically sound (or unsound, depending on one's moral stance) and agreed-upon research role is misleading, if not false. To wit, I often had conversations with police officers who took me to be among their ranks. Many times, policemen whom I had not previously met but encountered during a shift had no other explanation available for my presence other than collegueship, since we were meeting on "police-only" territory (e.g., the city jail, interrogation rooms, roll call areas, back rooms in the courthouse or hospital, or special "R & R" areas in particular districts such as the proverbial policeman's restaurant or saloon). And, to a civilian encountered during the course of a shift I was never anything but a policeman, although one in plain clothes. Short of wearing a clapboard sign proclaiming one's iden-

---

[32]Rubenstein (1973: xii) is, however, somewhat vague about the basis upon which he was permitted to observe the police when he notes: "Legal complications prevented me from becoming a sworn police officer, although I had fulfilled all the requirements at the Academy. . . . But I was permitted," he continues, "to go on the street as an armed observer." It is hard to tell from this quick description just what his status was in a patrol unit.

[33]Other works accomplished from a member role include the memoirs of former police administrators such as Ahern (1972) and Daley (1973). The writings of Joseph Wambaugh (1970, 1972, 1973, 1975) are also pertinent here, as are the stark, but forthright, works of Radano (1969, 1974). And a rather startling book exists written by a criminologist gone native, Kirkham (1976).

tity, there is no way for the field worker to be sure that his research role in the organization is in fact the role to which all others are responding.

This is not to say, however, that the researcher need not worry about establishing a role for himself within a department. Nor is it to say that the covert-overt, active-passive dimensions are irrelevant for his purposes. Rather, I have suggested here simply that there can be no pure type of research role. At best, only a dominant mode can be established. How dominant this mode turns out to be in practice depends not only on how long the researcher has to develop a role in the field but also on how deep the researcher wishes to penetrate into the lives of the observed, and on how large a part in the researcher's own life the study is to play. The longer the field worker has, the deeper the penetration; and the greater the involvement, the more blurred the lines will become between the various research modes and the more likely the working style of the researcher will reflect, as my style did, a mixed stance of part member, part fan, part spy, and part voyeur.

At any rate, without firsthand accounts of the research process itself— such as I have tried to produce here—we cannot even begin to understand the various models that guide field work in police agencies. More critically, we cannot begin to compare or evaluate the worth of given techniques in terms of the findings produced until we have a number of detailed descriptions of what, in fact, the field worker did when he was doing field work. In this sense, the world of ethnographers is as closed as the police worlds it sometimes penetrates. Like the more quantitatively oriented investigators in the social sciences, field workers too are guilty of implying by neglect that "data collection" itself is something of an automatic, dronelike activity, an aspect of research little deserving of detailed analysis. In other words, the implication that flows from the silence on this matter is that once the issues to be addressed have been selected, the level and targets of the investigation decided upon, and the procedural arrangements for access set up, the data will be forthcoming in a mechanical, trouble-free way. Goffman (1971) calls this the Gilbert Chemistry Set model of social research, and it fits many descriptions of field work as well as experimental or survey studies. Particularly in police settings, practitioners of field work have been remarkably cavalier about outlining their data-collection techniques. Perhaps this Epilogue will stimulate others to provide a more comprehensive account for the research that stands behind their results.

References

Adams, R. N., and Preiss, J. J. (eds.) *Human organization research*. Homewood, Ill.: Dorsey, 1960.

Ahern, J. F. *Police in trouble*. New York: Hawthorne, 1972.

Alex, N. *Blacks in blue*. New York: Appleton-Century-Crofts, 1969.

Banton, M. *The policeman in the community*. New York: Anchor, 1964.

———. Social order and the police. *The Advancement of Science*, 27, 1970, 48–56.

Becker, H. S. Whose side are we on? *Social Problems*, 14, 1966, 239–47.

———. Practitioners of vice and crime. In R. W. Habenstein (ed.) *Pathways to data*. Chicago: Aldine, 1970.

Berreman, G. D. *Behind many masks*. Ithaca, N.Y.: Society for Applied Anthropology, Monograph No. 4, 1962.

Bittner, E. *The functions of the police in modern society.* Washington, D.C.: U.S. Government Printing Office, 1971.
Bruyn, S. T. *The human perspective in sociology.* Englewood Cliffs, N.J.: Prentice-Hall, 1966.
Buckner, H. T. The police: The culture of a social control agency. Unpublished Ph.D. Dissertation, University of California, Berkeley, 1967.
Cain, M. *Society and the policeman's role.* London: Routledge & Kegan Paul, 1973.
Chevigny, P. *Police power: Police abuses in New York City.* New York: Pantheon, 1969.
———. *Cops and rebels.* New York: Pantheon, 1972.
Conklin, H. Ethnography. In D. L. Sills (ed.) *International encyclopedia of the social sciences,* Vol. 5. New York: MacMillian and Free Press, 1968.
Daley, R. *Target blue: An insider's view of the New York City Police Department.* New York: Delacorte, 1973.
Dalton, M. Preconceptions and methods in *Men Who Manage.* In P. E. Hammond (ed.) *Sociologists at work.* New York: Basic Books, 1964.
Dornbush, S. M. The military academy as an assimilating institution. *Social Forces,* 33, 1955, 316–21.
Douglas, J. *Investigative social research: Individual and team research.* Beverly Hills, Calif.: Sage, 1976.
Drodge, E. F. *The patrolman: A cop's story.* New York: New American Library, 1973.
Filstead, W. J. *Qualitative methodology: Firsthand involvement in the social world.* Chicago: Markham, 1970.
Fox, J. C., and Lundman, R. J. Problems and strategies in gaining access in police organizations. *Criminology,* 12, 1974, 52–69.
Frake, C. O. Notes on queries in ethnography. In S. A. Tyler (ed.) *Cognitive anthropology.* New York: Holt, Rinehart & Winston, 1969.
Freilich, M. *Marginal natives: Anthropologists at work.* New York: Harper & Row, 1970.
Glaser, B. G., and Strauss, A. *The discovery of grounded theory.* Chicago: Aldine, 1967.
Goffman, E. On cooling the mark out. *Psychiatry,* 15, 1952, 451–63.
———. *The presentation of self in everyday life.* Garden City, N.Y.: Doubleday, 1959.
———. *Relations in public.* New York: Harper & Row, 1971.
Gold, R. Roles in sociology field observations. *Social Forces,* 36, 1958, 217–223.
Gulick, J. Urban anthropology. In J. J. Honnigmann (ed.) *Handbook of social and cultural anthropology.* Chicago: Rand McNally, 1973.
Habenstein, R. W. (ed.) *Pathways to data.* Chicago: Aldine, 1970.
Harris, R. N. *The police academy: An inside view.* New York: Wiley, 1973.
Hersey, J. *The Algers motel incident.* New York: Knopf, 1968.
Hughes, E. C. Who studies whom? *Human organization,* 33, 1974, 327–334.
Johnson, J. *Doing field research.* New York: Free Press, 1975.
Junker, B. H. *Field work.* Chicago: University of Chicago Press, 1960.
Kirkham, G. L. *Signal zero.* Philadelphia: Lippincott, 1976.
Klockers, C. B. *The professional fence.* New York: Free Press, 1974.
Knapp, W. *The Knapp report on police corruption (in New York City).* New York: George Braziller, 1972.
Levi-Strauss, C. *Tristes tropiques.* New York: Atheneum, 1972.
Lofland, J. *Doomsday cult.* Englewood Cliffs, N.J.: Prentice-Hall, 1966.
———. *Analyzing social settings.* Belmont, Calif.: Wadsworth, 1971.
———. *Doing social life.* New York: Wiley, 1976.
Long, N. The local community as an ecology of games. *American Journal of Sociology,* 64, 1958, 251-261.
Lortie, D. C. Shared ordeal and induction to work. In H. S. Becker, B. Greer, D. Reisman, and R. T. Weiss (eds.) *Institutions and the person.* Chicago: Aldine, 1968.
Lundman, R. J., and Fox, J. C. Maintaining research access in a commonweal bureaucracy. Unpublished paper presented to the American Society of Criminology, 1974.
Malinowski, B. *Argonauts of the western Pacific.* New York: Dutton, 1961 (first published, 1922).
———. *A diary in the strict sense of the term.* New York: Harcourt, Brace & World, 1967.

Manning, P. K. Observing the police: Deviants, respectables and the law. In J. D. Douglas (ed.) *Research on deviance*. New York: Random House, 1972.

———. Rules, colleagues and situationally justified actions. In R. Blankenship (ed.) *Colleagues in organization*. New York: Wiley, 1976a.

———. The researcher: An alien in the police world. In A. Niederhoffer and A. Blumberg (eds.) *The ambivalent force* (2d ed.) Chicago: Drydon Press, 1974.

———. *Police work*. Cambridge, Mass.: MIT Press, 1977.

Maas, P. *Serpico*. New York: Viking, 1973.

Mather, L. M. Ethnography and the study of trial courts. Paper delivered at the Annual meeting of the Midwest Political Science Association. Chicago, April 1976.

McCall, G. J. *Observing the law*. Washington, D.C.: U.S. Government Printing Office, 1975.

McCall, G. J., and Simmons, J. L. (eds.) *Issues in participant observation*. Reading, Mass.: Addison-Wesley, 1969.

Merton, R. K. Insiders and outsiders. *American Journal of Sociology*, 78, 1972, 9–47.

Muir, W. K. *Police: Street corner politicians*. Chicago: University of Chicago Press, 1977.

Murray, W. *Previews of coming attractions*. New York: World, 1970.

Niederhoffer, A. *Behind the shield*. New York: Doubleday, 1967.

Pelto, P., and Pelto, G. H. Ethnography: The field work enterprise. In J. H. Honigmann (ed.) *Handbook of social and cultural anthropology*. Chicago: Rand McNally, 1973.

Polsky, N. *Hustlers, beats, and others*. Chicago: Aldine, 1967.

Powdermaker, H. *Stranger and friend: The way of an anthropologist*. New York: Norton, 1967.

Radano, G. *Walking the beat*. New York: World, 1969.

———. *Stories cops only tell to each other*. New York: Stein & Day, 1974.

Radcliffe-Brown, A. R. *Method in social anthropology*. Chicago: University of Chicago Press, 1958.

Reiss, A. J. Stuff and nonsense about social surveys and observations. In H. S. Becker, B. Greer, D. Riesman, and R. S. Weiss (eds.) *Institutions and the Person*. Chicago: Aldine, 1968.

———. *The police and the public*. New Haven, Conn.: Yale University Press, 1971.

Reiss, A. J., and Bordua, D. J. Environment and organization: A perspective on the police. In D. J. Bordua (ed.) *The police: Six sociological essays*. New York: Wiley, 1967.

Roy, D. The study of southern labor union organizing campaigns. In R. W. Habenstein (ed.) *Pathways to data*. Chicago: Aldine, 1970.

Rubenstein, J. *City police*. New York: Farrar, Straus & Giroux, 1973.

Schatzman, L., and Strauss, A. *Field research: Strategies for a natural sociology*. Englewood Cliffs, N.J.: Prentice-Hall, 1973.

Schein, E. H. *Coercive persuasion*. New York: Norton, 1956.

Skolnick, J. *Justice without trial*. New York: Wiley, 1966.

Suttles, G. D. Urban ethnography: Situational and normative accounts. In A. Inkeles, J. Coleman, and N. Smelser (eds.) *Annual Review of Sociology*, Vol. 2. Palo Alto, Calif.: Annual Review, Inc., 1976.

Sykes, G. *A society of captives*. Princeton, N.J.: University of Princeton Press, 1958.

Van Maanen, J. Observations on the making of police. *Human organization*, 32, 1973, 407–418.

———. Working the street: a development view of police behavior. In H. Jacob (ed.) *The potential for reform of criminal justice*. Beverly Hills, Calif.: Sage, 1974.

———. Police socialization: A longitudinal examination of job attitudes in an urban police department. *Administrative Science Quarterly*, 20, 1975, 207–228.

———. Breaking-In: Socialization to work. In R. Dubin (ed.) *Handbook of work, organization and society*. Chicago: Rand McNally, 1976.

———. Experiencing organization. In J. Van Maanen (ed.) *Organization careers: Some new perspectives*. New York: Wiley, 1977.

———. The Moral Fix. In R. B. Smith and P. K. Manning (eds.) *Qualitative Social Research*. Forthcoming.

Walker, T. M. *Voices from the bottom of the world: A policeman's journal*. New York: Grove Press, 1969.

Wambaugh, J. *The new centurions*. Boston: Little, Brown, 1970.

———. *The blue knight*. Boston: Little, Brown, 1972.

———. *The onion field*. New York: Delacourt, 1973.

———. *The choirboys*. New York: Delacourt, 1975.

Wax, R. *Doing fieldwork*. Chicago: University of Chicago Press, 1971.

Westley, W. A. *Violence and the police*. Cambridge, Mass.: MIT Press, 1970 (first a Ph.D. dissertation, 1951, University of Chicago).

Whittemore, L. H. *The super cops*. New York: Stein & Day, 1973.

Williams, J. R., Manning, P. K., and Redlinger, L. J. The police and illicit substance control. Preliminary Report No. 76-NI-99-0109, National Institute of Law Enforcement and Criminal Justice, Law Enforcement Assistance Administration. March 1977.

Wilson, J. Q. *Varieties of police behavior*. Cambridge, Mass.: Harvard University Press, 1968.

Appendix[1]

Selected Research Studies of Police: Published Works, Dissertations, Theses, and Works in Progress

Study	Method	Period of Research	Research Site
Published Works			
Alex, Nicholas. *Blacks in Blue*. New York: Appleton-Century-Crofts, 1969.	Interviews	1964–65	New York, N.Y.
Banton, Michael. *The Policeman in the Community*. New York: Basic Books, 1964.	Interviews Observation* Questionnaire	1960–62	Scotland; 2 medium-sized U.S. cities
Bayley, David. *The Police and Political Development in India*. Princeton: Princeton Univ. Press, 1969.	Interviews (students & public) Observations Records	1965–66	India
_____. *Forces of Order*. Berkeley: Univ. of California Press, 1976.	Observation Interviews Records	6 months (2 summers) 1972–73	4 prefectures in Japan: Tokyo, Osaka, Aomori, & Fukuoka
Bayley, David, and Harold Mendelsohn. *Minorities and the Police*. New York: Free Press, 1969.	Interviews (police & public)	1966	Denver, Colo.

---

[1]This appendix is based on Manning's (see below) selective review of the sociological use of field methods in police agencies. We should note, however, that the listing has been substantially revised for presentation here. Furthermore, as the reader will notice, information available on many of the studies is incomplete and sometimes quite imprecise. To wit, sites are often anonymous, the number of interviews conducted by the researcher is rarely available, and even the period during which the study was accomplished is occasionally vague. In the Appendix, question marks indicate our own doubts as to how to interpret a given aspect of a particular project. Finally, the references to published works are illustrative, not exhaustive, of the books and articles that may have evolved from a specific study. Our purpose is therefore to summarize the research, not the literature.

See: Peter K. Manning, The Researcher: An Alien in the Police World. In A. Niederhoffer and A. Blumberg (eds.) *The Ambivalent Force*. Chicago: Drydon Press, 1974 (103–121).

Study	Method	Period of Research	Research Site
			New York, N.Y. St. Louis, Mo.
Bercal, T. "Calls for Police Assistance . . . ," in Hahn (ed.), *Police in Urban Society*. Beverly Hills, Calif.: Sage, 1971: 267–77.	Analysis of calls to an emergency police department phone number	1968	Detroit, Mich.
Bittner, Egon. "The Police on Skid-Row: A Study of Peace-Keeping." *American Sociological Review*, 32 (1967), 699–715.	Interviews Observations	1963–64?	
_____. "Police Discretion in Apprehending the Mentally Ill." *Social Problems*, 14 (1967), 278–92.	Interviews Observations Psychiatric Records	1963–64	
Black, Donald J., and A.J. Reiss. Many studies for President's Crime Commission Report, 1966–68.	Interviews Observation Questionnaire	Primarily summer of 1966	"High-crime" Precincts: Washington, D.C. Boston, Mass. Chicago, Ill.
Cain, M. *Society and the Policeman's Role*. London: Routledge & Kegan Paul, 1973.	Observation Interviews (officers, officers' wives)	1962–63	English Rural County/Urban Center
Carte, Gene E., and Elaine H. Carte. *Police Reform in the United States: The Era of August Vollmer.* Berkeley: Univ. of California Press, 1975	Historical		
Cicourel, Aaron. *The Social Organization of Juvenile Justice.* New York: Wiley, 1967.	Observation Police and Probation Reports	4 years	
Cumming, Elaine, Ian Cumming, and Laura Edell. "Policeman as Philosopher, Guide and Friend." *Social Problems*, 12 (1965), 276–286.	Police Calls (incoming)* Interviews Observation	1961	Syracuse, N.Y.

*Major data source.

Study	Method	Period of Research	Research Site
Daley, R. *Target Blue*. New York: Dell, 1974.	Observation (Deputy Commission, NYPD,1 year)	1970–71	New York, N.Y.
Drabek, T.E. "Lab Simulation of a Police Community System Under Stress." Columbus: College of Ad. Science, Ohio State, 1969.			
Drabek, T.E., and J. Chapman. "On Assessing Organizational Priorities: Concept and Method." *Sociological Quarterly*, 14 (Summer 1973), 359–75.			
Drabek, T.E., and J. Haas. "Laboratory Simulation of Organizational Stress." *American Sociological Review*, 34 (April 1969), 223–38.	Observation Simulation	1968–69	
Gardiner, J. *Traffic and the Police*. Cambridge, Mass.: Harvard Univ. Press, 1969.	Official Statistics (traffic violations) Interviews (police chiefs, traffic officers, civic leaders) Questionnaires		National Mass. cities National
Harris, R. *The Police Academy: An Inside Observation View*. New York: Wiley, 1973.	Observation*	1969 (Feb.– April)	Rurban County, Mass.
Kornblum, Allan. *Moral Hazards*. Lexington, Mass.: Lexington Books/D.C. Heath, 1976.	Participant- observation, Records Interviews		
La Fave, Wayne. *Arrest: The Decision to Take a Suspect into Custody*. Boston: Little, Brown, 1965.	Observation Court and Police Records	1956–57	

*Major data source.

Study	Method	Period of Research	Research Site
Manning, P.K. *Police Work.* Cambridge, Mass.: MIT Press, 1977.	Observation* Interviews	1972–73	London, Eng.
Muir, William Ker, Jr. *Police: Street Corner Politicians.* Chicago: Univ. of Chicago Press, 1977.	Interviews Observation		
Niederhoffer, Arthur. *Behind the Shield.* Garden City, N.Y.: Anchor Books, 1967.	Questionnaire Observation	21 years	NYPD, N.Y.C.
Piliavin, Irwin, and Scott Briar. "Police Encounters with Juveniles." *American Journal of Sociology,* 70 (1964), 206–14. See also Werthman and Piliavin article in Bordua (ed.), *infra.*	Observation Interviews	18 months	New York, N.Y. Oakland and San Francisco, Calif.
Preiss, Jack, and Howard Ehrlich. *An Examination of Role Theory: The Case of the State Police.* Lincoln: Univ. of Nebraska Press, 1966.	Observation Questionnaire* Interviews	1957–58	Michigan
Rubenstein, J. *City Police.* Farrar, Straus & Giroux, 1973.	Observation	one year +	Philadelphia, Pa.
Skolnick, J., and J. Richard Woodworth. "Bureaucracy, Information and Social Control: A Study of a Morals Detail," in David J. Bordua (ed.), *The Police: Six Sociological Essays.* New York: Wiley, 1967.	Observation Police Records	1962–63	"Westville" (Oakland, Calif.)
Skolnick, Jerome H. *Justice Without Trial.* New York: Wiley, 1966.	Observation* Interviews Questionnaires	1962–63	"Westville" (Oakland, Calif.)

*Major data source.

Study	Method	Period of Research	Research Site
Terry, W. Clinton III, and David F. Luckenbill. "Investigating Criminal Homicides," in W.B. Sanders and Howard C. Daudistel (eds.), *The Criminal Justice Process.* New York: Praeger, 1976:79–95.	Records* Interviews Observation	1970–74	California County Sheriff's Office (same as Sanders and Daudistel, *infra*).
Van Maanen, J. "Observations on the Making of Police-men." *Human Organization,* 32 (Winter, 1973), 407–18. (See dissertations.)			
Webster, John. *The Realities of Police Work.* Dubuque: W.C. Brown, 1972.	Police Calls Time-Motion Data		"Baywood," Calif.
Westley, William A. *The Police: A Study in Law, Custom and Morality.* Cambridge, Mass.: MIT Press, 1970.	Observation Interviews	1949 (originally a disserta-tion, Univ. of 1951)	Gary, Ind. Chicago,
Whittemore, L.H. *Cop!* New York: Fawcett/Crest, 1970.	Observation Interviews (patrolmen & detectives)	1967–68	New York, N.Y. Chicago, Ill. San Francisco, Calif.
Wiley, Mary G., and T.L. Hudik, "Police-Citizen Encounters: A Field Test of Exchange Theory." *Social Problems,* 22 (October 1974); 119–27.	Interviews* 200 on-the-job interviews by 2d author, a working police-man at the time Observation		Chicago, Ill.
Wilson, James Q. "Genera-tional and Ethnic Differences Among Career Police Officers." *American Journal of Sociology,* 69 (1964), 522–28.	Questionnaires	1960	Chicago, Ill.
_____. "Police Morale, Reform, and Citizen Respect: the Chicago Case," in Bordua (ed.), *op. cit.*	Questionnaires	1960–65	Chicago, Ill.

*Major data source.

Study	Method	Period of Research	Research Site
_____. *Varieties of Police Behavior: The Management of Law and Order in Eight Communities.* Cambridge, Mass.: Harvard Univ. Press, 1968.	Observation (?) Interviews "Visitation"	1964, 1965 1966–67	Several middle-sized U.S. cities

Dissertations:

Study	Method	Period of Research	Research Site
Bacon, Selden, "The Early Development of American Municipal Police." Yale Univ. 1939. 2 vols.	Historical Study		
Black, Donald J. "Police Encounters and Social Organization: An Observational Study." Univ. of Michigan, 1968.	Observation Police Records	Summer 1966	Washington, D.C. Boston Mass. Chicago, Ill.
Brede, R. "The Policing of Juveniles in Chicago." Univ. of Illinois (Urbana), 1971.	Observation Juvenile Records	1970–71	Chicago, Ill.
Buckner, H. Taylor. "The Police: The Culture of Social Control Agency." Univ. of California, Berkeley, 1967.	Observation	1966–67	Oakland PD, Calif.
Coates, R.B. "Dimensions of Police-citizen Interactions: A Social Psychological Analysis." Univ. of Maryland, 1971.			
Cross, S. "Social Relationships and the Rookie Policeman." Univ. of Illinois (Urbana), 1972.	Observation Questionnaires		
Cummings, Marvin J. "The Frame-Up." Univ. of Colorado, 1967.	Observation	1967–69	[North] "Carolina City"
Fischgrund, Thomas H. "Policy Making on Decentralization in a Large Urban Police Department." MIT, 1977.	Interviews Questionnaires	1976–77	Cincinnati, Ind., Ohio
Ford, Robert. "A Meeting With the Man: An Analysis of Police-Citizen Encounters in the Core City." Univ. of Illinois (Urbana), 1972.			
Guernsey, E.W. "The State Trooper: A Study of an Occupational Self." Florida State Univ., 1965.			

Study	Method	Period of Research	Research Site
Guthrie, Charles R. "Law Enforcement and the Juvenile: A Study of Police Interaction with Delinquents." Univ. of Southern California, 1963.			
Harris, James. "Police Disposition: Decisions with Juveniles." Univ. of Illinois, 1967.	Interaction Analysis Observation (see Clark/Sykes study, *infra*)		Three midwestern cities
Lundman, Richard J. "Police-Citizen Encounters: A Symbolic Interactionist Analysis." Univ. of Minnesota, 1972.			
Maniha, John K. "Mobility of Elites in A Bureaucratizing Organization: The St. Louis P.D., 1861–1961." Univ. of Michigan, 1970.	Historical Research		
McNamara, John H. "Role Learning for Police Recruits: Some Problems in the Process of Preparation for the Uncertainties of Police Work." Univ. of California, Los Angeles, 1967. See also McNamara article in Bordua (ed.), *op. cit.*	Questionnaires	1960–63	NYPD, N.Y.C.
Pepinsky, H. "Police Decisions to Report Offenses." Univ. of Pennsylvania, 1972.	Observation	1971–72	Minneapolis, Minn.
Petersen, David. "Police Discretion and the Decision to Arrest." Univ. of Kentucky, 1968.	Observation Interviews (115) (traffic & patrol) Documents and Records	"400 hours"	"Metropolitan Police in a Border State"
Pizzuto, C.L. "The Police Juvenile Unit: A Study of Role Consensus." Brandeis Univ., 1968.			
Sanders, W. "Detective Story: A Study of Criminal Investigations." Univ. of California, Santa Barbara, 1974.	Field Observation (detectives) Interviews Photos	1972–73	California County Sheriff's Office
Saunders, C.R. "High and the Mighty: The Middle-class Drug User and the Legal System." Northwestern Univ., 1972.	Interviews (lawyers, students, narcotics agents) Observations	1967–70	Chicago, Ill.

Study	Method	Period of Research	Research Site
Smith, T.S. "Democratic Control and Professionalism in Police Work: The State Police Experience." Univ. of Chicago, 1968.	Questionnaire* Observation Police Records	1967	Maryland State Police
Tifft, L. "Comparative Police Supervision Systems: An Organizational Analysis." Univ. of Illinois, 1970.	Observation Interviews (police, citizen)	1968–70	Chicago, Ill.
Trojanowicz, Robert. "A Comparison of the Behavior Styles of Policemen and Social Workers." Michigan State Univ., 1969.	Questionnaires	1968	Michigan
Van Maanen, J. "Pledging the Police: A Study of Selected Aspects of Recruit Socialization in a Large, Urban Police Department." Univ. of California, Irvine, 1972.	Observation Interviews Questionnaires	1970–71; 1974	"Union City"
Ward, Richard H. "The Investigative Function: "Criminal Investigation in the United States." Univ. of California, Berkeley, 1971.	Historical		
Watson, N. "An Application of Social-Psychological Research to Police Work: Police Community Relations." American Univ., 1967.	Questionnaires Projective Tests Interviews		
Wenninger, Eugene. "Bureaucratization and Career as Determinants of Participation in Police Occupational Groups." Univ. of Illinois, 1966.	Questionnaires		
Wilde, Harold R., Jr. "The Process of Change in a Police Bureaucracy." Dept. of Government, Harvard Univ., 1972.	Historical Data*		Detroit PD, Mich.

Masters' Theses

Comstock, D. "Boundary Spanning Processes in Complex Organizations." Univ. of Denver, 1971.	Simulation (Drabek data)		

*Major data source.

Study	Method	Period of Research	Research Site
Daudistel, H. "Cop Talk: An Investigation of the Police Radio Code." Univ. of California, Santa Barbara, 1971.			California County Sheriff's Office
Dempsey, J.C. "Isolation of the Police Officer." Psychology Dept. Colorado State Univ. 1967 (cited in Tifft).			

Works in Progress

Study	Method	Period of Research	Research Site
Bordua, David. Univ. of Illinois, Urbana.	Observation, Organizational Analysis		Chicago, Ill.
Bayley, D. Univ. of Denver, comparison of arrest rates cross-nationally.	Observation Records Historical	1977–	
Carrier, John. "Women in Policing" (tentative title). London School of Economics and Political Science.	Interviews, Historical Research	1970–	London, Eng.
Chatterton, Michael. Manchester Univ.	Observation Interviews	1971–73	Manchester, Eng.
Clark, J., and R. Sykes. Univ. of Minnesota.	Observation	1970–71 (15 mo.)	Three midwestern cities
Ferdinand, T. Northern Illinois Univ.	Observation Questionnaires* Historical Research		Several Illinois cities Netherlands
Guenther, A.L. College of William and Mary.	Field Observation (homicide detectives)	1974–75	
Levett, A.L. "Organization for Order: The Development of Police Organization in the 19th Century United States." Univ. of Michigan, forthcoming. (Cited in Black, *op. cit.*)	Historical		
Manning, P.K. Michigan State Univ.	Observation (narcotics agents) Interviews	1974–75	Washington, D.C. (metro area)

*Major data source.

Study	Method	Period of Research	Research Site
Punch, M. Two studies of policing.	Observation (detectives and patrolmen)		Six U.S. metropolitan police departments
Redlinger, L.J. Univ. of Texas, Dallas.	Observation (narcotics agents)		Amsterdam, Neth.
	Interviews (narcs, drug users and dealers)	1968–69; 1974–75	San Antonio, Tex. Phoenix, Ariz. Detroit, Mich. Jacksonville, Fla.
Reppetto, T., John Jay. A History of Detective Work.	Historical		
Sanders, W., Univ. of Florida.	Observation		
Savitz, Leonard. Temple Univ.	Questionnaires (cohort analysis)	1975– 1967–	Florida Philadelphia, Pa.
Schiller, S. Chicago Crime Commission.	Observation (detectives)		Chicago, Ill.
Shearing, C. Univ. of Toronto.	Police calls (incoming)	1971–1972	Toronto, Can.
	Police Patrol	1975–	
Sherman, L.W. Yale Univ., selected case studies of police corruption.	Historical Records Interviews	1974–	Selected U.S. cities.
Walsh, James. Oberlin College.	Interviews* Observation	1969–	Amsterdam, Neth. London, Eng. Dublin, Ire. "4 American Settings"
Ward, David. Univ. of Minnesota.	Observation	1970–	Minneapolis, Minn.
West, J., Univ. of Bristol.	Observations Interviews	1972–	Bristol, Eng.
Williams, J., Manning, P.K., Michigan State Univ., Redlinger, L.J., Univ. of Texas, Dallas; Research Triangle Institute, N.C.	Observation (narcotics agents) Interviews Records	1976–	

REFERENCES FOR SECTION INTRODUCTIONS

Banton, M. *The policeman in the community.* New York: Anchor, 1964.

Bayley, D. and Mendelsohn, H. *Minorities and the police.* New York: Free Press, 1969.

Black, D. J. The social organization of arrest. *Stanford Law Review,* 23, 6, 1971, 1087–1111.

Black, D. J., and Reiss, A. J. *Studies of Crime and Law Enforcement in Major Metropolitan Areas,* a report to the President's Commission on Law Enforcement and the Administration of Justice. Washington, D.C.: U.S. Government Printing Office, 1967.

Chapman, S., and St. Johnston, T. E. The police heritage in England and America. East Lansing: Michigan State University, Institute for Community Development, 1962.

Chevigny, P. *Police power: Police abuses in New York City.* New York: Pantheon, 1968.

Clark, J. P., and Sykes, R. E. Some determinants of police organization and practice in a modern industrial democracy. In D. Glaser (ed.) *Handbook of criminology.* Chicago: Rand McNally, 1974.

Critchley, T. A. *A history of police in England and Wales, 900–1966.* London: Constable, 1967.

Cruse, D., and Rubin, J. *Determinants of police behavior: A summary.* National Institute of Law Enforcement and Criminal Justice, Law Enforcement Assistance Administration. Washington, D.C.: U.S. Government Printing Office, 1973.

Edelman, M. *The symbolic uses of politics.* Urbana, Ill.: University of Illinois Press, 1964.

Ferdinand, T., and Lucterhand, E. Inner city youths, the police and justice. *Social Problems,* 17, 1970, 510–527.

Geertz, C. *The interpretation of cultures: Selected essays.* Chicago: Basic, 1973.

Goffman, E. E. The nature of deference and demeanor. *American anthropologist,* 58, 1956, 473–502.

———. *Encounters: Two studies in the sociology of interaction.* Indianapolis: Bobbs-Merrill, 1961.

Hughes, E. C. *Men and their work.* Glencoe, Ill.: Free Press, 1958.

Jacobs, J. Symbolic bureaucracy: A case study of a social welfare agency. *Social Forces,* 47, 1969, 413–422.

LaFave, W. *Arrest: The decision to take a suspect into custody.* Boston: Little, Brown, 1965.

Lee, W. M. *A history of police in England.* London: Methuen, 1901.

Lundman, R. J. Deference in police-citizen encounters. *Social Problems,* 22, 1974, 128–136.

Manning, P. K. Rules, colleagues, and situationally justified actions. In R. Blankenship (ed.) *Colleagues in organizations.* New York: Wiley, 1977, 263–289.

———. *Police work.* Cambridge, Mass.: MIT Press, 1977.

Muir, W. K. *Police: Street corner politicians.* Chicago: University of Chicago Press, 1977.

Parks, E. From constabulary to police society. *Catalyst,* 6, 1970, 76–97.

Piliavin, I., and Briar, S. Police encounters with juveniles. *American Journal of Sociology,* 70, 1964, 206–214.

Radelet, L. *The police and the community* (1st ed.). Beverly Hills, Calif.: Glencoe Press, 1973.

Reiss, A. J. *The police and the public.* New Haven, Conn.: Yale University Press, 1971.

Reith, C. *A short history of the British police.* London: Oliver & Boyd, 1956.

Rubenstein, J. *City police.* New York: Farrar, Straus & Giroux, 1973.

Selznick, P. *TVA and the grass roots.* Berkeley, Calif.: University of California Press, 1949.

Silver, A. The demand for order in civil society. In D. J. Bordua (ed.) *The police.* New York: Wiley, 1967.

Skolnick, J. *Justice without trial.* New York: Wiley, 1966.

Sterling, D. *Changes in role concepts of police officers.* Washington, D.C.: International Association of Chiefs of Police, 1972.

Sykes, R. E., and Clark, J. P. A theory of deference exchange in police-citizen encounters. Unpublished paper, University of Minnesota, 1974.

Tifft, L. I. The "cop personality" reconsidered. *Journal of Police Science and Administration,* 2, 1974, 266–278.

Van Maanen, J. Working the street: A developmental view of police behavior. In H. Jacobs (ed.) *The potential for reform of criminal justice.* Beverly Hills, Calif.: Sage, 1974.

Whyte, W. F. *Street corner society.* Chicago: University of Chicago Press, 1943.

Wiley, M. G., and Hudik, T. L. Police-citizen encounters: A field test of exchange theory. *Social Problems,* 22, 1974, 119–127.